1001 B-29s Avenge Pearl Harbor

Memoirs of a Flight Engineer

Donald Cotner

iUniverse, Inc.
Bloomington

1001 B-29s Avenge Pearl Harbor
Memoirs of a Flight Engineer

iUniverse books may be ordered through booksellers or by contacting:

iUniverse
1663 Liberty Drive
Bloomington, IN 47403
www.iuniverse.com
1-800-Authors (1-800-288-4677)

ISBN: 978-1-4620-1412-5 (sc)
ISBN: 978-1-4620-1446-0 (dj)
ISBN: 978-1-4620-1413-2 (ebk)

Printed in the United States of America

iUniverse rev. date: 09/09/2011

TABLE OF CONTENTS

* Indicates one or more photos in these chapters

DEDICATIONS

To Jean, my wife since 4 December 1943,
and to our progeny:
Daughters: Donna, Laura and Frances
Granddaughters: Jill, Michele, Asila and Jamila
Grandsons: Adam, Connor and Sean
Great granddaughters: Nicole, Amy and Abigail
Great grandsons: Joshua and Paul
and all future offspring.
Here's the opportunity to read, if you wish,
what the old guy and his friends did in the Great War.

Having written, I hope, for other readers too. Thanks in advance to any person who honors my words, and my pictures, with time and attention.

A Word About Names:

Real history books make generals famous. In my little book, about one phase of World War II, I have written mostly about warriors of lesser rank.

I have tried to name each person in my stories, warrior or civilian. I have a good memory; I possess good records; and I have consulted many of my wartime comrades-in-arms. I believe most names that I have bestowed are accurate.[1] I regret any error, of omission or of fact, that I may have made.

Soldiers and sailors are sometimes awarded medals for valor. Others serve bravely, perhaps even to death, sans receipt of decoration. I believe that the reading of a name will be, for the moment, an award of recognition.

---

1 Those names which I have assigned to unknown persons, in the interest of the story, are marked with an asterisk.

DEDICATIONS

Part I: Photos, Prologue & Preview

A Photographic Introduction; Papers, Persons, Planes & Places

Lt. & Mrs. Cotner
Don & Jean

Monroe Studio, Tusla 9 MONTHS MARRIED

UNITED STATES ARMY

CERTIFICATE OF MARRIAGE

This certifies that on the

4th day of December.

in the year Nineteen Hundred and Forty-Three

Donald Lee Catner

and

Jean Marie Riesinger.

were united in matrimony by me at

Dwight Chapel New Haven according to

the laws of the State of Connecticut

William M. Greenf

Chaplain, Army of the United States

Witnesses

David M. Blacklock

Mrs. David M. Blacklock

Bonnie (Mrs. David) Blacklock, from Dallas; and, Jean Riesinger, from Tulsa, drove all the way to New Haven, on 1930's roads in the Blacklock's 1935 Chevrolet. David and Don were Aviation Cadet roommates stationed at Yale University. (Note: "Witness")

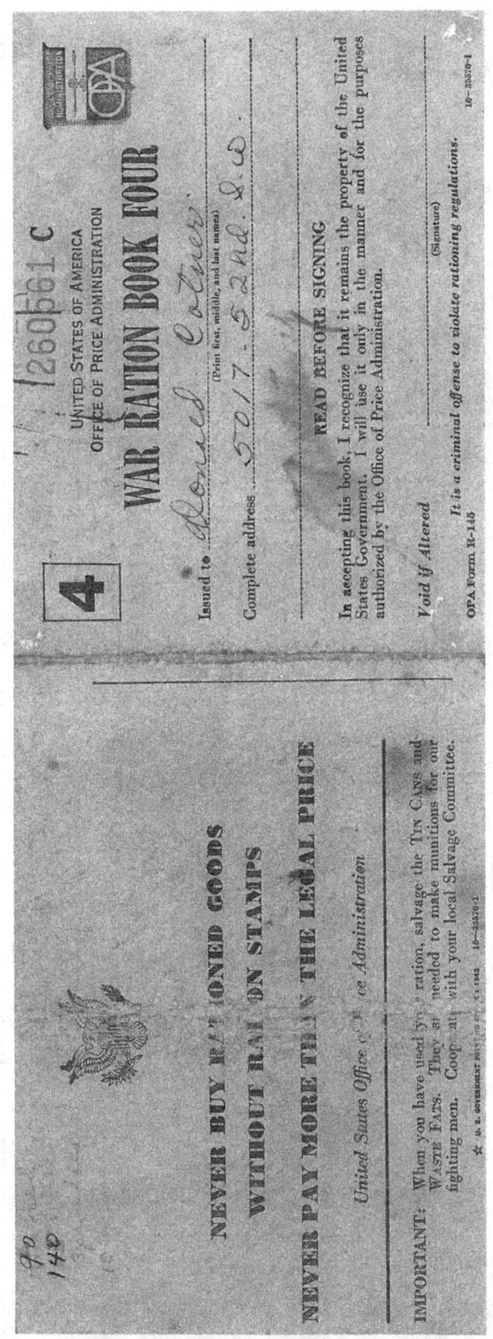

4

260561 C

UNITED STATES OF AMERICA
OFFICE OF PRICE ADMINISTRATION

WAR RATION BOOK FOUR

Issued to Donald Cotner
(Print first, middle, and last names)

Complete address 5017 - 52nd. S.E.

READ BEFORE SIGNING

In accepting this book, I recognize that it remains the property of the United States Government. I will use it only in the manner and for the purposes authorized by the Office of Price Administration.

Void if Altered ____________ (Signature)

It is a criminal offense to violate rationing regulations.

OPA Form R-145 16—35570-1

NEVER BUY RATIONED GOODS
WITHOUT RATION STAMPS

NEVER PAY MORE THAN THE LEGAL PRICE

United States Office of Price Administration

IMPORTANT: When you have used your ration, salvage the TIN CANS and WASTE FATS. They are needed to make munitions for our fighting men. Cooperate with your local Salvage Committee.

16—35570-1

Jean managed the food stamps. Don took care of the '36 Studebaker. We shared stamp responsibilities for other purchases.

From Jean's W.W.II Scrapbook

SECTION THREE THE DENVER POST—FIRST IN EVERYTHING—SUNDAY MORNING, JUNE 25, 1944 The Post Phone—Main 2121 3

New Air Force Battleship, B-29 Super-Fortress, Queen of Stratosphere

Mammoth of the Skies, Only a Dream in 1938, Begins Systematic 'Softening Up' of Jap Mainland for Invasion

UNCLE SAM'S mammoth super-Fortress, "queen of the stratosphere," that already ha struck terror in the hearts of the Japanese on their homeland, is shown above an at left in three striking perspectives. A pair of these 141.2-foot-wingspread dragon of the roving Twentieth air force (Hap Arnold's own) is shown in the large picture with a third (inset) photographed against the snowy slopes of Washington state's Mount Rainier.

Above is a closeup of the vaunted Boeing B-29 taken before the installation of propellers, a view which demonstrates the streamlining that gives the 300-mile-an-hour gian more aerodynamic refinement than any other military aircraft.

Newspaper Article, June 25, 1944, *Denver Post*

2 Freshly Minted B-29s

Aerodynamic perfection for a propeller powered plane.
Air Crops Photo

Capt. Harold Fiel's Lead Crew, McCook, NE, 4 March 1944

Kneeling: (L. to R.)
Don Connor, R. Gunner.
Seymour Schultz, Radio
Walt Calhoun, Top Gunner
Bill Smith, Radar
George Warn, L. Gunner
Rich Richardson, Tail Gunner

Standing: (L. to R.)
Claude Caldwell, Navigator
Charles Taylor, Pilot
Harold Fiel, Airplane Commander
Paul Malnove, Bombardier
Don Cotner, Flight Engineer

Air Corps Photo

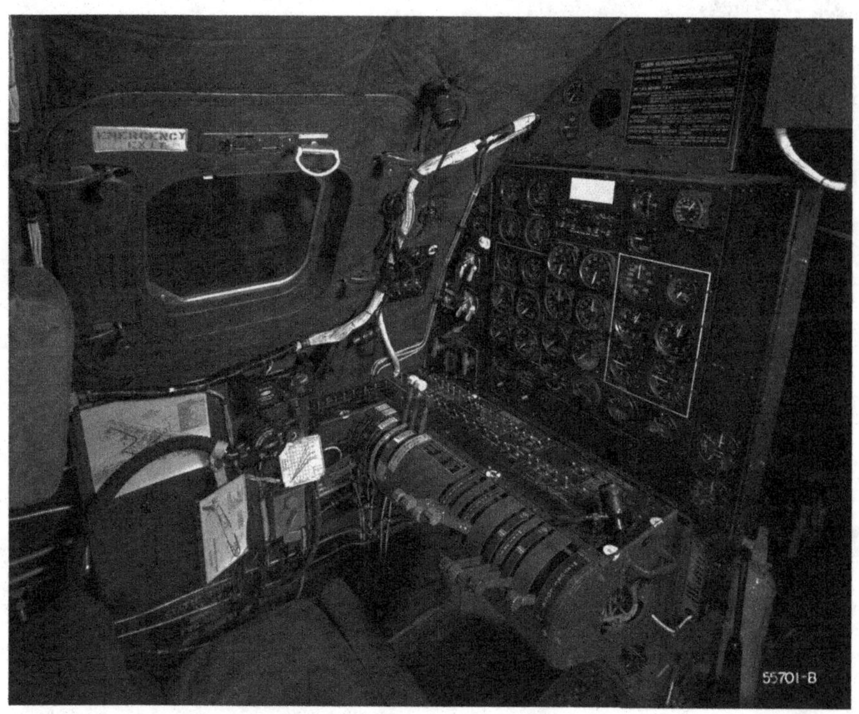

The Flight Engineer's Station

I ride aft of, and back-to-back with, the Pilot. Across the plane and through the Navigator's window I can see engines 1 and 2, and through a window on my left, engines 3 and 4. I monitor the engines by instrument readings and by sight and sound. I monitor, and keep a log of, fuel consumption. I compute and adjust engine power-settings on the half-hour, for maximum-range cruise-control. I am also responsible for in-flight maintenance, which is of limited scope. I can change fuses in some the electrical circuits; and, I can replace vacuum tubes in the computers. Each engine has an on-board computer regulating its two turbo-superchargers. As we burn fuel from each engines's wing tank, I replenish the tanks by pumping fuel, via the fuel transfer system, from the two 640-gallon auxiliary tanks (one hangs from the bomb racks in each bomb-bay).

Boeing Photo

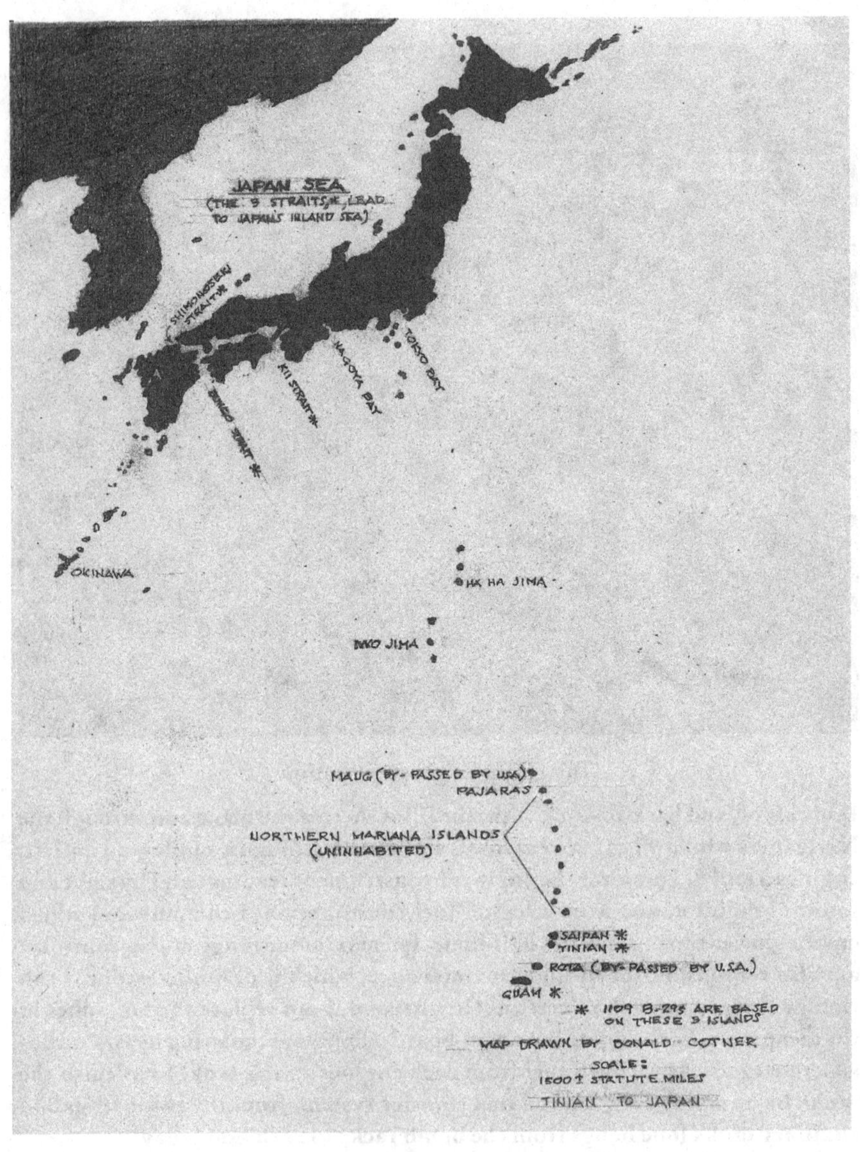

Map of The Pacific Ocean-Tinian to Japan
Credit: Don Cotner

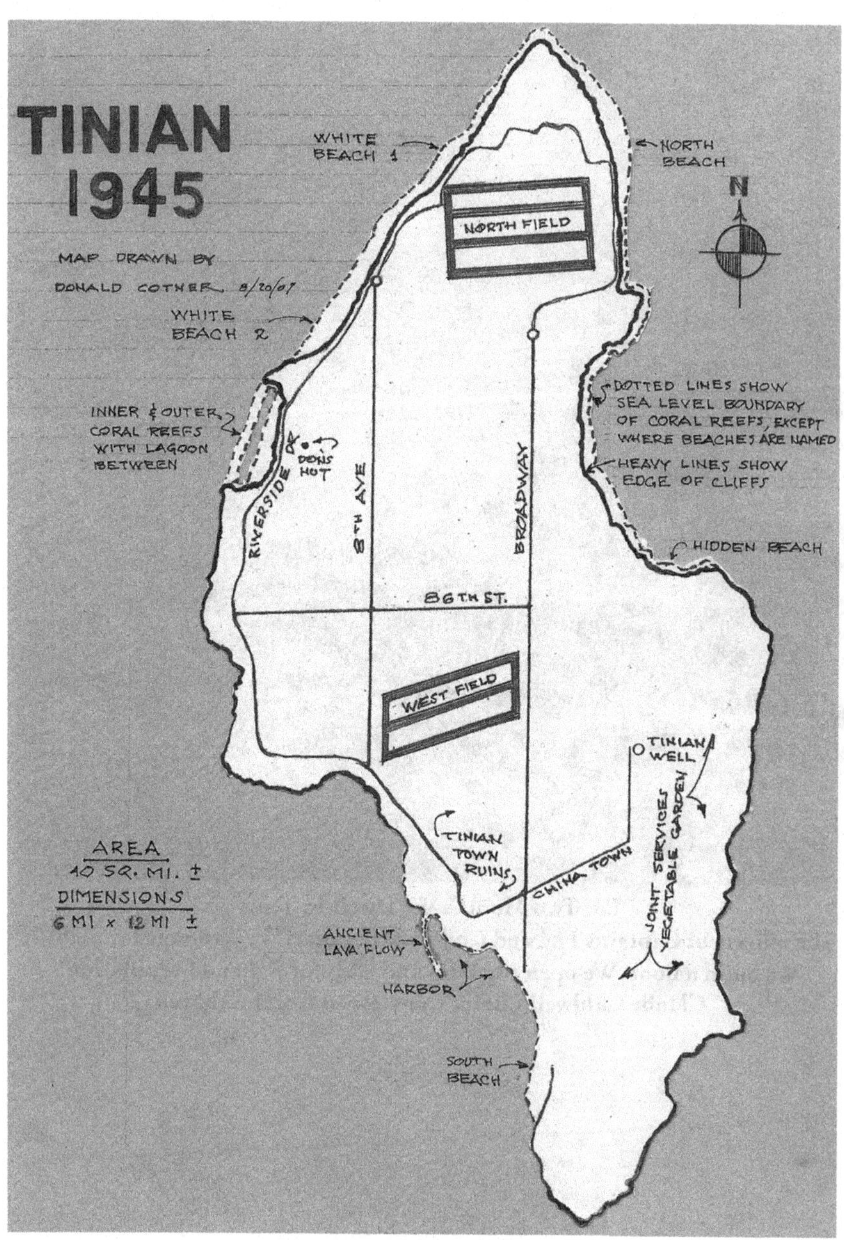

Map of Tinian, 1945
Credit: Don Cotner

For Two Months We Dwell In Tents
The officers of Captains Fiel and Curry share a tent. We scrounge for planks. We build a floor. We open the sides and ends for light and ventilation.
Claude Caldwell Photo, Courtesy of Coral Caldwell

The Wind Powered Washing Machine
M.V. Arnold, Navigator, Capt. Curry's Crew
Bill Duft, Bombardier, Capt. Curry's Crew
Don Cotner, Flight Engineer, Capt. Fiel's Crew

Claude and Don built this "appliance" from scrounged materials. In exchange for a fifth of whisky, a Sea-Bee forged a steel rod into a crank shaft. A motor pool mechanic traded us two ball bearing sets to fit the ends of the shaft, and 1 set to connect the crank to the plunger, all for a fifth of liquor. The Harbor was glad for us to haul away the lumber and the empty 50-gal aviation-gasoline drum.

Claude Caldwell Photo, Courtesy of Coral Caldwell.

The *Hon. Spy* on Tinian's North Field, 1945

Air Crew:	**Warn** L. Gunner	**Cotner** FL. Engr.	**Connor** R. Gunner	**Smith** Radar Op.
Gr. Crew: (Standing)	**Wesley** Electric Mech.	**Szarko** Crew Chief	**Kyger** Asst. C.C.	**Drigo** Radar Mech.

Claude Caldwell Photo, Courtesy of Coral Caldwell.

Hon. Spy and Claude Caldwell on Tinian
Engineer's window is above "*Hon. Spy.*" Pilot's window above "20th."

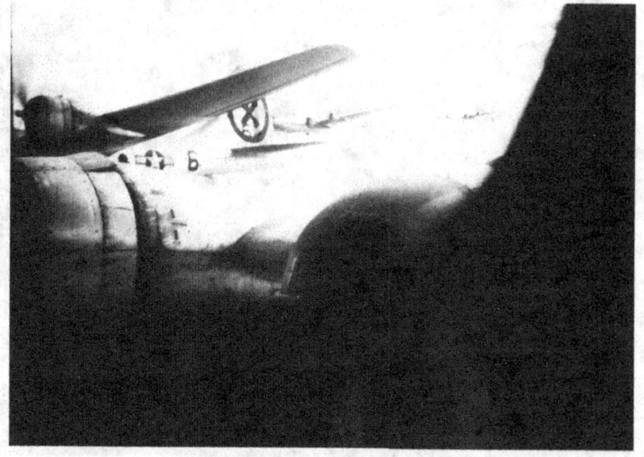

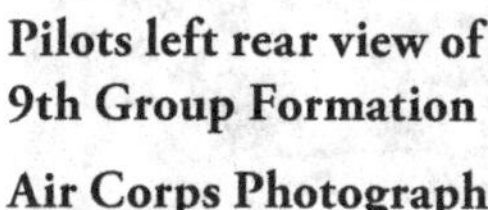

Pilots left rear view of 9th Group Formation

Air Corps Photograph

An Aerial View of Tinian, 1945

North Field (near) 9th Bomb Group and the 509th (A-bomb) Group. West Field, (far).

Air Corps Photograph

The See-Bees House the 9th Group in Metal Huts

Don and Crew's Hut, 1945" (far right)

1st Prize: Porch Deck and Roof; Bridge; Fence; and Garden.

Signal Corps Photo, Courtesy of Margaret Campbell (Boges)

Tinian's Red Cross Girls Are Party Guests of The U.S. Signal Corps, Co. 325

Back Row (L-R)
Lorene Whorton
Betty Band
Mary Woellwerts
Helen Klein

Front Row (L-R)
Ruby Hawkins
Sue Schroeder
Margaret Campbell (Boges)
Ruth Troxel
Kay Brennen
Bobby Gerlach

At 200 M.P.H., we fly 3,000 or more miles (round trip) to deliver our load.

Air Corps Photo

We Are Weary

Standing (L-R)
Claude Caldwell, Don Cotner, Chuck Taylor, Paul Malnove, Ted Littlewood, A.C.

Kneeling (L-R)
Don Connor, Bill Smith, Seymour Schultz, Walt Calhoun, George Warn, Rich Richardson

We have flown 29 missions, the last is with Capt. Littlewood. Our tour of duty is 35. *Will we survive 6 more?*

Air Corps Photo, Via courtesy of Larry Smith, Ed. 9th Bombardment Group (VH) History.

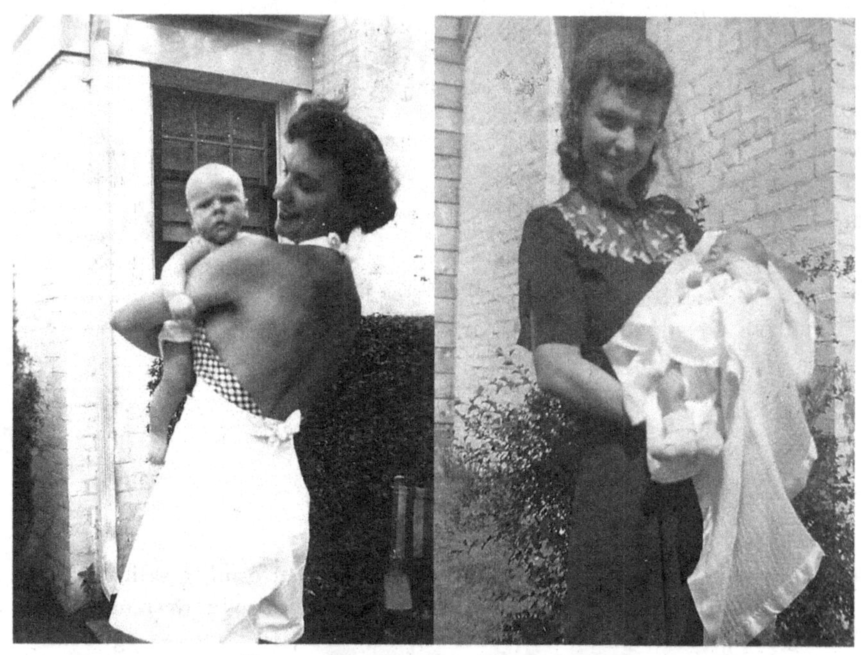

Donna Marie & Jean Marie Cotner

Tulsa is 8,000 miles from Tinian. When Will I See <u>My</u> Girls?

Credit: Emma Marie Riesinger, *Mother and Grandmother*

Our two engines, and our faithful airplane, are performing well, as we drone slowly but steadily on; but, there are hours to go between us and Iwo; and...I do not know if the fuel will last. In Bearden's plane, Sgt. Hal Worley, Right Gunner, with his own Kodak "Monitor" camera, clicks off a shot of old "574" sidling through the air with two paralyzed propellers.

Credit: Army Air Corps

A Patriotic Award, By Way of Prologue

Presented at an assemblage of "in-laws and out-laws" at the Herlig Family Reunion, 27 July, 2003

NARRATIVE

During the war time years of the 1940s, beautiful, energetic, patriotic eighteen-year-old Jean Marie Riesinger applies for work in the newly built and occupied Douglas Aircraft Factory, Tulsa, Oklahoma.

Her scores in the aptitude test are high. She demonstrates exceptional talent in mathematics. She rates "outstanding" in physical fitness. Douglas hires her immediately and assigns her to the Timekeeping Department.

Dressed in shirt and slacks, right leg cuff restrained by a steel clip, she rides a bicycle along the five and a half- mile circuit of intercommunicating aisle-ways serving the mile-long, 4,000,000 square foot shop floor. At each of the plant's 293 time-keeping stations, she gathers stamped cards and replenishes the supply of virginal cards. She returns to her office.

At her desk, she sorts cards, in accordance with classifications established by the Accounting Department. She totals hours, records sums, and routes reports to the accountants.

Miss Riesinger's rigorous accuracy and expeditious productivity is vital toward the success of Douglas' financial teams, as they negotiate complex contractual agreements with suppliers, and with purchasers, of goods and services. The prime product of worker pride is the swift and elegant twin-engine Douglas A-20 fighter-bomber.

On 25 July '41, at 9:00 p.m., Donald Cotner drives alone toward his home in the eastern outskirts of Tulsa. Lights are strung over the lawn at Yale

Avenue Presbyterian Church. It is an ice cream social. Knowing every item for sale will be homemade, Don, a Methodist, stops.

A pretty girl serves him cherry pie á la mode. He soon returns to the same young lady to order chocolate cake with chocolate ice cream. He sits and savors. The pretty girl comes over..."Don't you go to A. and M.?"..."Yes, do you?" Introductions and delightful conversation follow. So do a few ping-pong games. Before slow-working Don asks for a date, or even a phone number, Jean departs with her parents.

"O.K. Riesinger" is in the phone book. Jean and Don have their first date on 31 July. At 12:30 a.m., 1 August, in an Oklahoma cloudburst, Don drives his folk's Ford into a deep ditch near Jean's house. Jean's Dad rescues them. "Dad" takes Jean home immediately. It's twenty minutes to Don's house. Don can't escape. He hears a twenty-minute lecture. At home he gets a thirty-minute lecture from his mother, for leaving the car in the ditch.

Subsequent dates are blessed with good fortune...the shortened summer idyll ends. Jean elects defense work. Don forlornly returns to architectural studies in Stillwater, Oklahoma.

Declarations of affection flow from pens...Stillwater to Tulsa...Tulsa to Stillwater. Scripted, signed professions of passion document the binding, undeniable, indisputable, irrefutable truth of eternal commitment. Sans symbols of gold and stone, sans public utterance of ceremonial vows, their future is sealed.

On Christmas Eve of 1942, Miss Riesinger becomes engaged to Donald Cotner, U.S. Army Air Corps Reserve. On 23 May 1943, Don is called to active duty as an Aviation Cadet. He is assigned for training, as an Aircraft Maintenance Engineering Officer, at the Air Corps Technical Training School, Yale University.

On 27 November '43, Jean rides a Greyhound bus from Tulsa to Little Rock, Arkansas. There she connects with Bonnie Blacklock, wife of David

Blacklock, Don's cadet roommate. The two women drive 1,851 miles in Bonnie's 1935 Chevrolet, to New Haven, Connecticut.

At 1900 hrs. Saturday, 4 December '43, in Dwight Memorial Chapel, Yale Campus, Jean and Don are married by Capt. William Green, Chaplain, U.S. Army Air Corps. Bonnie is bridesmaid. David is best man. Dick Davis, a cadet comrade, and his wife, Marie, are present. In Jean's parents' absence, Don's Dad, George, gives Jean away.

At 1350 hours Sunday, 5 December '43, Professor William Colbert*, Don's Electronics Instructor, and his mother, Mrs. W.M. Colbert, host a reception in their New Haven home. Chaplain Green sends regrets. All other wedding celebrants attend. Don's mother, Vera, brings a home-baked three-layered "Pineapple Upside-down Cake"; it is her original-recipe specialty. Don wonders. *Can Jean cook? Will she learn?*

Gifts are few, small and inexpensive. Jean and Don appreciate them...But... Don has a guilt-tinged muse...*In our some-time future home...as she serves the punch...Will Jean ever be able to say, "This cut-glass bowl was a wedding present from my dear Aunt Birdie?"*

On Sunday, 5 December '43, at 1445 hours, David and Don's twenty-hour weekend leave will expire in fifteen minutes. With sorrowful good byes all around, the two men run to the campus.

At 1600, on New Haven's Town Green, to the music of the "Jersey Bounce" and the "St. Louis Blues", played by the Army Air Corps Band, led down the field by Colonel Glen Miller, the Cadet Corps passes in review. Bonnie and Jean wave as their husbands go by. It is a wave "goodbye" till 1800 hours next Saturday.

Jean and Bonnie return to their lonely rooms in an oversized antiquated firetrap of a lodging house, the only space near the campus they find for rent.

Bonnie's room is on the third floor. Poor Jean climbs a twisted staircase from floor three to her tiny gothic garret cell. She looks into her room. She cries. She sees one small window, an undersized single bed, a little table holding a few non-matching dishes plus a pot and a pan, hooks on the wall in lieu of a closet, a bare light bulb hanging from the ceiling, an open-flame two-burner cast-iron cook-top/space-heater sitting on a three-drawer chest.

The communal toilet room is on the third floor below. Its lavatory is Jean's single source of water. The lavatory and the tub, plus her portable nine by twelve-inch brass scrub board, are her main laundry resources. She hangs personal things to dry on a string in her room. Bulkier items she lugs to lines strung in the cellar.

Bonnie and Jean apply for war work. Whitney Blake Electric Company hires each of them.

Whitney Blake likes Jean's quick response to visual and auditive stimuli. She is assigned to Quality Control of message-line production. Whitney Blake winds the wire onto 1,001-foot reels and delivers it in million-foot lots to the U.S. Army signal Corps. The Corps uses the wire to establish and maintain battlefield communication systems.

3 March 1944: Don graduates from the Yale program and is commissioned 2nd Lieutenant. He is assigned to B-29 school at the Boeing Factory in Seattle. Jean and Don depart. They pause in the District of Columbia for a brief visit with Don's mother and dad.

4 March 1944, 2200 hours: Sans reservations, Jean and Don board a train for a five-night ride to Seattle. They learn that seating and sleeping accommodations are sold out. They sit up in the smoking car. Jean is allergic to tobacco smoke.

5 March 1944, 0100 hours: The conductor shakes Don awake, "I have an upper berth, if you and the lady wish to share it." We share. It's tight,

but we know this five-day cross-country trip is the closest thing to a honeymoon the Air Corps will ever grant us. We're young. It's fun.

In Minneapolis, passengers depart. New passengers board. Jean returns to our seat, "I met a woman in the ladies room. She was brushing rice from her hair. She barely caught the train after marrying a 2nd Lieutenant from Yale. They are the Delahantys...Eddie and Jane Don thinks, *Eddie Delahanty and his bride are on this train*?

Jean and Don, and Jane and Eddie, find a house to share in Seattle. Jean and Jane buy the groceries, cook the meals, and manage rationing coupons.

Counting the commute to the factory, Eddie's and Don's six-day week is long, but they are free every evening and all day on Sunday. The newlyweds enjoy Seattle.

30 May 1944: Don graduates at Boeing. The Air Corps assigns him to Flight Engineers School, Lowery Field, Denver, Colorado. Jean accompanies him. They find an apartment of their own. Jean manages the food rationing coupons alone. They buy a '36 Studebaker sedan. Don rides streetcars to Lowery to accumulate gasoline coupons. They use a few precious gallons of gas on sightseeing cruises. Jean and Don love Denver. They love each other.

8 Sept. 1944: The Air Corps awards Don his Wings and assigns him to the 9th Bomb Group for combat flight training. Jean and Don drive to McCook, Nebraska via Tulsa. They visit Jean's mother, Emma, father, O.K. (Otto Karl), and brothers, Frank and Teddy. Jean visits an obstetrician. Pregnant?...Yes.

Jean's Dad knows a filling station owner who gives them extra gasoline coupons. Sans fuel-supply worries, Jean and Don depart for McCook.

Jean and Don share a big farmhouse near town with Mrs. Smith (owner), Henry Smith (adult son), Okie Blugs (an Air Base M.P.) with Maggie (his wife) and Chuck Meeks (a 9th Group Bombardier) with Nancy (his wife).

Tenant couples share bathroom facilities. All wives and Mrs. Smith share laundry facilities, namely an ancient Maytag with a hand-crank rubber-roller wringer. Jean hangs her washing out to dry. It freezes. She thaws it in the house. She spreads newspapers to catch the drips.

All women share kitchen facilities, including a monstrous cast-iron-kiln-of-a-cooking-stove water-heater combination. Henry faithfully fills the firebox with timbers. Nebraska winter arrives early. Chill saturates the house. In bed we have mattress, comforter and bolster of feathers, plus youthful ardor, to keep us warm. Out of bed, we spend much time in the communal kitchen. When we become overheated, we retire to our own room to cool down before nesting into the feathers.

During daytime, 9th Group wives hang out at the Officers Club on base. Jean becomes a Charter Member of the *Pregnant Wives Club.*

The Officers Club throws a costume ball. Jean cuts armholes and leg holes in an olive-drab barracks bag. She is “Private SNAFU” (from a newspaper cartoon character. The acronym abridges an endlessly iterated soldierly lament, “Situation Normal, All Fucked Up”). Jean wins *Grand Prize, Best Dressed Woman.* The judges want to loosen the drawstrings and peek inside to prove her title is honest. Don doesn’t let majors and colonels pull rank on him, a lowly 2nd Louie, nor on his private little Private. Judges settle for a pat of her padded belly... from outside the bag.

20 Dec. 1944: Forty-five factory fresh B-29s are delivered to the McCook Air Base. A crew is assigned to each. Captain Feil gets Serial No. 224876. All soldiers are superstitious. The crew believes the sum of the last three digits is a lucky number.

21, 22 Dec.: Each crew inspects, test flies and accepts its airplane.

23 Dec.: The 9th flies in its first group-formation to Herrington, Kansas. (In training the forty-five crews had shared three B-29s, four B-17s, and

thirty-eight broomsticks.) Jean, with three pregnant passengers, drives the Studebaker. In Herrington, the Group has six days of "staging" for overseas duty.

25 Dec. 1944: Our holiday is poignant, and swift in passing. Past our window snow falls...and falls...It silences the little city...

Our room in the inn is warm and cozy...We lie on our bed...We glory in the beauty of our bare young bodies...The babe in the womb senses the touch of soft hands on Jean's sweet belly...

The babe moves...it kicks...Jean speaks the chosen names, "Merry Christmas, little Donna Marie. Merry Christmas, little Karl George. We can't know which till you get here". We have a pretty little tree here, just for you".

We meditate in awe and delight...We croon soft carols...We tell the babe of Christmases to come, but as we contemplate a future...we wonder in silence...as we wonder...

9 Jan. 1945: Jean and Don say goodbye. The 9th Group flies off to war. The heading is west. Destination is not revealed.

Jean's brother Frank arrives via bus from Tulsa. Frank chauffeurs Jean to Tulsa in the Studebaker.

After departing the California coast, Capt. Feil opens sealed orders, "We are heading for Tinian". The crew puzzles *...Tinian?...What is Tinian?... Where is Tinian?...*

25 February 1945: Don and his B-29 comrades-in-arms begin to earnestly assault Japan's home islands.

13 April 1945: Don, over Tokyo, delivers bombs; Jean, in St. Johns Hospital, delivers Little Cadet, Donna Marie. Jean's dad sends Don a wire.

1 August 1945: The B-29s, and the U.S. Navy, hold Japan quarantined, via blockade, from intercourse with any outside entity. Japan is defeated.

6 August 1945: *The Enola Gay* drops "Little Boy" on Hiroshima.

9 August 1945: *Bock's Car* drops "Fat Man" on Nagasaki.

2 Sept. 1945, 0840 hours: The 9th Group parachutes food and other necessities of comfort and weal, to American prisoners at a camp north of Nagasaki. It is Don's thirty-third, and last, mission.

2 Sept. 1945, 0840 hours, plus sixteen minutes: Japan surrenders.

11 Oct. 1945: At Jefferson Barracks, Missouri, Don is separated from service. He flies, via Braniff Airlines, to Tulsa. Jean, Donna and Don are united.

AWARD

For honorable and excellent service in the manufacture of arms, for suffering the sometime horrors of wartime housing, for enduring the necessities of material shortages and the officiousness of rationing, for comforting your special airman with love and the commitment of marriage, for regularly sending your husband messages of solace, cheer, and love across long months, and many miles, of separation, for bearing our babe sans the support of my presence, for braving the terrifying possibility that little Donna may never see her father, for the sum of all these things, though nearly sixty years late, I hereby award this Medal:

WOMEN ON THE HOME FRONT, 1941 THROUGH 1945
TO MY DEAR WIFE, JEAN MARIE COTNER
MATRIARCH OF THE HERLIG FAMILY

Donald Cotner
Long time ago 1st Lieutenant
U.S. Army Air Corps

From Dawn into Darkness, A Preview

First Published 1995, Chapter 6 – Mission Procedures, 9th Bomb History, Lawrence Smith, Ed.

5 June, 1945, 04:47: Dawn comes gently to the Southern Islands of the Mariana Chain. On Guam, Saipan and Tinian, earth and all earthly objects are dimly illumined by the cool lavender-gray radiance softly suffusing the air. At the island encampments of the twenty Bomb Groups of the five Bomb Wings, comprising the 20th Air Force, no reveille sounds, yet officers and men are summoned from sleep, some by the clocks of the diligent, some by the call of conscience, to the duties of the day.

On Tinian, in the 9th Bomb Group Encampment, men yawn and stretch. They relax, pause and rest a bit. They gather their wits. Goats, of a flock liberated from Japanese rule, goats gone half-feral and yet still half-tame, frolic and gambol through the streets and walkways of their adopted Bomb Group. The clatter of capering cloven hooves animates the men in the sacks. They sit on the edge of their cots, shoes in hand. They smash heels together, three times, hard! Ants and other night-dwelling shoe-creatures fall stupefied to the floor. They dash about in dazed frantic misdirection. In shoes and undershorts and with razor, soap and towel in hand, men head for latrines and washroom facilities.

Refreshed, shaved and dressed, officers and men hustle toward their respective mess halls. The warmer colors of progressing dawn are reflected from the western clouds. The air feels warm and moist, hinting at the heat and humidity of the tropical day to come.

Chow line appetites are whetted by the yeasty aroma of fresh-baked bread and the strong smell of percolating coffee. Cook Sergeants Bill, Charles and John Snyder work side-by-side on the serving-line. Dead-ringer triplets (drafted the same day), they retain their good-natured smiles, no matter how frequent the comments of hungry would-be comedians. Today, the hardworking early-rising cooks are also featuring scrambled eggs and bacon (egg powder reconstituted with Tinian well water, and smoked mutton strips from Down-Under), orange marmalade, and tropical butter (it neither melts nor spreads; but, cleaved with a sharp heavy knife, slabs are spackled with marmalade to a chunk of bread; delicious!). Other drinks are tomato juice (from five-gallon cans) and milk (also reconstituted from powder). Some men gripe, mainly to exercise a universal and immemorial soldierly privilege, but they know they eat well, considering the difficulties of climate and logistics.

Lt. Ed Delahanty, Flight Engineer on Capt. Wendell Hutchison's crew, and Sgt. Don Connor, Gunner on Capt. Ted Littlewood's crew, are among those airmen who opt to postpone breakfast in favor of a spiritual pre-flight tune up. They gather in the chapel created by Father Toomey, Chaplain of the 505th Bomb Group. In a secluded area, he has erected a portable, three-walled screen, open to the sky. His jeep is backed into the open end. He lowers the tailgate revealing the portable altar and other liturgical accoutrements essential to the Eucharistic rite. Father Toomey celebrates Mass. He prays the men will return safely. He confers General Absolution, sans confession, to all present. The men hurry to the mess halls. As the only Chaplain of the Roman faith in the 313th Wing, Toomey stows his gear in the jeep and hurries toward the 504th Group, scheduled next for takeoff, after the 9th.

05:55: Thirty-six flight crews, twelve each from the 1st, 5th and 99th Bomb Squadrons, the three Squadrons which comprise the 9th Group, begin assembling in the headquarters briefing room. Thirty-six ground crews, assigned to the planes scheduled to fly, plus the mechanics and specialists assigned to general aircraft maintenance, climb aboard G.I. troop carrier trucks. They ride to the 9th Group's flight line at North Field. The planes were fueled, the guns armed, and the bombs loaded the day before. Some ground crews, like that of M. Sgt. Joe Adams, had worked under portable lights (with portable generator) long into the previous night. They departed the flight line only after aircraft 820, "Daring Donna", was in A-1 mechanical shape for Airplane Commander Karl Pattison and his crew to fly today.

Aircraft 876, "Hon. Spy Report" will not fly this mission. With four new engines, and a just-completed 100-hr. inspection, the "Spy" waits in the Consolidated Maintenance Dock for an 11:00 a.m. test flight. Major John Cox, Group Air Inspector, and Capt. George Davis, Flight Test Engineer, must sign off on performance before the plane can be returned to combat service. Like tasters of the King's wine, M. Sgt. Maurice Szarko, Crew Chief, and Sgt. Bill Kyger, Asst Crew Chief, will fly as observers.

Szarko and Kyger will each receive the "Wright Medal", a sterling silver lapel-pin, which replicates the R-3350 engine. Presentation will be by Thomas Lazzio, Wright Aeronautical Company's technical representative, attached to, and bivouacked with, the 9th Bomb Group. The "Hon. Spy's" engines are the first set of four to remain operable for the specified 400-hour life. This morning Szarko and Kyger will help on the flight line, wherever they can, to get the mission underway.

I feel pride in these four engines. As the "Hon. Spy's" original Flight Engineer, I received them new from the factory. I "broke" them in. I operated them for the first 289 hours of their pre-overhaul span of life.

Today the ground crews perform the pre-flight tune-ups that will make each plane ready for combat. They top fuel tanks. They drain petcocks. They inspect and check piston extension in the Oleo landing-gear struts. They check tire pressures. They clean and polish windshields. They are proud of the beautiful B-29s assigned to their care, and they have great affection for the crews who fly them. They commit their most earnest integrity toward creating the safest mechanical conditions possible. They want those planes and the men to come back.

06:00: Lt. Col. Henry Huglin, Commanding Officer of the 9th Bomb Group, strikingly "West Point" in bearing, strides into the briefing room, accompanied by his staff of briefing officers. Major Harold Feil, 99th Squadron Operations Officer is first to spot Huglin, but air crewmen scramble to attention, even before Major Feil has finished sounding his crisp "Ten hut!" Huglin returns Feil's salute. He puts all "at ease" and "at rest". At twenty-nine, Huglin is the "old man", literally, as well as figuratively. By men whose lives are on the line, he is respected and appreciated for administering tough but fair discipline, and for his insistence on excellence in performance of duty.

Col. Huglin tells the men, "The 21st Bomber Command has ordered the biggest strike in the history of aerial bombardment. 504 B-29s, representing fourteen Groups, from the five Wings of the 20th Air Force, will drop 8,064,000 lbs. of incendiary bombs on Kobe, more bombs than 1,300 B-17s, flying from England, could drop on Germany. The objective will be to incinerate Kobe, and thus destroy what remains, after the 16 March raid, of the manufacturing and shipping capabilities of the largest and busiest industrial port city on the Inland Sea."

Huglin asks Major Frank Luschen, Group Operations Officer, to continue the briefing. Luschen unveils a large map of the Western Pacific. A line of red twine connects Tinian with the rendezvous area off the east coast of Japan. At rendezvous, the line turns west, then north to Kobe, then south-southeast to the coast, and back to Tinian. Luschen says, "Each crew shall make its own way north at 7000 to 7,800 feet altitude; and shall start climbing to rendezvous sixty miles offshore Japan." He puts his pointer on the line, "Rendezvous at 14:30 hours, by Group and by Squadrons: 5th Squadron at 13,000 feet altitude; 99th Squadron, 13,500 feet; 1st Squadron, 14,000 feet."

This gives pause in the minds of airmen. We well remember the first Kobe mission: the searchlights, the heavy flak, the night fighters. All missions to date have been flown under cover of night, or in daylight at 20,000 feet, or higher. *Will anti-aircraft fire be more accurate? Will Zeros reach altitude quicker? Will they stay with us longer?*

Col. Huglin senses the aura of apprehension abroad in the room. He stands, "The 5th Squadron will lead the 9th Group formation. Capt. McClintock will lead the 5th Squadron. I am flying with McClintock and crew." He signals Luschen, and sits down.

Luschen carries on, "Capt. Weinert will fly deputy-lead to McClintock's lead; Capt. Rogan will lead the 1st Squadron with Capt. Bertagnoli as deputy; 1st Lt. Bearden will lead the 99th, with Capt. Littlewood as deputy. I will fly with Bearden." Luschen distributes Pilot's flimsies, showing position of each plane in the formation, takeoff schedule, rendezvous, and target air speeds.

Capt. Leonard Brown, Group Intelligence Officer, unveils a large-scale map of the rendezvous/target area. He points out anti-aircraft gun emplacements. He warns, "Some guns are mounted on railroad cars, and thus may be located anywhere." Capt. Winton Brown, Group Weather Officer, predicts, "Clear skies in the target area; winds generally from the west all the way, with a tail wind component going north and a head wind component on the return leg, and a weather front, centered 100 miles south of Iwo Jima."

Capt. George Smith, Group Bombardier, tells bombardiers "Release bombs when you see McClintock's bombs fall," and he gives bomb arming instructions. Capt. John Nestel, Group Flight Engineer, hands out fuel log sheets and cruise control plans (charts showing scheduled engine power-settings). Nestel tells crews, "For maximum range cruise control, use a little more than charted power into a head wind and a little less while riding a tail wind." Capt. Jack Nole, Group Navigator passes out Navigator's "flimsies" (maps showing pre-planned headings), then at a signal from Huglin, Nole starts the count, "10, 9, 8, 7, 6, 5, 4, 3, 2, 1, hack!" We synchronize our watches. Col. Huglin wishes each man, "Good flying and good luck."

Huglin and McClintock hold a brief session with the Airplane Commanders and Pilots (20th Air Force titles for Pilot and Co-pilot), while the other airmen line up at the parachute counter. Each man checks out his own emergency equipment: parachute (with its personally tailored harness), survival vest (with its many pockets stuffed with water bottle, fishing tackle, tropical chocolate, knife, compass, map), and, "Mae West" inflatable life jacket. Wearing vests and jackets, and carrying chutes, clip boards, flimsies, etc, officers and men file outside and assembling by eleven-man crews, climb into the back of waiting trucks.

It's a crowded, rough ride to the flight line, but raucous ribald G.I. repartee makes it fun. The first truck pauses at the hardstand of Captain McClintock's B-29, aircraft "859", "Tokyo Kayo". The crew hops over the tailgate. McClintock reciprocates the salute of M.Sgt. Earl Newsted, Crew Chief. Saluting on the flight line is not mandatory. Importance of completing work performed under time restraints, and safety considerations, are of higher priority. When salutes occur they are in the nature of informal greetings. The aircrew performs regulation pre-flight inspections (second checks really): fuel tanks, oil reservoirs, bomb bays (each crowded with bombs and auxiliary fuel tanks). A mess hall truck pulls up. Mess crews distribute brown bag lunches. They put two large thermos jugs (water and tomato juice) into each compartment, fore and aft.

Capt. Richard Chambers, 9th Bomb Group Chaplain, drives up in his jeep. He invites all present to join in a word of prayer if they wish. Chambers is Protestant. All men join, whatever their faith. Chambers prays, "God of all faiths, God whose eye is on the sparrow, watch over these men today. Help them to fly to the best of their ability. Return them safely to Tinian. Amen." Chambers heads his jeep toward Captain Wienert and crew, at the hardstand of aircraft "284".

07:11: A jeep arrives. Col Huglin steps out. He returns salutes. He shakes the hands of McClintock and Newsted. McClintock reports, "Pre-flight completed; all O.K." Huglin says, "Let's go." The crew and ground crew, three men to a blade, push each four-bladed, sixteen-foot-seven-inch diameter Hamilton Standard Hydromatic propeller through two full turns to clear the lower cylinders of oil. Everyone boards. They batten hatches. With an "all clear" signal from Newsted, Lieutenant Dale Flocker, Bombardier, actuates the bomb bay door switch. Under a cylinder pressure of two tons/inch^2, pneumatically actuated pistons slap the doors instantly shut. Following their respective checklists, crewmembers perform the onboard pre-flight tests. All systems are in order.

07:15: McClintock says, "Start the engines." The ground crew stands clear. Lt. Russell Fee, the Flight Engineer, opens cowl flaps, sets throttles and fuel mixture controls to "idle-rich", energizes No. One starter fly-wheel for sixty seconds, turns on the ignition, and engages the starter. No. One propeller turns slowly, accelerates, and the engine comes to life. Fee sets No. One throttle at 800 rpm, (revolutions per minute), and starts engines two, three, and four. The low-register idle-song of the huge engines is music. Fee revs each engine up for magneto checks and gives McClintock the O.K.

07:21: The ground crew removes the chocks at McClintock's signal. He takes throttle control and proceeds along taxiways to takeoff position at the west end of Runway B. Other crews are following a similar procedure, each on their own schedule.

0:7:28: McClintock sets the brakes, gets tower clearance, says, "Prepare for takeoff" and calls for "takeoff power." Fee opens the throttle to the limit, while adjusting propeller pitch for 2800-rpm engine speed, and turbo-supercharger boost to forty-eight in. Hg intake manifold pressure. With a geared-down rpm ratio of seven to twenty, this means the propeller tips are traveling at 580 mph, (miles per hour), approaching, but not too closely, the speed of sound. The airplane quivers with tension as 8,800 horses strain to be free.

07:29: McClintock takes the throttles. He releases the brakes. Acceleration begins. The inertia of 137,000 lbs. gross-load, plus wing-flap/cowl-flap drag, gradually yields to propeller thrust. Lt. Art Landry, Pilot, calls off the indicated air speed as acceleration builds. A third of the way down the runway, the indicator reads forty-eight mph. This airplane is committed! If power falters now, it will not fly, and the hydraulic brakes will not stop it. It will roll over the edge of the eighty-five-foot precipice just 400 yards beyond the end of the runway and crash on the coral reefs below. The explosions, fire and smoke from thousands of gallons of 100-octane gasoline and thousands of pounds of incendiary bombs will be horrifyingly spectacular. The crew has seen it happen to other planes.

07:30:38: End of the runway, "144 mph. Good." McClintock eases the wheel yoke toward his chest. "859" responds. It clears the eighty-five-foot cliffs. Simultaneously, Bearden on Runway C, and Rogan on Runway D, are in the air. For the 9th Bomb Group, the mission is underway.

07:31:53: Wienert is airborne off Runway B. So it goes every sixty seconds on Runways C, D and B again, until thirty-five planes are in the air. Runway A is not used for takeoffs; it is reserved for any B-29 in trouble, which may need to come around for an emergency landing.

With four 8500-foot runways, and with 313th Bomb Wing air traffic, tiny Tinian's North Field is the biggest and busiest airport in the world. However, the 9th Group's formation will have one vacancy today. Aircraft "760" failed to pass pre-flight inspection.

07:43:41: Airplane Commander, Capt. Ted Littlewood, and his crew clear the cliffs. Lt. Chuck Taylor, Pilot, already has the landing gear on the way up. Littlewood noses down. He picks up a bit of airspeed as he incrementally works the huge Fowler wing flaps up into the wing.

With an eye on the temperature gauges, I, Lt. Don Cotner, Flight Engineer, close the cowl flaps, increment by increment, as fast as engine temperatures will permit. I lean the fuel-air mixture. Littlewood calls for the heading. Caldwell responds, "339 degrees." Following the numbers on the dial of the Westinghouse Flux-gate Compass, Littlewood turns toward Japan. He sets the course, and asks for climb power. I make the settings. The plane slows, but maintains good airspeed. By sight and by sound, I synchronize the engines, a task I perform every time I make a new power setting. We climb at 300 ft/min. Littlewood levels off at 7000 feet. Lt. Claude Caldwell, Navigator, adjusts the heading, in accordance with his latest calculation of position. Littlewood aligns the plane on course, adjusts the trim-tabs and sets up the Honeywell autopilot. I make cruise-control power settings. At 195 mph indicated air speed we join the stream.

This long leg of the mission is exciting only if mechanical malfunction occurs. We've been in the air only twenty minutes, and S. Sgt. Seymour Schultz, Radio Operator, has thrice told of hearing B-29s from the 9th report that because of engine failure, they are aborting the mission and returning to Tinian and Guam's 314th Wing, first off the ground today, has had an engine failure abort. Our Wright R-3350's are the most powerful (2200 h.p.) and most efficient (1.25 lbs./h.p. and 1.52 h.p./c.i.d.) aircraft engines in the world, but, the engine is of a new design and quality-control production bugs give us reliability problems. We think it is our misfortune that Dodge Motors has an Air Corps contract to build ninety percent of the engines. We, of course, are prejudiced. Dodge workers are striking for higher pay, while we are getting shot at. We hope our engines don't fail us at critical times. I listen to the engines droning steadily on.

We are lucky today. Our long leg is uneventful. In the aft compartment, ride four Gunnery Sergeants: Don Connor, Right Blister; Walt Calhoun, Top Blister; George Warn, Left Blister; and Rich Richardson, Tail Gunner. (Rich is at his battle station in the tail only in the target area). The Gunners each observe the air space around us. It would be stupid to collide with a friend. Capt. Littlewood demands strict compliance with Air Corps regulations. We like it that way. T. Sgt. Bill Smith, Radar Operator operates the equipment and monitors his screen. It is his only view. As we progress north-northwest, the various islands of the Mariana Chain, not always visible by eye, blip onto the radar screens. Radar is a good navigational aid, and the Navigator has a "slave" screen at his station.

In the forward compartment, Lt. Paul Malnove, Bombardier, who doubles as a gunner, watches air-space and assists the Navigator by taking drift readings on whitecaps through the Norden bombsight. The Airplane Commander keeps the plane in trim and on course. The Pilot takes a turn when called upon. Both men scan the skies. The Radio Operator monitors the airwaves. He too flies "blind". He gives the Navigator the broadcast Greenwich Time signals. The Navigator monitors and plots our course and position. He operates the LORAN equipment, another electronic navigational aid, and he has his own small Plexiglas dome in the top of the plane, through which he sights heavenly bodies via sextant. I ride aft of, and back-to-back with, the Pilot. Across the plane and through the Navigator's window I can see engines One and Two, and through a window on my left, engines Three and Four. I monitor the engines by instrument readings and by sight and sound. I monitor, and keep a log of, fuel consumption. I compute and adjust engine power-settings on the half-hour, for maximum-range cruise control. I am also responsible for in-flight maintenance, which is of limited scope. I can change fuses in some of the electrical circuits and I can replace vacuum tubes in the computers. Each engine has an on-board computer regulating its two turbo-superchargers. As we burn fuel from each engine's wing tank, I replenish the tanks by pumping fuel, via the fuel transfer system, from the two 640-gallon auxiliary tanks that hang from the bomb racks in each bomb bay.

Today, Lt. Phil True, Navigator on a newly arrived replacement crew, is assigned as a last-minute passenger for "orientation experience". He rides on the deck sans benefit of intercom gear. He squeezes between the forward gun turrets and the Navigator's table, where Lt. Caldwell has spread the flimsies, which chart the pre-set course. True and Caldwell try to confer. It is difficult. The navigator's station is tight for space when he's in it alone and the noise generated by the No. Two engine and propeller, just outside his window, is thunderous. Normally, a "passenger" can plug in a portable headset and be on the intercom line. I worry that True will have a long, lonely and dull ride.

Lt. Paul Malnove gets Captain Littlewood's O.K. to arm the bombs, thirty-two 500 lb. incendiaries in each of the bomb bays. Malnove removes his parachute and crawls from the forward compartment into the forward bomb bay through a small circular door in the bulkhead. In the bomb bay, space is tight, and catwalks are treacherous. Each bomb has a small propeller in the tail. Malnove pulls a pin to release the shaft. He counts the turns as he partially unwinds the propeller. The bomb is still safe. When the bomb is released, the windmilling propeller will set it to explode and ignite. With sixteen bombs armed, he departs the bay. Via ladder and handholds, he climbs into the thirty-four-inch-diameter tunnel at the top of the plane and crawls thirty-three feet to the rear compartment. He arms the sixteen bombs in the rear bay and returns to his station in the nose. He is sweating from his workout.

T. Sgt. Walt Calhoun, Top Gunner, and Central Fire Control Specialist, reports to Capt. Littlewood that he sees a good clear area to fire into. Littlewood gives the O.K. to test the machine guns. Richardson scrambles back to battle station. Under Calhoun's direction, each gunner fires a few rounds from his turret, via the gun-sight/trigger at his station. The B-29's CFC system has a nineteen-vacuum-tube computer that electronically controls the electrically-operated remote turrets. Using input data entered by the navigator, the computer calculates required trajectories, with allowances for aerodynamic characteristics (altitude, density and temperature of the air, etc.). No other airplane has such a system. Each gunner tries the impossible feat: to fire one round from each turret. Mission planners, to save weight in favor of bombs and fuel, give us only 100 rounds of ammunition per gun. A few good bursts and we will have shot our wad. We hope the Zero pilots never find out.

After the extremely loud, but fortuitously brief gun test, we really appreciate S. Sgt. Schultz, as he puts Saipan Sam on the intercom. Sam broadcasts from the Saipan station of the Armed Forces Radio Network. Before the war, Sam was Eddie Koontz, disc jockey for station KTUL in Tulsa, Oklahoma. I know this because I grew up in Tulsa. There is only one voice like that. Sam is a damned funny radio comedian. Right now he is sending us his disc jockey blessing, as he dedicates David Rose's "Holiday for Wings" (Sam's title) to the guys of the 20th Air Force.

In this phase of the mission, excellent performance of our duties and responsibilities is not incompatible with the art and practice of daydreaming. We muse on many subjects. We discuss some of these on intercom. Some of the single guys talk about sexual conquests. They seem to best remember, though, the ones who "got away". Capt. Feil, Smith, Taylor, Caldwell and I are married. I know each thinks of his wife. Their first act on boarding the plane is to place her picture within workstation line of sight. I do the same with a picture of my Jeannie holding our little Cadet, Donna Marie, our first baby, born Friday, 13 April, 1945, while I was flying the "Tokyo Arsenal Area" mission. We married men, and the single guys with sweethearts, don't talk much about sex, but my reveries are mostly about making love with Jeannie. I think, too, about little Donna. *Will I survive to be a daddy for her?*

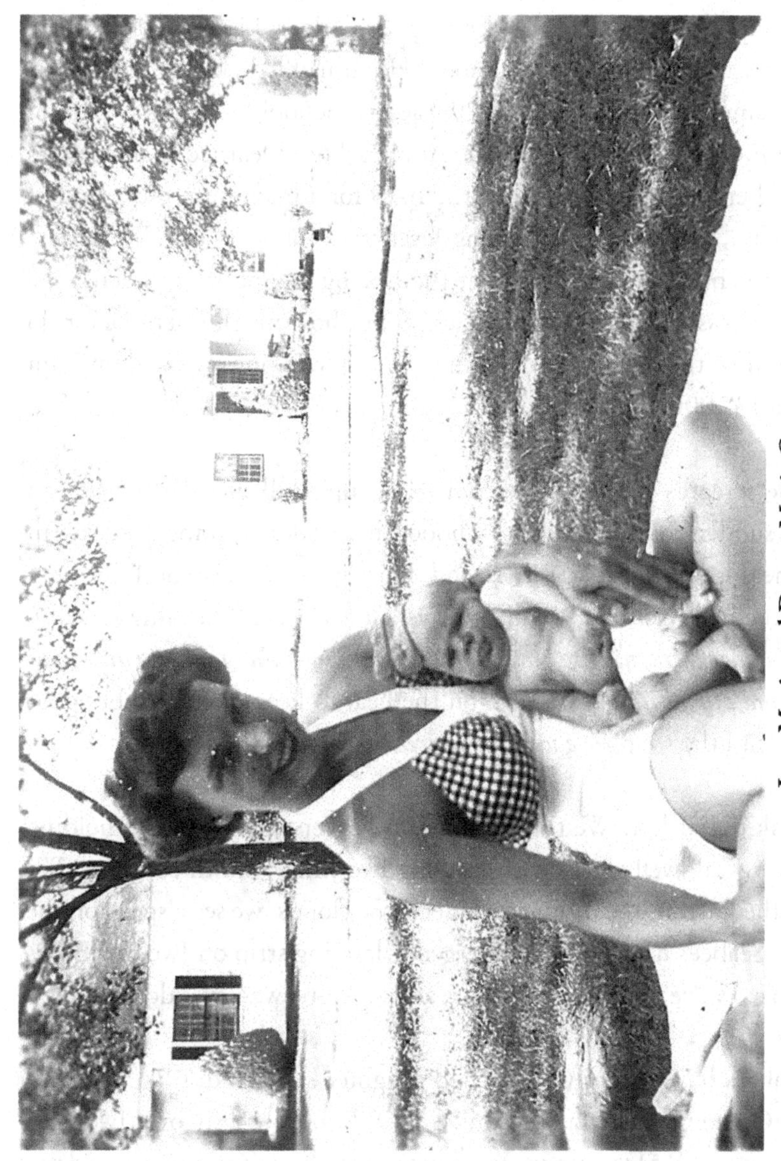

Jean Marie and Donna Marie Cotner
On the front lawn of Jean's parents' home in Tulsa, Okla.
Credit: Emma Marie Riesinger

11:33: We hit some rough air. We lose the sun. I look out my window. We're in a soup. We've hit the weather front. I can't see past our wing tips but I can see the wings flap up and down as the plane is buffeted by the turbulence. I turn and look over my right shoulder. Littlewood sits there calmly tweaking the autopilot knobs. His unruffled skill is reassuring. Then I remember the Boeing B-29 Factory School, which was part of the training the Air Corps gave me. At the school I learned that Boeing's structural engineers had designed the B-29 for a maximum gross load of 105,000 lbs., with an ultimate strength safety factor of 1½ to 1. We haven't burned much fuel yet. I know that the Boeing engineers considered the dynamic stresses induced by turbulence, but how much safety factor do we have when the extra g's of dynamic force are working on the aluminum skin of a 137,000 lb. B-29?

Malnove screams into the intercom, "Pull up! Pull up!" Before he can say it, a sudden roaring loudness whoooooshes under us going nose-to-tail and gone! I look around at Littlewood. He is gripping the wheel. He says, "What the hell was that?" Malnove says, "It was a B-29 heading south. *If it was an abort returning to Saipan or Guam, why didn't the crew avoid our course, and our altitude?* We turn on the heat to keep from trembling, as we peer into the soup. *Are we cold or are we still scared?*

We break out at last. We think we are in heaven, but we're still holding 7,000 feet. Caldwell says, "We're passing Iwo Jima." Smith confirms. We look to the East. In the distance, under some clouds, we see a speck on the sea. The Seabees have built an emergency landing strip on Iwo, for B-29s in trouble. We've never landed there, and we hope we never do.

The Seabees have recently completed a fighter strip, and a P-51 air-base facility. On some daylight missions, a B-29 Group will fly over Iwo, and lead a Group of P-51s to Japan. We don't worry about Zeros on those days. Unlike the Navy's carrier-based pilots, Air Corps pilots aren't trained in oceanic navigation. After they've chased Zeros out of the sky, and we've started "home", the Mustang pilots scramble to get on the tail of a B-29 for an Iwo escort. A Mustang pilot once asked Littlewood, "How come you guys always like to fly so slow?" but, we wonder, *How come we won't have Mustang cover today?*

Schultz can't get Saipan this side of the weather front. He picks up a Kobe station. When we are coming into Japan at night he gets Tokyo Rose. She speaks English well. She plays good American pop songs, especially love ballads. She tries to make us homesick. She tells us, "Give up and go home. Japan is winning the war. Give up. There's no use to die so young, so far from home, so far from the arms of your sweetheart. Give up." She's fun to listen to. We know the Japs are already beaten. They're just too damned stupid and too cowardly to surrender.

We can't stand radio Kobe in the daytime. Japanese music is discordant and slow moving, a bunch of off-key wailing and whining. There's no melody, no rhythm. We can't understand the speech, of course, and its sounds are not pleasant either. They're a boring monotone. No inflections. No accents. Every other phrase the announcer utters is "do mo are ee got oh," whatever that means. Schultz shuts off the sound. He keeps the radio compass tuned to the Kobe station, though. It, too, is an aid to navigation.

Radio Kobe didn't spoil our appetites. I can tell by the aroma drifting back from the nose, the guys up front are into their lunches. I open my brown bag, and find, not to my surprise, two large sandwiches (canned turkey, and peanut butter/orange marmalade) a huge dill pickle, celery stalks, carrot sticks, a big red apple and some fig Newton's. The turkey sandwich is juicy and delicious. The peanut butter is good, too, but hard to swallow. I reach around the back of my seat and hand my G.I. cup to Taylor. He fills it with tomato juice. Caldwell, True and Schultz call for juice. I pass their cups both ways. Everyone's thirsty. We knock off most of the jug of juice.

14:15: Littlewood calls for climb power. I make the settings. We climb at 500 feet per minute. We take turns using the relief tube. We anchor our parachutes to the one-man life rafts, which double as seat cushions. We make sure our oxygen masks are ready in case we lose cabin pressure. The B-29 is the first airplane to utilize cabin pressurization as an alternative to breathing oxygen at altitude. Richardson takes up his battle station in a tiny pressurized compartment in the tail. At 8,000 feet, cabin pressurization kicks in. We don't feel it, but we appreciate it.

14:28: We level off at 13,500 feet. I return the power to cruise settings. Littlewood takes throttle control. We don our heavy, cumbersome flak vests. We're just offshore, east of Japan. We see the Islands of Honshu to the north and Shikoku to the south. We see Kii Channel, which runs between the Islands, connecting the Inland Sea to the Pacific Ocean. Caldwell's navigation has been perfect. There is no cloud cover below our altitude. We can find Kobe visually.

Littlewood spots a partial formation. It's following the purple plume streaming from the smoke-generating device on the tail of McClintock's plane. Littlewood takes his place in the 99th Squadron as right wingman to the leader, Lt. Bob Bearden. Flying slightly higher, and a little to the left, the 99th will trail the 5th Squadron. The 1st Squadron will trail the 5th and the 99th high on the right. Flying at 190 mph CAS (Calibrated Air Speed), McClintock makes one more circle, and the formation is complete with thirty-six planes. Four planes with a big black "Z" on the tail have joined us. We know they're from Saipan, but we don't remember which Group "Z" represents. Why are they late? Did they not find their group? They are welcome. A full formation can defend better against fighters than a partial one.

Huglin and McClintock increase power. We follow. The dual turbo-superchargers on each engine give a real boost at altitude. The air speed is now 200 mph CAS. We're at fifty-six percent top speed. The B-29 is the world's fastest bomber. We wonder why we can't use some of that speed to get the hell in-and-out of there; but, more fuel...fewer bombs. Formation flying necessitates throttle jockeying. I have to make my best guess at how much fuel we're burning. Huglin leads us over the Kii Channel and over the Inland Sea toward Kobe. Connor sees eleven parachutes floating on the water.

Huglin turns north. Kobe Harbor leads us straight to the heart of the city. Earlier, arriving Groups have set Kobe's heart ablaze. Smoke billowing from the inferno on earth towers to the heavens above us. T. Sgt. Larry Smith, Central Fire Control Gunner on Capt. Wendell Hutchison's crew, from his excellent top-blister view, estimates the top to be at 40,000 feet and rising. A young man with a keen sense of the historical significance of current events, and with no Zeros in sight, Smith films the column of smoke with his personally owned 8 mm movie camera. Hutchison gave permission to bring the camera aboard after Smith promised not to shoot movies of Zeros.

Anti-aircraft guns have our altitude. Detonations batter our ears. Concussion waves jolt the plane. Shrapnel clusters (spent we pray) scatter rattling tattoos on the plane's drumskin-taut aluminum surfaces. I look at my picture of Jeannie and Donna. I read the words from the twenty-seventh Psalm. They were the text of Chaplin Chamber's Sunday sermon. I printed them on a card, which I've stuck on my instrument panel:

> "The Lord is my light and my salvation; whom shall I fear?
>
> The Lord is the strength of my life; of whom shall I be afraid?"

Huglin presses forward through the flak. Malnove opens the bomb bay doors. We reach the rim of fire. Bombs away! Our life rafts give us a stiff jolt in the butt, as the sudden liberation of energy stored in the aluminum-girder wing-spars springs the fuselage upward. Bomb bay doors snap shut. We stay in formation as Huglin and McClintock lead us around the column of smoke.

Hell erupts! All chattering shattering hell! Noise shock pains. Dust flies from every interior surface. Unannounced, the four fifty-caliber machine guns in the upper forward turret and the two fifties in the lower forward turret, explode into simultaneous action. Zeros rocket through the formation. We hang suspended, seemingly dead-still in the air, as Zeros whiz nimbly around us. Every time the Jell-O in my skull quits quivering, Malnove fires the six fifties again. There's never a warning. Over the target, gunners use their own intercom circuit. On the left, Warn calls for the rear turrets. He has a Zero in his sight. He tracks for three seconds. He fires. He sees his tracers go in. The Zero flies on. "Dang!" It's young Warn's strongest expletive. We score no kills. Connor and the other gunners see a B-29 in our formation burst into flames. It's one of the stray ducklings that chose to fly with us. Connor counts only eight blossoming chutes. He sees Zero pilots strafing the men hanging in the straps. He sees a giant fiery cross spiraling to earth. The Zeros break off. Huglin turns the formation toward the south-southeast to avoid the guns of Osaka, as we set course for the coast of Honshu, which is in sight.

We've done it again! Survived a mission. Twenty-three down; twelve to go! Don Connor switches intercom circuits. He says, "Gasoline is streaming off the No. Three nacelle." My instant fear , *Will it catch fire from the exhaust turbine wheels which run white hot*? I suggest to Littlewood that we shut down No. Three engine until we can find the source of the leak. He concurs. I close the throttles, turn off the ignition switch and close the cowl-flaps. Taylor pushes the feathering-button. A solenoid opens the feathering-valve. Hydraulic pressure drives a gear system in the spinner, which rotates the propeller blades to an aerodynamically stable position. Prop revolution slows, then ceases. Our airplane slows. We drop out of formation. Sgt. Don Van Inwegen, Tail Gunner on Bearden's plane watches it happen. He notifies Bearden. Bearden sends the 99th on with the Group. He and his crew risk their lives to drop back and fly "Buddy" with us. Littlewood, Taylor, Caldwell, Malnove and I confer. We head for Iwo. Littlewood asks Bearden to have Lt. Phil Klein, Navigator, help us fly the shortest course. I want to trade altitude for velocity in a long slow "power-glide". Littlewood agrees. He trims the plane. I make power settings by intuition and try to devise a rational fuel transfer plan.

Since we did not get seriously hit by flak or by any Zero's shells, and since no one aboard can see the source of the leak, I think the source must be in the No. Three engine fuel supply system. Connor thinks otherwise, because the quantity is profuse. From the tail, Richardson says, "I've got gasoline all over my left window." I can't see the stream of leaking fuel. I yield the point. I next suspect that No. Three wing tank has somehow ruptured and the gas is being sucked through the nacelle-to-wing "join-line". I commence a plan to distribute fuel from No. Three tank to tanks One, Two and Four via the fuel transfer system.

I monitor relative quantities by recording the length of transfer periods. I also monitor the fuel quantity gauges. Something's funny. I haven't yet added fuel to No. Four but the needle doesn't go down even though the engine continues to run. The transfer pump draws the needle down on No. Three, fast enough for quick detection. I pump from Four to Two for a time. No. Four needle doesn't move.

I now think gauge Four is not functioning, that tank Four is leaking and that airfoil aerodynamics is blowing fuel diagonally aft and inboard, across the bottom of the wing, until it reaches the No. Three nacelle. I keep No. Four running and continue to pump from Four to Two and One. No. Four engine soon stops from lack of fuel. The leak stops also, proving that it was No. Four. Taylor and I feather, and shut down No. Four. Now it won't be dangerous to run No. Three.

I open the throttles and turn on the ignition. Taylor pushes the button to unfeather the prop. The propeller blades do not rotate out of feathering position. He tries the button again; nothing happens. Littlewood reaches over and pushes it. Nothing. Malnove tries. Nothing. I try. Nothing, nothing, nothing! I take off my flak vest and my parachute and climb out of my seat. I squeeze my way around the turrets, past the navigator and radio operator to the back side of my instrument panel. I pull the feathering control-circuit fuse. It looks O.K. but I put in a new one. I use Schultz's intercom. I tell Taylor to press the button. Nothing, still nothing. I'm stymied. I go back to my station. There is some fuel left in No. Three tank. I set the system pumping into tanks One and Two. I don't know for sure how much fuel remains, because I don't know how much leaked overboard. End of mission dipstick readings have shown that my fuel consumption logs are more accurate than the fuel gauges in terms of quantity of fuel remaining. My log is now invalid. Can I trust the gauges?

The Air Corps, the Boeing Company, the Wright Company have given no information via publication or by oral instruction, on how to fly a B-29 for maximum range with only two engines on one side in operation. We are on our own. I increase power on each of my engines to retard our loss of altitude.

Capt. Littlewood does a marvelous job of keeping the plane trimmed and of maintaining the slow steady descent. Caldwell and Malnove work together to give me continuously updated ground-speed data. I now have time to apply the aerodynamic laws which relate horsepower to velocity, the physical principles which relate decrease of altitude to kinetic energy, the thermodynamic principles which relate internal pressures and external-load conditions to power-output of engines, the fuel-flow/horsepower - output data developed by Wright for the R-3350 engines, and the relation between indicated air-speed, true air-speed, and ground-speed, to derive maximum-range power settings.

Our two engines, and our faithful airplane, are performing well, as we drone slowly but steadily on, but there are hours to go between us and Iwo and I do not know if the fuel will last. In Bearden's plane, Sgt. Hal Worley, Right Gunner, with his own Kodak "Monitor" camera, clicks off a shot of old "574" sidling through the air with two paralyzed propellers.

Littlewood orders us to stow everything loose, in case we have to ditch. The rule in ditching procedure is to throw the loose, and thus dangerous, items overboard. Now, however, Littlewood does not want to open the bomb-bay doors. What if the induced drag would upset the delicate stability of the state of trim? What if we couldn't get the doors closed?

Littlewood yells at Phil True to stow the flak vests that had been hastily discarded and piled in disarray. There is no place to stow them. Each man usually stows his own vest under his feet; but, we're all too busy now. True struggles with the stiff and heavy vests. He is finally able to stuff each one into some pocket of space around the gun turrets. He's sweating now. Littlewood beckons True to his side. He says, "If we have to bail out, you go first." True is certainly gaining orientation experience.

Caldwell gives an E.T.A. of twenty minutes. We should be elated, but twenty more minutes will seem an eon. We've used up 10,500 feet of altitude and most of our gas, if the gauges are right. Number Two is on empty. I pump a shot from One to Two. Now both read empty, or maybe a hair above. I hope each tank has the same amount. It won't do us any good to have one engine running when the other quits.

Littlewood decides to hold 3,000 feet. I have to increase power. I'm reluctant, but I accept the command. I dread to boost the engines to a higher, steeper point on the fuel consumption curve, but I know Littlewood is right. There are eroded remnants of volcanic peaks on Iwo.

Malnove and Taylor sight Iwo. Littlewood doesn't like the low-lying cloud cover. Bearden doesn't have enough gas to linger. He radios Littlewood, "So long, Ted. See you on Tinian." He sets course for home. God, we feel alone.

Among the B-29s needing to stop at Iwo Jima that day, we are the long, late, last arrival. All other planes are safely landed and parked. By the time we finally get to Iwo, however, a Pacific rainsquall is sweeping the Island. The B-29 control tower tells Capt. Littlewood, "The field is closed. Ceiling Zero. Visibility Zero. Ditch or bail out at sea. The Navy will pick you up." The P-51 tower breaks in. "I see you on radar. I'll talk you down, if you think you can land on our 3,000 foot runway." Littlewood says, "We're coming in."

Littlewood is engrossed, every fiber tuned to the glowing green instruments, the voice in the headset, the response through the throat-mike, the aerodynamic forces manifested as tactile pressures through the wheel-yoke and rudder-pedals, the engine power and propeller thrust sensed through the throttle-knobs. In his hands, the great wounded bird responds with exquisite precision to each radioed correction of heading and inclination, while the man in the tower ceaselessly follows the pulsing-trace of our electronically illumined blip as it steadily "flies" through the glimmering translucence of the face of his scope.

During the eternity of our rain-shrouded circle, approach, and descent, I strain to see my two faithful engines through the watery slipstream coursing cross Caldwell's window. I listen with appreciation to the resonance of their rhythmic roar, yet dreading I might hear a first faint rumble of some throbbing irregular beat. I fix the instruments with hypnotic gaze, as though by force of will to maintain engine performance. The dials glare back with emotionless neutrality. I break off before I become entranced. I prepare for instant response, if Littlewood calls for emergency power.

In mute meditation we wait out the end of this endless flight, whatever that end will be. Our silent questions are our fears, our hopes, our prayers. *We won't run out of gas now, will we? An engine can't fail now, can it? The plane won't fly into the side of Mt. Surabachi, will it? Radar-guided landings usually work, don't they?*

Littlewood begins the final let-down. I remind him that a descent too steep can trap as much as twenty-seven gallons of fuel in each tank. Taylor calls out the altimeter readings. Littlewood orders, "Full flaps." Taylor responds. The flaps rumble back and down from the wings. Connor and Warn report, "Flaps full down." Our flight path flares. Littlewood adjusts the throttles. He orders, "Landing gear." Taylor flips the switch. The huge struts, with their two-wheel trucks grind down from nacelles Two and Three. The nose wheel and strut crank down from the fuselage. Struts clunk into place. Connor and Warn report; Taylor reports, "Wheels down and locked."

This is it. If we're off the mark, it's too late now. With gear down, and with so little altitude, our two valiant engines can't power a pull-up. There will be no second chance go-around. Oh Jeanie, I love you.

Littlewood sees the near end of the runway seconds before he touches down in a slightly bouncy, but deliciously safe landing.

Littlewood uses as much brake as he can without causing a skid on the wet tarmac. Our gross weight is now down to 68,000 lbs., half of what it was at takeoff. The brakes hold. We stop, just barely, at the other end of the runway. Ground crewmen guide Littlewood to a parking spot. He says, "Cut the engines." I do with alacrity. We open the hatches. Everyone disembarks. I intend to. Instead I fall asleep at my station. Malnove climbs back in to shake me awake. I'm stiff, but I make it to the good, good ground. It's Iwo, but we love it, and we say prayerful thanks to the Marines and G.I.'s who gave their lives here. They saved us. We huddle under the wings. The rain turns to a sprinkle. I walk under the right wing between engines Three and Four. I see the clean round hole in the bottom of the wing. It appears to be about an inch in diameter. It's closer to nacelle Four than Three. We won't be flying old "574" to Tinian tonight.

The ubiquitous G.I. troop carrier comes for us. We ride across the sands of Iwo Jima. We pass the sandstone hills honeycombed with Jap-dug tunnels. We get off at the transient overnighters encampment, sited somewhere on Iwo's western shore. We are issued blanket, pillowcase, towel and G.I. soap. We are assigned a cot in a tent. We shower. The water, piped hot out of the sand, is sulphurous and salty. We are not warned against soap. Neither water nor towel will remove the salted soap-scum. We rest on our cots. We itch, but we're too tired to scratch. Richardson says he saw a Zero explode. "The formation following ours got him." "Dang!" Warn sits up, "That was my dang Zero!" Connor and the gunners tell us about the chutes on the water, the B-29 going down, the eight parachuters, the strafing. It stops sprinkling.

A chow gong sounds. At an outside mess, we serve ourselves G.I. coffee, spam, mashed potatoes, gravy, green beans (from cans), G.I. bread, orange marmalade and tropical butter. We have canned pears for an extra desert.

We stroll toward the beach. Sulphurous steam rises where our shoes scuffle the sand. The sun has dropped below the low-hanging layer of clouds, and is beginning to descend below the rim of an earth, whose spherical curvature is so perfectly delineated by the vast Pacific's oceanic horizon. In the western sky, the clouds are breaking up. Distant clouds, fluffy and feathery, are lit with the pink, red and orange hues of the Pacific sunset. Nearer clouds, retaining a dark intensity, form weird fantastically lovely silhouettes, black and deep- purple, against the fiery glow.

Caldwell, who is Protestant says, "Connor, I'm sure glad you went to Mass this morning." Malnove says, "Me too, Connor, and since not one of the Chaplains on Tinian is a Rabbi, it's days like this that make Shultz and I glad you Christian guys worship Jehovah."

Capt. Littlewood rounds us up. He's hitched a ride for us to Tinian with a B-29 crew. They stopped on Iwo for minor repairs. They want to take off before dark. It's early dusk now, but with no air traffic, there is enough light. We grab our gear and scramble onto a truck. At the flight line we pile into the rear compartment of a 504th Bomb Group plane. We slam the hatch and the plane is rolling. We can't see out, but we relax and let the other crew do the flying.

It's dark when we land on North Field. For the 9th Bomb Group, the mission is accomplished. We ride in jeeps to the 9th Group Encampment. They will debrief us tomorrow. We walk to our huts. We wash off the soap scum with sweet Tinian well water. Back at our huts we hit the sack.

6 June, 09:30: We meet in the briefing room. We tell our story to the debriefing officers. They credit us with a completed mission. They will ask "Wing" to give Warn his Zero. The session ends. They leave. We linger.

Red Cross girls, Sue Schroeder and Kay Brennen, bring coffee and donuts. We dunk. We talk. We're survival high, but guilt nags. We've never named old "574". Someone says, "Nameless Lady". As comrades-in-arms, we each know that's her name, but with regret, we yield to soldierly superstition. We can't risk changing our luck by naming her at this late date.

On 10 June, the Lady without a name is returned to Tinian by a crew from the 504th Group, who left their plane on Iwo on the way home from the raid on the Osaka-Amagasaki urban area. We check out a couple of jeeps, and ride down to the flight line. M. Sgt. John Dreese, Crew Chief, and Sgt. Sherman McAffee, Ass't. Crew Chief, two mechanical aces, whose diligent expert care has made old nameless "574" such a faithful Lady, are installing new spark plugs, thirty-six to each engine. Dreese climbs down from the scaffold in front of No. Two. He grins as he points to the neatly painted "bomb" which McAffee has just added to the row of "bombs" under Capt. Littlewood's window.

Dreese says, "She'll be ready to fly on the next mission. They did a good job up on Iwo. Patched nine flak holes. Installed a new fuel tank and fuel-level sensor for number Four. A Zero got you from below with a twenty-mm cannon. For some reason the shell didn't explode, but by chance it hit the fuel-level sensor, and caused it to stick in a fixed position." Dreese pauses while we ponder. He continues, "You couldn't unfeather the number Three prop, because there was no pressure to actuate the hydraulic mechanism in the spinner hub. The pump's electric motor burned out when you feathered the prop. Those pump motors are fused on the control side of the solenoid, but not on the power side. You've got a new motor now."

That Zero pilot must have turned his nose up, on his way down, to fire one last pot-shot. He was lucky, but in the end, we are luckier; we've since survived one more mission (in aircraft "900"). Only three more to go.

PROQUOTES

"Ye shall hear of wars and rumors of war."

Jesus of Nazareth, Matthew 24:6.

"War is at best barbarism...Its glory is all moonshine. It is only those who have neither fired a shot nor heard the shrieks and groans of the wounded who cry aloud for blood, more vengeance, more desolation. War is hell."

General William Tecumseh Sherman
Attributed to a graduation address at Michigan Military Academy (June 19, 1879)

"In war there is no second prize for the runner-up."

General Omar Bradley

"No man is entitled to the blessings of freedom unless he be vigilant in its preservation."

General Douglas MacArthur

"Mr. Vice-President, Mr. Speaker, members of the Senate and the House of Representatives:

Yesterday, December 7, 1941 - a date which will live in infamy - the United States of America was suddenly and deliberately attacked by naval and air forces of the empire of Japan.

The United States was at peace with that nation and, at the solicitation of Japan, was still in conversation with its government and its emperor looking toward the maintenance of peace in the Pacific.

Indeed, one hour after Japanese air squadrons had commenced bombing in the American island of Oahu the Japanese Ambassador to the United States and his colleague delivered to our Secretary of State a formal reply to a recent American message. And, while this reply stated that it seemed useless to continue the existing diplomatic negotiations, it contained no threat or hint of war or of armed attack.

It will be recorded that the distance of Hawaii from Japan makes it obvious that the attack was deliberately planned many days or even weeks ago. During the intervening time the Japanese government has deliberately sought to deceive the United States by false statements and expressions of hope for continued peace.

The attack yesterday on the Hawaiian Islands has caused severe damage to American naval and military forces. I regret to tell you that very many American lives have been lost. In addition, American ships have been reported torpedoed on the high seas between San Francisco and Honolulu."

President Franklin Delano Roosevelt
Excerpt of speech to Congress asking for Declaration of War
(December 8, 1941)

Part II: Aero Assault

North of Nagasaki

1st ***published 2000, The Distinguished Flying Cross Society, Turner Pub. Co.***

2 September, 1945, 08:40: *The hell with it. Engine power is set. Littlewood has throttle control. The engines can run for a while without me watching little green needles do their little green numbers on a luminous lot of little green dials.* Via sequential contortions, I clamber into a crouch, with knees and feet upon my seat. I stretch up. I look down over the sill of my high window. I want my best view of this low-level bomb run. At 1500 feet above the valley floor, we are making our second pass over the target. The first has been in warning.

A ragged mob of the skinniest guys I've ever seen is frenetically cavorting in wild celebration. They are dancing, waving, yelling; but we can't hear them, even though Major Feil, commanding the mission, is flying as soft and as slow as a B-29 can go.

Willing or nilling, every earthbound ear in this end of Kyushu is hearing Harold Feil. In deliberately-delivered stentorophonic-decibels, electronically hurled to earth, Feil is repeating his first-pass message.

> "AMERICAN PRISONERS OF WAR!
>
> GREETINGS FROM THE COMMANDER-IN-CHIEF OF THE ARMED FORCES OF THE UNITED STATES OF AMERICA!

THIS IS MAJOR HAROLD FEIL...9TH BOMB GROUP... 20TH AIR FORCE!...YOU ARE NOW LIBERATED FROM JAPANESE AUTHORITY!

THE WAR IS ENDED!

AMERICA HAS WON!...JAPAN HAS SURRENDERED!

YOUR ORDERS ARE!...REMAIN IN THIS CAMP!...THE MARINES ARE ON THE WAY!...THEY KNOW THIS SITE!... THEY KNOW YOU ARE HERE!

REPEAT!...REMAIN IN THIS CAMP!...THE MARINES ARE COMING!

GOD BLESS YOU!"

In sixteen minutes, aboard the battleship *Missouri*, anchored in Tokyo Bay, General Douglas MacArthur, for the victors, and Foreign Minister, Mamoru Shigemitsu, for the vanquished, will sign formal surrender documents, drafted in U.S.A. terms. Every Nip, even that divine son-of-the-sun, Hirohito the Emperor, will be subject to the Governor of Japan, Douglas MacArthur.

None of us faults Feil for being sixteen minutes premature.

"Bombs away!" Food, clothes, soap, towels, razors, cokes, candy, gum and tobacco parachute downward, aimed to reach earth beyond the celebrating congregation of free men. Warn sees a failed chute-load of canned goods smash through a rat-shack roof. "Dang! Look what those dang cans did! Hope no one was in <u>that</u> dang barracks shack!" Connor sees it too. "They're all outside, George. First time around, I saw the strong guys carrying the weak guys out."

We're not far north of Nagasaki. For the sake of our guys below, we thank God this camp is, and was on August 9th, far enough.

Thank God "Fat Man" and "Little Boy" shocked sufficient sanity into that incredulously crazy collective-psyche, which is peculiarly Japanese, to enable these Rising Sun Samurai pretenders to admit inglorious defeat, and to accept ignominious degradation of lost Nipponese face.

Thank God Harry Truman is a real Commander-In-Chief. Thank God he had the wisdom and fortitude to make the awesome decision. He saved millions of lives.

Feil leads our sixteen-plane formation in a wide circle. The 9th Bomb Group, with the 1st, 5th and 99th Squadrons each contributing B-29s and crews, has the honor of flying this mission sans support of any other bomb, or fighter, Group.

Aligned for a twenty-mile final run on target. Feil orders emergency power. Littlewood opens the throttles, while I shift fuel-mixture controls to "auto-rich", increase turbo-boost pressure to forty-six inches of mercury, set propeller pitch for 2600 rpm, and synchronize the engines at 2,000 horsepower per engine.

Thunder from 1,152 air-cooled unmuffled cylinders, generating 128,000 horses, spinning 256 monstrous propeller blades, rumbles through Southern Kyushu's terraced hills. Vibratory waves of energy riffle the rice in the hillside paddies.

Following Feil, the formation swoops between the hills to 500 feet above the valley deck. Acceleration builds upon acceleration, upon acceleration. Feil's show of strength, speed, and power is to thrill the esteem-starved souls of our abused and abased buddies below, and to chill the mean brain of any vindictive-minded recalcitrant son-of-a-Samurai ninny in the vicinity.

At 375 mph, we near the camp. Feil orders a synchronous wing-waggling farewell. It's dangerous. We've never practiced. We crewmen think it is a fun ride. Each knows his own Aircraft Commander is an Airman's Ace, and any one of us will follow Feil in any B-29 adventure. I'm up on the seat again. I grab the top of the instrument panel for balance.

Our salute is returned. The parachuted box of furled flags is open. Each ground-bound comrade is waving "Old Glory". Each striped and spangled banner is a fresh incarnation of the hallowed colors. In myriad dancing manifestations, rippling facets of red, white and blue scintillate brilliantly in the dazzling illumination of the late summer sun. I sit down. I go back to work. I'm not the only one crying.

Feil zooms to gain a bit of altitude. We level off, and slow down to a 200 mph cruise. Feil leads us through a wide turn. He comes out on a due south heading. We fly over the Amakusa Sea, near smoking volcanic mountains on the western shore. Hydrogen sulfide stench fills the plane.

Feil climbs to the East. The air clears. Cockpits cool. Good. Our long flight home will be more comfortable.

Feil sets course for Tinian. He disassembles the formation. Littlewood and Donica buddy-up. We climb 500 feet, to the left, and return to compass heading. I check all instruments. I check the engines by sight and sound. I check our fuel supply. All is well. I relax. I meditate to the mantra of engine drone.

We're flying our last mission. It's number thirty-three. Capt. Littlewood and crew are listed for two more P.O.W. relief flights, but there is no mission credit in peacetime. We have no regret for falling short of the thirty-five required to complete an aerial-combat tour-of-duty. A soldierly dread, of the law-of-averages, has been lately seeping from subconscious internment into the wearisome reality of conscious cognizance.

With peace prevailing, averages have no dread. Missions of mercy make flying fun.

Off intercom, Malnove is in opportune earnest. "Can I fly the plane for awhile, Ted?" At Littlewood's "O.K.", Taylor scrambles to yield place, lest

Littlewood reconsider. After eight and a half hours, even the best seat in the house becomes wearisome. In haste, Taylor forgets to stoop. He knocks his noggin on the inner-curve of our tubular fuselage. There is no serious concussion of cerebral matter, as he buries his dome in the fiberglass-filled/nylon-covered, thermal insulation blanket, but the brim of his precious hot-pilot's hat is crumpled even closer to his ears. Taylor is elated at the increase in Air Corps panache he can now command.

In cautious consideration of the autopilot control panel, floor-mounted in the aisle, Taylor eases aft in a head-bowed shuffle. He slumps to his left side on the deck by my station. He draws his lank frame into a fetal pose, in best-fit accommodation to restricted space. A natural airman, his snores are soon in synchronous symphony with the four R-3350's.

Vibrations of "Taylor's Theme and Variations" joggle the memory molecules of my mental mush...*Amphetamine*!...With a slug of tomato juice, I gulp my pernicious prescriptive pill. I'm going to be damn sure Littlewood remains alert to monitor Malnove. I want no ugly-aerobatic aerodynamically-unstable aircraft-attitude to be inadvertently-induced by the accidental-antic of an amateur-aeronaut. We don't have that much altitude, nor do we have that much balance in Lady Luck's account.

Briefing for this mission started before midnight yesterday. The Flight Surgeon issues amphetamines to each crewman who must (or who elects to) remain awake for mission duration. With no back-up engineer aboard, I have no choice. Suddenly I see it, the source of my envy. *Who would be engineer, if I played pilot?*

I listen to the off-mike conversation between Littlewood and Malnove. It's a flying lesson. Good. Keeps their minds on business.

Caldwell is sharp and cool enough to play five-card stud with the big brass. He is our inside agent on "true" rumors. "Hey guys, you know in two or three months we'll be home, and out of the service. Do you suppose there'll be any jobs for bomber-crew experts?" Connor says, "Wow! Promoted all the way to civilian."

In silence, I visualize my Jeannie and Baby Donna. *I'll soon be a civilian husband and father.*

Littlewood doesn't comment. He hopes to be one of the few allowed to stay in the service. Why not? He's single. He's already a Captain. He loves to fly. The Air Corps has the best airplanes in the world. There won't be war for another fifty years, maybe never.

KAWASAKI, NAGOYA & FUSELAGE PHILOSPHY

It's intercom time for the rest of us.

Smith. You guys gonna wear your medals when you get home?

Connor. Yeah, a day or two. I'm anxious to get into civvies though.

Richardson. Me too, but I want to be a hero for a week, maybe. We can't wear `em here.

Warn. I saw a dang Colonel in the 58th Wing wearin' every dang medal there is. Everybody was dang-well salutin' that guy. Snickerin' later though. I'd hate to be in that dang guy's outfit.

As he often does, Warn inspires a pause.

Calhoun. Medals? The Distinguished Flying Cross is the only medal they gave us.

Warn. Yeah. I got six different dang orders, on six different dang dates, sayin', "Dear Sergeant Warn, you are such a brave and handsome young airman, us big brass hats of the 20th Air Force just have to give you one more dang Air Medal. By order of General Gung Ho." Dang, I better not say his name. I might get courtmartialed.

The crew seldom knows whether Warn is being funny or serious, but we are "dang-well" glad he flies with us.

Connor. You're young alright, George, You just had your eighteenth birthday; I guess that gal back in Memphis thinks you're handsome, at least in your uniform. But you're no braver than the rest of us. We fly these damn missions mainly because we don't know what they'll do to us if we say, "I'm not going."

Schultz. (*Inclined to seriousness*). Hey, don't make fun of the Air Medal guys, just because we get one every five missions.

Smith. It's more than just five flights. The qualification is that we flyers have to be put in harm's way on each of the five missions.

Calhoun. We qualified. We came back from every mission with a bunch of holes in the plane.

Cotner. We never said anything about it to you guys, but Littlewood, Taylor and I knew damn well we were in harm's way every time we went down the runway tryin' to get this overloaded firetrap in the air.

Smith. The Air Corps doesn't give credit for that kind of danger. Harm's way is defined as being in a spot where you can be injured or killed as a direct result of enemy action.

Cotner. You're just as dead if you burn up in fire caused by Air Corps action.

Smith. (*Also serious, and a true intellectual*). The Air Medal is awarded for Gallantry in Aerial Combat. It ranks with the Bronze Star. You respect that medal don't you, George?

Warn. O.K., O.K., I'll wear my dang Air Medals, if I can get some. Maybe I can trade one to some dang Infantry guy for a Bronze Star.

Caldwell. Don't worry George, you'll get your Air Medal, and at least five Oak Leaf Clusters to pin on it. At the Separation Center, they'll give you all the awards that haven't caught up to you. (*In confidential tone*). Don't spread this, or my tail will be muddier than a Nipponese dirt dauber's ass. Col. Huglin wants to be the one to tell the troops that everybody in the 9th Bomb Group will get a Presidential Unit Citation Badge with an Oak leaf Cluster.

Schultz. How many Battle Stars will we get to wear on our Asiatic-Pacific Campaign medal?

Caldwell. Four: Battle of Japan, Battle of Iwo Jima, Battle of the Marianas, Battle of the Carolines.

We pause as we review our experience with Pacific Island geography.

Richardson. (*Going back to the Unit Citations*). What's Harry Truman citing us for?

Caldwell. 15 April 1945...

Calhoun & Connor. ...Kawasaki! Kawasaki!

Caldwell. Kawasaki Urban Area...468 B-29s...low altitude...nighttime fire raid.

Smith. Yeah, and the 20th Air Force brass scheduled the 9th to be the last Group over the target.

Warn. Kawasaki...Dang...Dang...Dang! We dang well earned at least two dang little badges.

Caldwell. I agree George; but, the President only gave us one for that mission.

Connor. I saw three planes get hit with something. I think all of them went down. I know two of them did.

Warn. I saw one go down on my dang side. It was burnin'...burnin'... burnin...

Calhoun. (*Having had the best view from his center topside bubble*). I saw six get hit. Four went down. Two were in trouble when I lost them in the smoke column.

Kawasaki was our third mission with Lt. Karl Pattison as Airplane Commander, just selected from among the Pilots (20th Air Force shop-talk for co-pilot) to replace Major Feil, our original A.C. Kawasaki was Pattison's first mission as Airplane Commander, sans a rated A.C. flying check-pilot in the right-hand seat.

Caldwell. We didn't have to worry any more about Pattison being too young and inexperienced to be our new A.C.

Cotner. We damn sure didn't. When we flew into that stink-foul cloud of ink-black smoke, the updraft was so violent I looked at my rate-of-climb indicator. The needle spun around the dial 270 degrees, from zero to 6,000 feet per minute. I'd never seen it go beyond 700 f.p.m. before. The g force on my butt, and the "upside down" needle, gave me vertigo. Instant recall lit my wit and cooled my panic. Sans bomb-load, an upside down B-29 is structurally sound, and its "fighter-plane-type" carburetors will not fail the engines. I looked around at Pat to see how he was going to get us right side up again. He was flyin' by instruments, holdin' the wheel-yoke steady as a guy driving the wife and kids home from Sunday School.

Caldwell. If we had to lose Feil, when he got promoted to Operations Officer, we were lucky to get Pat.

Warn. There was one of those dang fireballs chasin' us. I tried my dangdest to shoot it, but it was closin' so dang-nab fast I couldn't track it. It was dang sure for gettin' us, `til we went into that dang smoke. I never saw it again after that. Guess it lost us. Dang-well it did.

We used to laugh when George told us he saw a dang fireball; but, enough gunners have reported seeing them, that even the Wing-level brass believe the Japs may have some new weapon. We hope they never build many of them.

Schultz. Szarko told me that the aircraft maintenance report says every one of the 9th Group planes that returned needed some sort of repair for damage caused by enemy action: flack, night-fighter bullets, ramming (balls-of-fire?), updraft.

Updraft? Can Kawasaki burning be counted enemy action? As we ponder, Caldwell gives a terse account of our side's human loss.

Caldwell. Lingle and Payne got shot up bad but at least they made it to Iwo and landed O.K.. Some men with Purple Hearts, but all alive. Malo, Sullivan, Jones and Carver were shot down. Four crews missing., forty-five men. Major Chapel was a passenger on Sullivan's plane.

Cotner. (*Memory cued by Caldwell's count*). Back at McCook, Major Chapel used to give me a ride out to the base every morning in his nifty blue Buick convertible. He didn't have to be on that mission. He volunteered. He was a leader who went where he asked his men to go. Harvey Glick on Sullivan's crew, John Scanlon on Carver's crew...those guys and I went all the way back to Aircraft Maintenance Engineering School at Yale, to B-29 school at Boeing, and to Flight Engineer's School at Lowry Field.

Connor. Right after the air-sea search failed to find any Kawasaki survivors, Major Waterman came by the enlisted men's quarters askin' where all the flight crewmen were.

Warn. Yeah. Like that dang X-O thought we'd tell him if we knew. That guy doesn't even wear his dang wings.

Smith. He <u>is</u> the Squadron Executive Officer, George. Flying status is not required for that job.

Connor. He was lookin' for volunteers.

Calhoun. Well, he'd just found six. Smitty, Schultz, Rich, Warn, Connor and I had to go next door with him, so he could watch us pack-up Carver's men's footlockers.

Schultz. That was tough duty. Last time we had been in their hut, we were all jokin' around tellin' tall tales.

Warn. I couldn't help you guys. I had to walk. Waterman saw me. He didn't stop me. He knew I was dang-well cryin'...why did I have to be the dang-fool idiot asshole jerk who was always kiddin' Donegan and Studeroth about their sweethearts goin' out every night with the dang-nab draft dodgers back home?

Richardson. It didn't take long to get all their stuff stowed away. It was a pitiful little bit really. In a way, it helped to get the pictures of wives, girlfriends and family out of sight.

Smith. I guess it helped, but waitin' in that hut for the G.I. truck to come, and lookin' at all those footlockers lined up on those empty cots, and readin' all those names stenciled in big black letters...SHIMEL...MARTEN... JENKINS...DONEGAN...STUDEROTH... CHRISTIANO...I felt like I was lookin' at a row of coffins in a morgue.

Warn. Yeah, and I came back just as that dang Waterman was makin' us hurry those footlockers onto that dang truck, so a replacement crew could move in.

Comments cease. The pause this time is perhaps for prayer.

Cotner. (*In silent muse, typical of the crew's thoughts*). *I'd pray, but what can we pray for; that forty-five men survived the flak, the bullets, the fires, the fall to earth, the crashes, and are "safe" in some filthy, foul Japanese prison* *camp? We've seen captured Jap films. We know what those little bastards do to prisoners.*

Richardson. (*Hoping for a break in the tough talk*). I don't know whether I want to know what the other Unit Citation is for.

Warn. (*Also hoping for a break*). Why does the President call it a Unit Citation?

Caldwell. Because it's awarded to everyone in the Unit, flyers and ground staff.

Warn. Even the dang cooks?

Caldwell. Yes.

Warn. I'm glad those dang guys get something. Gettin' up early every dang mornin'. Making the dang coffee. Peelin' all them dang-nab potatoes.

Shultz. I want to know what the second citation is for.

Caldwell. Well, the other Citation is for the fourteen mining missions the 9th flew to booby-trap the Shimonoseki Strait. You know, don'tcha, that the 20th Air Force Brass was kind enough to give that task to our Wing exclusively.

Warn. Well, thanks a dang-nab lot, Brass...Sir! I dang-well did not want to keep going back to the dang Shimono-dang-seki Straits. Them dang straits were poison. Them dang searchlights grabbin' us, and them dang night fighters. Man! Them dang-nab tracers comin' out of the darkness from every dang-nab direction there is.

Smith. I hope we get all our medals, but we'll be O.K., even if they never pass out the rest of them. I was reading up on medals over at Wing

Headquarters the other day. Consider yourselves genuine heroes. The first award of the Distinguished Flying Cross was in 1927, to then Captain Charles Lindberg, and the only civilian award ever made was to Amelia Earhart. That's good enough company for me. I damn sure won't be diffident about wearin' that medal, even when I'm a civilian.

Warn . Dang nab it Smitty, why don't you use the dang Queen's American like the rest of us? What does "not diffident" say?

Smith. Not retiring. Not shy.

Warn. S...H...Y?...Three letters...Dang.

Connor. (*Who keeps a journal*). I'm lookin' at my notes about our D.F.C. mission: "lead-crew, daylight-formation, 16,000 feet, Aichi Aircraft Factory, Nagoya."

Cotner. (*Interrupting*). Col. Huglin flew in our plane. I suppose he got the D.F.C. too.

Caldwell. If he did, it would be a bronze oak-leaf cluster. He got his first D.F.C. on March 4th for flying with Capt. McNeil on the 9th Group's second Tokyo mission.

Cotner. We were lucky as hell to have a brave Commanding Officer. He flew on seventeen missions, always with the lead crew.

Caldwell. Yeah, and he didn't have to. In fact, General Davies finally ordered him to slow down; made him fly no more than every other one of our scheduled missions.

Smith. Sometimes I felt I would have been a lot luckier to fly with a leader who was a coward like me.

Taylor. Yeah. At Aichi, we were briefed to go in at 20,000 feet. Huglin kept looking for daylight under the clouds, so Malnove could make a clear-vision run. He found daylight for sure, after we were all the way down to 16,000 feet. Malnove had clear vision. The ack-ack gunners had clear vision. The zero pilots had clear vision.

Littlewood. Listen guys, everyone on flying status in the Air Corps is a volunteer. We're here to win the war. Remember? I've seen the "recon" photos of what once was the Aichi Factory. We obliterated it. The Japs won't build airplanes, engines or anything else in that factory. Let's quit talkin' about bravery or cowardice, and just keep on gettin' the job done.

Connor. (*After a pause, comes back to his journal).* The zeros always gang up on the lead crew. They put four bullet holes in us that day.

Calhoun. Yeah, the little bastards knew our bombardier was too busy to fire the six fifty's at `em. They swarmed us head-on. They were mad damned hornets. I took over Malnove's six guns. I got some hits, but didn't slow `em down.

Caldwell. Malnove did value the clear-vision opportunity Col. Huglin gave him. Thirty-six B-29s dropped a hundred and forty-four 4,000 pounders, on his cue. Reconnaissance credited us with ninety-six percent destruction. That's what earned us the medal. They don't give the D.F.C. for mediocre results.

Smith. The rumor was that he was one of the sharp ones, when the brass put our crew together back at McCook.

Caldwell. That was no rumor; but, accuracy is damned difficult, and skill is hard to maintain. You can't guide the damn bombs after they leave the plane.

Warn. Dang. It looks like Gen. Le May, Leonardo Da Vinci, or somebody smart woulda thought how to do that by now.

Calhoun. Bombin' those damn piss-ant bypassed Japs on Rota on our "days off" was 200 hours of damn dull duty for gunners.

Connor. Aw, Walt, you just wanted somethin' to shoot at. I'm glad nobody or nothin' was shootin' at us.

Cotner. And Rota is only thirty miles from Tinian. We didn't have to worry about gettin' lost.

Caldwell. Or runnin' out of gas.

Cotner. Touché.

My attention becomes passive; my ear hears, but my thoughts are of Jeannie and little Donna.

Warn. If we'da had some Da Vinci dang bombs, I coulda had a day off to go to the beach once in a while. That big beach down south by Tinian Town is so dang pretty.

Tinian Town, a former Japanese city of 15,000 people, was flattened by pre-invasion naval bombardment.

Warn. I never got a dang chance to see North Beach up-close. It was small, but it sure looked good from the air.

Connor. George, you know both beaches are off-limits and guarded by Marines with rifles. South Beach is full of unexploded shells and North Beach is in the "Secret Zone".

Smith. And, after Hiroshima and Nagasaki, we know why it is so secret.

Warn. The beach I wished I coulda gone to is the one some dang guys call Hidden Beach. I heard the Seabees built it, with a bunch of dang sand from Guam.

Connor. That beach is off-limits too. It's a good thing you were so overworked. If you had gone there the guards would probably have shot you.

Warn. Just for watchin'? Dang. I wasn't gonna swim there. I dang-well don't even know how.

Smith. That's the nurses' beach, George. That's why the Seabees hid it. Thirty-seven nurses didn't want thousands of horny G.I.'s lookin' at `em in their bathing suits.

Warn. I bet they dang well wanted some of us guys lookin'. I heard most of `em didn't wear any dang bathin' suit at all. I'll bet it was 20th Air Force brass who didn't want us lookin'. They were dang well afraid we'd remember why we shouldn't take chances on dyin' while we're still a bunch a dang virgins.

Warn has bared the young soldier's direst dread: eternal loss, by death or worse, of his right to know carnal love of woman. We married men, of course, fear a more appalling fate, a future sans honey after once knowing the taste.

Calhoun. (*Returns to a bearable subject*). Well, luck saved our asses again at Nagoya. A Zero coming in low from the left damn near killed Warn and me. Damn near hit a bunch of wires and cables, too.

Warn. That was dang ugly noise, them dang slugs crunching through right past me. Wish I'd got that dang Jap. There were more of them dang Zeros than I could shoot at, especially with that dang-nab ice all over my dang-nab bubble.

Smith. Over at Wing, two of the neatest medals in the book are the Army's and the Navy's, Service Commendation Medals: beautiful colors and great bas-relief sculpture. Each is awarded for Military Merit, sometimes in a joint service operation. Our crew is qualified for the Army medal but I doubt if the brass will bother to nominate us. Now that the war is over, everybody is too busy scrambling to get home.

Schultz. I never heard of that medal.

Smith. It's not often awarded. It tends to fall through the cracks between participating services.

Calhoun. What did we do to qualify?

Smith. General Davies, Commanding Officer of the 313th Wing, in his Air-Sea-Rescue report of our crew's twenty-two and a half hour solo Superdumbo mission, "commended" us, and the crew of the Navy's submarine, for excellent work in our joint air-sea rescue effort toward saving the airmen on Joe Lewis' crew.

Suddenly we're not exultant heroes anymore. In silence we relive that fateful night in May.

SHIMONOSEKI, SUPERDUMBO AND THE SUBMARINE

23 May, 1945, 0212: In mid-zenith transit, a gibbous Nippon moon waxes nigh-toward full visible luster. Those stars perceivable hang snared within the supernal glow. Cockpit lumens are doubled via reflected intensity off the cloud tops below.

Sans benefit of generated light, I make my semi-hourly entries in the fuel-use log. With wind direction and velocity from Caldwell. I calculate a new maximum range cruising speed. I increase engine power via minor adjustments to propeller-pitch, throttle setting and turbo-boost. At 7,000 feet altitude, and 198 mph indicated air speed, we cruise toward target.

...

0212: Capt. Leon Smith, aboard B-29 "T. N. Teeny" (the name in honor of his beloved niece), flies at 210 mph, 500 feet above the clouds, 7000 feet above the Pacific Ocean entrance to Japan's Bungo Strait. Bungo's broad channel separates the main islands of Kyushu (the southernmost) and Shikoku (the easternmost). Navigator, Richard Daugherty, splits Bungo's radar image down the center. He gives Smith a heading of 332°-30', for the initial leg of the overwater route to the 9th Group's target for tonight, the Shimonoseki Strait.

Smith will lead the 9th Bomb Group in a twenty-eight-plane single-file raid down Shimonoseki Strait, the second-most heavily defended area of Japan. Each crew will parachute 14,750 lbs. of anti-ship mines into an individually assigned target location. Smith's target is Port Shimonoseki Harbor.

This is our Group's eleventh mining raid on this strategic waterway, which courses between the islands of Honshu and Kyushu, and connects the Inland Sea with the Sea of Japan. Our objective is to saturate the Strait with a diabolical assortment of high-explosive naval mines: mines rigged to float at various depths below the surface, mines with magnetic attraction for steel hulls, mines triggered to explode on contact, or to detonate as random chronological surprises. We men of the 9th are proud to be chosen weapons-deployers for this blockade, conceived, supplied and technically supported by the United States Navy. The goal is to deny Inland Sea industrial ports access to materials and supplies looted from Asian nations held in thrall by years of Japan's brutal, unprovoked wars of conquest.

Reconnaissance reports and photographs show that passage of vessels through the Strait has ceased. Success is dearly achieved by aircrews of the 9th.

• • •

0213: Caldwell gives an E.T.A. to target of 0229 to our crew's rendezvous with the sub. We maintain speed and course. Looking shoreward, through intermittent breaks in the clouds, we sometimes see the lights of Miyazaki and of lesser cities along the Eastern Kyushu Coast. We wonder why the Japs fight such a stupid war. Have they never thought of blackouts?

0214: A Littlewood announcement cues a rustle of dialogue.

Littlewood. I've got an IFF. It must be from the sub. It's gotta be on the surface. I wonder if they're gettin' our signal.

IFF, "Identification, friend or foe", is an electronic system of recognition used among allied air, sea and land craft.

Smith. (*Littlewood's Smith.*) Lieutenant Caldwell, look at that blip sixty-two miles dead ahead. I've been watchin' it a while. It zigs and zags now and then. Can't tell where it's headed.

Caldwell. It's the sub. Pretty near where it ought to be. Sure is a bright blip. Good work, Smitty.

0227: Tension sharpens as we approach.

Littlewood. Thank God for radar. We might not be able to get under this cloud cover. (*Slight pause.*) Schultz, make radio contact.

Schultz. Roger, Captain.

...

In the submarine control room.

Jack Hart. (*Radar Man, 2c, yelling up the ladder, control room to conning tower.*) Unidentified aircraft at 7,000 feet, approaching on direct course, five miles to sub.

Roy Anderberg. (*Quartermaster, 1c, stationed near the top of the short ladder, conning tower to bridge.*) Commander Grant, radar sees unidentified aircraft approaching at 7,000 feet, five miles out.

J.D. Grant. (*Commanding Officer, yells into the bridge microphone.*) DIVE! DIVE! (*He hits the dive button.*) AHOOO GWAH! AHOOO GWAH!

Voice and horn fill every space on and within the boat. Each submariner knows his pre-assigned duty, and instantly proceeds with performance.

...

Littlewood. Schultz?

Schultz. Yes, sir.

Smith. (*Frustrated into interruption.*) Damn! I lost my blip. Just blinked off. Must be an electronic aberration. Maybe I can get it back.

Littlewood. Schultz, is there a problem?

Schultz. Yes, sir. I'm tryin' to reach `em on 4475 kilocycles, encrypted. I'm calling "Wharf Rat", per briefing instructions. I get no response.

Littlewood. Is your radio gear workin' right?

Schultz. Yes, sir, according to instrument checks. Shall I try voice contact?

Littlewood. Not yet. Keep tryin' encrypted. Let's assume they're not far away.

• • •

Diesels silent, intake and exhaust ports sealed, electric motors revving "full ahead" on battery power, heading ninety degrees larboard to the still glowing phosphorescent surface wake, 100 feet below the surface, having obeyed a submariner's first law of defense, Captain Grant, now in the control room, has time to reflect.

Grant. (*To Bill Bruckel, Lt. Jg Communications Officer.*) That was probably our 20th Air Force friend. What's the fastest way to contact him?

Bruckel. Voice, sir. If we come up to fifty feet, we can raise number one mast and try to get him on clear channel VHF.

Grant. We'll do it. (*He turns to Toro's Engineering Officer, Lt. Jg Bill Ruspino, whose assignment on this watch is "Dive Officer".*) Raise depth to five-oh feet.

Ruspino. Raise depth to five-oh feet, aye, aye.

Ruspino steps to the dive-station. He repeats the order to the four men, each a Seaman 1c, on dive-duty: George Cassidy, stern-planes wheel;

Arnold Baldwin, bow-planes wheel; Don Allen, compressed-air manifold valves; and Mike Majoda, ballast-tank valve-levers.

Ruspino coordinates the maneuver, as he reads the attitude, motion and position of the boat reflected on the faces of the pertinent dials and gauges.

Ruspino. (*Reports to Grant.*) Boat in final trim at five-oh feet.

Grant. Five-oh. Aye. Hold her there. (*He raises the number 1 periscope...To Bruckel*). Make contact.

Bruckel. Make contact. Aye, aye...(*To Blayne Baker, Radio Man 2c.*) Raise the antenna and contact "Early Reveler" on VHF Channel Queen.

In clear channel communication, code names are chosen for difficulty of Jap enunciation, in case an interceptor relays a message.

Baker. Aye, aye. (*Raises antenna.*) CQ...CQ...CQ...Wharf Rat calling Early Reveler...Wharf Rat calling Early Reveler...Wharf Rat calling Early Reveler...Come in, Early Reveler.

Schultz. Wharf Rat...This is Early Reveler...Go ahead Wharf Rat. (*To Littlewood.*) Wharf Rat contacted me in the clear, Captain. How much shall I tell him?

Littlewood. Tell him we'd rather communicate in code. When you get him in code, get his identity.

Baker. Identify yourself, Early Reveler. We receive no IFF.

Schultz. I'll call you on 4475. Your IFF comes in strong.

Schultz and Baker exchange identities. Each reports.

Baker. (*To Bruckel.*) Early Reveler is 9th Bomb Group's B-29, Superdumbo, Captain Ted Littlewood, Aircraft Commander.

Schultz. (*To Littlewood.*) It's the USS Toro. Commander J.D. Grant is C.O. He sends greetings.

Littlewood. Good job, Schultz. Answer any questions you can. Consult me if you need to. My question is where the hell are they? Also, what are surface weather conditions? Did their radar pick-up our twenty-eight-plane flight headed toward Bungo Strait, about a quarter hour ago? Send my greetings to Commander Grant.

Schultz. Roger, Captain.

Schultz and Baker confer in code.

Schultz. (*To Littlewood.*) Toro dove; no IFF from us. Commander Grant says, "The wind is two hundred fifty-three degrees at sixteen knots. Swells are twenty feet high. I'm trying to hold coordinates thirty-two degrees, thirty minutes north and 132 degrees and thirty minutes east. That's about twenty-nine nautical miles off the coast. Cloud ceiling is estimated at 500 feet. The air is damp and cold."

Caldwell. (*Pause.*) That's about where the blip was when they dove.

Schultz. Here's more. Commander Grant says, "The sea current curves around the east coast of Kyushu and Shikoku, flowing northeast, sixty-seven degrees bearing, at one knot per hour. Water temperature is sixty-nine degrees. It's the famed Japan Current. It's cold, but warm compared to mid-Pacific water at this longitude...we're comin' up. Breaking surface now."

Smith. (*Interrupting again.*) There comes my blip.

Schultz. Toro got IFF's and radar blips from Capt. Smith's twenty-eight-plane flight. It passed seventeen miles north of `em. There was no contact. Toro didn't dive.

Littlewood. Give my thanks to Commander Grant. Tell him he's givin' us a great radar blip. We're gonna fly straight over him to get a radar drift reading, so that we can read the wind direction and velocity at our altitude, 7,000 feet.

We complete the procedure. Caldwell adds wind aloft data to his notes: 153° at ten mph..

Littlewood. Schultz, tell Commander Grant we're gonna fly a twenty mile diameter circle centered on Toro. We'll maintain altitude and slow down to maximum endurance cruising speed...Cotner, what is that in miles per hour?

Cotner. (*Calculates briefly.*) At current weight it's one hundred seventy-two miles per hour. Miles, not nautical miles. (*Reduces power*).

Littlewood. You got all that, Schultz?

Schultz. Roger.

Littlewood. Send it, and get me an A-O.K.

Shultz. Roger. (*Pause for transmission.*) A-O.K., Captain.

...

0229: Capt. Smith flies past mountainous Kunisaki Peninsula. He steers left, midway between Himo-shima and Iawi-shima, islands which flank the channel from the Inland Sea to Sua Bay. Out of the turn, Smith wends a mid-bay course, between the convoluted shorelines converging toward Shimonoseki Strait.

Through the mountain gap defining the Strait, a prevailing breeze from the Japan Sea, soft but persistent, banks clouds, from sea-surface to 6,500 feet, against Aso-Kirako, Futago-san, and lesser peaks along Kunisaki's spine. At lower heights, the Peninsula and a portion of Sua Bay's Kyushu shore is cloud shielded from crewmen's eyes.

Smith descends to 5,500 feet, his assigned mine-drop altitude. Successive planes will drop from higher levels. He calls for 230 mph speed, standard for each plane's mine-run this night. Flight Engineer, Jim Drake, increases power.

No cloud cover exists over the Shimonoseki Strait this night. The brilliant light of the near-full moon will enable our crews to make clear-sighted mine drops. For anti-aircraft gunners and fighter planes, the light will make ducks-in-a row targets of our aluminum-skinned B-29s.

The bay narrows. Ack-ack fire from shore batteries and gunboats begins.

• • •

Bruckel. (*To Arnold Baldwin, coming off duty on the bow-plane control wheel.*) Baldwin, relieve Van Auken on main-gyroscope watch. (*To Charles Van Auken, Electrician's Mate 1c.*) Van Auken, diagnose and repair our IFF system. It sends well, but it apparently does not receive.

Van Auken. Aye, aye, Lieutenant.

Van Auken proceeds, tools of his trade secure on his electrician's belt. He tests circuits for continuity. He measures characteristics of current flow in system components. He locates a break in the shielded wire connecting the signal-boost amplifier to the receiving antenna. He replaces the wire. Superdumbo's signal is immediately visible and audible.

Van Auken. It's workin' now.

Bruckel. Good work, Van.(*To Baker*) Tell Superdumbo we've repaired our IFF. We get a strong signal from them now.

...

We drone our endless circles. As we traverse the circuit, Caldwell cues Littlewood on wind-induced corrections. Littlewood tweaks the autopilot. We carry no mines, nor any bombs. In each bomb bay an auxiliary 640 gallon tank of fuel is suspended from the bomb racks. Each tank is spliced into the fuel transfer system. I can pump gas into any of the four wing tanks. We're 1300 miles from Tinian. With careful cruise control management, we can fly another 3,200 miles if we have to.

We marvel at the bravery of the *Toro* crew. Sixty days they spend at this assignment, then a few days R and R on a beach at Guam, as another sub, and another crew, takes over here. They hide underwater by day, but whenever B-29s are in Nipponese air they rise to the surface, prepared to help any plane in trouble,

...

Leading his linear phalanx in challenge to the moonlit Nipponese aerial gauntlet, Capt. Smith sees the lights of Port Shimonoseki ahead on the right. Smith and his crew reconsider the recurrent question.

Smith. Why do the damn Japs fight sometimes so smart, but most times so dumb? They know we're here; they've been shooting at us for an hour.

It has been ten and a half minutes by chronometer; but no combat veteran would say Smith lies.

Parobek (*Radar Operator*). Yeah, I've got the moonlit ventilation back here to prove it.

Port ahead on the right; it's target time. Smith yields control to Bombardier Rolland Blanchett and Navigator Richard Dougherty. At Blanchett's "Mines away!", Flight Engineer, Drake, pours on power as Smith flies a sharp-right climbing-turn toward 14,000 feet. At 180° he's on reverse-order exit-course: Sua Bay, the Inland Sea, Bungo Strait, out over the Pacific and home to Tinian.

Seventeen planes to the rear of Smith, Aircraft Commander Joe Lewis and his crew, at assigned mining altitude of 6,500 feet, fly on attack, steadfast to purpose, above the silvery ribbon of sea-strand below. Ahead and to the left burn the lower lights of Kitakyushu Harbor illuminating their personal target for this night's work. The iterative "why dumbs" go again asked, and again unanswered.

Lewis is experiencing the charmed-life effect of an apparent milk run, while Emmons ahead, and Hendrickson behind, are being repetitively rocked by the air-mass dynamics of near-miss flack-bursts. Cogitation on the mathematics of chance, and on the vagaries of fortune, resurrects other persistent whys.

Row *(Pilot)*. Oh!...Damn! Emmons just got bounced again. Hope no one is hurt. The plane seems O.K. The Japs can't fire anywhere near <u>us</u>. Is the twenty-third of May a Shinto lucky-day for odd numbers?

Dutrow (*Bombardier*). Are you talking about twenty-three or seventeen? Either way, I hope you got that backwards. We're not Shintos.

Fiedler (*in the tail*). I don't see how Hendrickson keeps on comin'. I thought once he was gonna do a barrel roll. Can a B-29 come out of a roll? He's still got all four engines runnin'.

Canova (*left Gunner*). Why aren't the fighters up? Do the Japs think there's too much light for night fighters? They could send the damn Zeros up tonight.

Stein (*Radar Operator*). Quiet. They might hear you. We don't want to change our luck.

Mine drop deadline is coming up.

Arnold *(to Dutrow).* Is there enough light to use the bombsight?

Dutrow. Yes. How's the radar picture?

Arnold. Radar's great. Shall we use the radar/bombsight procedure? It's your call.

Dutrow. Yes. Let's use R.B.P.

Arnold. Roger.

Many variables affect the trajectories of mines deployed by parachute: altitude, winds aloft and near the sea (chutes are rigged to open at 800 feet), mine configuration, and true components of aircraft velocity (direction and speed) with respect to the aiming point. The Norden bombsight manages most variables well. It is not, however, a chute-drop instrument. Teamwork is required between Bombardier and radar-aided Navigator. The 9th has acquired skill at placing mines on target.

Arnold (*to Dutrow*). Aim the plane at the shoreline, directly opposite the harbor.

Dutrow. Roger.

Via controls on the bombsight, and through electronic circuitry engaging bombsight-with-autopilot, he is now guiding the plane.

Dutrow. (*Peering through the scope, and fine-tuning the knobs.*) Cross hairs on course to aiming point.

Arnold. Roger. Looks good on radar. We're gettin' close. I'll give you a ten-count.

Dutrow. Roger.

He holds a steady course. Evasive action, severely limited for a long time, is not possible now.

Arnold. Ten...nine...eight...seven...six...five...four...three...two...one... hack!

Dutrow. Mines away!

...

0240 Hours:

Schultz. Captain Littlewood! I've got a Mayday! It's Warren Dixon, Lt. Lewis' radio operator. They're hit. They need help.

Littlewood. Get Lewis in the open.

Shultz. (*Makes contact on V.H.F. clear Channel Queen.*) There's static, but go ahead, Captain.

Littlewood. Can you hear me, Joe?

Lewis. Ted, we're hurt! We want to bail out over the sub!

Littlewood. We hear you, Joe, but talk as loud as you can over the static. (*To Schultz.*) Get Commander Grant on this channel. Have him listen... Joe, don't you want to try for Iwo, or the cruiser? The cruiser is only 300 miles down the line toward Iwo.

Lewis. It's bad Ted! We put our mines in the harbor. They got a direct hit on us before we could close the bomb-bay doors. No. Two is shot off. No. Four is dead. No. Three cuts out. The flux-gate compass is out. The gyro-compass is unstable. Arnold took shrapnel. Dixon and Dutrow used sulpha compresses, got the blood stopped. They gave him a morphine shot. He can't navigate, even with a compass. The left forward bomb-bay door is gone; we can't ditch. We gotta get outta this wreck. Take us to the sub, Ted.

Littlewood. We'll come get you, Joe. Do you know where you are, and where you're headed?

Lewis. We're trying to make it back to Bungo Strait. Stein is guidin' us by radar. He's trackin' the south coast of Sua Bay. I turned left after we got hit to keep out of the way of the other B-29s. We damn near flew into a big mountain. Now we've got cloud cover on this side of the bay. Row has Arnold's map. He thinks he sees the lights of Yukahashi through a hole in the clouds at three o'clock. I'm indicatin' 156 miles per hour. Can't quite hold altitude. Down to 6,300 feet.

Littlewood. Have you got `em spotted on your map, Caldwell? Talk to Joe.

Caldwell. Joe...Stein, how far are you from Shimonoseki?

Stein. Fifteen miles. We're twelve miles from Kitakyushu Harbor.

Caldwell. That is Yukahashi. I know exactly where you are. Keep following the shore till you get around Kanasaki Peninsula.

Lewis. Row wants to cut across the peninsula directly to Beppu Bay.

Row. Caldwell, on my map the peninsula is a huge round blob. It looks like we could save a hundred miles, but Stein says he can't find Beppu Bay.

Caldwell. You'll have to go all the way around the peninsula. Too many 9, 000-foot mountains. That's why Beppu Bay is in radar shadow. Stein, can you see the peninsula on your scope?

Stein. I can see a huge semi-round glob about sixty miles ahead.

Caldwell. That's it...Joe...Stein...you can veer to the left of shore, and fly a straight line tangent to the peninsula. That'll save a few miles. Follow the shore again around the peninsula till you get on the east side, then straighten out on what you best judge to be a south-southeast course.

Lewis. We don't have a damn compass.

Caldwell. Stein, when you can see water on the scope clear to the end of radar range, you'll be headin' south-southeast. You'll see Kyushu near on the right, and Shikoku farther away on the left. Joe, if the clouds permit, you'll see it visually.

Lewis. Stein, Row, you guys got all that? Can we do it?

Row. It'll be up to Stein. We're so socked in now, I can't even see the wing tips.

Victery. (*CFC Gunner, from his top bubble*), I can't see the top of the stabilizer.

Stein. I can do it, Lieutenant.

Lewis. Ted, Caldwell, thanks, we're gonna do it. Stein, gimme direction.

Stein. Start a slow left turn. I'll straighten you out when we get on course.

Littlewood. Joe, we're already on our way. Cotner, give us some speed.

Cotner. Roger, I'll set up a 265 mile per hour cruise. We can hold that for a long time without ruining an engine.

Littlewood. 265's O.K....Joe, is your IFF workin'?

Lewis. I think so, Ted. The test lights burnin'.

Littlewood. The sub says ours is O.K. If it's cloudy where we meet, we'll need all the help we can get, findin' each other. We're gonna burn all our lights. We'll turn on the landing lights when we get closer. You'd better burn your lights too. The Japs can probably find us anyway, if they decide to come after us. Hang on, Joe. We're in contact with the sub.

Grant. Joe, this is J.D. Grant, Commander U.S.S. Toro. We'll hold position. We have to zig and zag around a bit, but, we won't stray far. Littlewood knows where we are. He'll get you here.

Lewis. Thanks guys; but, God...damn...it! Hurry! My engineer's got number one on emergency power. Wright guys say fifteen minutes is all the engines can take goin' that hard. If this plane keeps sinkin', I may ask Yarewick for takeoff power. Wright gives an engine three minutes max on that.

Littlewood. Joe, save takeoff power for a last chance try. You might be able to trade altitude for power when we get closer to the sub. Don't worry about emergency power. Do what you have to do. None of the Wright tech-reps volunteered to ride with you on this mission, did they?

Lewis. Thank God Row is big and strong. When No. Three cuts out, it'll take both of us to hold the wheel and rudder.

Littlewood. We're doing 265, Joe. Hang on. Keep all your guys lookin' for us. We're gonna be a little above you on your left. (*To crew.*) Everybody stay on watch for Lewis. As we approach, they will be below us on our right.

(*To the Navigator.*) Claude, can you figure a meeting time and place; and, how soon we can get Joe back to the sub?

Caldwell. Yeah. Gimme a minute, Ted. (*He calculates.*) O.K. I got it.

Littlewood. Joe, Caldwell's got some info. I'll let him tell you. Go ahead, Claude.

Caldwell. Joe, your whole crew may want to hear this. We'll meet you in about thirteen minutes. You will be approaching the Inland Sea mouth of the Bungo Strait. The lights of Beppu and Oita should be at about three o'clock. Hope it's not cloudy there. It is cloudy here. From the meeting point to the sub will be about twenty-four minutes.

Lewis. We got you, Claude. Thanks.

• • •

Safely in our own plane with all four engines running smoothly and powerfully, we feel great empathy for our buddies trying to fly in their stricken bird: the aerodynamic drag induced by gaping bomb-bays and other flak damage, the flight-plane instabilities caused by the asymmetrically applied forces of drag, lift and thrust. Thirty-four minutes to the sub will seem long to us, but it will be ceaseless torture for them.

Caldwell and I think of Joe Lewis on the football field, where he always seemed to be on the opposite side in our pick-up games. He wasn't big, but he was tough and faster than a crazy rabbit. He shot craps the same way, maybe even tougher and faster. Richardson played on the 9th Group softball team with him. Joe is the only guy I can think of who played both games.

We wonder about Maurice Arnold. *What chance does a bleeding wounded man have to survive a bailout into the cold, cruel Pacific? Why is he in that airplane? He's the navigator on Captain McNeil's crew. McNeil wasn't scheduled for this mission. Is Lewis' navigator in sickbay? Did fate nominate a replacement: big, likeable, gentlemanly, M.V. Arnold?*

Then there's Yarewick, trying to get power from his engines. Can I suggest something that might help No. Three run more steadily? It must be an ignition or a fuel, problem. A fouled spark plug is the only ignition problem for which in-flight correction may be possible. A richer fuel-air mixture may flush oil from a fouled plug. Conversely, a leaner mix will cause an engine to run hotter and perhaps burn a plug clean.

To richen?.....or to lean?...

First richen...a richness induced engine stall is less probable than a stall effected by a mix too lean; and, a too-starved/too-hot combustion chamber is more likely than a richer, cooler chamber to cause failure of feverishly reciprocating engine parts. Since Yarewick's got so little power, and I can't experience the symptoms, I hesitate to propose advice. I decide I owe him my best thought.

Cotner. Ted, ask Joe if I can talk to Yarewick.

Littlewood. Joe, Cotner's willing to talk to Yarewick if you and Bill want him to.

Lewis. Let him talk.

Cotner. Bill, Don Cotner here. Maybe number three will run a little smoother for you if you nudge the mixture control toward rich. It's worked for me. Take it easy though. Watch and listen closely. If the engine starts to stall, lean the mix a tad.

Lewis. What do you think, Bill?

Yarewick. Cotner's the Squadron Flight Engineer; let's try it.

I smile in small chagrin at a title bestowed by Major Harold Feil, the new Operations Officer of the 99th Squadron. Capt. Feil, the original Airplane Commander of our crew, was promoted when Major Chapel was shot down over Kawasaki. Feil likes me. I think he is doing what he can to mentor me.

The cited position, Squadron Flight Engineer, has no M.O.S. number, and no listing on the Table of Organization. It carries no additional pay, rank or authority. It came with no prescribed duties, and I have not delineated any but if it bucks up Yarewick and Lewis, they can call me anything they want.

Lewis. I'm gonna gamble on Cotner and Yarewick. Thanks, Ted.

Yarewick makes the adjustment.

Lewis. Ted, it sounds better.

Cotner. Joe...Bill, if number three responds, I suggest you run it on climb power and set number one for a little less than that. That should let you hold altitude and get a little more speed and easier control. One and Three should run a long time on climb power.

Lewis. Roger, thanks, we'll try it.

Yarewick makes the power settings.

Lewis. It's working great. For the first time I feel like we're gonna make it to the sub. We're hitting' 175 now.

In an interval of interplane radio silence, flying at a true closure rate of 499 mph, corrected for wind and altitude, each aircrew concentrates toward successful implementation of our fateful aerial rendezvous.

Littlewood. Schultz, is our Aldis lamp aboard?

Schultz. Roger, Captain.

Littlewood. Plug it in and check it out.

Schultz. It's workin', sir.

Littlewood. Bring it up front to Malnove. Plug it in at his station and show him how to use it. We'll need you back at the radio. I'm gonna let him use it for pointin' and flashin'. If there is radio malfunction, we'll get you up here to send Morse.

Schultz. Roger.

Schultz squeezes around the turrets and past Caldwell. He crawls on the deck past me, goes forward between Littlewood and Taylor. Malnove plugs in the lamp. Schultz instructs him in its use.

"Lucky" men among the Lewis' crew are those whose aviational and navigational accountabilities obsess their sensibilities.

Smith watches the sometimes-sparking No. Three engine, ready to report the first sign of fire.

Yarewick nurtures the faltering strength of the stricken bird's propulsive energy toward maximum sustainable production of flight supporting thrust.

Stein conducts a million cloud-piercing particles in wave-like ballets of emanation, reflection, reception and transmutation, as showers of sparks strike the rounded retina of the bird's electronic eye. He monitors the green-glowing image in its faithful delineation of sea-and-shore, ahead-and-below.

Responding to Stein's continuous correction of direction, Lewis and Row guide the frail fractured falcon along the aerial arc of a near-perfect circle, as they tenuously trace the circumference of the Kanasaki bulge...

After an eon of cloud-bound claustrophobic confinement, in traverse of an endless coil, a glimmering perception of shroud-density dissipation elates the crew.

Canova. My wing tip! Hey guys, I can see the glow when my wing light blinks.

Smith. (*Right Gunner*). Me too, and I see lights on the shore through holes in the clouds.

As the plane wends onward, visibility improves.

Canova. I see lights below on the left. There must be boats on the water.

Row. I hope they can't see us.

Lewis. Can anyone see any lights on Shikoku yet?

Canova. I see a long string of lights way off on the water, or maybe on the shore.

Stein. Hey Joe!...Lt. Littlewood! I'm lookin' a hundred miles. There's no land ahead! Nuthin' but water. It must be the beautiful Pacific.

Lewis. We've been coming out of the clouds. We're close to the peninsula on the right, and I see a big island on the left. Must be Shikoku. We seem to be on a southward course toward the Bungo Strait. Can you hold it Stein?

Stein. Yes. I can keep you pointed toward the middle of the strait.

Lewis. Good, because there are more clouds ahead.

Littlewood. (*On intercom*). Caldwell, did you follow that conversation?

Caldwell. Yes.

Littlewood. Can you plot Lewis' course, from where he is, through the middle of the strait?

Caldwell. Yes.

Littlewood. Keep us about three miles parallel on the Shikoku side.

Caldwell. I'll try Ted; but, I can't guarantee we won't be on a collision course. We'll have 300 feet altitude between. Let's pray our altimeters are both readin' right. Wish to hell we had radar altimeters.

Littlewood. Does your three-ought-six rendezvous ETA still hold?

Caldwell. Roger, about four more minutes.

Littlewood. Malnove, start flashing the Aldis lamp...Taylor, landing lights on...Crew, all interior lights on.

Crew. (*In a virtual chorus*). Lights on.

Littlewood. Joe. Are you hearing us?

Lewis. We hear you. Four minutes to rendezvous. You're all lit up. Aldis is flashing. We're down to 6,100 feet. Number three misses occasionally. We're damn near out of the clouds now, but there are clouds ahead. We may be in them with you. Our right landing light is on. The left doesn't operate. We're watching for you.

Littlewood. Roger, Joe. We're dropping down to 6,400. We'll try to be three miles to your right. Our clouds are thinning. Maybe we'll meet in the clear.

Engines drone. Pilots grip wheels. Tempus stagnates. Men's strained, searching stares go blankly rewarded.

Calhoun. We're breaking out of the clouds.

Dutrow. Joe! I see them! They just came out of the clouds. They're damn close. They're goin' to pass damn near straight over us.

Jubilation! Jubilation! Conscious emotion is amplified by extra-sensory currents transmitted man-to-man and plane-to-plane.

Littlewood. Joe. Glad to see you. God! Damn! What the hell saved us from a collision? I'm gonna zig right, zag left, make a counterclockwise one-eighty, come around behind you, pass you, slow down to your speed. I'll maintain three hundred feet above you and lead you to the sub. O.K.?

Lewis. Roger, Ted. We'll do our best to follow you.

Littlewood. Cotner, give me emergency power. I want to get in position before we get back in the clouds. Be ready to slow down.

Cotner. Roger, Ted.

Littlewood. Caldwell, take the Aldis lamp back to the rear compartment. Show Richardson how it works. Richardson, meet Caldwell by Smith's station and take the Aldis lamp back to the tail with you. Flash it at Lewis so he can follow us in the clouds.

Caldwell/Richardson. Roger.

A surge of g-force claps its grasp upon us, as Littlewood cranks Superdumbo into the tautest coil we've ever turned.

Caldwell and Richardson are clamped in place. When the g's permit, the two struggle through, over and around intraplane obstacles. Caldwell sheds his parachute to climb into the thirty-three-foot tunnel to the rear. To speed the way, he neglects to drag the chute behind him, in rare non-compliance with Air Corps Regulations.

By will and by skill, Littlewood holds the helm against centrifugal powers of a turn so tight that Boeing bans it. Superdumbo, defying designer admonition to flyers, buckles no skin, sprains no spars, strains no struts, fractures no ribs and ruptures no rivets, as it carries us safely through.

Littlewood. Joe, we're directly behind you and a little above. What is your airspeed?

Bruised, but not broken or bleeding, Caldwell and Richardson return to their respective stations.

Lewis. I'm readin' one-seventy-three, Ted. I will try to hold that. I may occasionally have to lose a little altitude to do it.

Littlewood. Sounds like the safest way to trail me. I'm gonna fly over you and try to maintain your speed, after I get in front. Keep me posted on altitude.

Superdumbo moves into position. The planes enter the clouds.

Lewis. Three hundred feet is too high, Ted. Row and I have to strain too much to look up. Can you come down to twenty feet above us?

Littlewood. O.K., Joe. Comin' down. Good idea. We can see each other better in case the clouds get really thick. (*To himself.*) *I don't want to worry Joe or anyone else, but that's damn close. Hope to hell there's no turbulence ahead.*

Littlewood. Richardson, can you see Lewis? Are you flashin' the Aldis? Is he flashin' his?

Richardson. Roger, I'm flashin' right on the nose. I see my reflections. The bombardier is flashin' at me.

Littlewood. Guide me Rich, on altitude and speed. I want to fly like our two planes are tied with a string.

Richardson. Roger.

Littlewood. Joe, if we can stay close enough together, this will work. You follow my course and I'll adjust to your speed and altitude. We'll be in the clouds all the way, but we can do it. It's only about twenty-four minutes more. You feel O.K., Joe?

Lewis. Roger, except for Arnold, we're all O.K. We're gonna make it.

...

On the Toro Bridge, Commander Grant turns toward the conning tower hatch.

Grant. (*Yelling, off mike*). Anderberg, Littlewood's found Lewis. He's leadin' him here by Aldis lamp. Be here in about twenty-four minutes. Tell those with rescue duty assignments to be ready.

Anderberg, standing on the bridge ladder, head above the hatch, yells his response with an aye, aye. He turns, bends his head, and tells the helmsman in the conning tower. He bends further and shouts the message down the shaft to Lieutenant, Jg Bill Ruspino, in the control room. Via telephone, Ruspino passes the word throughout the crew. Cheers amplify. The metallic tube resonates.

The sub's bridge is integrated into the telephonic intercommunication system and a voice-tube connects bridge to control room. Naval tradition, and Sub Captain preference, is to relay all messages, bridge/control room, via voice through the highest-ranking enlisted crewman, the Quartermaster.

. . .

Smith. (*Littlewood's Smith*). Lieutenant Caldwell, that blip about seventy miles dead ahead looks like the sub.

Caldwell. That must be it. It's in Grant's zone.

Via radar, Caldwell visualizes the shortest route toward the sub. He verbally advises Littlewood.

Lewis, Row and Yarewick, intermittently shedding precious altitude, valiantly trail Superdumbo's tail.

Richardson, tuned in hypnotic ocular focus, senses "string-tautness" and counsels his Captain.

Superdumbo turns, speeds, slows and dips in precise response to Littlewood's corrective commands.

Time remains in stasis. Forever is still forever.

. . .

0321: Down to 5500 feet, the string-tied, cloud-shrouded tandem-pair flies through Pacific Ocean air. Caldwell takes a radar drift reading on Okino-shima, an islet in Bungo's mouth. He estimates wind aloft: 263°; 19 mph.

Caldwell. (*In his head.*) *Wow! The wind out here has rotated 110° and picked up nine miles per hour.*

Littlewood. Commander Grant, Littlewood here. We're departing Bungo. We have Toro on radar, and we have your IFF. Do you have ours?

Grant. Aye. We have it. Glad to have you back.

Littlewood. Lewis is with us. We're in the clouds. He's trailin' our lights.

Grant. Aye, Littlewood. We've been copying your conversation. Great flying both of you... Lewis, we're ready to welcome you and crew aboard. We've got hot coffee and doughnuts ready, shot of whiskey, steak, anything you want.

Lewis, Thanks, Commander.

The "new" Navy bans hard liquor aboard all vessels. Old time captains know the value of daily grog to sailors under stress. Commander Grant is an experienced submariner. He knows sea-stress, and undersea-stress. During pre-sailing weeks in port, he skillfully manages "unawareness", as each crewman gradually hoards his stash.

Navy prohibition is to officers and enlisted men, but officers are "gentlemen" by Declaration of Congress: ergo, dichotomy in Grant's mind, and resolution in his "old-timer" policy:

1. Each Toro officer personally manages his own "spirital" account;
2. Shortly after Toro sails on war patrol, Grant appropriates every "enlisted-bottle". He secures a communal-cache in a locker he reserves for this purpose. He keeps one key. He gives the other to Lieutenant Robert Poage, Toro's Executive Officer;
3. Daily, Grant, and/or Poage pour two neat shots in a coffee mug for each enlisted man who comes by the galley at the end of his watch. Water is the chaser. Commander and Exec maintain a precise "grog-log". Log security is rigorous.

Littlewood. Joe, there are things you need to know before you bail out. I've held back, because we've both been too busy flyin' and, I didn't want you and your crew worrying longer than you had to. What you've got below, Joe, is twenty foot swells, sixty-nine degree water, cold damp air, sixteen knot wind...Did I get it right, Commander Grant?

Grant. Littlewood's correct, Joe; and, sixty-nine degrees is warm enough to attract sharks. We've seen a few. It might be best to get in rafts if you can.

Littlewood. You may want to fly on to the cruiser, Joe. We can make it in less than two hours.

Lewis. We might make it halfway and run out of gas or altitude. We don't know how much fuel is runnin' out of flack holes in our wing tanks. We don't know how long we'll have two engines workin'. The swells may be bigger and the sharks hungrier by the cruiser. We'll get out here, where we've got a friend in the water.

The crew stoically suffers the dire dialogue. It quashes each man's silent hope, that successful flight to the sub would have presaged a plan to proceed to the cruiser, and from there to try for Iwo. No man wants to desert the comfort provided by the B-29's thin-skinned cocoon, and by the presence of comrades. Each man dreads solo confrontation of terrors that lurk outside in dismal, murky void.

Loyal to Joe Lewis, respectful and trustful of his experienced judgment, they make no protest. They prepare pragmatically, and with prayer, to accept their airplane Commander's decision, and to do their best to survive.

Littlewood. Roger, Joe.It's your call. We'll help you. Let's plan bailout procedure. What do you want to do, Joe?

Lewis. We just want out. Let's fly straight to the sub and jump.

Littlewood. Everyone out on the first run?

Lewis. Roger, we'll be all ready to jump. You tell us when.

Littlewood. Roger, Joe. Caldwell will do it direct...O.K. Claude?...O.K. Joe?

Lewis. Roger.

Caldwell. Roger, I'll give you a ten-count hack, Joe. I need everyone's approval of a landing spot.

Lewis. Right on deck, or as close as possible.

Littlewood. Have you done this before, Commander?

Grant. No. We've pulled guys out of the water, but they were ship-sunk sailors, or ditched fighter pilots.

Caldwell. Joe, I think the best spot is a half mile south-southeast of Toro. If I try to get you closer, you might hit the sub. At twenty feet per second that'll hurt bad. The ocean current will carry you to Toro in less than thirty minutes.

Grant. That sounds good to me. We've got two Aldis lamps. They make damn powerful searchlights. We'll watch both sides.

Lewis. (*The crapshooter speaking*). I know the odds against you, scoring a bulls eye, Claude. I'll take `em. We'd rather break somethin' than drown. Put us on board, if you can.

Littlewood. Roger, Ted.

Caldwell. Roger.

Grant. Aye, aye.

Caldwell computes bailout numbers. *It's parachuting-a-mine déjà vu, except Malnove can't use the bombsight, and when will a man pull a ripcord? In dark, dank vapor surround? With cold, bottomless, black brine below?...Posing the question posits the answer...Damned soon.*

Caldwell averages wind vectors, computes fall time and chute-drift vectors.

Caldwell. Joe, I've got some bailout information for you and your crew.

Lewis. Roger, Claude, we're listening.

Caldwell. Ted?...Commander Grant?

Littlewood and Grant. We hear you.

Caldwell. When I say "Jump," clear the plane as soon as possible. Fall time from 5,000 feet will be four minutes and ten seconds. I've figured wind drift on that, so pull the rip-chord as soon as you think you're clear of the plane and other jumpers. During fall, you'll drift one-point-three miles laterally. You'll hit the water near the sub. Any questions?

Lewis. Everybody got it? Row?

Row. Roger.

Lewis. Dutrow?

Dutrow. Roger.

Lewis. Arnold?

There is no response.

Dixon. He's not wearin' his mike, sir. He restin' on the deck. Dutrow and I are gonna have to help him get out.

Lewis. Is he conscious?

Dixon. He's conscious, but he's not very alert. He shouldn't be jumpin'.

Lewis. Does he want to go down with the plane?

Dixon. No, he's said a coupla' times to help him get out.

Lewis. Will he be able to pull his ripcord?

Dixon. Says he will. Says don't worry about him. He can take care of himself.

Lewis. Can you rig up any kind of line to pull it automatically?

Dixon. I can't think of anything we've got to use. It'd have to be strong enough to pull the cord, but weak enough to break away.

Lewis. If you can find a line, you or Dutrow could hold it till it pulls the ripcord then drop it.

Yarewick. Dixon, I've got about three feet of number ten electric wire I carry in case I have to jump a solenoid, or tie something up that's rattled loose. If you have four or five feet of spare radio wire, maybe you can splice somethin' up that will work.

Dixon. Roger, I can splice your wire onto Arnold's intercom cord. That'll give me about ten feet. Is that enough?

Yarewick. I know damned little about parachutes, but Caldwell said pull the cord as soon as you clear the plane.

Dixon. O.K. Hand me your wire. I'll do it.

Both men reach around Yarewick's instrument panel. Dutrow has been using Arnold's intercom gear. He unplugs it and hands it to Dixon.

Dixon. How you feelin', Lieutenant?

Arnold. (*In whispered moan.*) O.K.

Dixon. We'll be jumpin' soon. Dutrow and I are gonna help you through the compartment door. You just fall out the bomb bay. I'm gonna pull your ripcord.

Arnold. O.K.

Dixon. When we get in the water, we'll help you get in your one-man raft. Caldwell is gonna put us right on the sub.

Arnold. Claude can do it if anybody can.

Dixon. Lt. Lewis, I've got a line rigged. I've told Arnold what we're gonna do.

Lewis. Good work, Dixon.

The air-corps supplies its airmen with the best parachutes in the world. The harnesses of chutes issued to combat crewmen are tailor-made to personal measurements. The air-corps spends minimum time on jumping instructions. No jumps are made in practice. Colonel Huglin, with cooperation from Coast Guard Commander Hoffman*, Port Tinian Harbor Captain, arranges for 9th Group flyers to get a brief simulation of bailout experience. Every man on Lewis' crew, and most men aboard Superdumbo, is remembering a fateful April afternoon.

. . .

The remnant of an ancient lava flow forms Tinian Harbor's north-side breakwater-pier. On rails, at piers-end, stands the mobile harbor-crane. A line of 9th Group Airmen winds back from crane to shore, and curves along the beach.

In turn, we buckle a parachute harness, sans silk umbrella, over our Mae West vest. Via a pair of ring-clips, a tightly packed one-man life raft (our "seat-cushion" aboard the B-29) hangs from the harness, butt-high suspended.

In turn, Seabee Len Jensen*, Seaman 1c, slips the upper harness strap onto the hoisting hook. Swiftly, we sweep upward 100 feet, swoop out over the harbor, and drop in controlled descent. At twenty feet per second, we fall at "open-chute" velocity.

We try to remember instructions:

1. Unsnap the ring-clips.
2. Pull the cord to inflate the raft with CO_2.
3. Drop the raft.
4. Unbuckle the harness.
5. Tumble forward ten or fifteen feet into the water.
6. Pull the cord to inflate the vest. (Warning: In a true jump, don't inflate the vest until you are clear of the silk and its shroud lines.)
7. Swim to the raft and climb aboard.

Many men are still pondering instructions when they find themselves in the water. The water is warm. The surf is soft. For swimmers it is a fun game.

Non-swimmers are dunked in a panic of flailing, struggling, liquescent terror, inhaling and ingesting lungfuls and bellyfuls of suffocating, nauseating oil-soaked seawater.

None die, but swimmer and non-swimmer alike thank God that he will never have to make a real jump.

...

All around athlete, superb swimmer, compassionate commander, Joe Lewis, despite absorption in his piloting problem, reprises a vision of the harbor-water exertions of his floundering, non-adept crewmen, Yarewick, Fiedler and Victery. *Damned Air Corps. Shoulda taught these guys to swim, before they ordered them to fly over half the damn Pacific...The damn Navy's worse. I'll bet three-fourths the guys aboard Toro can't swim.*

Lewis. Sergeant Victery and all you men in the rear compartment, listen up. Victery, you're in charge back there.

Eighteen-year-old Staff Sergeant Victery has one month in grade over Staff Sergeant Stein.

Chorus. Roger, Lieutenant.

Lewis. Caldwell is gonna give us the word. When he says, "jump", I'm gonna hit the bailout button. At the alarm, get the hell out through the bomb bay, fast! Victery, organize the jump procedure. Strong swimmers should go first and be ready to help the non-swimmers. Any questions?

Victery. We'll do it, Lieutenant. We've never heard the jump alarm. Can we hear what it sounds like?

Lewis. O.K. I'll turn it on, but don't anybody jump now for Christ's sake.

He releases the safety and punches the button...No sound...Again...No sound...He punches repeatedly...Hard...Nothing.

Lewis. Victery, did it go off back there?

Victery. No sir.

Lewis. The God-damn Japs got our bailout bell. Wonder if they fucked-up the bomb bay doors? Fiedler, are you still in the tail?

Fiedler. Yes, sir.

Lewis. On your way forward, open the rear exit door. Leave it open. When you enter the pressurized compartment, leave the bulkhead door open. If the rear bomb bay doors won't open, you guys will have to scramble out the back. You won't have time to waste on stickin' door latches.

Fiedler. Roger, Lieutenant.

Lewis. Victery, get your men on the gunner's intercom circuit. Arrange a jump sequence. Line `em up by the bomb bay door. Stay on the intercom at your station. Switch to my line and report.

Victery. Roger, Lieutenant.

Lewis. Victery, as ranking non-Comm, you're last man out. O.K.?

Victery. Yes, Lieutenant.

Victery. (*On the Gunner's channel*) Is everyone on this channel? Canova? Smith? Stein? Fiedler? (*Each answers*).

Victery. Swimmers out first. In the water, get ready, soon as possible, to help the non-swimmers. I'll stay on intercom. I'll give the signal with a loud, "jump," and with a strong tap on the shoulder. Pass it along to the front of the line. Any questions?

Chorus. No, Sarge.

Victery. Here's the jump sequence: First, Smith; second, Canova; third, Stein; fourth, Fiedler. Any objections?

Chorus. No, Sarge.

Victery. Fiedler, get out of the tail and up here in line.

Fiedler. Roger, Sarge.

Victery. (*Switches back to the Airplane Commander's channel*). Lieutenant, we're ready.

Lewis. Good job, Victery. Stand-by.(*To crewmen in the front compartment.*) Here's the plan for us up front. The bailout bell is busted. Stay on intercom. Dixon, you are ears for Dutrow and Arnold. You three go out the forward bomb bay. At my command "jump" everyone gets out fast, but in sequence. Arnold goes first with help from Dixon and Dutrow. Don't forget his rip-cord. Dutrow is second and Dixon, you're third. You two get Arnold out of the water and into his raft as soon as possible. Dixon, tell me when you're going out the door, so Yarewick, Row and I can go out the nose-wheel well. You got that, Dixon?

Dixon. Yes Sir, Lieutenant.

Lewis. Yarewick, when you hear, "jump", get out of your seat, stand on the deck between Row and me, and open the deck-hatch over the nose-wheel. When the nose-wheel is down, jump out the well. O.K.?

Yarewick. Yes Sir, Lieutenant.

Lewis. Row, when Caldwell starts his count, I'll give the command, "nose-wheel". You lower the nose-wheel. When I hear that everyone but you and I are out, you get out damn quick. I'll hold the plane till I see you go. O.K.?

Row. O.K., Joe.

Lewis. (*To Crew*). All of you. Good luck and God bless you.

Chorus. God bless you, Lieutenant.

. . .

0325: Caldwell checks chute descent computations. He marks a jump-target-dot on his radar scope. He reads angle and distance, Superdumbo to dot. His ETA is 0329.

Caldwell. Ted, correct course one half degree to the left. We're four minutes to bailout.

Joe hears...His crew hears...Perception of time's progression reverses polarity. Stagnation flashes into acceleration. Tinian Harbor visions of near-death-encounter flare inside Fiedler's skull. His voiceless prayer speaks for all... *four minutes...oh God...I'm not ready...I'm not ready.*

Lewis. Roger, Ted. We're ready.

Grant. Aye. We got it Littlewood. Do you have Azimuth coordinates you expect them to drop out of the clouds at? We estimate cloud ceiling to be 1,000 feet above us.

Littlewood. Can you answer, Caldwell?

Caldwell. Roger, Ted. (*He calculates, then speaks).*Commander Grant, Azimuth angle and distance from Toro should be eighty-three degrees and a quarter mile.

Grant. Eighty-three degrees by a quarter mile. Thanks, Caldwell. We'll focus our Aldis lamps on that spot.

Caldwell. (*To himself*). *I've been giving info like I know what I'm doing. Everyone seems to believe I'm accurate. My answers are guesses. I would have to know wind direction and velocity at 500 feet altitude intervals to make an accurate calculation*. (*To Grant).* I suggest Commander, that you sweep as big an area as you can with your lights.

Grant. Aye. We'll fan out from your reference point. If we see where they're comin' down, we may be able to pick `em up pretty quick.

Caldwell. Three minutes.

The tandem B 29s fly on.

Caldwell. Two and a half minutes. Ted, correct the course one half degree to the left.

Littlewood. Roger.

Lewis faithfully follows Littlewood's lead.

Lewis. Row, open the bomb bay doors.

Row. Roger, Joe. (*He hits the emergency bomb-salvo button, at his station.*)

Smith. (*Signals to Victery*). Rear bomb bay doors open.

Victery. Rear bomb-bay doors open, Sir.

Dixon. The right front bomb bay door only opened part way. It's stuck at about a forty-five degree angle. We'll have to dive out toward the left side. There's plenty of room to make it, Sir.

Caldwell. Two minutes.

Lewis. Two minute warning.

Smith opens the door in the bulkhead separating the rear pressurized compartment from the rear bomb bay. The Venturi effect of the three-foot diameter hole accelerates the cold slipstream. At 200 miles per hour, wind saturated with decibels from the two engines roars into and through the rear compartment, and out the rear exit door. Shivering is no shame now. Smith fights the wind to sit at the door. He pushes both feet through the hole. He rests each foot on the narrow catwalk just inside the bomb bay. With each hand he grips the circular doorframe. He flexes forward at the waist, and forces his head and shoulders against the wind, through the door into the bomb bay.

During this maneuver, Canova spots the breath-inflation tube at the top of Smith's Mae West.

Canova. (*To himself*). *My God! His mouth-tube is open. When he pulls the chord to open the* CO_2 *canister, it's all gonna rush out the tube.* (*To Smith, in his loudest yell.*) SMITTY! YOUR TUBE'S NOT TIED AND ANCHORED!

The men, especially Smith, hear the wind and nothing more.

Canova. (*To himself*). *If I punch him, he'll jump. It's too soon.*

He watches Smith in fascination. The tandem flies on.

Caldwell. One minute.

Victery. (*To the men*). ONE MINUTE.

The men hear the wind. Nothing more.

Smith looks back, over the left shoulder, into the compartment. He reads Canova's frantic signal for attention.

Canova. (*Points to his own tube and uses exaggerated mouthing to silently enunciate*). YOUR TUBE IS OPEN. YOUR TUBE IS OPEN.

Smith. (*Looks down at his tube. Looks at Canova, signals a left thumb up, mouths)* THANKS.

Smith folds the tube flat, screws the knurled knob tight, tucks tube and knob into the protective pocket, snaps the pocket. Without looking back, he salutes again with his left thumb.

Caldwell. Thirty seconds.

Lewis. Thirty seconds.

Victery. Thirty SECONDS!

Caldwell. (*Repeated by Lewis and Victery*). 10...9...8...7...6...5...4...3...2...1 ...Jump!

...

In the rear, Victery soundly punches Fiedler. Fiedler punches Stein. Stein punches Canova. Canova launches a vigorous blow. The plane shudders and shifts. The blow is feeble on Smith's shoulder.

Smith. (*Turns to Canova and mouths*) *ARE YOU SURE? ARE YOU SURE*?

Canova. (*mouths*) *YES!...YES!...JUMP!...JUMP!...JUMP!*

Canova lands a solid thump. Smith curls down at the waist. He dives forward into the bomb bay. He falls into the night below.

...

One, two, three, Canova. Stein and Fiedler exit in Smith's train.

Victery. Lieutenant Lewis. Smith, Canova, Stein and Fiedler are out of the plane. I'm going now. Goodbye.

In his haste to jump, he misses Lewis' acknowledgement.

Lewis. So long, Victery. See you aboard Toro.

Up front, Dixon grips Arnold's rigged-up ripcord in his left hand. One at a time he lifts Arnold's legs into the bomb bay, through the circular bulkhead door. Dutrow tries to lift the inert mass of Arnold's flaccid upper-body into a sitting position, just inside the door. Dixon fears to drop the ripcord. He gives Dutrow a one-arm assist. Three arms are not enough.

...

Dixon. Arnold's too heavy for us, Sir. It'll take one man in the bomb bay, and two in the compartment to get him out.

Lewis. Roger, Dixon. We'll go around again. I'll need Yarewick and Row on station till we start the jump run. I'll send Yarewick back to help you then.

Littlewood. We hear you, Joe. I'm turning left. We'll come around again on target. Toro is still on our radar screen. (*To Toro*). We got five out, Commander. They should be breakin' out of the clouds in three or four minutes.

Grant. Aye-aye, Littlewood. We're watchin' for them.

...

All five chutes perform perfectly. Suspended in downward drift through dank and dark void, wind driven into dynamic pendulous oscillations, each man knows absolute loneness. No man sees another. No man sees the sea, the sub, or the circling super-fortresses.

Each man wonders at the drone of the tandem planes continuing in circumferential flight.

...

Lewis. Ted, I'm losing airspeed. It's the drag of the open bomb bays. I'm afraid to shut the doors. Might not get `em open again. I don't want to stall out.

Littlewood. Keep your speed up, Joe, even if you have to lose some altitude. Richardson is still watchin' you from the tail. He gives me good directions. I'll stay with you. It won't be long now.

It is long to Lewis, Row, Yarewick, Dutrow, Dixon and Arnold.

Caldwell. Four minutes to bailout. Correct the course a half-degree left, Ted.

Littlewood corrects. Lewis follows.

Caldwell. Three minutes.

Lewis. My altimeter now reads 4,700 feet and falling.

Caldwell. Two and a half minutes. Correct course another half a degree left.

Lewis. Yarewick, open the nose-wheel-well door, then go back to help Dixon and Row.

Yarewick. Yes, Sir, Lieutenant.

Caldwell. Two minutes.

Lewis. Two-minute warning.

Dixon climbs out into the forward bomb bay. He hands his intercom gear to Yarewick. He clutches Arnold's ripcord within his left-handed vice-grip on the aluminum jamb of the bulkhead door. He braces his left foot against the edge of the partially open right side of the bomb bay door.

Caldwell. One minute.

Yarewick. (*Off mike to Dutrow, Arnold and Dixon*). One minute.

Caldwell. Thirty seconds.

Lewis. (*To Row*). Lower the nose wheel.

Row. Roger.

He pushes the switch. Lewis and Row hear the gear grind down into place. The plane bucks.

Lewis. (*To Row*). Get up. Get ready to jump at my hand signal.

Row stands by the opening to the nose wheel well. Alone at the controls, Lewis can't hold the plane. Bucking becomes violent.

Lewis. (*Not waiting for Caldwell*). Jump! Jump! Jump! He signals Row.

Row flexes knees, in preparation to leap through the wheel-well. The plane yaws and banks. Row struggles for balance. He falls. His right elbow bangs into the bottom rung of the well-side aluminum ladder. The elbow hurts. Worse, impact, from the six-foot free-fall, jambs Row's humerus into his shoulder socket. By instinct, he reaches for the ripcord with his right hand. His shoulder throbs. His arm has no strength. He pulls the cord with his left hand. His chute opens. He descends in pain. He ponders chances. Can a one-armed parachutist survive in the sea?

Yarewick and Dutrow lift Arnold by his armpits. They push him feet first into the bomb bay. Dixon supports Arnold's head and neck in the crook of his right arm. He pushes Arnold's legs and body toward the open side of the bay, with his right foot. Yarewick and Dutrow give a final shove. Arnold falls clear of the plane. Dixon almost goes with him, but he clings to the handhold until he feels the ripcord release the pilot chute. He slides down the forty-five degree right door into space. Yarewick and Dutrow quickly follow. All chutes open and function. Arnold, Dixon, Yarewick and Dutrow join their descending comrades.

The hard jolt of the chute opening stirs Arnold into consciousness from his drug-induced semi-coma. His wounds tear. He feels the shock of pain. Bleeding resumes. He is not aware of bleeding. The pendulum swing soothes. Morphine regains control. He floats downward in pleasant, partial torpor.

Lewis struggles with the wheel yoke and rudder pedals. No. Three quits. Electric power fails. Lights extinguish. Radio dies. Lewis tries to dive for speed. Desperate for engine power, he opens the throttle on No. One. The plane shudders, shakes, stalls, spins.

Bound by centrifugal force, incommunicado, in utter darkness, without even the glow of instruments for company, Lewis falls in accelerating spirals toward the sea. He listens to the whine of his runaway engine, and the scream of the rushing wind. Before dizziness overcomes his brain, he thinks, "*Thank God, they all got out.*"

Richardson. Captain Littlewood, I've lost Lewis. All the lights went out. The plane went down in a diving turn.

Littlewood. Keep searchin'. Have you counted the parachutes?

Richardson. I never saw a single parachute. I had the Aldis lamp focused on the nose. I think I saw Lieutenant Row get out of the pilot's seat. I'm not sure. I couldn't see inside because of the glare off the Plexiglas.

Littlewood. I heard Joe telling everybody to jump before Caldwell started his count. Joe never explained, or said goodbye. I'm sure he was busy and in a rush. I assume they all left. Forget the search. Relax Richardson. You did a hell of a good job. (*To himself) I'm gonna recommend Richardson for promotion*).(*To Toro*). Commander, you've got six more comin' down. They'll be through the clouds in about three minutes.

Grant. Aye, Littlewood. We missed the first five. I presume they're in the water now. We'll do our best to spot these men in the air.

Littlewood. We're gonna climb out now, and circle you above the clouds `til daylight. What time is dawn?

Grant. Gimme a second (*Yells to Anderberg*). What time is sunrise?

Anderberg. (*Yells the question to the navigator below, and the answer back to Grant.*) 0509.

Grant. O.K., Ted, sunrise is 0509. Dawn is brief at sea. My guess is 0500, or maybe 0502 if the clouds are still here. At your altitude, it might be 0455 or so.

Littlewood. Roger, thanks. At dawn, I'm gonna let down about 1,000 feet per minute. It'll take us about six or seven minutes to get under the clouds, if the ceiling doesn't change. What do you predict?

Grant. I predict the ceiling won't change. I can give you a better estimate of its altitude when we have some daylight.

Littlewood. I'll appreciate that.

Superdumbo climbs steadily to 7,000 feet, about 500 feet above cloud top. We set up again to maintain a twenty-mile diameter circle at maximum endurance speed, down to 169 miles per hour, now that we've burned eleven and a half hours' worth of fuel weight. We have nearly three hours before we can go down and search the sea.

Littlewood and Grant agree to keep clear channel contact open, but to use it only for urgent communication.

...

Lewis' plane smashes into the water. A human observer would have perceived the splash and noise as cataclysmic concussion. Unconscious, Lewis senses no part of his violent death. The dark, deep ocean rolls on.

Healthy swimmers Smith, Canova, Stein, Dixon and Row find idiosyncratic enjoyment in their dangling descent, through surreal surround. Each man calmly reviews remembered recommendations, with application to his personal plan for entering the sea.

Non-swimmers Yarewick, Fiedler and Victery, tense with apprehension, do not appreciate their swaying, swinging fall through dismal, spectral aura. Anxiety overrides attempts to remember and plan.

Arnold takes placid pleasure in his undulating downward drift. He serenely accepts the future. He vaguely wonders why the air should seem colder the farther he falls.

The pain of his useless right arm and shoulder rules big, strong, brave Row. Taut harness straps restrict his attempts to find relief and comfort. Each tethered oscillation brings new torture. Severity of suffering paralyzes his brain. His thoughts are fitful; his plan incomplete.

Bursting through the bottom of the clouds brings the shock of reality to each chutist, with the exception of Arnold, who dreams on. Rate of fall appears to accelerate. An increasing roar of gigantic swells is perceivable. Perception induces calm men toward agitation. Perception intensifies discomfort of apprehensive men.

No man gauges height above the sea surface. None sees; it is too dark. None can gauge by ear; none has experience. If a man drops from harness too soon, free fall will kill. If drop is late, entanglement will drown him.

Wind velocity increases. Oscillation amplitude grows. Smith sees the swells. He waits for perfect timing. He is wind-spun 180° in an accelerating pendulum downswing. He is knocked breathless by back-side collision with the rushing rise of an upwelling billow. A thought flashes. *Was I that low?* Wind in the canopy drags him up, and through the top of the huge wave. He swallows salt water. He flies through the air. He bangs the next wave. He unsnaps his right side life-raft clip. He unsnaps his harness. He frees his arms. The wind drags the harness roughly from his legs. The life raft goes with the wind. Smith sinks. He pulls the cord on his Mae West. The life jacket inflates.

Coughing, sputtering, vomiting, he rises. *I'm saved.* He realizes he's floating too low in the water. After a long struggle, he removes his shoes. With careful timing he manages to breathe. He seems to ride in the troughs. The top of waves blow onto him. *What the hell, I'm wet anyway. I'll make it.*

Canova misjudges height. He hits the water gently in a trough. His canopy collapses over him. He tries to swim clear. With water-soaked shoes and clothes, he's too heavy to swim. He has to inflate his Mae West. He is entangled in shroud lines. His many pocketed C-1 survival vest is in the plane, but he has carried the survival knife. He cuts himself free. He is unable to free his life raft. He removes his shoes. *I'll make it.*

Stein remembers Caldwell's advised time of descent. He remembers the noted time when he jumped. Reading the phosphorescent dial of his air-corps-issue aviator's watch, he tracks his fall. With expert timing, and perhaps great fortune, he drops his life raft in the bottom of a trough and tumbles in almost on top of it. He inflates his vest, and climbs into his raft. *I'll make it.*

For a fearful non-swimmer, Fiedler judges height well. He drops his raft, timely. He escapes his chute. He inflates his Mae West. In compensation for inability to swim, he wears his C-1 survival vest, a mistake. The wet vest, shoes and clothes drag him under. Frantically occupied in gasping an occasional breath, he can't paddle toward his life raft. There is no way to remove the survival vest from under the inflated life vest. With energetic urgency he flails arms and legs in a desperate struggle to keep his nose above water. The battery-operated lamp is the only survival article he can access from the C-1 vest. He clips it to his Mae West. He switches it on.

Victery, like Smith, has a vicious, wind-driven collision with the side of a swell. Unlike Smith, his swimming ability is nil. Out of his element, he fights the enemy ocean. He fears its chilling embrace.

Still dreaming, Arnold comes down gently in a trough, and his chute settles softly upon him. Weak and cold from loss of blood, his efforts are feeble. Cold submersion brings him to sufficient consciousness to try, and to think a curious thought. *If I survive, will I survive drowning or hypothermia, or both?*

Dixon and Dutrow, strong swimmers each, encounter ferocious forces of wind and wave. Each loses his life raft. Each is able to save himself by inflating his Mae West. Each is desperate to find Arnold and Yarewick, whom they know will need help. Each man's search is limited to an occasional glimpse into the next trough as he is thrown to the crest of a raging billow. All search is vain. Each sees no one.

Yarewick hits the water during a brief lull in elemental savagery. A non-swimmer, but strong athlete (his brief rookie season as a starting pitcher for the St. Louis Cardinals being interrupted by the military draft), he manages survival via Mae West, but sans raft.

Row cuts his chute early and free-falls too far. The jolt knocks the wind from his lungs. It shocks his shoulder into intense spasms of piercing pain. His raft vanishes. With strong will, and stout left arm, he is able to inflate his life vest.

Ten men float. None has seen any other man since leaving the plane. Each wonders, *What will come next? How soon will it come?*

About an hour into the water, after one of many wave-crest float-ups, Smith looks over the top. He thinks he sees the glimmer of light at the bottom of the next trough. It is "real" light, not the phosphorescent glitter he has seen every time his paddling and kicking, or wind force and sea force, has disturbed the brine. *Is it hallucination*? He swims to investigate. The light is from Fiedler's survival lamp, dim now with dissipated voltage. Fiedler floats on his back. There is no sign that he breathes. Smith rights Fiedler. He tries for an hour to resuscitate his comrade. He applies all he knows within limits of the watery situ. In exhaustion, Smith reluctantly gives up. Clutching a strap of Fiedler's Mae West. He floats in silent vigil. He leaves the lamp burning. It flickers dimly.

Canova spies the dimly lit scene, and swims down the slope of a wave.

Canova. Smitty. You're the first man I've seen. Are you O.K.? Who's with you?

Smith. (*Roused from awed reverie.*) It's Fiedler. He's dead. He was dead when I found him. God, I'm glad to see you, Duke. You're the only one I've seen besides Fiedler.

Canova. Are you sure he's dead?

Smith. I worked for an hour. He never breathed once.

Canova examines Fiedler. He attempts resuscitation for half an hour.

Canova. (*Giving up*). You're right. He's dead, poor guy. At least he made a good try. I was afraid he was too nervous to do this good.

Smith. I think that C-1 vest dragged him too low in the water.

Canova. I tried to talk him out of it in the plane. He thought any aid he could get would help.

Smith. I've noticed that I'm higher in the water holdin' onto his strap. Do you really agree that he's dead?

Canova. Oh, he's for sure dead.

Smith. What do you say we let him loose and share his Mae West and survival vest?

Canova. O.K. If we pray for his soul.

Smith. Can we make it silent prayer?

Canova. Yeah, we should.

They remove both vests and the lamp. Each prays for his comrade. Fiedler's body disappears into the deep. Smith and Canova float a little higher. Breathing is a smaller struggle.

Canova. Let's see if we can find any spare batteries in the pockets of this C-1.

Smith. (*After they find batteries, tropical chocolate, ocean-water dye and other survival items*), I feel guilty using these things.

Canova. Yeah, it's like Fiedler is sacrificing his life for ours.

Despite implications of self-censure, each man's hopes toward rescue are buoyed.

• • •

Aboard Toro, Commander Grant turns to his Quartermaster.

Grant. Anderberg, have those men standing by organize themselves into two Aldis lamp search parties, with alternate hour deck duty for each party. We're gonna search by Aldis till daylight. We'll be sweeping the wave tops, lookin' for airmen to pop up. First party report on deck pronto.

Anderberg. Aye, aye. (*He peers down the conning tower into the dim red glow of the control room, and repeats the order.*)

When the gong signaling nightfall sounds, all interior lights on a submarine switch to red. This protects night vision in case men are called to emergency duty topside.

• • •

Aboard Superdumbo:

Littlewood. Attention, crew. There's not much we can do till we get some daylight. While we are circling, remain at your station. Maintain watch for Jap aircraft. We can't help the guys in the water if we get shot down.

In the sea. On the sea. In the air. Time, for young American men, again stands still.

0456: Faint gray light peeps over the 6,500-foot cloud tops on the eastern horizon. Littlewood addresses his crew.

Littlewood. O.K., men. We're goin' down. If we find room under the clouds we'll be flyin' search patterns. (*To Toro*). Commander Grant, we've got a little light up here. We're startin' down. Keep me posted on the clouds and the light.

Grant. Aye, aye. We've got a little bit of dawn light now. I will be able to tell you more in a few minutes. I suggest slowing your rate of descent at about 3,000 feet.

I reduce power, and close the engine cowl flaps to conserve heat as we descend at about twice our usual rate. Littlewood levels out and circles at 3,000 feet. We're in the clouds.

Littlewood. Commander Grant, we're at 3,000 feet. What's below us?

Grant. I don't think the ceiling changed, but I read it a little different in daylight. It looks to be twelve to fifteen hundred feet.

Littlewood. Good. We'll start flyin' our search patterns at 1,000 feet.

Grant. It's still three minutes to sunrise. We'll get more light then.

At the gong, Toro's interior lights turn from red to daylight-white.

Littlewood. Roger, comin' down to 1,000. (*To Cotner.*) When I level off, Don, set up a speed about halfway between maximum endurance and stalling speed.

Cotner. Roger.

We level off. I set up a cruise at 153 miles per hour. Littlewood starts the first leg of his first pattern. Except for Littlewood, this will be the first sea search for the crew. Littlewood has flown B-17s in search of Navy pilots, down in the Atlantic off the Florida coast.

Littlewood. (*To crew.*) Flying a search is like plowing a field. We'll fly a straight line for twenty-five miles, make a tight one-eighty and fly fifty miles in the next row, turn again and repeat. A man in a Mae West will be hard to spot in an ocean this rough. (*To Caldwell*). Claude, watch heading, distance and altitude for me. Correct me and tell me when to reverse course. Plot the area searched. I'm gonna be watchin' the ocean.

Caldwell. Roger. (*To Smith.*) Smitty, I want to use the breakwater wall at Nobeoka Harbor as a point of reference. The blip is bright. Can you keep it in focus?

Smith. Roger.

Grant. We'll search too. We'll zig and zag and change speeds frequently. There are shore batteries at Nobeoka.

Littlewood. Roger. When we find someone, we'll guide you in to bring him aboard.

Grant. Aye, aye. (*On the bridge, to the Executive Officer*) Lieutenant Poage, halt Aldis lamp search and continue the one-hour alteration of deck duty for the search and rescue parties.

Poage. Aye, Sir.

Poage moves onto the deck and notifies the men. In passing he tells Anderberg. Anderberg relays the order below.

Among the eleven men aboard Superdumbo, six have a good view below: Malnove, Littlewood, Taylor up front, Warn, Connor and Richardson in the rear. I am monitoring the engine instruments. I steal as much time as

I dare to get up on my knees, on my seat, to stare down over the sill of my high window. Caldwell can't abandon his monitoring assignment. Schultz has no window. Calhoun has no downward view from his topside bubble. Smith has no window. Viewer or non-viewer, no crewman speaks.

Caldwell. Ten minutes. Reverse course. New heading: north, twenty-three degrees, fifteen minutes east.

Littlewood. Roger.

Our course runs parallel to Kyushu's relatively straight eastern coast. The shoreline is clearly visible. Semi-tropical, with pine forested mountains behind, it is beautiful country, but we are in no mood to admire anything Japanese. Vista details become more sharply defined (and so does Superdumbo) with the progression of time.

We hope we can soon complete a successful rescue and depart for Tinian. We know Toro's crewmen feel the same. Their departure, however, will by Naval Order be limited to a dive and brief undersea voyage. Their new below surface hideout must be within a fifty-mile radius. They shall have to be on surface duty for the next B-29 mission.

We continue our run. We remain silent.

Littlewood. (*To the crew.*) This is no time to be bashful. If you see somethin', speak up. If you're not sure what it is, we can come around and check it out.

Chorus. Roger, Captain.

Caldwell. Twenty minutes, Ted. Reverse course. New heading is south, 102 degrees and thirty minutes west.

Littlewood. Roger.

Caldwell, Ted, I can see by radar that the wind has picked up speed and swung around. It's almost straight on-shore. If you set up the autopilot for the straight-run heading, I can use my direction control to keep us on a radar-tracked course.

Littlewood. Roger. I'll set up the autopilot soon as I come out of this turn.

Warn. (*Five minutes into the run*). Dang. I see somethin' down there. Is it a man?

Chorus of searchers. Where George?

Warn. It was straight below me. I don't see it now. Dang waves are too dang high.

Littlewood. We'll turn around and take a look. Caldwell, can you take us back over the spot?

Caldwell. I'll try. Make the turn and set up north, twenty-two degrees, thirty minutes west.

Littlewood brings the plane around and onto course. Caldwell makes minor adjustments.

Warn. I dang well did see somethin'! There it is again!

Malnove. I see somethin' dark.

Connor. There's somethin' there.

Littlewood. Could anyone tell what it is?

Chorus. No, Sir.

Littlewood. I'm gonna come back again at 500 feet. I'm turnin' off the autopilot. I won't have enough altitude to correct any electronic piloting error. Guide me back, Caldwell.

Caldwell. I'll try, but if we find the same spot, it's luck, not me.

Warn. It's a dang log.

The chorus agrees.

Littlewood. I didn't want to fly this low, but I'm going to. We'll save time.

At 500 feet the search continues. We are surprised to find so many logs, wooden crates and other floating debris.

Grant. Littlewood, we picked up two planes on radar. They're over Bungo Strait at 1500 feet, headin' this way, makin' about 200 knots. Naval intelligence says the Japs don't have radar.

Littlewood. Let's hope intelligence is right. At 200 knots, they're not fast enough to be fighters. I'm gonna stay and shoot it out with them.

Superdumbo's gunners have mixed feelings. They will have somethin' slow to shoot at for a change, but even a slow plane can shoot fast bullets.

Connor. I see them, just under the clouds toward Bungo.

Warn. I see `em. Come on, you dang Japs.

Grant. I'm gonna order a dive in two minutes if neither your gunners or mine can identify them. A two hundred mile an hour dive-bomber is too fast for us.

Connor. They're turnin' around and goin' back.

Warn. Come on back and flight like men, you dang Jap cowards.

Calhoun. (*With a good view from the top bubble*). Those aren't military planes, least not any I learned in gunnery school.

Warn. I'd like to shoot `em anyway. Dang.

Grant. We followed you. Our radar confirms your visual. They're leavin'. Now we can get on with our job.

Superdumbo, never having gotten off course, continues the search. Connor observes small boats putting out from shore. Their crewmen spot Superdumbo and sail a rapid retreat. We speculate that the B-29 has perhaps become a symbol of awe to the common folk of Japan.

0628:

Caldwell. We've been flyin' patterns for an hour and a half. How long can we stay here, Don?

Cotner. (*Calculates*.) Seven and a half hours, if we go home to Tinian. Ten and a quarter, if we spend the night on Iwo.

Littlewood. We'll find `em before long.

Malnove. I hope so. This is wearin' me down. You see a man in the water ahead, and he turns into flotsam when you get there.

• • •

Smith and Canova, in search of warmth and a comfortable position, have created a back-to-back sandwich. The third Mae West is the filling. Fishing line from a C-1 pocket is the binding. Great hope at 0530 has become discouragement. Each has asked many times, why don't they just fly over here and see us? Dazed and numb with cold, vigilance wanes.

Facing north at the moment, Smith rests his neck on the Mae West and his head against Canova. He opens his eyes. He sees an apparition.

Smith. Look, Duke, it's a plane.

Canova. It's the Superdumbo. Damn, let's pour the dye.

He opens the lid to seawater dye. It's orange. It spreads.

Malnove. Ted! There's a spot of orange dye! Dead ahead! It's spreadin'. There's a guy! No! Two guys!

Littlewood. Hallelujah!

He makes a tight turn. He flies back toward the men in the water. Superdumbo wags its wings.

Smith and Canova. They see us! They see us!

Littlewood. Commander Grant, we've found two of `em. We'll circle. Steer toward us. We'll bring you close.

Grant. Anderberg, Littlewood's found two men. We're goin' after them. Tell the talk-man to announce it to all hands. Get the second rescue party on deck.

Anderberg Aye, aye, Sir.

He yells it down to the control room.

Grant. (*To Quartermaster*). Orders for the control room. Radar give the helmsman and me bearing and distance.

Anderberg. Radar bearing and distance for helm and bridge. Aye, aye.

Tate. (*Miles Tate, Radar Tech 1c, repeats the order, reads his scope and yells.*) Bearing three oh oh four degrees. Distance eight point oh four knots.

Anderberg yells the angle and distance to Grant and to the helmsman, Walton Toups, Seaman 1c.

Grant. (*Via phone and telegraph needle, to the Maneuvering Room.*) All motors forward flank speed.

Response is verbal, visual and by sense of accelerating motion. Toro turns toward the bearing. It speeds to the rescue at twenty knots per hour.

Superdumbo circles. Richardson, unable to see what's happening ahead, continues to search toward the rear.

Richardson. I see another one! He's in his raft!

Littlewood. Where is he?

Richardson. About half a mile toward shore from the other guys.

Connor. Yeah, I see him. I think the first two guys are Canova and Smith. I can't tell who this is.

Warn. Dang, I can't find him.

Connor. You're on the wrong side of the plane, George. You'll see him as you come around.

Superdumbo continues. Crewmen on the right side of the plane spot the man in the raft. Littlewood gives him a wag of the wings.

Littlewood. Commander Grant, we've found a third one. He's only a half a mile away.

Grant. Good!

Gunner's Mate 2c, Shel Wilber, from his fifty-caliber machine gun near the bow, spots Canova and Smith.

Wilber. I see `em Skipper. (*He points.*) Right over there about an eighth of a mile.

Grant. Good eye, Wilber, I see them.

He maneuvers the boat for a slow-speed pass. The pair soon floats about two yards off the starboard mid-beam.

Don Koll, Gunner's Mate 1c leads the crew of the four-inch gun on the rear deck. Don Shreve, Gunner's Mate 1c is leader of the five-inch gun crew on the "cigarette" deck, forward of the bridge. He acts as gun Captain for the three guns.

Shreve watches from his station. Koll and Lieutenant Jg Hugh Simcoe stand mid-beam at the boat's edge. Each hurls a life preserver on a rope. Canova grabs one. He works his head and shoulders into the preserver donut. He grips it with both hands. He hugs it to his chest. Koll and nearby hands reel him in. Smith connects on the second toss. Simcoe, with help, reels.

Toro and the men in the water vary in response to wave dynamics. Toro goes up, men come down. Men go up. Toro comes down. Banging and scraping on Toro's plates, Canova manages to push off with his feet. He gains traction from the cargo net draped against the hull.

Waterlogged, pickled in brine, Canova is hauled aboard, out of water into raw wet wind. A fitful chill aches his teeth and shakes his bones. Chief

Pharmacists Mate, "Doc" Neidlinger, bundles him into a thick, wide wool navy-blue-blanketed bear hug and carries Canova across the deck and up the short ladder to the bridge. With Anderberg's help, he slides Canova through the hatch and down the ladder onto the conning tower deck. Cradling the exhausted man in taut embrace, with support from submariners below, Neidlinger descends the ten-foot, open-rung vertical ladder to the control room deck. He guides and sustains Canova in a blanket-wrapped shuffle across the deck and into the Wardroom. "Doc" exposes Canova's left arm. He injects morphine.

Steward 1c, Bill Rivera, pops out of his tiny galley. He has warm brandy and hot beef broth on a tray. Doc helps Canova swallow brandy. Brown spoon feeds broth. Three spoonfuls and Canova's asleep. Doc and Ensign John Duff carry Canova down the passage.

Duff. (*Reading the dog tag.*) Put Canova in my bunk.

Neidlinger. Aye, aye. He carries Canova across the three-foot space to the bunk. He lifts him into the bunk. He straightens and tucks the blanket.

Still in the water, Smith emulates Canova's footwork on the cargo net. Simcoe hauls rope. Simcoe and Smith strain to clasp right hands.

Toro rolls to starboard. Simcoe slips. He shifts for balance. He drops the rope. Touching fingertips part. Faster than thought, Smith floats free in the sea.

The roll reverses. The starboard hull rises. The sea rushes in. Undertow engulfs Smith. He looks up. The hull crashes down. His life vest and the life-preserver doughnut, rope attached, buoy him against the bottom. Toro's forward motion scrapes and bumps him sternward.

Glissando/crescendo! Near inaudible hum from Toro's idling propulsion system winds into screaming wail, as four, 1000 watt, induction motors, and twin sets of propeller shafts, reduction-gears and drive-screws, whine in accelerating spin. Smith's skull resonates with vibrations so readily transmitted through marine-grade steel and dense-hard water.

In jumbled rotation, questions tumble through Smith's cranium. *Where are the damn propellers? Will I get out from under this damn submarine? Will the damn rope get caught in the propellers? Will they look for me again? Can they find me again? Am I gonna drown? Where are those God damn propellers?*

The hull rises. Smith gulps air and brine. He coughs and pukes. The sea spits him out. Strangling spasms suffocate...death's hovering devil senses a command from home. *NO!*

Smith recovers respiratory and gastronomic equilibrium. He watches Toro's stern depart. he seeks a sign from aboard...he sees no sailor, nor any signal.

He searches the sky...*GONE .The plane is GONE.* He hears the engines... *FADING... Superdumbo heads for Tinian*...Or, so the sound registers in his bollixed brain. Hope perches on a wingtip...*A A B A A N D O N N E D.*

But Smith is not forsaken. Superdumbo crewmen see him disappear and reappear. They guide Littlewood in a sharp turn toward a quick fly-over. Connor, Warn and Malnove all see Smith wave a return to Superdumbo's wing-wag salute.

Grant brings Toro around, through telephonic communication with his helmsman, Don Allen, in the conning tower. With guidance from Littlewood, Grant has Allen on re-rescue course.

As final approach nears, Grant phones an order, "Bridge, maneuvering room, all motors idle." He simultaneously sets his telegraph pointer a hair forward of the "stop" sector-line. John Spain, Electrician's Mate 1st Cl. responds "Maneuvering-room, all motors idle, aye, aye." He matches

Grant's "analog command" point-to-point, on his telegraph dial. He cuts current flow to ten amps on each of the four motors.

Grant will concede reduced speed for a rescue attempt. He will not stop. Acceleration time from stop to maneuvering speed is dalliance too dire. He must maintain dive readiness and torpedo dodging mobility. He must not give shore batteries opportunity to zero-in on a stationary target.

Ed Hary, Torpedoman 1c and Ed Logsdon, Fireman 1c, grateful for the fresh air break, are on forward and starboard lookout duty. From their posts near the top of the conning tower they spot Smith. They give Grant micro adjustments to bearing and distance. The gliding boat soon has Smith starboard abeam. Boarding this time is swift and pure.

Fourteen minutes after his unintentional inspection of Toro's hull, Smith lies warm, dry and asleep in Ensign L.A. Davis' bunk; Littlewood circles Stein; and Grant is underway toward the next rescue, all motors at "flank-speed".

Wilber. (*Spotter again, from his forward machine gun position.*) Here's another one. He's sailin' along in a little rubber raft.

Grant precisely places his boat alongside Stein. Shreve is at the rail.

Shreve. Ahoy, sailor. Want a ride on a submarine?

Stein. (*In better shape than his mostly submerged buddies.*) Sure, if you're goin' my way.

Stein and Toro yo-yo out-of-sync, until Stein is hauled aboard. He's wrapped navy style and hustled below. He is soon morphined, brandied, brothed (he lasts through ten spoonfuls) and bunked.

...

Eight aviators are still down in the Pacific.

Superdumbo resumes the heading. We pursue the search. We cover the sea from sub to shoreline. Gun emplacements can fire at us. They do not. Japs with rifles can fire. They don't. We fly past Nobeoka.

Warn. Where are all the dang little Jap guys?

Malnove. Yeah, it's a damn dead town.

Caldwell. They must all be in some sort of bomb shelter.

Smith. (*In a joke.*) None of them are on radar.

Calhoun. The B-29 has `em buffaloed.

Richardson. Thank God. I wish the Japs in the big cities were too scared to shoot.

We search other areas of the sea. We search for weary disappointing hours. We find no downed airmen.

1058: Since takeoff from Tinian yesterday at 1710, Superdumbo has been airborne sixteen hours and forty-eight minutes.

Since receiving Lewis' Mayday call, Littlewood has flown two tedious stints on continuous manual control. He feels that the piloting exigencies of this flight demand the skill and judgment acquired during his thousands of hours of multi-engine experience.

Littlewood. How many hours of gas do we have left, Cotner?

Cotner. At maximum range cruising, we have eight and a half hours; longer if we split the time between max range and max endurance. We have two options: keep searching until fuel to Tinian becomes a factor, about three and a half more hours, or search six and a quarter hours and fly to Iwo.

Littlewood. (*After contemplation*) Sounds like enough gas to make a fast flight to Iwo or Tinian if we leave now.

Cotner. Roger. If we do that, I suggest we limit speed to about 230 or 240 miles per hour, in consideration of engine reliability, now and for future flights. (*To Caldwell*) Two forty will get us to Tinian in about five hours, won't it?

Caldwell. Yes, depends on the winds. Do we have enough gas to climb around in search of tailwinds?

Cotner. Yes.

Littlewood. (*To Caldwell*) Good idea.

Littlewood uses conservative good judgment, which is how good young airmen become good old airmen. To continue the search, he trusts neither his own weary reflexes nor Taylor's inexperienced abilities. Taylor came to the crew immediately from Cadet flight school.

Littlewood. Cotner, give me climb power till I level off at 3,000 feet, then set up a 240 mile per hour cruise.

Cotner. Roger.

Littlewood. Caldwell, give me the heading to Tinian.

Caldwell. Roger.

Littlewood. Crew, we're goin' home.

The crewmen are sad. They want to continue the search.

The crewmen are glad. They've reached the limit of effective "sea-sight". In every trough they see "monsters, mermaids, goblins, and things".

The crewmen feel relief that this decision will never be on their conscience. For special relief I turn to thoughts of Jeannie and the babe she carries.

Littlewood makes a climbing turn over Toro.

Littlewood. Goodbye, Toro; goodbye Commander Grant; goodbye crew. We thank you for all you have done for us B-29ers, and for your faithful performance of your air-sea rescue assignments. When they wake up, give our best wishes to Canova, Smith and Stein. Tell `em we'll see them on Tinian.

Grant. Goodbye to you, Captain, and to your crew. You were indeed a super Superdumbo. We'll take good care of your boys.

Grant watches our wing-waggle farewell salute, as we take up our course for Tinian.

Grant. (*To Toro crew, despite lack of air cover*) Continue the search.

Charles Van Auken, Electrician's Mate 1st Cl., U.S. Submarine Toro Rescuee

19 years old in 1945

U.S. Navy, Courtesy of Mark H. Van Auken, son of Charles Van Auken

Air-Sea Rescue Participants Speak, Boston Reunion of the 9th Bomb Group

Standing (L. to R.)
Rescuee: S. Sgt. Bob Canova, Left Gunner, Lt. Joe Lewis' Crew
Rescuers: Lt. Jg. Bill Bruckel, Communications Officer, USS Toro
S. Sgt. Don Connor, R. Gunner, Capt. Littlewood's Crew
Lt. Jg. Bill Ruspino, Engineering Officer, USS Toro
1st Lt. Don Cotner, Flight Engineer, Capt. Littlewood's Crew

Sitting: Herb Hobler, Pres. 9th Bomb Gp. Association

Credit: Jean Cotner

Beeman

We find a forty-mile an hour tail wind at 10,000 feet. On compass heading 159°, we race homeward at 295 miles per hour, sea-surface speed. The *U.S.S. Toro,* briefly a mote on Richardson's retinas, vanishes. Due west, the ruptured cone of Kagoshima Volcano exhales its eternal exhaust.

Richardson. (*Crammed long hours inside his tiny compartment.*) Captain, can I come up to the rear cabin?

Littlewood. Are there any Zeros in sight?

Richardson. No sir.

Littlewood. O.K. Come on up.

Richardson plugs his mask into a portable aluminum oxygen can, climbs from his tiny compartment, crawls and walks through seventeen feet of unpressurized fuselage, opens the cabin door, and joins the company of crew-mates. He stacks flack-jackets to clear deck space. He lies on his back beside Calhoun. The pair will later relieve Connor and Warn from observation duty.

To the limit permitted by our responsibilities, the rest of us seek mental repose. With that inexplicable faculty for synchronizing brain waves, which seems innate among members of successful aircrews, we unite the focus of our meditation on Beeman.

Beeman's yarn spins its thread, through quick pieces of history, on the wheels inside my brain case.

Since a few millennia ago, a People...Polynesian?...perhaps?...flourish, in unsophisticated bliss, on four small islands, southernmost of an isolated string, which punches through the surface in a remote region of Earth's most vast ocean.

Violent storms sometimes sweep these isles, thrilling the People's spirit, and intensifying appreciation of long calm interludes...

Interludes when soft breezes, fragrant and pure, caress grove, meadow and strand. Fresh water, cool and clear, flows forth from ancient rock formations. Sun and clouds alternate on nature's timetable to send warm rays and gentle rain.

Shore waters teem with edible creatures. Indigenous plants, some wild and some primitively domestic, afford bounteous harvests of fruit, nuts and vegetables. There is no threat of discomfort, nor of danger, from flora, or from fauna. Temperatures are perfect for the unclothed fashion.

Tasks necessary for sustenance are brief and pleasant occupations. Supple and handsome men, women and children sport on sunny, sandy beaches, swim in gentle warm surf, nap in the shade of flowering trees, scud across rolling crests of spirited waves in swift, agile canoes, each fitted with tri-cornered sail and outrigged stabilizer. Couples make innocent free love, nap, make love again, nap once more, make love again, through spans of unmeasured time.

6 March, 1521, as counted on the Calendar of the Pope of Rome. Three black ships stain the southeastern horizon. They become dark floating giants as they bear nearer and nearer the three-mile-wide channel that separates the two most northern islands from the southern four. The invading vessels veer toward the smaller, more verdant of the pair.

Men of the People muster in 1001 canoes. They sail their fleet, swiftly in greeting, toward the aliens encroaching from the outer limits of oceanic space. The islanders skillfully maneuver in-and-about, all-around, as they graciously escort the visitors to the harbor.

Femao de Maghalhaes, leader of the weird invaders, drops anchor. His men lower his longboat and slowly and clumsily row him to shore. He proclaims, to the welcoming throng, his proud discovery of their puny island. He says, "Your home is now the property of King Charles the First of Spain, whose right to possession of discovered lands is the decree of His Holiness, Pope Alexander the Sixth. This land and its sisters shall now be called the *Islas de las Velas Latinos* (Islands of the Lateen Sails)."

7 March 1521, Magellan is eager to continue his quest to be the first explorer to navigate the earth's circumference, a commission awarded by King Charles in gratitude for switching allegiance from Portugal to Spain.

After sailing ninety-nine days, sans landfall, from the western coast of Southern *Tirre Firme* (later to be called South America). Magellan spends this day trading trinkets to the "stupid" People for provisions.

Despite the impossibility of verbal communication, Magellan establishes a trade agreement: Trinkets for Food and Water. Some People-persons gather an armload of fruit, nuts or berries and stash it on the beach. Other persons fill the ship's jugs with spring water and lug them to the shore. Each person receives a beaded-bauble. In comparison to Magellan's "barter-samples", "payment-baubles" are small, void of sparkle, artless of design and clumsy of construction. For the People, the contract is broken. They quit.

Crewman are thus required to harvest, haul, load longboats, row to ships and hoist to decks. The People watch. Magellan's men's miserable spirits become meaner.

With sneering, ironic humor they call the People *Chamoro*. In Spanish it means skin-head. All of the People, of both sexes, wear untrimmed hair on face, head and body. There is no metal, nor any ore, on any of the islands. Having no ethnologic memory, and no recitative or written records of any other land, or of any other humans, the People do not recognize the bigoted racial slur implicit in the Spanish word Chamoro. They like the music of the syllables. They accept the name.

8 March, Magellan's sailors finally stow all provisions aboard the three vessels.

9 March, Magellan weighs anchor. He sails due west. He looks back. He says, "Adios *Islas de las Ladrones*" (Islands of the Thieves).

16 March 1521, Magellan sails into the passageways of an archipelago... COGNIZANCE ...ELATION..."I know these islands! I was here with Captain Albuquerque, on the 1511 Portuguese expedition! I know the way west to Lisbon. I've been around the world!...I'm the first man!"

17 March 1521, Magellan in a fervor of reverence toward Charles, his newly sworn Liege Lord, and in an ardor of awe for his God., dedicates a dual quest. He claims islands for King, and souls for Christ.

27 April, Magellan is killed in a fight with a tribe whose Chief prefers his own God.

Spaniard Juan Sebastian de Elcano inherits Command of the Commission. He claims possession of Magellan's personal logbook of route-notes and cartograms. He sails eastward. He rounds the Cape of Good Hope. He heads north.

7 September 1522, Elcano drops anchor of his single remaining caravel into a Spanish harbor. His report to the King includes discovery of the *Islands of the Thieves*, and of the westward route to the 7001-island archipelago (later to be known as the *Philippine Islands*).

Elcano does not tell the King that he led a mutiny, a mutiny inspired by fear of sailing into a narrow rock-bound passage on the south Atlantic coast of *Tirre Firme*, or that Magellan quelled the mutiny, sailed through the passage and into the Pacific Ocean.

For being the first man to circumnavigate the earth, the King awards de Elcano a medal, a globe sculpted of gold, and inscripted in Latin: "Primus

Circumedisti me". The King also confers a promotion to Captain, a raise in salary and a bag of golden Ducats.

Authorities decide that Spain must have a military garrison on its new islands. New Captain Elcano leads the establishing expedition. He knows Spanish soldiers and sailors will demand fish every Friday, but will refuse it on any other day. He sails around Good Hope to the "Philippines". There he loads breed-animals, cattle, swine and goats aboard. He continues eastward to the largest and most southern of the Islands of the Thieves.

Elcano commands the People to become herders, and to supply the garrison with beef, pork and mutton. Communication is almost impossible, but a few natural linguists on both sides, with the help of dramatic enactments, eventually understand the elementary premises, if not the fine details, of each side's proposals.

The People refuse. *Work? Work for dirty, stinking, weird invaders? We don't need work. What is work?*

Force and the threat of great violence cannot persuade the People. Elcano sails once more to the "Philippines". He returns with men, women and children, whom he has learned will be servile.

The People never accept Spanish occupation. Those on the southernmost island revolt. Armed with wooden fishing spears, but with vastly superior numbers, they slay every Spaniard on their island.

The Spaniards, however, have ultimate weapons: European bacteria and viruses. Ninety percent of the People, and of the Filipinos, on each of the four islands die. Those surviving the plagues inter-mate and begin to meld racially, culturally and linguistically, toward becoming a new native ethnic group.

Spain adopts Chamoro names for the inhabited islands. From south to north these names are Guam, Rota, Saipan and Tinian. Against minor resistance, Spain reestablishes the garrison on Guam.

Politicians in Spain gain favor with their Queen. They change the name of the *Islas de las Ladrones* to the *Islas de las Marianas.*

31 July 1898, Spain surrenders in its war with the United States of America. The U.S.A. declares the Philippines to be an American Protectorate, and Guam to be a Territory. The U.S. claims no other Mariana Island.

Impoverished Spain sells Rota, Saipan, Tinian and the northern string of unpopulated Mariana Islands to Germany.

In World War I, Japan opportunistically joins the allies. She defeats those Germans stranded in the Marianas. After the war, against strong protest by the U.S.A., the League of Nations awards possession of all the Mariana Islands except Guam to Japan.

Japan fortifies its three occupied islands with defense installations. These include anti-aircraft/anti-seacraft gun emplacements and shore-patrol gunboats. Saipan and Tinian each have an airfield, with fighter and bomber planes and crews.

On Tinian, the Japanese allot the minimum acreage needed to feed the island's population to provisional agriculture and animal husbandry. They clear maximum acreage of forest to plant sugar cane, a cash crop. They import Koreans to toil as slaves in the cane fields. Tinian's Chamoros migrate to Rota.

A village on Southern Tinian, near the harbor and the beach is ever known as "Tinian Town" or the appropriate linguistic equivalent, by the People, the Chamoros, the Spaniards, the Germans and the Japanese. Tinian

Town's population is about 17,000 persons: 9,000 military, 3,000 Japanese civilians, and 5,000 Korean slaves.

7 December 1941, while Japanese envoys are in the District of Columbia, discussing peace, for an Asia long terrorized by Japanese military aggression, Japan, in cowardly surprise, attacks Pearl Harbor. On 8 December, Japan attacks Malaya, Hong Kong, the Philippines, Wake Island, Midway Island and Guam. Except for Pearl Harbor and Midway, Japan sustains these battles to victorious occupation.

During the days and nights of March 5 and 6, 1942, America and her allies engage Japan in terrible naval warfare, the battle of the Coral Sea. Japan claims victory, but, loses so many ships the war's momentum reverses.

American soldiers, sailors, marines and airmen relentlessly advance from New Guinea, island by island, toward Japan. In fierce fighting the U.S. takes Guam and Saipan. Strategists elect to bypass Rota. Intimidated Japanese troops make no attempt at intervention when the U.S. Navy transfers Rota's jubilant Chamoro population to Saipan.

Dawn, 19 July 1944, Tinian Town residents find the largest naval armada ever assembled deployed offshore. A five-day bombardment hell flattens the town. A few deserting soldiers, some civilians, many Koreans and most animals hide in the cane fields. Lt. Col. Takashi Ogata, Commanding Officer, rallies his surviving troops to defend the harbor and the beach against the coming American landing assaults.

24 July 1944, 0530: The 2nd Marine Division forms a line of attack. The line moves toward Tinian Town beach. Col. Ogata brings forward all reserves. The battleship *Colorado* takes twenty-two hits from Ogata's six-inch guns. The destroyer *Norman Scott* takes six. Skipper Seymour Owens,and sixteen others die. Forty-seven men are wounded. The *Colorado* and the *Norman Scott* retire to Saipan. The cruiser *Indianapolis* replaces the *Colorado*. The line of landing craft approaches shoreline. Ogata orders mortar fire. The

Marines retreat. They re-board the troop carriers. The fleet, battleships and all, sails away. Japanese soldiers cheer. They celebrate another victory over the cowardly Americans. Ogata...? He wonders.

At the same time, the 4th Marine Division, supported by battleships, cruisers, et al., forms a line of attack. The landing craft move toward two northern beaches, "White One", sixty yards wide and "White Two", 160. Battleships and cruisers fire point-blank. P-47s from Saipan, strafe and drop napalm.

0750: The first wave comes ashore. Waves continue every four to ten minutes. The 2nd Marines arrive from the south. They join the assault.

1749: Fifteen thousand, four hundred and sixteen Marines, their arms and supplies, are on the plateau atop the eighty-five-foot cliffs, firing their 75MM howitzers.

After dark, the Japanese make the "ritual" bonsai counter-attack. By dawns-light, body-count score is 2,041 (800 wounded) Nips to 549 (472 wounded) Americans. Any American death, or life-force harm, is tragic. This assault is the least dire of all our Pacific Island conquests. The Generals call it the most successful. A few Japanese surrender. A few hide in the forests or in caves. Most die. Col. Ogata commits harakiri.

Via search and bullhorn pleas, Americans offer sanctuary to all creatures secreting themselves from the terror. No soldiers, no animals, three civilians and 2,861 Koreans accept succor.

Seabees are soon ashore. They commence construction of North Field, which will become the world's largest airbase, with four 8,500-foot runways. They build all ancillary structures, roads, mess halls, etc., requisite for combat operation of B-29s by men of the 313th Wing of the 20th Air Force.

18 January 1945, 1303: 1st Lt. Raymond Johnson lands his B-29 on North Field's runway A. Johnson and crew are the first of the 9th Bomb Group's

Air Echelon to complete the aerial deployment from our combat training base at McCook, Nebraska. Each of the Group's forty-five crews flies in its own newly delivered B-29, on an individual flight basis, on an 8,900-mile odyssey, with stops at Herrington, Kansas, Ogden, Utah, Sacramento, CA, Honolulu, and Kwajalein Island. Other 9th Group crews, including ours, arrive early afternoon.

An earlier arrived cadre issues first priority supplies: C-rations for evening and next-day meals, army cot with pillow and blanket, gas mask, helmet, forty-five caliber automatic pistol and bayonet knife. A tent goes to the designated leader of each twelve-man unit. Capt. Feil, our crews' Airplane Commander, receives a tent. He elects to share it with the Lieutenants of his crew, and with A.C. Capt. Curry and his Lieutenants.

Feil selects a site on the 99th Squadron's allotted area. The ten of us drag the tent to the site. Sans instruction, experience, and as it appears, intelligence, we struggle with ropes, poles, and canvas. Then... our first Mariana Island sunset begins.... Folds and "unfolds" of G.I. specification canvas sag to earth. We stand in wonder, as the colors of nature's palette combine in continuing permutations, to illuminate sky and sea-surface in glorious radiance from limit to limit of the curvilinear panorama.

We give up. We unfold our cots. We spread our blankets. We sit. We sup on C-rations. We lie down. Conversations commence. They die. At dawn we come awake. *This is not Nebraska...*

Dawn yields to sunrise. From a different but equally elegant pallet, sunrise melds and splashes its hues across the heavens. In appreciation, we linger dreamily in the sack. *It has been eons since I woke up with Jeannie.*

We breakfast at a mess tent with tables, benches, coffee and fresh baked bread. From my stash of C-rations, I select a can of eggs and ham.

We erect the tent. We move inside. We can't live in it. It's too hot. It's too dark. It's too dusty, being sited on the soil of a recently bulldozer scalped cane field. We inspect the construction and the rigging. We are inspired and energized. Capt. Feil requisitions a G.I. truck. He pilots us to Tinian Harbor. The Captain of the Port is happy to reduce his growing pile of discarded packing lumber. We transport a load.

We partially disassemble our tent. We extend all side and end canvasses horizontally from the eaves. From our stash we select and install boards to build a rough but serviceable floor.

Other tent dwellers copy our ventilating and lighting system, but none are willing to perform floor construction toil. We gloat in comfort in our breezy, bright, pollution-free environment.

It is too soon dawn...too soon the fall...the fall which pride has preceded. Four hundred cloven hooves race through our opened walls, clatter the length of our reverberant floor, and gallop out our open-ended tent. Malnove sits up, "Look out! Here they come again!"Here come...there go...we need sleep. We want sleep. Will those damn goats never stop?

They stop. We sleep, but the flock does not forget. In blea-a-tific unison they recite a psalmatic passage. *Oh, great god, Pan, glorious it is to gambol in thy name.* The goats return. They prance another percussive paean to Pan.

The flock adopts the 9th Group. Of all the capriods they have ever known, in person or in genetic encodement, men of the 9th are the only creatures who have ever erected a holy temple (our tent) dedicated to the one true lord of life.

Daily at dawn, the flock displays devout devotion to deity, via resolute celebration of requisite rites. Devotion we can forbear. Ritual we revile. This night we build barricades. Next night we weave snares. There is no barricade a goat cannot climb, no snare a goat can't eat. End to end we align our cots along our perimeter. These goats do not fear us. They love us. With speed and agility, they leap our cots and our snoring carcasses. Kids too young to venture a vault, scramble beneath, bumping our butts in the rumble.

We hate these goats. We sleep with bayonet knives unsheathed. In dim early light, we slash toward sound and smell. We score no kills, no probables, nor any psychological intimidations.

We consign these goats to eternal damnation, with masterful soldierly curses. We load our pistols. We lurk in the sack. We do not sleep.We remove the ammo, and store the pistols. Dumb as we are, we're not that stupid.

We surrender. Goats win. We learn toleration.

We know not where the goats abide in the heat of the Tinian days. Our uniform is socks, shoes and boxer style G.I. undershorts. We add cotton khaki short pants and open collared short sleeve shirts when duty calls us outside our tented area. Tinian's goats are never shorn. Their uniform is pure wool. We learn empathy.

In early evenings, solar radiation wanes, ocean breezes waft. The flock regularly returns, probably from some forested retreat. Bleating their baa-aah-aahs, and their maa-aah-aahs, they race along the pathway. They leap atop tent flaps. Several tents host "king of the mountain-goat" competitions. Who has more fun: goats or us caprioids?

We learn respect...then admiration...then pride...then love. *Are they not our goats*?

On certain days, 200 or more itinerant peddlers roam Tinian's roads and streets. These enterprising entrepreneurs are enlisted men from each of the eleven military specialty units which provide ancillary service support to the 20th Air Force: artillery, infantry, Seabees, etc...

Their merchandise is anything in their possession, lawfully or unlawfully. Examples are airplane models crafted from machine gun shells, jewelry crafted from seashells, jewelry crafted from machine gun shells, carpentry-services (including labor and materials). A Seabee builds double-deck bunk beds for our crew. The "springs" are interwoven strips slashed from brand new inner tubes intended for G.I. trucks. The bunks are more comfortable than G.I. cots, by an order of ten and they relieve our crew from the press of people in a tent too small. From a Seabee who introduces himself as Pete Ayers, Tulsa, Oklahoma, I buy a "rising-sun silken flag, taken from a dying soldier". Sale ended, we talk. Pete is two years older than I am. We find no mutual Tulsa friends; but, we feel an "Okie" bond.

The peddlers' clients are aircrew officers. When the B-29s are parked on North Field, the peddlers know that many fliers will be in their tents, playing cards, dominoes, checkers...Are there not ways to gamble on any game?

In the enlisted men's club, beer that is rated 3.2% alcohol is sold in bottles. A man can get drunk on 3.2 beer; but he is then limited to three activities, none of which is initiated by volition, but by the autonomous nervous system. These activities are: 1. Pissing, 2. Puking, or, 3. Pissing and puking simultaneously. Unfortunately, or perhaps fortunately, it is not possible for a man to amass a sufficient cache of bottles to partake in the joy arising from these activities, but many men hold it axiomatic that, with access to hard liquor, they could have even more fun than officers, who no doubt sip strawberry daiquiris from stemmed goblets, small finger extended in delicate decorum.

Officers are gentlemen by decree of Congress. An Air Corps policy perquisite of all officers is permission to form cooperative clubs, through which liquor can be purchased, one fifth of hard liquor per week per officer. We pay $1.05 per bottle, which carries no federal or state excise tax.

We don't know if governmental taxing authorities approve tax-free liquor, or if we are drinking bootleg liquor. Since the bottles are sealed, and none of us have gone blind, we have no wish to know. Neither do the peddlers, nor their friends, nor their customers.

A fifth of liquor is the medium of exchange. Its standard of value is $20.00 U.S., but an officer who sells to an enlisted man for cash, forfeits honor. We know who the scrooges are among us. We call them cowards.

Most liquor is consumed within the week acquired. On the first night preceding a day when no mission is scheduled, we gather in an empty tent. With bottle in hand, we sit on the ground, back against the tent walls. Each man imbibes at his own pace. The banter, though convivial and funny, is an exchange of disparagements. As consumption increases, slurs become more demeaning, and thus more hilarious.

Someone begins the first bawdy song. Each man sings from youthful lust, and with uninhibited gusto. Never having been a member of a college fraternity, I am astonished, and delighted, to learn that there is so great a number of ribald ballads. None are about fidelity of love between man and wife; nevertheless, each song makes me long for my Jeannie. I think of her enjoyment when I teach "Roll Me Over in the Clover", and "I used to work in Chicago" to my beautiful naked lady.

A few drunks possess sufficient power of will to cork their bottles and search out their sacks. Others reach an oblivion that crumples them onto the earth from where next day's minimal relief of stupor, enables self-discovery that they are roasting in a stinking basting potpourri of sweat, urine, remaining contents of an uncorked bottle and stale vomit.

The sagacity of congressmen, the probity of military policy-prescribers and the accuracy of an axiom are thus confirmed.

Two airplane Commander gentlemen take their liquor or leave it: Capt. Emmons and 1st Lt. Spaargaren. The latter is Norseman by name, and berserker by body build. We call him Sparky, what else. Emmons, Sparky and their officer crewmen dwell in the tent next to ours.

Among the peddlers, Seabees are the canniest and most creative. One day we hear a Seabee/Sparky negotiation. We join the watchers. The Seabee has a baby-goat kit. The kit consists of a newborn kid, barely able to bleat. Accessories include a baby-sized bottle with milk, a nipple fashioned from a rubber glove, and a U.S. Navy storehouse-sized box of powdered milk.

The kid is irresistible, but after last night's empty-tent soiree, who has a bottle of liquor? Emmons and Spaargaren do. Each was on duty; Emmons as Officer of the Day, Sparky as Mail Censor. Emmons is not present now, having made a cliff-face descent to swim in our stretch of beachless ocean. By default, Sparky thus becomes the nanny of a goat.

Sparky is intellectually ignorant of goats, especially of the science of goat husbandry, or perhaps more appropriately stated, the art of kid mothering. He is, however, instinctively and emotionally the perfect mother. The baby is bleating his best to convey his great need of a ready teat, and of nannily affection. The kid's bond is instantly fixed, and so is Sparky's.

Sparky sits on his cot, goat in the crook of his muscular left arm. He lovingly cuddles the kid against his powerful hair-covered pectorals. In his right hand he holds the bottle. He brings the nipple to the kid's questing mouth. With sweet tenderness, Sparky croons, "rock-a-bye kiddie, sweet little kiddie." The kid sucks lustily and gazes up into Sparky's eyes. The mutual emotion mists the eyes of both mother and son.

In this state of motherly bliss, Sparky muses on a name for his darling son."*Billy"...obvious, but trite...It must be special. Some variation of Billy? "Bill"... "William"..."Willy"..."Will". Better, but too contrived, besides, everyone would still call him Billy..."Rambler"..."Wreckie"..."Techie"*. (Sparky had a year at Georgia Tech before being called to active service from the Air Corps Reserve.) Capt Emmons returns from his swim. "*Beeman*"!...*That's it.*

Emmons. (*Astounded and amused in equal parts*). What the hell!

Sparky. I got him from a Seabee, Beeman! I've named him after you! The poor little orphaned tyke needs a godfather. Will you take care of him if anything happens to me?

Beeman, i.e., Capt. Emmons. Can't you give him back to his real mother?

Sparky. The Seabee wouldn't tell me how or where he got the kid. He just guaranteed he was a real goat and in perfect health.

Capt. Emmons. Where the hell are you gonna keep him?

Sparky. In the tent.

Capt. Emmons. Did the guys agree to that?

Sparky. I think they're all playin' softball or somethin'.

Capt. Emmons. We're gonna have to vote, and a blackball is a veto. It's pretty damn crowded in here now. Where the hell can he stay?

Sparky. I'll see that he's not in anyone's way.

Capt. Emmons. How the hell can you do that?

Sparky. He can sleep in my sack till he's older.

Capt. Emmons. Where the hell are you gonna sleep?

Sparky. He's gotta sleep with me anyway while he's so young.

Capt. Emmons. You don't know a goddamn thing about goats, do you?

Sparky. I already know I can raise Beeman. And I know he'll be a damn good little goat.

Capt. Emmons. Goats don't know what's good or bad, and they damn sure don't give a damn.

Sparky. Beeman's smart. He'll learn.

Capt. Emmons. It's too damn soon to tell if he'll be smart. Anyway, even a smart goat smells like a goat.

The discussion is still going nowhere, when the crewmen return from the softball field. Being anxious to grab soap, towel, clogs and a clean pair of shorts before heading for the shower, they work their way through the throng surrounding and inside their tent. Exerting their right as tent mates to know, they move to the inner circle.

Being by now favorably inclined toward members of the genus Capra by virtue of devotion to our adoptive flock, non-residents of Capt. Emmons tent are inwardly in support of Sparky's plea. We want that little goat in our back yard, especially if he lives in someone else's tent. From exchanges of individual viewpoints, we progress into a coordinated coercive lobby, in, and surrounding the tent.

Consideration of the scene...the tiny beastie at suckle on an Airplane Commander's breast, looking up with furtive doubt, at a mob of great gorillas, is unrelievedly poignant.

Capt. Emmons. (*With attempted gruffness, but in emotionally broken voice.*) Even my own damn crew is against me. O.K. I give up, but you'll be sorry.

Diapered in G.I. towels, Beeman lives in Sparky's arms for the next twenty-four hours. Wherever Sparky is required to be, Beeman is there too, including visits to the latrine, the shower, the mess-tent. For permission of mess-tent presence, Sparky asks Capt. Erskine, 9th Group Mess Officer.

Erskine. It's O.K. by me. Better ask Col. Wright.

Wright. (*99th Squadron C.O.*.) I'll ask Col. Hall.

Hall. (*9th Group Operations Officer.*) I'll ask Henry.

Col. Henry Huglin, 9th Group C.O. knows how, and where to bend a rule. Better still, he knows when not too. He knows how the officers and men of the 9th feel about little Beeman. Stern as he sometimes seems to be, Huglin loves the little kid, too.

Huglin. O.K., but issue an order to Capt. Erskine, that no local goats shall be served <u>on</u> our mess tables. We don't want to eat any man's pet.

Like any mother's, Sparky's arms get tired. He tries Beeman on the ground. For a baby, the little legs are strong, the prances perky, the legs long. Does he not have the wild genes of a Luzon-Highlands mountain goat? Nanny and kid are still inseparable. Bleating and trotting under, around and between Sparky's feet, Beeman still goes where Sparky goes.

Beeman flourishes on the double-strength blend of G.I. milk concocted by his nanny. He matures emotionally and accepts his tent-mates as uncles. He will permit other men to hold him, if they put the nipple to him.

We begin to fly practice missions to by-passed Rota, thirty miles to the south. We destroy all gunboats, all gun-emplacements. We occasionally spot marooned Jap troops. We ignore them. We practice proficiency toward real missions ahead.

The Rota missions are brief individual sorties. Spaargaren flies an early one. It is the first separation of nanny and kid. Beeman hides under Sparky's cot. He bleats piteously and continually. Neither godfather, nor any uncle can comfort him. Not even with the nipple.

Maturity progresses. Curiosity and eagerness toward physical exercise inspire Beeman toward short excursions from nanny. We in the neighboring tent are honored and delighted to be visited first. He discovers our floor. He dances a little jig. We applaud. It alarms him. He dashes home and leaps onto nanny's cot. Assessing no harmful effect, he returns. We want to pet him and hold him. We try to catch him. We discover that, though quite small, he is a real goat. He escapes from our encirclement.

Beeman retreats to nanny's cot. He calms down. We people believe goats are stupid, and they are, but they think goat-thoughts very well.

Beeman meditates.
Teasing godfather, uncles and large apes is fun. He returns. He dares us. The game is on. Beeman doesn't tire. We do.

Beeman visits other tents. He loves to jump onto cots. He shuffles his hooves and sniffs around. Lt. Richard Steinberg, Bombardier on Capt. Curry's crew, is at the flight line taking pictures of his ground crew. Steinberg is a 6'-5" tall, broad-shouldered and deep-chested Brooklynite, he has seen a goat in a zoo, but before Tinian, nowhere else.

Steinberg returns, camera hung from his neck. He is ecstatic to find Beeman prancing on his cot. Too excited to focus, he points and shoots, just in time to catch Beeman as he leaps from the cot, while simultaneously releasing a full salvo of tiny goat-bomb pellets.

Steinberg rushes in for close-up reconnaissance. He is delighted to rate Beeman a "ten" for accuracy. Steinberg harvests the pellets by hand. Inspiration strikes.
I'll enlarge this photo and frame it. I'll put these pellets in a glass vial and mount it on the frame. I'll call it "Bombs Away, Tinian, 1945".

24 February 1945: The Seabees complete construction of North Field's fourth and final 8, 500-foot runway. Next day the 9th Group celebrates. We inaugurate our aerial campaign against Japanese homeland targets. We strike Tokyo-Bay port installations. From now on we will fly real missions, earnest missions.

Beeman's little brain painfully ponders the mystery of Sparky's frequent and lengthy disappearances. Occasionally, godfather Emmons comforts and feeds him. More often it is one of the apes. Until his nanny returns, he piteously bleats his solitary suffering as he forlornly searches the mostly empty tents of the 9th Group area.

Beeman still nurses. He will have to until he matures. His sign of maturity will be appearance of a typical rounded goat-belly. Until then, milk will be his only source of protein. With development of the belly, a bacterial culture will spontaneously proliferate within the plump expanse. Powerful enzymes will enable Beeman to forage upon and produce sustenance, including protein, from a long and weird catalog of dietary substances, most of which will seem to be inedible to us apes.

• • •

Superstition is a soldierly condition, even among men of education, who are expected to reason rationally.

Lt. Spaargaren is scheduled to fly on the 13 March Osaka Urban Area mission. Some crewmen suggest that Beeman fly as mascot in case thirteen is an evil omen. Sparky thinks, *What if I say no, and someone gets hurt*?

At the boarding, Sparky spreads Beeman's nesting towel on the deck, between the airplane Commander's and the Pilot's chairs. Beeman snuffles a bit and snuggles into the blanket. Sparky instructs him to "stay" an obedience command he has never heard before. Flight Engineer, Frank Schehr, starts the engines. Beeman trembles at the noise and vibration, but,he does not flee. He stays. The folds and aromas of his blanket comfort him. Sparky taxis the B-29 into takeoff position.

Schehr winds each engine up to its 2,200 horsepower max. The plane throbs and pulses into its takeoff run. Beeman leaps high in panic. He comes down into Sparky's lap. Pilot Robert Reinert takes over. His takeoff is perfect. Sparky nestles Beeman again into the blanket. He takes control of the plane. He levels out on course to Japan. He sets up the autopilot. Each plane is flying individually toward a Honshu offshore rendezvous point. The Group will assemble into battle formation, fly over Osaka, drop bombs, fly to the Pacific, then break formation. Each plane will fly individually to Tinian on auto pilot.

The auto pilot control panel is mounted horizontally, an inch above the deck, between Airplane Commander and Pilot. Controls consist of knobs and switches. Beeman rises. He clambers onto the autopilot. He stands, rear legs to the rear, front legs forward. Urine splashes down, puddles and seeps. It seeps...wires, switches, rheostats, relays, and coils all crackle and spark. Vacuum tubes shatter...urine fries, sizzles and spits...stinking steam rises. The B-29 climbs, falls off, yaws, rolls, then instantly reverses these instabilities and recovers.

Sparky. (*To Reinert and Bob Filson, Bombardier.*) Immobilize that damn goat. Tie him up. Put him in a sack...something.

Reinert and Filson. Roger.

Sparky. (*To Schehr.*) Come turn this damn autopilot off, Reinert and I will try to maintain flight.

Schehr. Roger. (*And almost immediately*) Autopilot off.

Sparky. Thanks Schehr. I'm glad our engineer knows the B-29. You saved our lives.

Schehr. O.K., Lieutenant.

Sparky. (*To himself in an ugly dilemma.*) *Shall I abort? Get this thing back on the ground; save everybody's life; get all officers court-martialed...me for treason...the others for abetment? I could fly the mission manually. Lead-crews only use the auto pilot over the target anyway.* (*to Schehr*) Frank, what are chances the autopilot can start acting up again?

Schehr. No chance, sir, even if the switch shorts itself into an "on condition". I pulled the fuse. No way it can get any current.

Sparky. Thanks again, Schehr. You and Tilson got something to confine Beeman in?

Schehr. Roger, Lieutenant; we're gonna wire him shut, inside a flak vest.

Sparky. Good. Use my vest. (*Musing as he flies on.*) *If enemy action or airplane malfunction brings us down, fate will be my punishment, and my absolution of sin. If we drop our bombs on the enemy, and make it back to Tinian, I probably will be the only one punished, but punished for a less serious military crime.*

Sparky and crew put their bombs on target. They return safely to Tinian. Sparky is enervated from the fourteen hours (*which he refuses to share with Reinert*) of manually piloting the big plane. Punishment of fatigue is the bliss of atonement.

Sparky confesses his sins to the debriefing officers. Since it ends fairly well, they think it's a funny story.

Lt. Col. Wright, Commanding Officer of the 99th Squadron, who needs every trained crewman he can get, does not ground Spaargaren. Instead, he writes a letter of condemnation, a copy of which will remain forever in Spaargaren's personnel file. Sparky will not make Captain for a long time, perhaps never. The letter recommends that, after the war, Spaargaren be court-martialed or sued in Civilian Court, and made to pay $33,149.00, the cost of the ruined autopilot control system.

Sparky grounds Beeman and forbids him to fly again. The crew is loyal to Sparky, and points out that they hurt the enemy and all survived. Perhaps it was because Beeman <u>is</u>, after all, a lucky mascot. No one will ever know otherwise.

The 9th flies regularly to Japan. Some crews return. Some don't. Beeman's belly grows. He disdains the bottle. He eats weeds, dried cane stubble, our dirty underwear if we carelessly give him opportunity. Seabees (in line of duty) build us Quonset hut domiciles. We are able to shut the doors on goats and they don't like to climb on corrugated, galvanized-iron barrel-vaulted roofs.

In what we suppose will be the last time we see Beeman, he is sniffing and snorting the escutcheon of Gwendolyn, a ewe in estrus, as she leads him into the forest.

I trust that, when this great war is ended, someone will record Beeman's part in events, significant perhaps, in the history of man and animals on one small planet. Maybe Beeman is even of war-winning significance to young volunteer American B-29 crewmen, who regularly pour terrible vengeance upon Japan, young Americans who for the salvation of sanity, need to express tenderness toward a fellow creature,even toward a goat.

Beeman lives with Gwendolyn in the grip of bliss so compulsive, no goat can resist, except a brief, rare moment of rest and recuperation becomes sometimes an inexorable absolute. While on R.& R., Beeman remembers his uncles.

25 May 1945, 1132: Staff Sgt. Nick Bonack, Radar Operator on Captain Stanley Black's crew, and Staff Sgt. Larry Smith, Central Fire Control

Gunner, on Captain Wendell Hutchinson's crew, are in their Quonset hut, playing a bastardized game we call two-handed hearts. They pause. They listen. A small clan of animals makes a cloven-hoofed sound track across their south-porch deck.

Bonack puts his cards on the table (a 2' x 2' square of plywood, portable from cot to cot). He goes to the screen.

Bonack. Hey, Larry, it's Beeman, with three ewes. Man, he's still growing.

Smith. Got a harem, huh? Must be all that double-strength U.S. Navy milk that Lt. Spaargaren nursed him on. (*Now at the screen wall*). I've got my camera. Let's go out. I'll get a picture of you with Beeman and his new ewe friends.

They open the door. The ewes jump off the porch, trot ten feet, turn and wait for Beeman.

Smith. Maybe we can get the harem another time. I want to get you and Beeman now. He may never come back again.

Bonack. Yeah. His horns aren't very big yet. Some of these big gruff billies have horns five times the size of his. He might get killed defending his harem.

Smith. Can you get him to come with you into the sunlight?

Beeman understands the request. It is already hot at this hour, but he proudly poses broadside, full-sun, belly in grand display. Bonack kneels. He embraces Beeman in affection.

Smith. Smile Beeman. Smile Nick. Good. (*He clicks one shot*).

Bonack. I'd like to have a print of that one, Larry. I want to send it to my girl.

27 May 1945: Ten crews return from saturating Moji Harbor, Shimonoseki Strait, with anti-ship mines. *Thunderin' Loretta*, Capt. Black's B-29, and Bonack, do not come back.

22 June 1945: Prints at last in hand, Larry Smith mails a print of Beeman and Bonack to a beautiful young lady in North Carolina.

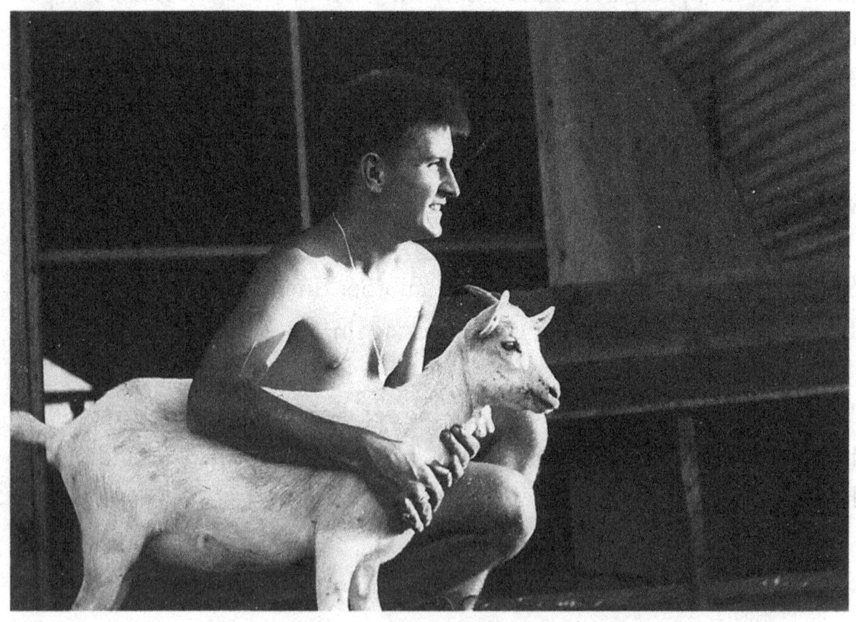

Nick Bonack and Beeman
Credit: Larry Smith

Five and a Half Miles Over Tokyo

Caldwell turns us from poignant memories of Bonack and Beeman, as he questions, "You guys haven't forgotten our first mission have you?"

...

25 February 1945, 0717: A portentous hour is here. Thirty-two B-29s are in formation, departing Tinian, on course to Tokyo, 1,000 feet above the Pacific. It is the 9th Bomb Group's first mission to Japan.

We are ready. With a total strength of forty-five planes, with eleven men per crew, we represent 101,000 hours of military training. We bring more than one million hours of life experience with us to this most earnest hour of war.

We are of a generation who, as schoolboys, sang, "Columbia the Gem of the Ocean", "My Country Tis of Thee", "The Star Spangled Banner" We pledged our allegiance to the flag every day. We have had a love affair with the airplane. Our heroes are the Wright Brothers, Eddie Rickenbacker, the Barnstormers, Lindberg, Wiley Post and Will Rogers, Roscoe Turner, Jacqueline Cochrane, and Amelia Earhart.

Aboard Capt. Harold Feil's B-29, the Flight Engineer, that's me, reprises memories, typical of men my age.

17 October, 1923: Seventeen months into life. I'm in my father's arms. Mother, father and I pause on the path of an Arkansas forest glade. I hear a new noise, an engine in the sky. I search upward...A double-winged thing-a-machine clears the pine tops, engine humming, paddles thrumming. It elegantly sails above the glade. "Bird car-car!" I laugh, "Bird car-car!". Is this a memory? Or a vision infused via long-term iteration of a parental boast?

17 September 1927: I am five years old. In our *Model-T Ford* we drive to Tulsa's McIntyre Airport. We join a waiting throng. I ride on my

Dad's shoulders. A plane lands, taxis, parks. A tall slim man steps out. A mechanic brings a scaffold. The slim man climbs and inspects his engine. He turns. He waves. The crowd roar crescendos. A man turns to my Dad, "Lindy did it on one wing and one engine". Dad buys a small metal replica of the *Spirit of St. Louis* and gives it to me.

17 September 1929: I discover pulp magazines. I beg my Dad for coins. I collect stories of World War I aerial dog fights.

17 September 1930: I walk the aisles of Exhibition Hall at the Oklahoma State Fair. I discover a display of precisely crafted small-scale replicas of airplanes. I remain till closing. I learn about balsa wood, model airplane glue, paint, plans and kits. I have a new hobby. I build *Spads, Nieuports, Fokker D-7s.*

17 September 1931: I graduate to rubber band powered flying models. I build frames of balsa sticks and ribs. I cover them with shrink-fit paper-tissue. Beauty is in their response to the laws of aerodynamics.

17 September 1932: Dad buys me a tiny one cylinder, two-cycle, air-cooled internal combustion engine. I build, crash, and rebuild many balsa and tissue flying machines.

17 September 1935: Wiley Post and Will Rogers are killed. Post's *Lockheed Orion* crashes on take-off, from a small lake in Alaska. Engine quits fifty feet into the air. Bad gasoline. Lake is 100 yards inland from the Arctic Ocean, twelve miles east of Barrow. Congress and the nation observe one minute of silence.

1936 - 1939: Tulsa Central High School: Math, Science, English, History, and Art.

1939: Oklahoma State University and a dilemma: Aeronautical Engineering or Architecture? I choose Architecture.

7 December 1941:Infamy.

January 1942: I enlist in the Army Air Corps Reserve.

September 1942: My scholastic advisor permits me to substitute seven units of aeronautical engineering for six units of French.

25 December 1942: Jean Riesinger and I become engaged.

23 May 1943: I report for duty as an Aviation Cadet, Non-flying. I train to become an Aircraft Maintenance Engineering Officer.

September 1943: The Air Corps sends me to Yale University for technical training.

December 1943: Jean Riesinger and I marry on Yale Campus, Capt. William Greene, Chaplain.

2 March 1944: I graduate from Engineering Officer Training and receive commission as 2nd Lieutenant. I volunteer for flying duty. The Air Corps sends me to the Boeing Factory School to study the B-29.

June 1944: I graduate from the Boeing Factory School. Army Air Corps sends me to Flight Engineer's School at Lowery Field, Colorado.

September 1944: I graduate and am awarded silver wing insignia. Air Corps assigns me to 9th Bomb Group for combat training. I report to McCook, Nebraska Air Base. Capt. Harold Feil, Airplane Commander, assembles a crew. He chooses me to be Flight Engineer.

25 February 1945: We're here. We're ready. When we return to Tinian, we'll only have twenty-four missions remaining to complete our tour of duty.

On Captain Feil's crew, intercom comments on the morning's briefing commence.

Connor. This is it. You guys scared?

Warn. I ain't scared, but I dang sure am thoughtful.

Smith. What're you thinking about, George?

Warn. This ocean is mighty dang big. We gonna have dang well enough gas?

Calhoun. I'm scared, and I'm thinkin'...Both.

Richardson. We know what about, Calhoun.

Calhoun. You're right, it's that little gal I met in Wichita that night we got our last leave. How come I fall in love on my way overseas? I may never see her again.

Warn. Did they say we'd have enough gasoline?

Connor. I'm sure they told Lt. Cotner.

Warn. (*Switches intercom circuits*). Lt. Cotner, we got enough gas to get to Tokyo and back?

Cotner. Hang on a minute, Warn. (*To Capt. Feil...off mike*). Should we ask everyone to get on our circuit till we get near Zero territory?

Feil. Let's all communicate on circuit one, until further order.

Crewmen. (*As the order spreads.*) Roger, Captain.

Cotner. Don't worry about fuel. We're carryin' only three 500 lb. bombs in each bomb bay. There is a 640-gallon auxiliary fuel tank in each bay. That's plenty.

Feil. Since this is our first mission, there are some unknowns. Planners are giving us an edge on safety factors. We'll bomb at 29,000 feet. Jap fighter ceiling is 24,000 feet. Flak maximum height is 26,000 feet.

This reassures the crew. We lapse into silence.

• • •

0944: On Airplane Commander John Hobaugh's B-29, *Nip Nemesis*, engine No. One suddenly drops 400 rpm. The plane slows, loses altitude. Lt. Warren Heiser, Flight Engineer, increases power on Two, Three and Four. He speaks on intercom.

Heiser. Captain Hobaugh, number one has swallowed a valve. We'd better feather it.

Hobaugh. Roger, Heiser. We'll do it.

Heiser shuts off fuel flow, ignition, and turbo-boost. He closes the cowl flaps. Lt. Alvin Miller, Pilot, pushes the feathering button. He releases it as soon as the propeller blades reach aerodynamic neutrality, and engine rotation ceases.

Hobaugh. (*To Sgt. Carey Raymond, Radio Operator),* Contact Captain McClintock's Radio Operator. Tell him we've lost number one engine. We're aborting. Get McClintock's acknowledgement.

Raymond. (*Proceeds with instructions*). Capt. Hobaugh, Capt. McClintock acknowledges. He wishes you a safe return to Tinian.

...

On Capt. Feil's plane, Schultz relays Hobaugh's abort message. Warn says, "Dang."

Warn, feeling compelled to speak further, and forgetting he is on circuit one, comes forth from contemplation.

Warn. I'm still thinkin', dang it.

Connor. About Hobaugh's abort, gasoline, or that little gal in Memphis?

Warn. Yeah, her too. She hasn't written in three dang weeks.

Connor. She's just a sophomore in high school. They don't draft high school students, and only a few of them enlist. She's got plenty of boyfriends.

Warn. But she told me she loved me.

Connor. All the young girls say that. Remember, Juliet was only fourteen years old when she said it to Romeo. They get smarter when they get older.

Warn. I'm thinkin' about this dang 3,100-mile flight, too. Each crew was supposed to do a 3,000-mile non-stop flight during our dang training at McCook. We tried twice. Once we had to land at Colorado Springs, and once at El Paso. There ain't no dang place to land today.

Feil. We'll make it. The B-29 is the best airplane in the world. This one is brand new. It's ours. Those three we shared at McCook with forty-four other crews, were early models, full of bugs, maintained by ground crews who were learning. Only two out of forty-five aircrews completed the 3,000-mile training flight. We're the best crew in the Group. I handpicked each one of you.

(*After a pause.*) I need your help. We'll be in formation eight and a half hours today. Taylor and I want an immediate sound-off if any plane drifts too close. Stay on alert.

1002: An engine on Airplane Commander, R.B. Jones' B-29, "Dottie's Dilemma", swallows a valve. He is forced to abort.

Schultz relays this info to Capt. Feil and crew. Warn tries to be silent. Some of us hear his hushed "two". No one acknowledges it.

We rumble on toward Japan. It's hot at 1,000 feet. The B-29 has no cabin cooling system. Feil and Taylor are the only ones with operable windows. They keep them shut to reduce drag and conserve fuel.

I make the engine power settings, and try to maintain the fuel-use log. It's difficult. I have to make guesses. In formation flight, Feil and Taylor have throttle control. They juggle velocity constantly to maintain position in the formation.

We enter clouds and rainsqualls. The sun disappears. We loosen the formation. Captain McClintock orders all lights on, interior and exterior, including landing lights. Dense drops splatter their weight upon our wings. They pummel a pulse against our thin-skinned fuselage. *Do we fly within the drum-set of a demoniacal timpanist who inexorably pounds forth the Coda of a Mahler Symphony?*

Thirty-knot gusts bounce us hard...up...and harder down. Airplane commanders shut off autopilots. Human touch allows greater pitch and roll, more slip and yaw, but it is softer and less stressful on the structural systems of an overloaded B-29.

We burst out into sunlight and McClintock tightens the formation. He orders lights out. Music comes on. There's too much static north of the cold front. Schultz tunes Saipan out. Caldwell says Iwo Jima is now 100 miles to the east. Smith can't check him on radar. We're too low.

• • •

1008: Engine No. Three on Airplane Commander Bob Bearden's B-29, "Old 900", catches fire. Bearden and his Flight Engineer, M. Sgt. Robert Tilman, feather the engine and shut it down. Tilman turns the engine fire-extinguishing system selection switch to No. Three. He pulls the fluid release handle. He can still see flames blowing through the cracks in the cowl flaps. He releases the second, and last, squirt. Smoke and flames cease. Bearden notifies Capt. McClintock that he is aborting.

Schultz again reports to our crew. Warn's, "three", is a little bolder. The crew remains silent.

Maybe they're not proud of their thoughts. I'm not. If we will have to abort, I hope it is soon. The farther we get from Tinian, the more dire will be the return trip, in an ailing airplane.

Schultz tunes into the Armed Forces radio station on Saipan again. We try to listen to Abbot and Costello. Static is worse. Schultz tunes Saipan out.

1057: Schultz reports the abortion of 1st Lt. Raymond Johnson and crew, another valve swallowed.

Warn. (*In no muted tone*). That's four.

Calhoun. God damn it, George!

Smith. We can count. George.

Capt. Feil. We're all in this plane together. The calmer we react, the safer we're gonna be.

Halfway between Iwo and Japan we hit a second weather front. It's different. We hold our 1,000 feet of altitude. Clouds are about 500 feet above us, except that now and then we fly through wispy tails that drift down to us.

The deeper our ingress, the crisper the chill that cramps my anklebones. I slip my sheepskin half-boots over my oxfords. I put on my leather jacket. I know now why the meteorologists sometimes say "cold-front".

We look up into the beauty of an amorphous multi-dimensional universe, whose murky froth is infinitely traversed with ever-opening, ever-changing, ever-closing, spume-surfaced spaces. A faint eerie-blue light glows in all voids.

CRACK!!!

All four propeller-discs glow with eerie fire. Individually, it's terror. Collectively, it's horror.

Warn. Number one and number two are on fire!

Connor. So are number three and number four!

Calhoun. All four are on fire!

Cotner. It's only "St. Elmo's fire". It's not uncommon to airplanes, or to ships at sea. I saw it over Colorado a couple of times, when I was in Flight Engineering School.

I'm still shaking, but I have a duty to my crew. I'm lucky. I studied the phenomenon in physics and aerodynamics classes, again at Yale, and once more at the Boeing school. But...thunder was never so loud before...even in an Oklahoma electrical storm.

Warn. What the dang hill exploded?

Cotner. We were struck by lightning.

Warn. Don't lightning set planes afire?

Cotner. No.

Warn. It set the *Hindenburg* afire. I saw the dang newsreel.

Cotner. Our aluminum skin protects us. The *Hindenburg* had a cloth skin, and it was filled with hydrogen. One tiny spark and it was gone.

Warn. We got oxygen, 100-octane gas, motor oil, hydraulic fluid, and a thousand dang bombs.

Cotner. You're right George; they're all hazards but we don't have sparks... from lightning that is. Tomorrow we'll go down to the flight line and I'll show you the cable system that bonds all parts of the plane together so that electrical charges will flow across, instead of sparking across parts that are isolated from each other.

WHACK!!!

St. Elmo's aura burns brighter. Silence ensues.

Warn. How come St. Elmore's fire don't set the engines afire?

Cotner. No sparks. I'll explain it tomorrow. We'll all get together at the Red Cross shack for coffee and donuts. O.K.? *I'm glad I brought my aerodynamics and physics texts. I need to review what I think I know about ionization*. (*To the crew*). The thunder is the worst thing. We're so close to the lightning we get no damn warning. It scares me as bad or worse than it does you, but just think how lucky we are to see this awesome display. How many people in the world will ever get the chance to do this?

We fly into the sunlight. All too soon our celebration of the rite of St. Elmo's Fire ends. I hold up my hand. I spread my fingers. *There is no blue glow. Was I expecting glow?* We continue the mission.

...

1517: Half an hour beyond the second weather front, Lt. Nat Patch, Navigator, calls on intercom.

Patch. Captain McClintock, we're on course to the initial point of climb. ETA is five minutes. Climb heading is 329 degrees.

McClintock. Roger, Patch, Are we on schedule?

Patch. We're two minutes late, Captain.

McClintock. That's damn close. We'll make that up easy. Good job, Patch. (*To Sgt. Claude Allen, Radio Operator.*) Allen, send an encrypted message to all 9th Group radio operators, "Airplane Commanders, we start our climb in approximately four minutes."

1522: We climb.

...

1539: 1st Lt. Tutton's No. Four engine catches fire. M. Sgt. John Chambers, Flight Engineer, shuts it down and extinguishes the fire, as 2nd Lt. Rick Gerolau, Pilot, feathers the prop.

Tutton. (*To Navigator, 1st Lt. Bert Sharrow*). Sharrow, how far are we from the target?

Sharrow. A 100 miles.

Tutton. (*To Chambers*). Can we climb to 29,000 feet on three engines?

Chambers. No sir.

Tutton. (*To Sharrow*). Can you find us a good target of opportunity?

Sharrow. That bay out your left window is Suruga Bay. Shizuoka is an important port city. In my opinion, sir, there are no good targets when we only have three engines.

Tutton. Thanks, Sharrow. Take us to Shizuoka. I wanta get credit for a mission. I don't want to fly this far to abort. (*To Sgt. James Walker, Radio Operator*). Notify Capt. McClintock's Radio Operator we've lost an engine. We're gonna bomb Shizuoka.

• • •

1542: At 10,000 feet we encounter wispy mist. A minute later, we are enshrouded in dense fog.

McClintock. Allen, send this, encrypted, to all radio operators: Airplane Commanders, burn all lights. Spread the formation. If we find daylight by 30,000 feet, close the formation for a bombing run. Do not climb higher. Repeat. Do not climb higher than 30,000 feet. Allen, get an acknowledgment from each Airplane Commander.

Allen. Roger, Captain. (*He sends, receives and reports.*) Captain, all Airplane Commanders receive and acknowledge.

1605: At 27,000 feet, we break through into brilliant sunshine. Cloud-top reflection blinds. McClintock orders a check of the formation. Allen reports that all twenty-eight remaining planes respond, but that Wienert, Scheafer, Cox and Loy are still in the clouds, and aren't sure where. McClintock instructs Allen to tell those four that we're going on without them.

1606: At 27,500 feet.

Patch. Captain, we're caught in one hell of a damn blow. I hope it's not a hurricane. It hit us about 500 feet above the clouds. I estimate wind velocity at 150 miles per hour and its direction to be twenty-two degrees, E.N.E.

McClintock. Something's goin' on. I've never seen this before. Never flown this high before. The B-17 ceiling was 25,000 feet. I'm still holding 329 degrees on the gyrocompass. I'm crabbing left between fifty and sixty-five degrees to do it. I can't check wind speed. (*To Allen.*) Get me voice contact with all B-29s.

Allen. Roger, Captain. (*Allen complies and reports to McClintock.*) The entire formation is on clear channel. You can go ahead now, Sir.

McClintock. Attention all Airplane Commanders. We are flying in an extremely rapid wind. I hope to hell it's secular. He pauses, but no one laughs. (*To himself*) *Guess these guys don't know their Japanese history...* If it turns gusty, it will be dangerous. We'll have only a twenty-three-plane formation. Fill in the gaps, but spread it out. Allow at least 150 feet between planes. Drop your bombs when you see mine go. (*To Patch.*) Use the radar procedure, and tell Friedman when to salvo the bombs.

Patch. Roger, Captain.

1609: At 29,000 feet we level off in "spread" formation. Patch, using his "slave" radarscope image of land and sea, guides McClintock across the Sagami Sea and over Tokyo Bay. Per briefing instructions he avoids possible locations of anti-aircraft guns, i.e., the Islands of Mikuru, Kozu, Miyake, Nii, To (Toh) and Oshima, and the shoreline cities of Tateyama, Misaki, Minato and Yokosuka.

...

1614: Airplane Commanders Wienert, Scheaffer, Cox and Loy emerge from the clouds. Wienert leads as they try to overtake the formation.

1624:

Wienert. (*On intercom to Lt. Thomas Petrulas, his Navigator*). Tom, we aren't gonna catch `em. What's our secondary target?

Petrulas. I can't recognize the secondary. The Island of To is the third target. I see it on radar. It's about ten miles ahead, five degrees to the left.

Wienert. Guide me in. We're gonna bomb it.

Petrulas. Roger, Captain. Try seven degrees left. We've got a strong crosswind. (*To Lt. Dale Flocker, Bombardier*). Get ready. I'll tell you when to drop `em.

Flocker. Roger.

Not wishing to be alone on their first visit to Japan, Scheaffer, Cox and Loy follow Wienert.

...

1647: Looking past Kamakura on the eastern shore, toward the western shoreline, Patch sees a blip five miles south of Chiba. He studies...*Is this our target? Damned if I know. But it must be. If it ain't, I don't know what the hell is.*

Patch. Captain McClintock, at Yokohama turn right to gyrocompass heading oh-two-oh degrees. Out of the turn it will be fifteen miles to target. Oh God, with this tail wind we'll only have two minutes to get the bombs off.

McClintock. Do the best you can, Patch.

1649: McClintock leads his unwieldy formation into a space-time devouring turn. He takes up heading oh-two-oh. Patch concentrates on the blip.

Patch. Captain, correct the heading two degrees right.(*To Sampson Friedman, Bombardier*). Get ready, "Sampie". We're closin' damn fast. I'm gonna yell bombs away in less than thirty seconds.

McClintock and Friedman. Roger.

Patch. 10...9...8...7...6...5...4...3...Bombs away.

Friedman. (*Echoes.*) Bombs away! He toggles his six bombs. He records the time: 1650.

Some of the formation's bombardiers drop their bombs immediately. Many are slow...unprepared by the unexpected brevity of the run and by the incompleteness of the countdown.

Patch. Captain, turn to gyro heading oh-nine-oh. It's sixteen miles to the Pacific Coast. The way this wind is pushin' us it'll be less than two minutes.

McClintock. Roger. Do you think we hit anything?

Patch. I'm not sure that blip I was tryin' to hit was even the damn target. I think we scattered bombs all over the peninsula. Maybe some of them hit something. I let you down, Captain.

McClintock. How fast do you really think that wind is?

Patch. I haven't had a chance to make a good estimate. Right now I'm thinkin' it's about 250 miles an hour.

McClintock. It's not gusty. Let's ride it out to sea about a hundred miles before we turn home.

Patch. Good idea, Captain.

• • •

Aboard Captain Feil's Crew.

Richardson. (*Tail Gunner.*) (*Watches anti-aircraft shells bursting in a line behind us. He switches from the gunner's intercom circuit to circuit one.*) Ha, ha, ha! The Japs are shootin' at us, but they can't catch us.

Taylor. (*Pilot.*) How the hell do they know where we are? Intelligence says they don't have radar. They can't see us through the clouds. Can they hear us?

Feil. (*Airplane Commander.*) They probably saw the bombs fallin' out of the clouds and tracked `em to the ground. They guessed we would turn due west to get out to the ocean.

Malnove. (*Bombardier.*) I didn't think they could shoot this high.

Feil. How high are they shootin', Rich?

Richardson. The flak is burstin' 500 feet above us, Captain.

Smith. (*Radar Operator.*) It sounds like someone's throwin' gravel on the unpressurized section behind me.

Warn. I hear that dang gravel on the roof. Hope that ain't what flak sounds like.

Richardson. Naw. It can't be flak. They're chasin' us, but droppin' further behind.

Caldwell. (*Navigator.*) The Pacific Coast line is just ahead. We'll soon be out of ack-ack range.

Malnove. There's flack ahead. It's 1,000 feet above us, and it's on our course.

Schultz. I hear gravel on the roof again. It's over the front bomb bay. I don't think it's comin' through.

For six minutes, we ride the streaking air stream. We see no more flak bursts. We hear no more gravel on the roof.

…

1658:

Patch. Captain, we're 100 miles east of Honshu. The heading for Tinian is one-five-nine-degrees on the gyrocompass. This damn wind looks like it's gonna blow forever. It's not a hurricane. It doesn't bend one damn degree. It's gonna give us a hellish head wind component. I suggest we let down in a hurry to just above the clouds.

McClintock. Roger, Patch. Will do.

He descends at 1,000 feet per minute. Not having disbanded the formation, he trusts the formation to follow. He levels off at cloud top. All twenty-three planes are still with him. They follow.

McClintock. I think we're out of that freak wind. I'm only readin' about ten degrees of crab now. Rather than lead the formation into the clouds, I'm gonna hold this altitude. Whata you think Patch?

Patch. You're right, Captain. We've still got head wind. Let's hold altitude and heading, for a while. I'll shoot the sun now, and again in half an hour.

Maybe I can get a reading on head wind velocity. Shootin' the sun is not as accurate as shootin' a star though.

McClintock. Sounds good to me. How's it sound to you, McFee?

Russell McFee. (*Flight Engineer.*) It's O.K. But, we can't fly all the way to Tinian in a head wind. It only took us about half an hour to climb through these clouds. We should be beyond them soon. Then we can start lettin' down about 100 feet per minute, till we run out of head wind, and maybe find a tail wind.

Patch. Yeah, once we get into clear air, we might be able to get a drift reading, through the bombsight, on a white cap. And, when it gets dark, I can shoot a star.

McClintock. That's a hell of a good plan, men. Let's do it.

McClintock starts the slow descent. Forty minutes later, at hour 1738, and altitude 23,000 feet, they come out of the clouds. Patch and Friedman make their observations and calculations. They average their results and report their estimation of wind speed-and-bearing to be ten miles per hour directly on. McFee says that's too much. McClintock implements a steeper let down.

At 19,000 feet, Patch and Friedman report a five mph tail wind. McFee recommends leveling off to save altitude in case we need to search again later.

McClintock contacts all Airplane Commanders on the clear channel. All report that they are O.K., with no injured crewmen and with plenty of fuel. McClintock disassembles the formation with, "We'll see you on Tinian."

• • •

Aboard Capt. Feil's plane, we release a bit of tension.

Feil. (*Checks out the plane and the crew.*)Caldwell, how's our course, position and E.T.A.?

Caldwell. We're on course to Tinian. We've diverged toward the east from the planned return route, but it's insignificant. By dead reckoning, our position is about where it should be. Using Patch's and Friedman's wind estimate, my E.T.A. to Tinian is 2318. Compass heading is still 159°.

Feil. Cotner, how's the fuel?

Cotner. My log shows we have 991 gallons. Only seventy-five gallons less than was scheduled for us at this point. Those head winds goin' into Yokohama hurt us. The tail winds, after we turned, helped, but we didn't spend enough time flyin' with the wind to balance the fuel burned flyin' against it. I'm confident we'll have plenty to get home on. *Did I say home*? *I guess from now on, Tinian will be home.*

Feil gets a report from each member of the crew. Each is in an optimistic mood. Each reports his equipment is functioning properly.

Warn. Lt. Cotner, tell me about St. Elmo's Fire. I can't wait till tomorrow.

Cotner. I'll try, but remember, I'm no expert. I'll try to keep it in terms of the way we experienced it. When the difference in the static electrical charge between a cloud and our airplane gets high enough, the gasses in the air become ionized at a point, probably at the point of highest potential difference between the cloud and our plane. The gasses glow and begin to transmit electricity. This process almost instantaneously develops into a conducting path from cloud to plane, or as we say, a bolt of lightning strikes the plane. And on its way it "cracks-the-whip" on a lot of air molecules...we call this thunder.

The electricity delivered to the plane flows through the aluminum skin. Aluminum is a much better conductor than air. The electricity is attracted to the magnetism generated by the rapidly rotating and reciprocating iron parts of the engines. It flows from skin to engine, through the grounding cables...no sparks, remember...and then to the propeller blades,out to the tips. The electromotive force is still strong enough to cause air gasses to ionize and glow along sharp edges of the propeller blades. I've read that the glow lingers for as long ninety seconds. Does that seem about right to you, Warn?

Warn. Yeah, by dang, it does.

Cotner. Well anyway, by the time the electricity reaches the propeller, it no longer has enough energy to initiate lightning bolts. But by then, another bolt strikes the plane.

Warn. Dang. You're right, Lieutenant. We really are lucky. I hope we run into St. Elmo's Fire every time we fly to Japan. Thanks for explaining all that stuff.

Cotner. You know, Warn, by the time you go back to school after the war, they may have entirely new theories about stuff like this.

Warn. But Lt. Cotner, what is ionization or whatever you call it? And why does electricity make gasses glow?

Cotner. You ask the right questions, Warn, but you ask the wrong man. I don't know the answers. But we can see that it works when we look at a neon sign. There the gas is inside a sealed tube, so that it doesn't diffuse into the air. A different gas is used for each color. The electricity is continuously applied, so the glow is constant. After the war you should study science, Warn. You're a natural.

Malnove. (*Looking ahead.*) We're coming up on that cold front again. The clouds are several thousand feet below us. I don't suppose lightning strikes up does it? After your great lecture, I'd like to encounter St. Elmo's Fire again too.

Cotner. We've got twenty-four 3,000-mile-plus missions to go. I bet we'll see it now and then.

Malnove. What I'm most curious about is those damned high-velocity winds. Do you have a meteorology lesson you can give us on where the hell they came from?

Cotner. No. Capt. Feil has more hours in the air than anyone on this crew. Ask him.

Feil. (*Who has been listening.*) Good job on St. Elmo's Fire, Cotner. I've experienced it several times, and I've heard it explained, but you're the first one who made sense about it. In the Airplane Commander's briefing, they talked about high winds. We were forbidden to fly higher than 30,000 feet. You know 33,200 feet is considered to be the absolute ceiling for B-29s. We've been told the controls get pretty mushy at that altitude; that turbo-boost decreases.

Captain Brown, 9th Group weather officer, talked about high winds in the Airplane Commander's briefing. The 58th wing flying out of India has gotten into very high winds at 32,000 feet over Japan. Brown thought we would be O.K. at 30,000. He also told us that B-17s and B-24s got into headwind trouble at 25,000 feet a couple of times trying to get back from Berlin on a westward heading.

Brown said both the Japs and the Germans have supposedly published papers in meteorological journals in their respective countries. Each discovered the winds via unmanned weather balloons.

Each is trying to suppress information now. He expects to learn a lot about all manner of weather phenomena during the course of the 20th Air Force's aerial campaign against Japan.

Warn. What if these Japanese winds and the German winds are connected into a stream that goes all the way around the world?

Feil. I've never heard that idea before. I've never heard of really high winds over the U.S. either, except in tornadoes or hurricanes. The winds over Japan today are not from either of these storms. You may have something, Warn. I'll ask Captain Brown about it. Keep on wondering.

Warn. What are the dang chances that we'll have to abort yet?

Taylor. (*Who seldom converses, but chooses to now.*) It's too late to abort. We've already dropped our bombs on the target. If we go down in the ocean now, we'll still get credit for the mission. There'll be crews who saw us drop 'em.

Connor. It's only called an abortion, George, when we have to turn around before we hit the target.

We cross both weather fronts. We remain above the clouds. We hit rough air, but it's not bad. South of the second front, Shultz is able to get Radio Saipan. He puts it on the intercom. It's pop tunes: Glen Miller, Harry James, Tommy Dorsey, Bing Crosby, The Andrews sisters. The sun goes down...colors...colors...colors...We're still at 19,000 feet; at this altitude Pacific sunsets extend forever. Caldwell reports that we're on course and on time. I repeat that we have plenty of gas, and that the engines are operating perfectly...*We're going home.*

2140: Capt. Feil begins a let down.

Cotner. Captain, we've got extra fuel. Do you want to maintain power and get home early?

Feil. No. Let's fly maximum range cruise control. I don't mind landing with extra fuel in the tanks. I sure don't want to be in the air in some kind of emergency wishin' we hadn't wasted fuel.

Cotner, Roger, Sir.

I reduce power on all four engines. I have to close the cowl flaps to maintain operating temperature. As we lose altitude, the sun sets in a hurry. It's eerie to perceive the descent by so many of the senses: the growing darkness of the sky and the sea, the muted sound of the engines and propellers, the shifting force of gravitational pull body-to-plane and plane-to-body, pressure changes in cranial cavities.

Caldwell's course leads us straight to Tinian. The movies are still playing at the outdoor theaters. Capt. Feil orients himself by the light of the seven screens dispersed about the island. He finds the runways by the headlights of G.I. trucks. He makes a smooth landing. He brakes to slow the plane. He taxis. He parks. I cut the engines.

Each man goes through his disembarking checklist. Tasks accomplished we climb down to the ground. I realize how much I love this little island. I kiss the earth. So do we all.

Master Sergeant Maurice Zarko, and his ground crew, shake our hands.

Zarko. You guys had me worried. You're the last crew back. Everyone else has been here a while. I hope my airplane didn't hold you up.

Feil. No, the plane flew perfectly.

Cotner. We have the 20th Air Force's best Airplane Commander. We had enough gasoline to race a bit at the end, but Capt. Feil played it safe. Thanks, Captain.

A truck takes us to headquarters. We turn in parachutes, bombsight, tail-guns. Red Cross Girls Kay Brenan and Sue Schroeder give us a shot of whiskey with a water chaser.

The debriefing officers are tired. They tell us the 9th has no losses. They've heard all the stories already: high-winds, weather-fronts, high winds, no fighters, high winds, flak at high altitude...They make it quick for us.

We walk to our huts. We shower. We hit the sack. I worry. *Why didn't they tell everyone at briefing about the rapid air stream? Is withholding information about danger gonna be policy?* .Then I talk to Jeannie. *We flew our first mission today, honey. All planes came back safely. No one got hurt. I love you, sweetheart.* Repose hits me...Fatigue hits me...Whiskey hits me...I sleep.

BLITZ ONE, TOKYO

Aboard Capt. Littlewood's plane reminiscence continues, as we fly on course toward Tinian. We're still returning from our 2nd September Prisoner of War Supply-drop mission.

...

26 February 1945, 1003: I come awake. I'm tired from yesterday's mission. I lie for four or more minutes on my back, then I remember who, where and when I am. I climb out of the sack. I knock the ants out of my shoes. I perform ablutions. I dress. I go to brunch. Capt. Erskine, 9th Group Mess Officer, did not permit the Seabee's to dismantle the Officers' mess tent, even though he now serves three scheduled meals a day in conventionally constructed mess hall buildings, one each for officers and enlisted men.

Brunch is a self-service repast. The menu is all you can eat of fresh baked G.I. bread, tropical butter, orange marmalade plus plenty of hot G.I. coffee. Brunch hours are anytime between breakfast and lunch. We appreciate the privilege of Capt. Smith's informality.
I fill a cup from Capt. Smith's bottomless urn. I inhale. I sip. I open my eyes. Capt. Feil, Caldwell and Malnove are together at a table. I join them and we all say hi.

Feil. What did you think of the mission?

Cotner. Well, we're alive, and I believe the plane is in good condition.

Feil. Yeah. It sure as hell flew well. *(To Caldwell)* What's your thought, Claude?

Caldwell. A navigator hasn't got a chance in winds that fast. If we're gonna fly in that kinda stuff very often, they're gonna have to give us some kind of ultra-rapid calculating device.

Feil. That was a nightmare. I'm glad we had no collisions or damages.

Malnove. Jap planes can't reach us and Jap flak doesn't hurt us. I think twenty-four more missions will go by before we know it.

We believe Air Corps authorities speak truth when they tell us twenty-five missions is a tour of duty. It will be after our twenty-third mission that we will hear, "Replacement crews are arriving too slowly. Your tour is extended to thirty-five missions."

Cotner. After I eat, I'm gonna go to the line and check on the plane. Anybody want to go with me?

Feil. I do. I'm through eating. I'll go check out a Jeep from the motor pool, and drive back to pick you up.

Claude, Paul and I are hungry. We try to acquire calories before Feil gets back. We each butter-and-marmalade a slab of bread, dunk it, and slosh it down with even more coffee.

Malnove. Wait a minute. We don't need to get sick. Capt. Feil won't be late for lunch. If we get back before lunch, we can have a second brunch.

Caldwell. You're right. He is punctilious. It equates with honor to him.

Cotner. He hopes to stay in the Air Corps after the war. He <u>is</u> a true military leader, and his punctuality and devotion to duty raises the odds on our crew's survival.

Feil honks. We grab a hunk of bread, run outside and vault into the Jeep. Feil pilots us to North Field over Tinian Roads: 8th Avenue, 42nd St., Broadway (the Seabees' road engineer is a native of Manhattan Island).

We arrive at Parking Stand 52. Master Sergeant Maurice Szarko, Crew Chief, and Sgt. Bill Kaiger, Ass't. Chief, run to greet us. We hop out.

Szarko. I'm glad you guys came. I've got a coup'la things to show you. See that bomb Kaiger painted on the nose, under Capt. Feil's window.

Feil. That's beautiful, Kaiger.

Caldwell. Yeah, you're an artist, Kaiger.

Kaiger. Naw, I've got a stencil.

Cotner. But you have an artist's sense of composition. I visualize twenty-four more sprouting from this one. You chose the right spot.

Malnove. Keep 'em up-to-date Kaiger. I want to take a picture home with me.

Air Crew Collective. Thanks, Kaiger.

Szarko. Come look.

He stoops under the fuselage. He shuffles into the front bomb bay.

We follow Szarko past the open bomb bay doors. We stoop, shuffle, and stand. We look up.

Feil. My God. Look at the damn holes.

Caldwell. I see seven. Is that all?

Malnove. You want more?

Szarko. There's more. Look in the roof over the wing.

(The wing extends through the fuselage at mid-height and separates the two bomb bays longitudinally.)

Caldwell. I see 'em. They're not very big.

Malnove. You want bigger?

Cotner. Did they hit anything vital? A wire, a tube, a cable?

Szarko. Five came through the rear bomb bay. One knocked the insulation off of some wires to the rear running lights. If the bare wires had shorted, you would have lost some lights, and a short can start a fire. These wires didn't short of course.

We all move under the fuselage into the rear bomb bay. We look.

Feil. Damn.

Crew chorus. Damn...Damn...Damn...

Feil. Cotner, did you have any indication that these wires were hit?

Cotner. No. When lights <u>do</u> go out, the guys who can see them tell me. If they short out, it may blow a fuse. Every time we get out over the Pacific, on every mission, I'm going to check each damn fuse. I had no idea that "gravel-on-the-roof" noise meant that flak might have come through. It sounded like it bounced off. Thank God this is a harmless lesson. I'll tell Captain Nestel (*Group Flight Engineer*), we engineers need a training session.

Feil. Didn't the engineers get any training about "gravel-on-the-roof"?

Cotner. No. It was never mentioned. Not in the Engineers Training Manual or in any training lecture. One lucky thing is that these holes can be patched without damage to the plane's structural integrity.

Szarko. I've got the sheet metal men coming. I hope they get here. There's a lot of pressure to have the planes ready to fly tomorrow.

Feil. Good. The sooner we complete our twenty-five missions, the better we'll like it. (*Looks at his watch*) Oh damn, it's 1115. We'll be late for lunch.

We're suddenly hungry. We depart.

At lunch it's barbecued mutton chops, again. Some guys groan. The chops are not from Tinian goats. Australia sells them to Uncle Sam. The grumble is that mutton and lamb is the only meat they send. Excellent fresh fish is now and then flown in from down-under, but the grumblers will not admit that fish is meat. They want beef. *Are they not real live American men?*

There is a joint-services vegetable farm on Tinian. It's irrigated from the well. Good things grow there. We eat well.

Lunchtime rumors circumnavigate the room, clockwise and counter-clockwise. They meld into one "true" consensual rumor: we will fly tomorrow. The one "true" origin is the flight line, no doubt.

Flight crewmen go to bed early and sober tonight.

27 February, 1945: The true rumor is counterfeit. No B-29s will fly today. A photo/weather reconnaissance B-29 returns to Guam. The report goes straight to 21st Bomber Command Headquarters, "Damage assessment not possible. Tokyo still socked in."

28 February: Same report.

1 March, 2 March, 3 March: Same…Same...Same.

4 March: The 9th Group puts twenty-three B-29s in the air, in a daylight raid at 25,000 feet on the Nakajima Aircraft Factory, Tokyo. Our crew is

not assigned to this one. Nineteen crews make it to Tokyo. Cloud cover is dense. No crew finds the factory. Via radar, seventeen crews bomb the secondary target, "Tokyo Urban Area". Lts. Klemme and Bearden bomb Shizuoka and Maug as "Targets of Opportunity".

5 March, 6 March, 7 March, 8 March: Rumors? Yes...Reports? No.

9 March, 1945, 1600: Col. Huglin, 9th Group C.O., opens the flight crew briefing.

Huglin. Gentlemen. This message is from the Commander of the 21st Bomber Command, General LeMay. He and his staff have evaluated photos of the 25 February mission against Tokyo Bay Targets, and the fourth of March mission intended to be against the Nakajima Aircraft Factory. General LeMay declares each of these missions a failure. He declares high-altitude, precision-bombing strategy of Japanese targets to be a failure.

General LeMay orders 324 B-29 crews to return to Tokyo tonight, twelve crews from each Squadron of each Group of Tinian's 313th Wing, Saipan's 73rd Wing and Guam's 314th Wing. General LeMay <u>commands</u> us to hit the target. He ensures our success; he assigns bombing altitudes of 6,400 to 7,800 feet.

Flight Crews...*Silence....Silence.....Silence...*

Huglin. With courage, we cannot fail. General LeMay gives us nine square miles of Tokyo's Koto District as target. Koto is a mixed occupancy area of homes, commercial buildings and industrial buildings. Most homes, and many commercial buildings, are made of sticks and paper. Roofs are of thickly thatched straw. The war-industry factories are made with bare-steel structural frames, covered with corrugated-steel wall and roof panels. The conflagration we create will ignite any building in the path of the Koto firestorm. Each B-29 will carry a total of 16,000 pounds of M69 and

M47A2 incendiary bombs. At 500 pounds each, that's thirty-two bombs per plane. Incendiaries are filled with jellied gasoline, plus sufficient TNT to ignite and dispel glowing globs of viscid adhesive goo.

Cotner. (*Thinking) I don't like to hear this.*

Huglin. None of us wants to burn homes and to kill innocent people. We will of course obey orders. Here is my philosophy. We are fighting toward extinction, or surrender, with an enemy who has started a war we have to win. Many of the homes we will destroy house families who serve as parts-fabricating contractors to the war-industry factories of the neighborhood. Many of the civilians we will kill are designers, and/or builders, of weapons. All are supporters of the Japanese economy. The sooner we can force surrender, the fewer Japanese and Americans will be killed.

Flight Crews... *Silence, Silence, Silence...plus a unanimous nodded assent... But we wonder: why did the Air Corps ask Boeing to build a high-altitude bombing plane? Why has all our training been spent learning how to use it, for that purpose? Won't most of us die? Personally, I don't wish to go on this mission,.but...I know I will. I did volunteer for flying duty.*

Huglin. Our best defense is surprise. The Japanese have seen B-29s a number of times since the first raid on 15 June 1944, by forty-eight planes of the 58th Wing, flying the hump from India, and refueling in China. The 73rd Wing began bombing from Saipan on 13 November 1944. Weather and/or photo reconnaissance B-29s fly overhead daily. All these planes have flown at high altitude, during daylight hours. No incendiary bombs have been dropped. No planes have flown over Japan at night.

Cotner. *I wish General Hansel was still Commanding Officer of the 21st Bomber Command.*

Huglin. Intelligence tells us the Japanese will be confused, unprepared and unable to adjust anti-aircraft gunnery toward low-flying targets.

The firestorms will immediately overpower their undermanned and underequipped fire suppression units. (*He pauses briefly.*) Major Luschen please continue.

Luschen. (*Group Operations Officer*) Thank you Col. Huglin.

Luschen passes out flimsies to airplane commanders, navigators, and flight engineers. An aide pulls down a map of the Pacific, Tinian to Japan, and a large-scale map of Tokyo.

Luschen. Each of the 324 B-29s participating in this mission will fly an individual sortie. Clouds are not expected but there will be no moonlight. Details shown on the flimsies must be followed exactly. We want no collisions. Three hundred and twenty-four B-29s converging on a relatively small area, flying sequentially, in the dark, with all lights aboard extinguished, must each be precisely flown.

Cotner. *The more I hear of this mission, the less affection I have for General LeMay.*

Luschen. First Wing in the procession is the 73rd. Their lead squadron will start the fire. Each successive airplane's aiming point is any unburning area on the edge of the fire.

Cotner. *With choices like that, what will keep B-29s from crossing paths?*

Luschen. The 313th Wing flies second. Our first takeoff is five minutes after the 73rd's last takeoff. The 314th's first plane will reach Tinian from Guam five minutes after our last plane is in the air. Takeoffs, within each Wing, are scheduled at seventy-five-second intervals. If you do the arithmetic, you'll see that bombs will be falling on Tokyo for more than five hours. It is possible that the Japs will bring in night fighters from elsewhere in Japan. You will have 100 rounds of ammunition per gun. If you're sure a night fighter is attacking you, shoot at it in short bursts, or you will soon be out of ammo. The limit on ammunition will save weight for bombs.

Cotner. *The more I learn, the more ill feeling I have toward General LeMay.*

Luschen. Maintain the stream of planes in order of takeoff. There will be no time or place to rendezvous and realign this linear formation. Fly at the altitudes and velocities prescribed on the flimsies.

If you must abort, advise the Commander of the plane following you, via voice, on clear channel. Depart the line in a descending 180° counter-clockwise turn. Fly back to Tinian at 2,000 feet on a course parallel to the Tokyo bound stream, maintaining five miles separation to the west.

Cotner. *God damn. What Jr. Birdman of a mission planner thinks 324 B-29s will maintain a seventy-five second interval flight pattern through 1600 miles of Pacific Ocean air, just because 324 air-speed indicators are each showin' the same numbers. New as I am to aeronautics, I know that every flight instrument has an allowable tolerance for error. I visualize the total debt for discrepancy allowances coming due in one grand collision event over Tokyo. No doubt the burning B-29s will ignite a glorious holocaust. I hate General LeMay...I hate, too, his eternal cigar. As we are all falling into the fire, shall we each light up a damn stogie?*

Luschen. (*Takes his pointer to the Tokyo map*) This is the Tokyo Port Area, on the northwest corner of Tokyo Bay. You navigators and radar operators who flew on the 28th of February may recognize it from your radar view on that day.

The Sumida River flows in a winding course, east to west, six miles north of the Port. The river turns south and flows in a nearly straight line to its mouth, in Port waters. (*Moving his pointer.*) This is the Ara River. It flows south and empties into Tokyo Bay east of the Sumida.

The 73rd Wing's aim point is between these two rivers, five miles north of the Bay.

Due to surface winds, wherever they may blow, and succeeding bomb drops, wherever they may fall, the fire can spread in any direction. It may leap the Sumida River. It may then spread south toward this conspicuous landmark. Who will tell me what it is?

Several voices. The Imperial Palace Grounds. *(Our crew thinks Captain Feil was first. We are proud.)*

Luschen. Good. The grounds are defined by an encircling moat. Very visible by daylight, and by its radar image. Each aircrew man is charged with daylight recognition. All navigators and radar operators are charged with radar screen identification. No B-29 crewmember shall harm any part of the Emperor's property with bomb or bullet, nor shall he transmit any literal expression of opinion toward the Royal Eminence via excretion of urinary waste through the B-29 relief tube system.

Out of respect for Major Luschen's rank, crewmembers titter, giggle and snicker. A few brown-nosers guffaw, howl or roar. The joke was new when the first military crewman had to take a leak in a WWI primitive biplane bomber. In a B-29, the relief tube drains to the atmosphere beneath the fuselage.

Huglin. Excuse me, Frank. I want to add emphasis. This order comes from the Commander-in-Chief. After the war the U.S. will have to govern Japan. The President will appoint a Military Governor. The appointee will need a surviving Emperor for the accomplishment of governance, an Emperor who has not lost face and who retains respect of the people. So no bomb in the garden, on the buildings or in the moat.

It's O.K. to fly over the Palace Grounds on the way to other targets. We want the Japanese people to know we are capable of bombing their Emperor any time we choose to.

Back to you, Major Luschen.

Luschen. Thank you, Col. Huglin. (*To aircrews*) So, men. It's o.k. to fly over Imperial Grounds. Just don't drop anything.

Luschen gives the floor by turns to the Group Officers of Navigation, Meteorology, Engineering, Armament, etc., for the completion of details.

He dismisses us for an early supper. We report back for parachutes and flight gear. We ride to the flight line in trucks. We make preflight inspections. We pull the props. We climb aboard. We start engines, taxi and take-off, all on schedule, except Capt. Curry, who aborts take-off.

At scheduled altitude of 3,000 feet, and speed of 195 mph indicated air speed, thirty-five 9th Group B-29s play follow the leader. It gets too dark to see the plane ahead but we see its running lights. We fly into cloudbanks. We lose the plane ahead. We come out of the clouds. One time we come out and almost ram the tail of a B-29.

We are supposed to maintain radio silence, so instead of asking this suddenly appearing Airplane Commander who he is and why he is here now, Capt. Feil asks for speed. I give him power for a fast cruise. He goes around, then turns back into line. I slow us down to our assigned 195 mph. We seem to be doing O.K. so long as Capt. Feil and Taylor can follow the running lights. The Captain is constantly juggling the throttle to maintain the interval. It's nerve-tightening flying for him. It wastes fuel. The Air Corps has given us no method of determining fuel use rate for throttle juggling flight. I try to time and record fast and slow intervals. It's tiring. I am uncomfortable with the accuracy of my log.

I wonder how we'll make it through the two weather fronts ahead. We'll be in rough air with no lights visible through the clouds to follow. A somehow humorous question enters my head. *What am I doing here?*

I'm scared inside the weather fronts. We bounce around in wind, rain and darkness. *Are we about to fly up Capt. Keene's tailpipe? Is Lewis flying up ours?*

Somehow we make it through. It's not far now to To (Toh) Island, our initial point. Per Capt. Feil's request, I give him climb power. We climb to 7,100 feet, our bombing altitude. The Ninth Group is last among the 313th Wing planes. The 314th Wing is not far behind. They'll bomb at 7,800 feet. I worry about them dropping incendiaries on us. B-29 altimeters are even less accurate than are their air-speed indicators.

At To, we follow the line into a leftward turn. We come out on a course to the Port of Tokyo. Feil notices the plane ahead has increased speed. We're supposed to fly the bomb-run at 210 mph indicated air speed. I give him 210. The Port, across the Sagami Sea and then across Tokyo Bay is 150 miles from here. We can see red glow in the distant sky.

We fly past Oshima Island. Keene ahead extinguishes his running lights. Feil turns ours off, per briefing instructions. He strains to stay in line by the glow of the eight turbo superchargers pumping up Keene's four engines.

Feil's eyes are adjusting. We're now 100 miles away, but flames are climbing the sky. He can begin to see silhouettes of planes ahead. He thinks the line may be breaking up.

Smith. (*On intercom*) Lt. Caldwell, look on your radar screen. I've got a great picture of the Imperial Palace. It's ahead of us at eleven o'clock.

Caldwell. Wow. It looks like a distorted bull's-eye. Beautiful image, Smitty.

Malnove. I can't see it visually, but,I'd sure like to drop some M-47's on it. I'm sure you could tell me where and when, Claude.

Feil. Congratulations, Smith and Caldwell. You've met your radar recognition requirement. Listen, Crew. We've got a serious situation soon ahead. Don't try to find the Palace visually. We'll find it on a later trip. I want everyone to concentrate on his job. Gunners, search the sky for B-29s and night fighters. Let me know as soon as you find either. Understood? Respond when I call your name

Calhoun. Roger.

Warn. Roger

Connor. Roger

Richards. Roger

Feil. Malnove, you're a gunner until I tell you I'm on course to the drop-spot. Then make your drop by intuition. Don't use the bombsight.

Malnove. Roger.

Feil. Cotner, keep the engines runnin'. Be ready to increase power if I ask for it. Maintain your fuel use log as best you can.

Cotner. Roger.

Feil. Caldwell, be ready to give me an escape heading as soon as we get beyond the fire.

Caldwell. Roger.

Feil. Smith, keep giving Claude a good radar picture of what's below. He will need it to get us back to the Pacific.

Smith. Roger.

Feil. Schultz, keep monitoring the encrypted channel in case something significant comes in.

Schultz. Roger.

Cotner. *Thank God for Captain Feil. I was apprehensive as hell. I'm sure the other guys were too. I still wish I were not here, but we're the best crew. These guys will do it like Capt. Feil says. We may get hurt, but we won't hurt ourselves.*

Captain Feil keeps following the B-29 ahead of us. He thinks now it might be Capt. Reynolds' plane. He doesn't know how the lineup got out of order but whoever is flyin' this plane is holdin' speed steadier. Maybe Keene just took the wheel from his Pilot. Well, that makes it easier for Capt. Feil and me. The red sky glows brighter the closer we come.

Malnove. I see silhouettes of planes against the fire. They're spread all across the sky.

Feil. Good. Keep searchin' and reportin'.

Calhoun. There's searchlights and ack-ack ahead.

Connor. One poor guy is caught in a searchlight. He's catching a lot of anti-aircraft fire.

Schultz. I hear "gravel on the roof" again, only louder this time.

Warn. There's a B-29 on fire about 9:00 o'clock.

I check my instuments, then steal a look, across the deck, out Caldwell's window. I see the burning B-29. It rolls left and falls off into a spin. I say a prayer for the crew, whoever they are. Warn reports the spin. I feel a sort of guilt that they got hit and we didn't. *We're not safe yet* . I check my instruments. All engines perfect. I look out Caldwell's window again to check No. One and No. Two. I'm chagrined. I forgot to check them when I was watching the burning B-29.

I look out my window to check No. Three and No. Four. *They're beautiful.* I see a B-29 to my left and above. *What's he up there for? Has Guam caught up with us*? I see short Bursts of tracers going into him. *Short bursts?...Is that from a B-29*? I can't see the plane that's shootin'. Of the plane gettin' hit, one wing bursts into flame. I get back to my instruments. I hope there are no night fighters out there. I deeply hope it wasn't friendly fire. If I ever get shot down I earnestly hope it's by an avowed enemy, doin' his soldierly duty, rather than by a cowardly comrade shootin' at any plane he sees, lest it might be an enemy.

Richards. I see a B-29 goin' down...on fire. A B-29 shot him.

Smith. I'm glad I can't see out.

Calhoun. I was scared before. Now I'm terrified.

Malnove. There's a strong wind from the northeast. I can tell from the direction the smoke and the flames are blowin'.

Feil. We'll soon be heading into that smoke. Hope we'll be able to see.

Feil. Keene, or whoever that is ahead, is peelin' off to the left. I'm gonna look for a bare spot off to the right. Gunners, help me find one.

Malnove. Captain., look toward the fire about one o'clock, just about due north. It's about half a mile wide and a mile deep. If we hit near the far end of that space, we will help keep Tokyo burnin'.

Feil. Roger, Malnove. I'm eyeing that spot. Let's do it. Soon as we get to the middle I'll turn north.

I guess our turn to drop is comin' up. Hope all those poor damn Japs are in an air raid shelter. I remember newsreels of Londoners spending nights in the underground rail tunnels. Tokyo has some huge sub-surface rail terminals plus lots of neighborhood stations. Miles of rail lines criss-cross below the ground. Tokyo authorities have had time to prepare for civil defense.

Feil turns due north.

Calhoun. Capt. Feil. A B-29 went straight over us. It was about 500 feet higher and fifty miles per hour faster. I couldn't get an angle on its tail insignia. It seems to be racing us to our target.

Feil. Probably is. We'll damn sure report him at debriefing. He ought to be grounded, and worse. Caldwell, note the time, altitudes and air speeds. Someone in the 314th Wing is in a hell of a hurry to get through this mission. Taylor, watch that nut.

Caldwell and Taylor. Roger.

Jap anti-aircraft gunners are serious. They impose a pattern of bursts that we will have to fly through. It ain't 4th of July colors. It's red flames showing through dirty smoke puffs. They catch us with a searchlight. They hold us in the glare. It is serious psychological injury. We expect a direct hit any second. But, after a sixty-three second eternity, the lights leave us, and focus on those 314th Wing guys who passed over us. The ack-ack goes with the light. Are the Japs afraid he'll get out of range before they can shoot at him? We are less angry with him. He is a good decoy.

Malnove. He's droppin' his bombs on our target.

Feil. I'm gonna go in to the east of his fire. (*He maneuvers and lines up again..)* We're on a bomb run again.

Connor. It's sure gettin' hot in this plane.

Warn. Lt. Malnove, any danger of those bombs goin' off before we get rid of them?

Malnove. It is hot and gettin' hotter. The fire is damn fierce and thanks to our friend from the 314th, we're gonna have to fly right over it. It'll take 553 degrees to ignite the bombs.

Cotner. The wings'll start foldin' up before we get that hot.

Feil. I'll climb outa here before it gets that hot.

I think again about the people below. *Thank God they're all in shelters.*

• • •

Americans, even General LeMay, won't know what is happening on the ground until after the war is over.[1] Tokyo authorities, at the direction of the military, forbid the use of subways, or of the few governmental buildings that are somewhat fire-resistant, as air raid shelters. What if presence of civilian refugees stymies passage of a train, or thwarts military utilization of a building? These evil Samurai Bushida authority fools issue a shovel to each household, and ask the residents to dig their own shelters. Most houses are built three to a lot. There is room for but a few foxhole-size "shelters" per lot. The fools tell the people to fight the fire at their own house, and to help neighbors. To accomplish this purpose, the fools issue each household a barrel of water and a mop to beat flames with.

Women, who haven't heard from soldier husbands in months or years, put their babies and children into foxholes. They pile on a few rotten boards for a roof. They flail at flames with their mops. Their mops soon burn to nubs. The women flail jellied gasoline onto themselves. The lucky ones die of smoke inhalation. The happiest die without hearing the screams... of their children.

Some families try to beat the fire to the Sumida and Ara Rivers. Many of the narrow twisted streets are dead-ended. All are jammed with people and abandoned carts. The B-29s keep coming. Fires start ahead, and on both sides. Some people reach the rivers. The bridges are too hot to walk on. The Asakusa bridge over the Sumida River, near the geisha houses (the really fun geisha houses) smolders...smokes...groans...collapses. The fires are jumping the rivers.

The estuary rivers are of torpid flow. They absorb fire-heat well. Their waters are hot. They cool no torsos. They slake no thirsts. Citizens lie down in neat Japanese accumulations along the banks. They die.

Eighteen year old Tadashiro Takugawa* is slow of mind. Each branch of the military has rejected his enlistment attempt. He does tedious tasks well, at an electric parts assembly plant. His grandfather is keeper of the local fire-warden bunker. Tada "helps" the old man. The wardens check in at the 12:06 a.m. first siren. Each departs on his route through the city. Tada watches the endless hell-borne aerial procession. At 2:45 a.m., he asks the grandfather,"Ojii San, why do we fight a country so great, it can build an airplane as powerful as the B-29?"

Ojii San yearns to confirm the truth he hears from his grandson's heart, but, not trusting Tada in his honest, dim-witted naiveté, to keep safely silent, he says, "Remember, Tada, Japan is winning the war."[2]

...

Feil. (*Flying toward our new target*) Drop 'em when you think best, Malnove, but drop 'em short rather than long. I don't want to search for a new target where the fire is burnin' so hot, north of the burned-out area.

Malnove. Roger, Captain, me too. (*Measuring distance by eye,he allows for the intervalometer setting of fifty yards between bombs. He doesn't bother to correct for the fifty mph head wind. He's seen enough to believe that no one,* *including General LeMay, will criticize our effort on this mission.)* Bomb bay doors coming open.

Schultz. (*Looks through the porthole into the front bomb bay*) Front bomb-bay doors open.

Connor. (*Looks through rear porthole)* Rear bomb-bay doors open.

Malnove. *Better short than long. Better short than never...Better now than later....* Bombs away.

Each time, the intervalometer trips the shackles on a bomb. We get a jolt in the butt, as the wings snap straighter from sudden loss of load.

Warn. (*Counts the jolts*) Twenty-eight, twenty-nine, thirty, thirty-one, thirty-two. Hooray!

Malnove closes doors.

Schultz. (*Looks through the porthole*) Front bomb bay closed. All bombs gone.

Connor. (*Looks*) Rear bomb bay closed. All bombs gone.

Feil. Listen, Crew, we will fly over fire and through smoke. When we are clear, Lt. Caldwell will give us directions to the Pacific Ocean. Stay vigilant. We'll have a chance to relax when we're on course for Tinian.

Everything turns suddenly black. We feel more g's on our butts than a roller coaster gives at the bottom of the big drop. Oily smoke fills the cabin. The stench is evil. I've never smelled barbecued human flesh, but I know by intuition that few, or none, of the Japanese citizens made it to a bomb shelter. We rise rapidly. My rate-of-climb indicator and my altimeter confirm the g-force receptors in my hind-end. I am disoriented. I have no flight indicator instruments. I turn, and lean to the right. I look at Capt.

Feil. He's holdin' the wheel, kinda lettin' the plane fly itself. I think maybe we're upside-down, but Captain Feil is right-side-up so I must be also. I don't think to time our climb. It seems we're in climb mode forever. At 10,500 feet we fly out of the smoke. The foul odor lingers.

Feil. Smith, you o.k.?

Smith. I'm good. I'll need a little while to get the radar tuned up.

Feil. Caldwell, you o.k.?

Caldwell. Yes, soon as Smitty gives a picture I'll figure out how to get out of here.

Feil. Cotner, you and your engines O.K.?

Cotner. Roger. We got a great ride and some free altitude.

Feil. I'll hold altitude, course and airspeed; I'm goin' to call the roll. If you're O.K. and the plane and equipment at your station is O.K., Roger, "all O.K" (*He proceeds and gets all O.K.'s*) Stay on watch; there may be planes at all altitudes, and at all speeds and headings.

Cotner. Capt., is the ban on running lights still in effect?

Feil. The flimsie didn't get specific on that. We're still gettin' light from the fire. When we get in the dark, I'll turn 'em on.

Smith. I've got a good picture now. It shows the coast.

Caldwell. Yeah, that's great, Smitty. Captain, set up a heading of sixty-eight degrees on the gyrocompass. It will take us north of Tokyo Bay, across the peninsula, and over a lake. We'll cross the coastline between Omigawa and Hokoda. At the coast turn to ninety degrees; hold it for ten miles. Set up 164 degrees to Tinian; it's about 1650 miles. After I can get an idea of wind velocity, I'll give you an E.T.A.

Feil. Sounds great, Caldwell. Let me know when we get beyond the Bay. I'll turn on the running lights. (*To Cotner*) Let's hold 210 mph till we get on the Tinian heading, then switch to maximum range cruise control.

Cotner. Roger, Captain.

We make the first turn. We begin to leave the fire and smoke behind... *Thank God*...But, the surviving Japs will have to live with the fire, the ashes and the carbonized carcasses.

We turn toward Tinian. I'm exhausted. I can't stay awake. I swallow my amphetamine pill.

We're alive. My hatred for General LeMay is only smoldering now. I decide to keep it secret. Maybe that's the proper function for commanding generals, to give us dumb soldiers a figure to vent emotions upon.

I think about Jeanie, and our unborn child. Thoughts bring no calmness, peace, or repose. I invite visions and feelings of love and sexual fulfillment... Visions and feelings, always present in my reveries, sans conscious summons.

I get instead...anxiety, apprehension, dread. *Will I survive twenty-three more missions? What will happen to Jeanie and our baby? Dead or alive, I shall be a father...Will I ever be a daddy?*

In dark humor, I glare at my instruments. *Well, at least they are normal.* I read my watch: 4:12 a.m.

Caldwell. (*Interrupts intercom silence).* My E.T.A. for Tinian is 0840.

Cotner. *Oh, God, four and a half hours.*

0524: Faint light invades the cockpit. It steadily blossoms. I realize what it is. For the first time in my twenty months of flying, I am aloft as dawn arrives.

Warn. (*Whose left gunnery position is now facing east*). Dang! What a ding-dang-dilly sunrise.

Malvove. Glorious.

Calhoun. Amen.

Taylor. Golly damn.

Feil. Best aerial sunrise I've ever seen.

Caldwell. Thank God it's still on schedule.

Others of us have no easterly window. I look past Caldwell, out his window. I see warm sky colors. Do I see pink glow on Caldwell's face? It must be imagination. As I watch, color whitens and illumination brightens. But, heaven's radiant display does not dissipate, nor dispel, my dour disposition.

Do molecules of unclean Tokyo smoke cling to the sensors of my nose and tongue? Or does an obscene memory hang in my brain?...Or is there a difference?

I try a leftover bite of my peanut butter sandwich. *It's not what I want.* I fish a cigarette from my pocket...I light...I puff...I stub... I envy my crew-mates sunrise chatter on the intercom. I pour coffee into my cup...I sip. *I never did like cool coffee.* I search my pocket for a piece of tropical chocolate. *I must have eaten it all.* I find, instead, my other amphetamine capsule...*I've never taken two...but I feel a pull...or is it a push?* I wash the pill down with cold coffee. If I expect to be cheered, it doesn't work...

I read my watch again and again. By 5:54 my left wrist trembles. I extend my right hand. It's trembling. I have done well on the Army's marksmanship ranges. Instructors have credited my steady vigor...now I am taut, stretched, tense, strained, keyed up, on edge. *Is my blood quavering in my veins and arteries, or is it imagination.*

I perform my duties. *I hope I'm doing well...I think I am...Why do I have uncertainty?...What shall I do?...Tell Captain Feil?...What can he do?*

I decide not to worry him. I've done this to myself. I do not believe I'll lose cognitive capability or physical proficiency, except that I'll have to be cautious of fine-tuning adjustments to propeller-pitch, manifold-pressure, throttle-position, etc., when I make engine power settings.

I count my pulse: seventy-four beats per minute. *Is that high?* My remembered resting pulse is sixty. *Am I at rest now*? I've never before taken my pulse in the air. I have no aerial base line.

The hours to Tinian are agonizingly slow in passing. Every task, every thought, includes anxiety, apprehension, and anguish...

0659:

Caldwell. (*Startles us again*). Smitty has Pajaras on radar.

Feil. Glad to hear that.

Warn. What the dang-hill is Pajaras?

Caldwell. It's the northernmost island of the Mariana chain, about 330 miles north-northwest of Tinian. It is 100 miles due east of us right now. It proves we are right on course and still on schedule for our 0840 E.T.A.

Feil. Good navigating, Claude.

Everyone is survival happy, except I am still dominated by my miserable non-comprehendible apprehensive mood. I bum a chunk of chocolate from Caldwell. He tosses it across the plane. I fumble the catch. It falls unwrapped down onto the well-deck, by my right foot. I retrieve it. I scrape it. I gnaw off a chunk with my right-side incisors. I wait for saliva to soften it. I crumble it with molars. It yields no joy...I wish Captain Feil would say, "Let's burn a little gas, and get this plane home".I refrain from telling him we have enough gas to do this. Feil flies silently on.

0838: Capt. Feil's landing is perfect. He taxis. He parks. We clamber to earth. A truck takes us to debriefing.

Red Cross girls, Sue Schroeder and Kay Brenan, give us coffee and donuts. I don't want coffee. *Sue and Kay are so pretty, so sweet, so happy to see us, I can't disappoint them.* My taste buds shriek, *This stuff is poison.* I drink every drop.

Two medics offer us a shot of whiskey. My stomach rebels at ingesting additional chemical substance. *I'm glad it's easy to say no to them.*

At debriefing we tell our story. We learn that Capt. Keene and Lt. Hardgrave ran out of fuel. Each had to ditch in Northern Mariana waters. Rescue searches for each crew are underway.

0931: Debriefing officers dismiss us. We walk to our huts. I take a shower. The water truck has just filled our elevated tank with fresh water from Tinian's well. In about five hours the sun will have warmed it. The cold shower sharpens my raw edge.

I skip brunch. I hit the sack. I intend to sleep many hours. Instead I lie wide-eyed, focusing on the ceiling of our hut...I close my eyes...They stare at the inner-side of my lids.

1145: My buddies go to lunch. I choose sleep. *Why can't I get sleep?*

1430: No sleep yet. I'm still trembling, and now I'm trembling while sweating from the damn afternoon heat.

1500: The Flight Surgeon's office is open now for sick call. I get dressed. I walk to the Medic's tent. The orderly admits me to see Capt. John K. Eppes, 99th Squadron Flight Surgeon.

Eppes. C.O.T.N.E.R. Cotner?

Cotner. Yes, sir. I can't go to sleep.

Eppes. How long have you been awake?

Cotner. Well, I woke up on the 9th about 10:00 a.m. and flew on the Tokyo mission that night. I've been in my hut tryin' to sleep since debriefing. I've been awake about thirty hours now. Can you give me a sleeping pill or something, Captain?

Eppes. Didn't you do some napping on the mission?

Cotner. No sir, I'm the Flight Engineer. There's no one to take my place. That's why I took the amphetamine pills.

Eppes. Did you take both of them?

Cotner. Yes, sir.

Eppes. What time did you take them?

Cotner. The first one about 0200 and the second about 0530.

Eppes. How much coffee did you drink?

Cotner. A lot. I don't keep track.

Eppes. How much liquor do you drink?

Cotner. I drink my fifth each week. Usually in a binge. I never drink on the day or night before a mission; nor on a mission day. I don't drink beer.

Eppes. How long have you had that cigarette cough?

Cotner. About three years, I guess. I've been smoking about five years. I don't remember how long I've had the cough.

Eppes. (*Takes my blood pressure, counts my pulse*). 138 over 79...69...Pressure and pulse are abnormally high for a young airman like you.

Cotner. *Yeah, I remember 105 over 70 and a pulse of 59.*

Eppes. (*Listens to my chest, looks at my tongue*). You're the kind of man who should quit smoking.

Cotner. But, Captain Eppes, I enjoy smoking.

Eppes. What you "enjoy" is the satisfying of your addiction to a poison. Smoking will kill you.

Cotner. My Dad hates it that I smoke. He calls cigarettes "coffin nails".[3]

Eppes. Cotner, I'm givin' you no sleeping pill. No medication of any kind. You've got an overdose of bad substances. It'll wear off eventually. Go back to bed. You'll fall asleep. I'm leaving you on flying status but I'm lookin' you over real good at your next six month's physical exam. Quit smokin', and no binge drinkin'. Never take more than one amphetamine pill.

Cotner. Why do I get two pills then?

Eppes. Take the second one, Cotner, only if you have to stay awake to save your life. Maybe you've been awake in a life raft for hours, and need to continue beating off the sharks.

I walk back to my sack and climb in. I stare at the ceiling. It's the same as before. I check my watch often...Night arrives...I hear my buddies come in from the Officer's Club...I listen to a couple of card games...The lights go out...I clock the dark hours: 10:17...10:35...11:01 ...11:20...I yawn...11:39...I go to the latrine...11:43: back in the sack...I stretch...*yawn*...

---

1 Toyohiko Kagawa, the world-noted Japanese convert to Christian evangelism had long preached a "social-gospel" in pre-war Japan. During the war he was sent to prison because he apologized to the people of China for Japan's invasion of their country.

In 1950 Kagawa toured the U.S.A. He told Americans of the agony inflicted upon Japanese people by firebombs, and of the poverty they were suffering as they struggled to restore their cities. Americans thronged to his appearances. Kagawa asked the American people to contribute to a Japanese relief organization he had founded. Americans were generous.

Jean and I heard Kagawa twice, when he came to Tulsa, Oklahoma. We were moved. We pledged support. We sent modest funds regularly, until acknowledgment ceased in 1953...Was Kagawa in jail again?

2 The knowledge to compose the "ground-level" passages, pp. 11 and 12, comes from reading The Night Tokyo Burned, Hoito Edoin, St. Martin's Press, N.Y., N.Y. Tada and his grandfather are my inventions. Edoin at age seventeen experienced and survived this holocaust. Perhaps he saw my plane fly over.

3 After the war, I try many times to quit smoking. On 1 Jan. 1948, I quit...forever. Thank you, Capt. Eppes. Thanks, Dad.

Blitz Two – Abort Mechanical

11 March 1945: Following the "Blitz of Tokyo", I wake up too late for breakfast, too late for brunch, and almost too late for lunch. By a powerful sprint I arrive at the Officer's Mess Hall barely in time to be served. I sit by Captain Feil. He is with a group of his Airplane Commander buddies: Rogan, McNiel, Hutchison, Lewis and Bearden. The A.C.'s acknowledge me with a greeting. Being a smoker, and earnestly breathless, I can only respond with a feeble unmilitary seated salute. The Commanders nod. I hope it is in understanding. They then ignore me to continue their post-mortem review of the Blitz.

I listen. Airplane Commanders have a good view of all that is in front, above, to the sides and below the airplane. I have a good view of each engine.

I learn .Bertagnoli, B.E. Cox, Curry and White had to abort. Jarvis had to bomb To as an alternate target. No one was shot down but on the way home, Capt. Keene and Lt. Hardgrave ran out of fuel. Each had to ditch in Northern Mariana waters. Air-Sea Rescue searchers have found Hardgrave's crew. All men are safe, currently bound for Saipan aboard a Navy PB-Y. The search for Keene's crew is still underway...

Lt. Jack Jewett, Flight Engineer on Keene's crew, is my buddy. Jack and I were in the same graduating class at Yale. He and his wife, Polly, were married on the 4th of December 1943, the same night Jean and I were married by Chaplin Greene, on campus. Polly is a New Haven girl. They were married in her church. Polly is pregnant. I'm troubled for Jack, and for Polly. *Isn't it too early in the 9th Group's war for people to be getting killed or to become missing in action*?

Feil and his friends carry-on. I hear variations on the theme of our own crew's experience: "One helluva fire"..."A god-damn hot one"..."Le May will be happy"..."He'll be so damn happy we'll fly nothin' but blitzes from now on"...

After lunch I ask Captain Feil to have another coffee with me. I need his concurrence on a procedure I hope to institute.

Cotner. Captain, I'm guessing that you have a lot of multi-engine flying hours.

Feil. I've got a total of about 300 hours on B-17s and B-24s, plus about thirty B-25 hours.

Cotner. In those planes you had all the engine controls and instruments and you were responsible for engine operation, as well as for piloting the plane.

Feil. That's right, but I like Boeing's idea of giving engine-operation plus fuel-use-management to specially trained guys like you. I think we'd lose fewer B-17s and 24s if there were Flight Engineers on their crews. B-17 and B-24 pilots have too damn much to do. The B-29 is twice as big, carries three and a half times the bomb load, and all its systems are much more complicated, so a Flight Engineer is a necessity.

Cotner. The problem is, the Flight Engineer's station is the only place anyone can operate the engines from. What if flack or bullets get me? You or Chuck would have to move back to the engineer's station to run the engines, and to change the power settings every half-hour.

Feil. I might be able to do it. In an emergency, I will try. Chuck can't do it. He was sent to the 9th Group directly from cadet flight school. He's had very little multi-engine experience or training and I don't want to be pretending I'm Flight Engineer, while Chuck is alone up-front trying to be Airplane Commander.

Cotner. I'd like to train one of the gunners to take over in case I'm knocked out.

Feil. Sounds good to me. Got anyone in mind?

Cotner. I'll need to talk to them. In my opinion, we can spare one gunner when we're not over the target. I'd like to check out Richardson, Warn and Connor.

Feil. Why not Calhoun?

Cotner. Well, as Central Fire Control Gunner he rates one stripe above the others. I don't want them to think I'm playin' favorites. But, if none of the other three want it, or if I think they aren't qualified, I'll give him a chance. He's an Iowa farm boy. They usually have mechanical experience.

Feil. I agree with everything you say. I approve the idea. You handle it on your own.

Cotner. Thanks, Captain.

Feil. Just remember; we can't offer any stripes, or pay, as an incentive. There's no spot on the Table of Organization for an Assistant Engineer.

Cotner. Roger, Captain. I'm gonna get started. I'll keep you posted.

It's unwritten custom that neither officers or enlisted men unnecessarily invade each other's quarters. I hurry over to the 99th Squadron Headquarters tent. I tell Major Watterman, Squadron Executive Officer, that I need to see Sergeants Calhoun, Connor, Richardson and Warn of Captain Feil's crew.

Watterman. What for?

Cotner. (*Lying a bit.*) Captain Feil wants me to drill them on some in-flight crew procedures. I think, *why in hell did the 99th draw Watterman for an Exec? That ground-lubber is too damn jealous of anyone who flies. I guess it's because it seems in the Air Corps, a flying corporal outranks, de facto, an administrative major. He is also scared witless that 9th Group Officers and men might fraternize.*

Watterman. Where will you meet?

Cotner. (*Thinking.)I want to tell him it's not his concern .but...I'll butter him up a bit..* Do you think, sir, that the outdoor theater will be a good neutral place?

Watterman. Yes, but keep it brief.

Cotner. Thank you, Major.

I rush off. I find the men resting in their tent. They come with me to the theater. In a patch of shade, we sit on sand bags, which at movie time, serve as theater seats. They listen to my proposal. They like the safety aspect. They respond.

Warn. I did dang good in gunnery school. I love the remote controlled guns on the B-29. I want to dang-well shoot down Jap fighter planes.

Richardson. I'll try it, if no one else will but I don't think I have the talent to be a good engineer.

Calhoun. I don't want to take a chance on losin' my Central Fire Control rating.

Connor. I want to do it. I'm a good auto mechanic. I hope to learn all I can about airplanes. I'd like to start on tonight's mission.

Cotner. Tonight's mission? Damn. Is that on the bulletin board?

Connor. Well, the only thing on the bulletin board is "briefing at 1700 - all listed personnel". We're on the list.

Cotner. I'm so tired, I assumed we wouldn't fly tonight. You guys are good soldiers, and, per orders, check the bulletin board. Thanks, you may have saved my ass. Let's all go take a nap then...Yeah, Connor, we'll start tonight.

11 March 1945, 1700, Briefing:

We arrive early. Only an idiot would be late. We are confronted by a large suspended map. An arrow labeled "target for tonight" points to Nagoya, a city on Honshu's eastern coastline about halfway between Tokyo and Osaka.

A tune, and a phrase enter my mind: *Nagoya...Nagoya...I hear you calling me.* It's the refrain from "Nagoya" a song I often heard on the radio in the early 1930s. The melody is beautiful, and dreamily slow. To me it evoked then, and does now, a picture of a romantic and sleepy oriental village: thatch-roofed paper-houses on winding narrow garden-lined streets, trotting men in loin-cloths and coolie hats, pulling rickshaws, geishas in kimonos carrying parasols...

Col. Huglin. (*At the podium*). Congratulations Gentlemen. The 20th Air Force's Blitz of Tokyo was successful. Recon photos, taken this morning, show that fifteen point eight square miles, ten percent of Tokyo's area, is burned to the ground and that smoke is still rising on the edges of the burned area. General Le May is pleased. He is so happy that he hopes to improve results on tonight's Blitz of Nagoya, a large industrial city. He has set bombing elevations at 5,000, 6,000 and 7,000 feet. He compliments each airman who flew over Tokyo. He wishes you even greater success at Nagoya. Major Luschen, please continue.

Cotner. *5,000 to 7,000 feet? Damn...Nagoya...Nagoya...La la la lala la.*

Luschen. This is another 324 B-29 mission for the 20th Air Force. The 9th Group will again send thirty-six B-29s. The 314th Wing from Guam will lead. Saipan's 73rd Wing is second. Tinian's 313th Wing flies last.

Cotner. *If I have to go, I'd rather go in at 7,000 feet than at 5,000 or 6,000 feet...Last sounds better than first or second...Nagoya...Nagoya...*

Luschen. We'll fly individual sorties again. Capt. Scheaffer will lead. Take off precisely as scheduled on the pilot's flimsy and stay precisely in line all the way till after you drop your bombs on the edge of the fire.

Cotner. *Please do...Nagoya...Nagoya...*

Luschen. If you must abort, follow the same procedure as last time: descend left 180° to 2000 feet, five miles west.

Cotner. *It worked last time...Nagoya...Nagoya...I can't stop humming this. Fortunately I'm keeping it inaudible.*

Luschen. General Le May has changed the intervalometer setting from fifty yards to 100 yards. He thinks we probably wasted some bombs at Tokyo by dropping them too close together.

Cotner. *So, we'll be sitting-duck-targets on a bomb run for twice as long a time and distance...Nagoya...Nagoya...Am I the only one humming this?...*

Luschen. There will be no "sacred" targets to worry about at Nagoya.

Cotner. *What about us targets in the air? We're damn sacred....scared too... Nagoya ... Nagoya...*

Luschen. Gen. Le May believes we will again surprise the Japs. He thinks they will not expect us to fly again so soon.

Cotner, *I damn sure didn't expect it...Nagoya...Nagoya...I do not want to blitz Nagoya...*

Luschen yields the floor to the meteorologists and other specialists to fill-in the details. Major Luschen wishes us good luck and Col. Huglin dismisses us with, “Good flyin’ men.”

I remind Connor to bring paper and pencil for note taking.

Routine repeats itself: early supper, parachutes and flight gear, trucks to the flight line, pre-flight inspections, pull props, climb aboard, start engines, taxi, and takeoff. It is routine, except that five crews discover at the flight line that their B-29s are not ready to fly so soon again.

• • •

1930 hours: Thirty-one ready crews in their thirty-one ready B-29s are on their single-file way to Nagoya. Capt. Feil, at number twenty-two, follows Capt. McNiel and leads Capt. White. In transit we fly again at 3,000 feet and 195 mph air speed.

An hour into the flight, Capt. B.E. Cox tells Capt. Scheaffer that he is aborting. B.E. Cox swoops left, down and around. Capt. Feil repeats the message. Warn starts a count. His gunner buddies don’t let him finish. I ask Connor to come up front. He arrives shortly. Capt. Feil hears greetings. He looks around.

Feil. Hi Connor. Where’s your parachute?

Connor. I left it in the back, Sir. I was in a hurry to get here.

Feil. We’re training you as an “emergency” engineer to increase the crew’s safety prospects. We don’t want you breaking Air Corps Safety Regs during training.

Cotner. I failed to remind him, Sir.

Feil. That <u>was</u> a failure. (*To Connor*) Go get your chute, Mae West and life raft.

Connor. Sir, the tunnel is too little to crawl through with all that on.

Feil. You're right. Connor, drag it behind you.

Connor. Yes, sir.

Connor departs.

Cotner. Captain, the crew is glad that you enforce the safety regs. I appreciate it. But I've heard Connor say that he doesn't know how to swim. That day last September at McCook, when we practiced with rafts and Mae Wests in that farmer's pond, Connor and other non-swimmers had trouble clambering out of deep water into their one-man rafts. He might do better in an emergency just depending on his Mae West to keep him from drownin'.

Feil. I'll ask him. *Damn, he's not answering his intercom. I'll call Warn. No, there he is.*

Connor. Yes, sir.

Feil. Would you feel safer in the water with, or without, your one-man raft?

Connor. Without it sir. I'd rather just use the Mae West.

Feil. O.K. You don't have to bring the raft up-front with you then.

Connor. Thank you, Captain.

Connor returns from his round-trip excursion of the thirty-three-foot tunnel. I pat the deck on my right.

Cotner. Sit here, Connor. Get in the habit of watching the instruments, and lookin' out at the engines.

Connor. Roger.

Cotner. (*With pride in "my" engines*). The Wright R-3350 is the largest (3350 cubic inch displacement) most powerful (2,200 horsepower), most efficient (1.25 lbs./h.p. and 1.52 h.p./c.i.d.) aircraft engine in the world.

Connor. Wow, my hot-rod Ford V-8s got only eighty-five horses.

Cotner. From our experience, and from the travails of the 58th wing flying from India in 1944, we know that the 3350's durability is fragile.

Connor. Is that because Dodge is buildin' em?

Cotner. Partly, but bear with me for a history lecture. Are you comfortable?

Connor. Yes, sir.

Cotner. In 1938 the Air Corps invited U.S. aircraft companies to submit preliminary designs for a bomber that was bigger, faster and of longer range than the B-17. The Air Corps liked Boeing's concept.

Connor. Good.

Cotner. In 1940, not anticipating the need to ever bomb Japan, the Corps asked Boeing to build two XB-29s, two YB-29s, and a number of production B-29s.

The largest available power plant was the R-3350, being developed by Curtis Wright, but by Boeing engineer's calculations, 8,800 horsepower was not enough.

Connor. Damn. That seems like enough power to haul several freight trains.

Cotner. Freight trains don't have to fly very high. Well, Boeing offset this limitation by using extensive wind-tunnel tests, on a number of successively refined models, as a design-process to create an exceedingly clean and efficient aerodynamic shape.

Connor. Is that why the B-29 is such a good lookin' airplane?

Cotner. Yes, as a flying machine it is a perfect illustration of Le Corbusier's dictum that "form follows function".

Connor. Who's Laycorboossay?

Cotner. He's a French architect. Anyway...Boeing used the same wind-tunnel/model-system to derive a closely cowled and precisely directed airstream, to flow around and through the cooling fins of each cylinder head.

Connor. Didn't the improved aerodynamics solve the problem?

Cotner. Yes, it did.,but today, in the Mariana Islands, the Air Corps commands us to load the B-29 far beyond the capacity Boeing was given as design criteria. (*Wups, I damn near said Gen. Le May commands us... Nagoya...Nagoya...Why do I associate Le May and Nagoya in my head*?)

We can fly this overburdened airplane, on 3,000+ mile missions, only by operating the engines at higher power per unit of slipstream velocity than Wright and Boeing allowed for.

Connor. So it's the Air Corp's fault.

Cotner. Is that what I said? Well, the engines do overheat. And they fail. We call the most common failure "swallowing a valve".

Connor. We've heard Airplane Commanders reporting that failure.

Cotner. When an engine begins to get too hot, a small part called the exhaust-valve retainer is the first piece to burn up. When it goes, the valve falls, or is sucked, into the cylinder. There are two exhaust valves per cylinder, eighteen cylinders per engine, four engines per airplane. That's 2 x 18 x 4 = 144...144 chances for one of any plane's engines to swallow a valve.

Connor. How do the Commanders know they've swallowed one?

Cotner. Their Flight Engineers tell them. That's why we have to monitor the instruments so faithfully, especially the tachometers, and the cylinder head temperature gauges. (*I point out the tachs and gauges*).

Connor. When an engine swallows a valve, doesn't it make a loud noise?

Cotner. I'm sure it does, but you can't hear it in here, above normal engine roar. We shut the engine down before the piston, poundin' on the loose valve, inside the cylinder, beats the engine up.

Connor. How do you know when a valve gets swallowed?

Cotner. The tachometer suddenly drops about 200 or 300 rpm. Sometimes it runs steady at that lower r.p.m. Sometimes it's low and wavering. The cylinder-head temperature-gauge sensor is attached only to the No. One cylinder. Often it's some other cylinder that swallows the valve.

Connor. Is rpm drop our only clue?

Cotner. Sometimes we also see a drop in intake-manifold pressure. The turbo-chargers have an electronically controlled governor. If the manifold pressure gauge also shows a drop, we check the vacuum tubes in that engine's manifold-pressure governor. If a tube is burned out, we replace it.

We can then restart the engine, and check the manifold-pressure. If the manifold-pressure is normal, we let the engine run.

Each engine has two magnetos to produce spark. If one magneto malfunctions, rpm's will decrease. It's almost impossible to positively diagnose a swallowed valve, but when the rpm drops, standard and safe procedure is to shut off fuel and feather the prop if you have three good engines left. But if necessary, you can use a slow-running engine to get you home. It will still give you some power.

Connor. Do you think I can learn all this?

Cotner. I'm sure you will, but I'm gonna take a break right now. I'll let you sit in my seat a while and watch the instruments and the engines. Sitting on that deck is tiresome. I've gotta go use the relief tube. I'll be right back. Then we'll talk about the second most common engine failure.

I take off my headphones and throat-mike. I climb out of my seat. I take off my parachute. I read my watch: 9:15 p.m. I look out the nose. In the dark ahead I see the running lights of Capt. McNeil's B-29. I work my way around the upper and lower gun turrets, which intrude into the cabin space. I squeeze past Caldwell's little table.

Cotner. Hi Claude, how's it going?

Caldwell. Good. On these single-file flights, all I have to do is keep track of our location by recording headings, speeds and times. Capt. Feil's following Capt. McNeil's tail. Do you think there's an extra gunner I can train to be emergency navigator? Connor is certainly a rapt pupil.

Cotner. He's a rare apt one, too.

I proceed to the tube...With relief. I sigh and look over at Schultz. He's facing his radio gear. He's wearing his headphones. He's absorbed with his electronic dials and knobs. I don't interrupt him. I head back toward my seat. Connor hears me talking again to Caldwell. He watches me squeeze around the upper turret. I look past Connor. On No.Three engine nacelle, I see fierce flashes of fire suddenly shoot from each cowl-flap opening. I watch turbulent prop-wash, plus 200 mile-per-hour slipstream winds, instantly beat wildly burning 100-octane aviation fuel, into a froth of superheated plasma.

In the black of night, brilliant close-range glare hurts my eyes. My squint is extreme. Yet, vision is real. Vicious flames violently attack our plane's vulnerable wing, and its stored volume of explosively volatile gasoline. Connor reads my face. He looks out at No. Three.

Cotner. LET ME IN, CONNOR!

Connor. Yes, Sir.

Swiftly we swap places. I close No. Three throttle. I cut off No. Three turbo boost. I shut off No. Three ignition. I shut No. Three cowl flaps. I set the fire extinguisher valve to No. Three. I pick up my throat mike and hold it against my larynx.

Cotner. TAYLOR! FEATHER NO. THREE!

Taylor. Roger.

Cotner. Captain Feil, there's a fire in No. Three. Taylor is featherin' it. I'm gonna put the fire out.

I watch No. Three prop slow down. The inferno fights to escape the nacelle. I see spits of flame and gusts of smoke bite through the imperfect seals of the aluminum cowl-flap edges. The prop stops. I pull the extinguisher handle.

I start a silent count. *1, 2, 3, 4, 5, 6, 7, 8, 9, 10, 11, 12, 13, 14,15*. Nothing changes. I don't know why I count. It's not part of the procedure. I count again, one through fifteen. *Is that half a minute*? I don't know how fast I'm counting. I count again, 1 through 15...*Nothing? Do cowl-flaps sometimes yield to intense heat? Do they melt, or burn away? There is one more shot of extinguisher fluid. The procedure says for the engineer to use his judgment. Use the second shot to finish off the fire? Or save the second shot for another fire?* No guides toward judgment are given. I start another count...*1...2...3...4.* I determine to pull the handle again at fifteen. *5...6...7..., If I don't get this fire-out, why worry about the next one?...9...10...11,* I decide to pull now... *Wait...Do I see a flicker?...Yes!...another...and another.* Intensity dwindles...I think I've got it...I wait...I watch last traces of fire and smoke retreat into the nacelle...they vanish.

Cotner. Taylor! Is there any fire in No.Three from up front? Calhoun! Do you see any fire in No. Three?

Taylor. No.

Calhoun. No.

Cotner. Capt. Feil, I think the fire is out. I used one shot of fire extinguisher fluid. I've got one shot left. I'm gonna save it in case this fire comes back, or another engine catches fire.

Feil. Roger, Cotner, good job.
(*To Schultz*). Get me Capt. Scheaffer on clear-channel.
(*To the crew*). We had a fire in No. Three. It's out now. We'll fly back to Tinian.

Schultz. Roger, sir...Go ahead, Sir.

Feil. Capt. Scheaffer, this is Capt. Feil. I'm aborting. We had a fire in No. Three. It's out now.

Scheaffer. Roger, Captain. Good luck.

Feil. Malnove, salvo the bombs.

Malnove. Roger...Bombs away...Bomb-bay doors comin' closed.

Schultz. Forward doors closed. All bombs gone.

Warn. Rear doors closed. All bombs gone.

Feil makes the prescribed 180° turn with a change of altitude. Caldwell gives him the heading toward Tinian.

Cotner. Capt. Feil, I'm going to set up a conservative three-engine cruise control.

Feil. Roger, go ahead.

Cotner. Connor, just observe what I do, this time. I'll talk you through a power setting change on our next mission.

Connor. Roger.

Cotner. Can you guess, Connor, which mode of engine failure is the B-29's second most common?

Connor. That sounds like a leading question, Sir; so, the answer must be catchin' fire. I for sure know fire is the scariest one.

We're at 2,000 feet. No. One and No.Two are running smoothly, and in perfect sync at 2100 rpm No. Four is running well, at 2500 rpm.

The difference in engine power is my attempt to give Capt. Feil partially balanced thrust on the right and left sides of the plane. It's not perfect. Feil has to crank in left-rudder-trim, but not so much trim that the autopilot can't handle it. Capt. Feil is happy.

I send Connor back to his right-gunner's station. I ask him to keep watch on engines Three and Four from that perspective. On the intercom, I ask Warn to do the same for One and Two. I ask Calhoun to watch all four engines. I tell them that I have only one shot of extinguisher-fluid remaining; that sometimes one shot is not enough to suppress an engine fire and that if we should have another fire, I want to douse it immediately.

Chatter on the intercom tells me the crew is happy, despite some small regret that we used preparation time, flying time, and survived one more take off, but earned <u>no</u> credit toward a completed mission.

Dis-synchronicity of revolutionary velocities between the four propeller blades on the right and the eight blades on the left creates an acutely agonizing arrhythmic pulse that pounds the eardrums of us creatures caught between.

But, I'm happy...*Nagoya... Nagoya...In a few hours we'll be safe on good old Tinian ground. I didn't have to blitz Nagoya. The crew thinks I'm a hero...I did nothing but use a standard procedure that some intelligent engineer somewhere...Boeing?...Wright?...Kidd?...Air Corps?...worked out.* I thank them all whoever they are. I thank all the people who designed the fire-suppression system components .I thank all the men and women who built them...and those who installed them...

I thank Col. Huglin, who, during training back at McCook insisted that each air-man master the instruction-manual for his crew-position and whose "West Point" system of "public pop-quizzing", of randomly selected trainees, provided positive propensity toward sincere preparation...

And...I am proud that I knew the procedure so well, and performed it so readily.

I relax and hum my inevitably recurring refrain...*Nagoya...Nagoya...I hear your call*...I think of Jeannie...But...I watch my engines.

A Little Local R. & R.

12 March 1945:

Following our six-hour interrupted attempt to fly to Nagoya, my lovely six-hour sleep is interrupted by Captain Curry and his crewmen, who trek across our reverberant tent floor after returning from their <u>successful</u> round-trip Nagoya excursion. They fall exhausted into their sacks. Their tired bones become soon asleep. My languorous brain barely registers that their snores begin...ere...its slumberous small self sleeps deep again.

Rested and relatively happy, I wake in time for a leisurely brunch. At 0930 hours, I join my crewmates in a special debriefing of the aborted crews.

Our crew's session is short. I report the fire and they tell us we get no mission credit. They rate our brief flight as "abort-mechanical".

This comforts me. Had they thought it was due to crew-member goof-up, namely mine, they would have rated it "abort-personnel", and, they would have put a memo in my file, detailing my stupidity, cowardice, or whatever deficiency of soldierly conduct they would blame me for.

I don't care if I never make "General", but I do not want a paper-in-my-file to keep me from becoming "1st Lt." as soon as possible.

We learn there were three other abortions. Lt. Johnson's was rated "abort-mechanical", (No. Two swallowed a valve). Lt. Loy and Capt. B.E. Cox each got an "abort-personnel". In neither case was a "culprit" named, or his misdeed made public.

I wonder about the "abort-personnel" policy. *Won't the whole crew feel defamed? Will not the innocent leak the accused person's name and report his "accursed-crime" in defense of their own honorable, brave and wise deportment?...*

I check the bulletin board. No briefing today. No duties at all are posted for Feil's crew, except that Malnove, Taylor, Caldwell and I are the censorship crew for tonight. Air Corps Lieutenants, by turns, draw the assignment of censoring the outgoing letters of all 9th Bomb Group enlisted men. I go back to the tent.

Caldwell wants to toss a football. We check one out. It's a one-on-one mismatch. He has a large right hand and a strong right arm. He throws long. I throw short. He gets bored. I get tired. We quit.

I find Captain Feil.

Feil. Hi, Don. Nice to have a day off, isn't it? What do you have planned?

Cotner. No plans yet, but I want to talk to you about abort-reports.

Feil. O.K.

Cotner. It seems to me, the rating "abort-personnel" may hurt morale.

Feil. Well, the 99th Squadron C.O. calls a meeting about once a week for the Operations Officer and the Airplane Commanders. "Abort-ratings" came up last meeting. We've got to have them, you know.

Cotner. I suppose so.

Feil. We are in the Army. Every Commander, of every rank, has to report his successes and failures to the next level of command. The more we know about why we fail, the better training we can provide.

Cotner. I see why those in command need reports, but do we crewmen need to be privy to personnel failures?

Feil. Yes. If flyers thought every abort was mechanical, they might lose faith in the airplane and in the maintenance crews. What if the ground crew gets blamed for some air crewman's goof? What about their morale?

Cotner. O.K., Captain, I'm convinced. Thanks for straightening me out.

Feil. I'm glad you're concerned. I want you to know I'll fight for you if I think they're tryin' to pin a bum rap on you. It's the Airplane Commander who decides to abort. With our crew, I can't imagine ever having to abort for any reason, other than mechanical failure.

I return to the tent. Bill Duft, Bombardier on Lt. Johnson's crew, is there. Duft, from a neighboring tent, is looking for a gin-rummy game. Since we'll have only a half-hour before lunch, I agree to play. Duft is a talkative little Irish guy. His hometown is McKee's Rocks, Pennsylvania, a suburb of Pittsburgh. He has no Irish brogue, but his speech is... well ... interesting. For example, he addresses a small group as "you-uns" instead of "you-all", like all us normal Okies and Arkies do.

We go to lunch. After lunch Duft seeks another gin game. I decline. I lie on my sack.

Karl Pattison, Pilot on Capt. Curry's crew, asks me to go swimming. Back home, I am a strong swimmer...in pools, lakes and streams. I've never swum in an ocean. In physical training at Boca Raton, Florida, they used to run us "basic-training" cadets to the nearby Atlantic beach, make us practice judo on each other, then rinse off the sand in the sea. I never had time to find any water deep enough to swim in.

I jump up and change into swim trunks and tennis shoes, copying Karl's attire, except that he carries swim goggles. I have never owned or used a pair. We head west out of the 9th Group area.

For 200 yards we follow a path through a crop of native grasses, sprouting through the stubble of a former Japanese cane-field. We cross Riverside Drive, another Manhattan street name.

Past the "Drive" we walk twenty yards to the edge of the cliff. On hands and knees, I peer over. It is vertical...or maybe a little steeper. Captain Winton Brown, our 9th Group Meteorologist (and by default our Geographer/ Geologist/Oceanographer) has told us it is 125 feet to the sea level coral ledge. He said, "Don't try to climb down or up." Since his auxiliary "appointments", if he has any, are not in writing, those airmen idiotic enough to scale the perpendicular facade, feel they have not disobeyed a "real" order.

Karl locates a rope he and other swim buffs have anchored to lower branches of a big bush. He starts down. He has done this before. I watch his technique. He holds the rope in his left hand, as an emergency reserve. He uses rocks and/or roots as right handholds, and as toeholds. I follow. About thirty feet down, a familiar question reprises itself. *What the hell am I doing here*? At sixty feet down I run out of rope...I find a "successor rope". Karl, ten feet below, is holding it in his left hand...*How did he do it?...* I'm a little bit miffed. *Why didn't he demonstrate the rope-change maneuver? I guess he figured I'm smart enough to decide the best way to do it.*

I fix my left-handed grip on the first rope. I feel with my feet for solid and stable footholds. I test their support. I grasp the new rope in my right hand. I release the first rope. I grasp the new rope in my left hand. I find a rock for a right handhold. I rest...I resume descent. I come to the end of the second rope. Karl is standing on the coral shelf.

Karl. Good goin', Don.

Don. I'm not down yet.

Karl. You've got 15 feet more. This is the place where most of the injuries happen.

Don. But it's not vertical anymore.

Karl. That's why it's so dangerous. Guys get careless. That slope just below you is about forty-five degrees. It's made from pieces of coral that have sloughed off the cliff face. That's what makes the cliff so steep.

Don. Well, you made it safely.

Karl. I'll talk you down. Get onto the slope in an all-fours position...Good, now creep down backwards on your hands and feet. Keep your arms and legs off of the coral. It has sharp edges.

Don. Thanks, Karl; here I come.

I make it to the reef. I search the cliff...left...and...right. We're in a cove. I guess it to be about half a mile each way to the headlands.

Karl. What are you looking for?

Don. An easy way up.

Karl. (*Pointing up along the rope*). This is the easy way. If you don't climb out here, you cross the coral to the seawater lagoon. You swim across the lagoon, to the outer reef, walk across coral again to the open sea, dive in and swim six miles south to the beach...with your tennis shoes on.

Don. Tennis shoes?

Karl. You never want to put yourself in a place where you might have to walk across coral barefoot.

Can you swim six miles without resting?

Don. No, but aren't there resting places along the way?

Karl. Only if you climb up onto the coral. That's hard to do without hurting yourself. The waves out there will hurl you against the sharp corners of the coral reef.

Don. How deep is the water?

Karl. Well, these Islands have risen from the deepest bottom in any of earth's oceans. It's called the Marianna Trench. It's seven point five miles deep. We're on a coral shelf attached near the top of a mostly under-sea mountain.

Don. So, do we swim out or climb out?

Karl. If we swim and make it to the beach, we might get blown up tryin' to get onto and across the beach.

Don. And, if we don't blow ourselves up on an unspent invasion-bombardment shell, we'll get caught on an off-limits area, by the Marine Beach Patrol, which means at best, a letter in our personnel file...Let's climb out.

Karl. Don't worry. Everyone who's been down here has climbed out.

Don. But have any of them been smokers?

Karl. Sure, ninety-eight percent of the guys in the Air Corps smoke.

Don. You don't.

Karl. I was on the water-polo team in high school. Never got started smoking. You'll make it back to the top O.K. You're strong. You'll just have to catch your breath when you come to the good stopping places. Let's swim.

I follow Karl toward the ocean. We walk across the coral. It hurts, even with tennis shoes on. Thirty yards out we come to the lagoon, a salt-water filled chasm. It's fifteen yards of calm water, then more coral. Then crashing waves and splashing spray.

With his goggle strap in hand, Karl dives. He slips his goggles over his eyes as he continues down into a seaweed forest. I catch occasional glimpses through the "foliage". He dives deeper...deeper...deep...He disappears...*Is he exploring a cavern*?

I sit down on the coral edge, with my feet in the water. I intend to ease my way in. Salt water seeps into bleeding cuts on my thighs, and on my butt. I change my mind.

I struggle back to my feet. I cut my legs on the coral. I stand. I dive as shallowly as possible. I don't know what lurks in the dark jungle Karl is exploring. *Where is Karl .He can't hold his breath that long, can he?...I know I can't rescue him...or .should I say, I cannot imagine that I will rescue him...*

Karl pops up. He treads water. I tread.

Karl. Come on down, Don. It's beautiful.

Don. I can't open my eyes under this water. The salt burns `em.

Karl. I saw several octopi and a conger eel.

Don. Aren't they dangerous?

Karl. Naw.

Don. I'm content to look down and see the beautiful fish.

Karl. There's usually a family of squid around here; they are certainly beautiful.

Don. What about giant squid and giant clams?

Karl. Didn't see any. I think the Marianas are too far north for those.

How buoyant the water is...how pleasant the temperature...what fun it is to tread water and to paddle around. There are five squid. . .did they find me?...Is this the "family"? Two are about nine inches long. Three are small - Mom, Dad and the kids?

They are aware of me. I see them watching me. If I don't move toward them, they don't move away. I try to gently move closer. They maintain a distance, just beyond reach. They propel themselves via a rippling wave motion of their "wings", a sine wave that progresses fore to aft, on each side of their body. *Karl is right. They are graceful and lovely. Do I sense a communicating intelligence or do I wishfully imagine it?*

My rapturous oceanographic existential state of bliss is interrupted, as Karl rises suddenly beside me.

Don. You scared away the squid.

Karl. You found them. Good.

Don. Let's be quiet. I want to see if they'll come back.

Karl. They disappear instantly when they want to. They squirt a jet of water out of their mouth, and they emit a cloud of black "ink" that obscures their trail.

Don. That's it all right. Can you tell me what those appendages are? They move in waveform on the sides of their bodies.

Karl. I don't know the scientific name. I call them wings.

Don. That's what I call them.

Karl. I don't know when they'll come back, if at all. We don't have time to wait. We need to conserve energy for our climb out. That's a lot of work.

The reference to "work" takes me back to my first semester of engineering physics, and the study of the science of mechanics, wherein work is measured in foot-pounds, i.e.: one foot-pound of work is accomplished when a one pound mass is raised one foot. I look at the cliff.
My engineering ego can't resist calculating the work I'll do climbing out. *I weigh 135 pounds. One hundred pounds times 125 feet equals 12,500 ft. lbs. Thirty-five pounds is about 1/3 of 100 lbs; and thus 1/3 of 12, 500 ft. lbs. is about 4,200 ft. lbs. When I climb to the top of the cliff, I will have done nearly 16,700 ft. lbs. of work.* It scares me but I don't know what to compare it with. *As a thin and wiry cadet, I accomplished the rope climb easily on the obstacle course and.I was a smoker then also.* I decide I <u>can</u> get up and out.

Don. You're right, Karl. Let's get out of here.

Karl . I'll show you how to get on the coral without getting too many cuts.

Don. I'll watch you.

Karl is supple and sinewy, a six-foot four-inches tall young man. He puts both hands on the coral. He lowers himself into the water till his forearms are forty-five degrees below horizontal. Simultaneously, with great power, he gives a scissor-kick, and a double-arm lift. He swings his right leg out of the water, clears the edge of the coral and puts his right foot down. In this three-point stance he hefts his left foot onto the coral. He stands.

I try...Ouch!...I knock my lower ribs on the corner of the coral but I make it onto the reef. Some blood runs down my belly. Who cares? It wasn't too bad for a first try. We walk gingerly toward the cliff.

I notice for the first time that Karl is wearing a watch on his left wrist. *I'll be damned. We can time our ascent.*

Don. Karl, how come you're wearin' your watch?

Karl. This is my skin-diving watch. It's waterproof to 100 feet.

Don. You're from Tucson. Where do you dive there? What is skin-diving?

Karl. I spend summers at my Grandmother's. She lives in California. Skin-diving is underwater exploration, done without protective equipment. I choose to wear goggles. Some California purists think goggles are for sissies.

Don. You're damn good at skin-diving.

Karl. It's a hell of a lot of fun.

Don. I might like it better if I had goggles but I'm not goin' to ask my wife to send me any. She's too pregnant. Are you married?

Karl. No. There's a skin-diving girl in California I like a lot. We write.

Don. Where in California does your Grandmother live?

Karl. In Modjeska Canyon.

Don. Never heard of it. Is it a real canyon? Where'd it get a name like that?

Karl. It's a Polish name. The canyon is named after my Great-grandmother, Madame Helena Modjeska. She had a house and several acres in a beautiful valley in the canyon. She and her second husband, Charles Bozenta, a Polish Count, were the first non-Indian people to live in the canyon.

Don. If your Great-grandfather was a Count, how come they migrated to the U.S.?

Karl. My Great-grandmother was a beautiful young woman. She was an actress, a singer, and a dancer. She performed in plays, musical plays, operettas and operas. She also did recitals. She was popular all over Europe. A promoter arranged an American tour. She was a hit. She toured the U.S. for years. My Great-grandparents enjoyed life in this country. They prospered. They discovered this uninhabited, unspoiled canyon wilderness, with a stream running through it, with live oaks among its flora, and with deer, wolf and mountain lion amongst its fauna. Who would want to be Count and Countess in Europe, when they could be Adam and Eve in a Southern California Eden?

Don. But, you are Polish royalty?

Karl. No. Gustav Modjeski was my Great-grandmother's first husband. They were each Polish, and neither was royal. She kept "Madama Modjeska" as her stage name, after she married the Count. My mother was a Modjeska until she married Sidney Pattison, a U.S. citizen. So, I am an American but I was christened Karolek. I changed it to Karol in the sixth grade and to Karl in high school.

We arrive at the cliff.

Don. I propose that you go up first, and wait for me at the top. That way you can get quick help in case I need to be rescued. I won't start till you're on top.

Karl. O.K. I think that's over-caution but I'll do it, if you want it that way.

Don. I'd like to compute the average horsepower I generate on the climb. Will you time my ascent and my rests? Time yourself and I'll compute horsepower for you.

Karl. That'll be fun. I'll do it. Here I go.

Karl starts up. He moves fast. *He's a competitor. I'll bet he wants to generate two or three times the horsepower that I do.* I intend to watch how he climbs but he's soon so high that my neck gets tired.

I can't find a comfortable place to sit or lie down. It's hot as hell, with the afternoon sun bouncin' off the cliff and the reef.

I have a horrible thought. I'm gonna get one severe sunburn. They "officially" warned us about this Tinian sun in our orientation lecture, delivered in our first hour on the island. If we miss any duty because of sunburn, they dock our pay, and of course, a letter goes into our file.

Don. (*Yelling*). I'M COMING UP NOW!

Karl. OKAY!

It's not so bad when you're motivated. About thirty-five feet up, I find good "holds" and a protrusion to lean my left hip against. I stop. I need to breathe deeply.

Some pebbles hit my shoulders. They're small but I worry *What if some big sharp rocks come down? What if Karl slips and falls? .He'd knock me off the wall.* That ghostly thought haunts me again...*What am I doing here?*

Ambition returns. I climb. I rest a couple of more times, then Karl grabs my hand and helps me onto the top.

Don. Thanks, Karl. It was fun. I earnestly appreciate your instruction, your guidance and I really needed that last lift.

Karl. I'm glad you liked it. You want to rest a minute?

Don. No. I wanna get back and get out of the sun.

Karl. You don't show any redness.

Don. I used to get sunburned when I was a kid in Oklahoma. Once redness shows, it's too late. You're already burned.

Karl. O.K. Let's go.

He jogs. I follow...we're soon in the shower. We're lucky. The water-truck driver has just filled the shower tank with fresh, cool water from Tinian's pure, pure well.

Back in the tent, Karl comes by. He hands me a piece of paper. I read: "K - 24':13"; D - 32':45"." I open my physics book to "Work". Out loud, I read a note I had made in the margin. "If you want to measure your horsepower, run up a short flight of easy steps as fast as you can. If you are a light-weight, track star you might generate 4 h.p.". Karl shrugs.

I show him the horsepower formula: H.P. equals work (in foot pounds) divided by time (in minutes) and by 33,000. Obviously, horsepower generated on a difficult but slow climb will be puny. Karl shrugs. I shrug. I apologize for my poor memory of physics.

I relax in my sack...I meditate *.I resolve never to descend the cliff again. The time in the water was fun, especially when I was with the squid. .but I'm soon to be a father. I shouldn't risk injury, no matter how much fun the swim was*...I think of Jeannie and the Babe...I fall asleep.

Caldwell wakes me for supper. My skin doesn't burn. Maybe I'm O.K. We talk.

Don. Claude, I went skin-diving with Karl Pattison today. It was fun.

Claude. Yeah, I've heard it is.

Don. Don't you do it? You're a Californian.

Claude. I live in Redding. That's Northern California. It's a long way from the ocean and the water at beaches up there is icy cold.

Don. So, do you do your swimming in a pool?

Claude. Yeah. It gets hot in the summer. Carol and I love to swim at the Country Club pool.

Don. Are you guys golfers?

Claude. Yeah, do you and Jean golf?

Don. No, we play tennis but we are public court players.

Claude. What are you gonna do after the war?

Don. Well, I haven't decided whether to stay in the Air Corps, or go back to school.

Claude. I'm goin' back. I've got a B.A. but I want to go to law school.

Don. I don't know if I can support my wife and child and make my grades. I don't know whether to go back to architecture, or switch to aeronautical engineering.

Claude. Well, let's just concentrate on one mission at a time and get through our twenty-five so we can go home.

Don. You know, the Japs are beaten. If they had any brains they'd surrender now before we burn the whole damn country down.

We walk back to the tent. I rest on my sack. Malnove and Taylor are there.

Malnove. What time you guys want to start censoring?

Taylor. Damn, I want to go to the movie tonight.

Cotner. What's playin'?

Taylor. *Meet Me in St. Louis.*

Caldwell. Herb Boerner saw it over at the 505th's theater. He said it's damn good.

Malnove. Let's all go the movie, and do the censoring after.

Taylor. If we want a seat for the first show, we'd better go now.

Cotner. Let's go.

Caldwell. Roger.

We hustle down to the theater. We get good seats. We shoot the breeze while the crowd gathers. We watch the sun set. In the Marianna's, that's the best show of all. It's soon dark. The movie shows begin.

The newsreel shows a war bond rally at Rockefeller Center. It makes me think of my mother and dad. Every cent they absolutely do not need to live on goes toward the purchase of war bonds. They each donate a pint of blood every month to the Red Cross. They have invested their only son in the war. They want him to have the best possible chance to survive.

The next story is spring training in Florida. A one-armed guy, named Pete Gray, is gonna play right field for Cleveland.

Patton is chasing the Nazis out of Italy. The commentator says we are winning the war but I thank the fates that I don't have to fight on the ground in winter-wet weather, or in any weather.

Finally, they show a group of B-29s flyin' past Mount Fuji. It's not us; no big black Circle-X's on the tail; but we cheer like it is.

They give us the "Three Stooges" for a comedy. Every time Moe sticks his fingers in Curly's eyes, or hits Shep on the head with a brick, our 9th Group "full-house" crowd roars out guffaws, and howls out belly laughs, just like I used to do when I was ten years old watchin' the "Stooges". But after inflicting horrible hurt on our enemy and living the terror of being a target, violence is somehow not so funny.

Meet Me in St. Louis comes on. It more than makes up for the Stooges. It's humor is warm and gentle. The movie ends. We depart to the music of Les Brown, with Doris Day, in a recording of "Gonna Take a Sentimental Journey."

Our foursome heads for the 9th Group Headquarters tent. A large box of letters awaits. We will read it all before we are through. Our orders are to remove with scissors any information that may be of aid to Japan. There is a written list of specific items such as troop strength, armament strength, mission targets, losses, etc. Beyond that, we are authorized and commanded to clip anything not mentioned in the list that some bright young G.I. may have thought to write about, if in our opinion, it is hurtful to the U.S. war effort.

Ninety-five percent of the mail is love letters, mostly to sweethearts, some to wives. The other five percent is to parents. I despise this duty. *Why am I, just because I'm an officer, thought to be wiser, and more patriotic, than my enlisted comrades? Why should I be privy to intimate writings, of a man's deep, deep feelings, for the woman dearest to his heart?*

First of all, I screen from my purview the names of writers and receivers, to the extent possible. I scan the letters rapidly. Nothing catches my eye. I put each letter, intact, back into its envelope. Tokyo Rose already knows more about us than anybody on Tinian, except perhaps the highest-ranking officers. Caldwell, Malnove, and Taylor clip enough snippets to satisfy the authorities that we are sufficiently "chicken-shit". We report to the Officer of the Day. "Letters are censored, box locked, Sir."

We walk to the tent. Everyone is asleep. We soon are in our sacks. Taylor snores. Caldwell and Malnove breathe deeply...I lie awake.

I sit up quietly on the edge of my cot. By flashlight I write to Jean. I thank God that officer's mail is exempt from censorship: at least they tell us it is. My expressions of sexual love and longings are ardently explicit. I would not want some of my asshole-type "superiors" to have them in their hand, or worse, in their head.

I thank her for her sweet letters, for the snapshot of her beautiful pregnant-belly self, for the box of oatmeal cookies with raisins. I don't tell her we couldn't eat them because they tasted like the bottom of the deep foul hold of some British cargo vessel.

I'm glad I have so many recreational experiences to report. I tell her about gin rummy with Bill Duft, football with Claude, whom she knows, cliff climbing and swimming with Karl Pattison, whom she knows not. I make the cliff less steep, and the coral less sharp. She needs no extra stress. I describe Karl's skin-diving, of which I believe she knows nothing. I tell her I didn't dive, and don't want to; so, "send no goggles". I tell her that *Meet Me in St. Louis* is a good movie. Three actresses play "strong-women" roles - Mary Astor, Judy Garland, and a new child actress, Margaret O'Brien. She looks about seven years old but she holds her own with Astor and Garland. They are three sisters, in a story set in St. Louis during the 1904 World's Fair.

I write that "I don't know if you get to go to movies or not, but I know you will like this one".

I write a similar, but shorter letter to my mother and dad.

Personal delinquencies assuaged, I fall asleep.

BLITZ THREE – OSAKA

13 March 1945.:

I wake up early. I walk to the brunch tent. I enter. Lt. Ken Lobdell, Flight Engineer, on Capt. White's crew, walks out.

Lobdell. Hi, Don. You'd better grab a quick brunch.

Cotner. Good morning, Ken. Why? What's my rush?

Lobdell. Nestel has posted a flight engineer's meeting at 0900.

Cotner. What's the subject?

Lobdell. None was given.

Cotner. Thanks, Ken. I'll see you there.

Lobdell. There's also a 1700 briefing for thirty-three crews. Your crew is on the list.

Cotner. Where do we go tonight?

Lobdell. The memo didn't say. Bye.

Cotner. Bye.

I grab a cup of coffee. I drink it "mess-hall" black. Capt. Smith serves it "percolator-hot". I add a little "milk" (powder stirred in water), so I won't scald myself. From coffee and orange marmalade on G.I. bread, I devour a four-minute brunch. I run to the briefing room.

John Nestel, Group Flight Engineer, passes out a packet of papers headed "XXI Bomber Command, Engine Operation, 25 February 1945". The first page is titled "Engine Operating Limits". It tabulates maximum allowable manifold pressure for revolutions per minute from 1400 rpm to 2400 rpm and corresponding manifold pressure settings at altitudes from 1,000 feet to 30,000 feet, at 5,000-foot intervals. It also lists Brake Mean Effective Pressure and Brake Horsepower.

Nestel. Take this table with you when you fly. Be sure to observe the maximum manifold pressures.

Cotner. *Of course we will. We do now. These aren't any different than the maximums we've been using.*

Nestel. (*Hands out the rest of the packet*). Some of you may know that engineers from Boeing and Wright have been making fuel consumption test flights. This is the report of their tests.

We know them well. They are Civilian Attaches to the 9th Group. Thomas Lazio, of Wright Aeronautics, is my friend and mentor in engine operation. Their B-29 was equipped with special instruments such as fuel-flow meters and carburetor air temperature gauges. We don't have these instruments in the planes we fly in combat.

I scan the charts. There is a page for every altitude from 1,000 feet to 30,000 feet, at 1,000 feet intervals. Each page lists values for each of the variables shown on the "Engine Operation Limits" page including "Brake Mean Effective Pressure" and "Brake Horsepower". Additional data shown is: 1. Gross Weight (including contents) of the airplane, 2. Carburetor Air Temperatures (with formulas for estimating this temperature from outside-air temperature and density, 3. Fuel Comsumption per Engine in gallons per hour.

Nestel. There are no orders on the use of these charts. So, file these papers. They are too complicated to waste time on. We'll continue to fly by the power settings on the flight engineer's flimsies.

Instantly I protest, albeit introspectively. *But!...with this data and with wind and atmospheric information from Caldwell I can compute fuel consumption per sea-level mile, at any current power setting. . .and at the next lower setting, if the wind is with us...or next higher, if we are flying into a headwind. I can thus decide whether or not, and by how much, to change power for the best fuel economy.*

After the meeting I explain this to Nestel. I expect him to show interest.

Nestel. How do you know this?

Cotner. It's aerodynamics.

Nestel. We studied aerodynamics in flight school. They taught nothing about this.

Cotner. I joined the Air Corps Reserve in 1942. The Corps asked me to continue my college studies in architectural engineering until called to active duty. I got the opportunity to complete the fouth year of my five-year curriculum. During that year, I got school permission to substitute seven units of aerodynamics for six units of French. Professor Vincent Young damn well taught me.

Nestel. Well, we're gonna fly by the flimsies. I'm not gonna be responsible for changing anything.

Cotner. If I write the idea up, you can forward it through channels for consideration, can't you?

Nestel. No, I won't do that. It's too complicated.

Cotner. I'll teach classes in it.

Nestel. No.

Cotner. Yes, Sir......*Sir.*

I'm not the only Flight Engineer who has a professional jealousy demon gnawing inside his heart. On 15 February 1945, an order from XXI Bomber Command reached Col. Donald Eisenhart, 9th Group C.O. (at that time[4]). The order instructed each Group Commander to promptly fill the newly authorized position of "Group Flight Engineer," with a well-qualified man.

Each of us Flight Engineer Officers has twelve months in grade as a 2nd Lieutenant. Each has graduated from: 1. The Army Air Corp's Aircraft Engineering School, at Yale University, 2. The Boeing Factory School, at Seattle and, 3. The Air Corp's Flight Engineering School, at Lowery Field, Denver.

Each of us had also been required to submit a transcript showing a minimum of two years study, with B+ grades, in an accredited civilian engineering college to qualify for the program. Each of us has had six months "combat-training" as a Flight Engineer assigned to a crew, at McCook, Neb. Army Air Base.

John Nestel joined the 9th Bomb Group early in 1945 as pilot on a replacement crew. Col. Eisenhart read on Nestels' educational record that he had one semester of Mechanical Engineering study at Purdue University on his transcript. Eisenhart named Nestel to be "Group Flight Engineer"...Why?...

I resolve to use my new charts and graphs on tonight's mission. I go to my tent. I take my new charts and my aerodynamics textbook back to the brunch tent. In a quiet corner, fortified with coffee, I study.

4 Mar. '45, Col. Eisenhart was promoted to 313th Wing Hdqters. Lt. Col. Huglin was promoted to become 9th Grp. C.O., and soon to the rank of Colonel.

I find, and remember well, the information I absorbed while preparing for Vincent Young's rigorous exams. I hear the "Little Prof." (whom we students liked, in spite of his tests) say in his rich profundo voice, "Other variables, weight, wing surface, coefficients of lift and drag, being held constant, the horsepower required varies as velocity to the third power." Professor Young not only said it. He held us responsible for being able to derive the formula for "horsepower required" on a test.

I reason: *weight will change every second we burn fuel...but...for a 60 minute or shorter period, the weight of fuel consumed will be small in comparison to the gross weight of the plane including contents. Wing surface will remain constant. Lift and drag coefficients vary with angle of attack, but only by an unnoticeable amount during an hour of flight. For practical purposes they too can be neglected.*

My personal bitterness seems justifiably more severe than that of other engineers, because, in addition to my pursuit of standard aerodynamics study, being eager to learn everything possible, I had volunteered for zero-credit work in "Special Topics of Aerodynamics". It was taught by Dr. Ainsley Diamond, the proud young genius, with Ph.D.s in Math and Physics from MIT, who was head of the Mathematics Department at Oklahoma State.

I had to learn advanced aerodynamics plus advanced math, including "The Theory of Equations having Complex Variables" (such as the square root of negative numbers) and "Conformal Mapping Transformations". Still, I try to keep my bitterness non-malignant and unbiased. It's not Nestel's fault, and he is otherwise a good guy. Maybe both he and Donald Eisenhart are each trying to do an assigned job they don't have the background for, or probably the wise Colonel knew that keeping each trained engineer flying with his crew is better "war strategy" than assigning some one capable Flight Engineer to "fly a desk". Also, fairness (in terms of promotion and/or of death opportunity) to any individual soldier is not a consideration.

That's the Army. It's probably life. Maybe I'm fortunate to learn so young. I know I'm lucky to have so many good and well-qualified officers as my superiors.

I take my book, my writing tablet, my slide rule and my new and now precious documents back to my tent. With my buddies I go to lunch. After lunch it's back to the tent.

After studying, I take a shower. This time the water is warm from the sun's radiation...satisfying and relaxing. I lie down in my sack. I fall asleep.

1630 hours: Taylor wakes me. I get up. I dress. I gather my gear. Captain Feil, Taylor, Malnove, Caldwell and I walk to the briefing room. We sit with Schultz, Calhoun, Connor, Warn, Smith and Richardson. Other crews arrive. The arrow on the map points to Osaka, another large industrial city.

1700: Col. Huglin strides in. Group staff officers follow. At someone's "ten-hut", we stand. Huglin puts us at ease. We sit. He proceeds to the podium.

Huglin. Welcome gentlemen. General Le May congratulates you for your raid on Nagoya. Based on your debriefing reports, this may surprise you. It did me. Your reports were accurate, and from my perspective your stories were not tales of great success. The fire seemed less intense than that at Tokyo. Pictures show that one point eight square miles of Nagoya are burned; considerably less than the fifteen point eight square miles at Tokyo. General Le May thinks it is a good result. He assigns no blame to aircrews for inflicting less damage at Nagoya.

Cotner . *Here comes the huge "however".*

Huglin. General Le May lists four causes for our comparatively poor performance:

1. To their credit, Nagoya authorities cleared broad fire-stop lanes through the city.

2. Fire suppression crews responded more promptly and performed more proficiently than those at Tokyo.

3. Surface winds were seven miles per hour, considerably slower than the winds at Tokyo.

4. Our bombs fell too sparsely and, he accepts blame for the decision to increase the intervalometer setting.

Cotner. *Our leader accepts blame? Am I to be required to reassess General Le May's character?*

Huglin. Col. Luschen, please continue.

Luschen. Thank you Col. Huglin. Good evening gentlemen. As you see, we're going to incinerate Osaka tonight. It will be another 324-plane raid. Our Wing, the 313th, will be first over the target and the 9th Group has the honor of leading the Wing. The mission will again be flown in single-file formation, with succeeding planes dropping their bombs on the edge of the fire. So you see the necessity for accuracy and the opportunity to demonstrate proficiency.

Cotner. *Yes...yes...yes...*

Luschen. Col. Huglin has assigned pathfinder responsibility to five of the Group's fifteen lead crews. He wants to assure that at least one lead crew will survive possible attrition from abortion or enemy action.

Cotner. *Good.*

Luschen. The five lead crews are those of the following Captains: 1. Curry, 2. Shenefiel, 3. Chapman, 4. McClintock and 5. Feil.

Cotner. *Feil...Good...Being early over the target will mean less hazard to our being, and less horror for our vision of the calorific cataclysm below.*

Luschen. Capt. Curry will drop his bombs at 0200 on 14 March. The time interval between successive planes is one minute and fifteen seconds.

Cotner. *0200?.Opposite from the little pig, who built the brick house, and who always fooled the wolf by starting each day's joint-venture earlier than on the previous day, we keep bringing our fire later each mission...Do the Japs know about the "Three Little Pigs"? Or, is it Le May's purpose to add an hour of terror to each successive mission?*

Luschen. We shall proceed to the target at 5,000 feet altitude and we shall bomb from that altitude.

Cotner. *I'll still choose first-over.*

Lushen. After bombs are released, each plane shall make a climbing left turn to a due-south heading. Level out at 10,000 feet. Over the Pacific, each crew shall make its own way back to Tinian.

Cotner. *I can see it now.*

Luschen calls in the specialists. Their comments are similar to those made for previous blitz missions, except for that of Captain Brown, Group Meteorologist.

Brown. Our three "weather" B-29s, flying from Guam, have been outfitted with improved instrumentation. The crews have implemented new procedures that enable them to process data and formulate forecasts quickly. This report came in via short wave just fifty minutes ago. In forecasting, speed enhances reliability. They say, that on our return from Osaka at 10,000 feet,we will have a thirty-mile per hour tail wind, all the way.

Assembled Air Crews. Yea! Hooray!

Cotner. *Thank you meteorologists...Thank you, Captain Brown.*

...

2100: At 5,000 feet, we are well into our single file flight toward Osaka. Each plane is connected, in the cloudless night, via each Airplane Commander's vision of the running lights of the plane ahead. Winds are neutral, permitting Lts. Paul Gudgel, navigator, and George Marshal, flight engineer, of Capt. Curry's crew, to follow precisely the mission flight plan as it is delineated on their respective flimsies.

Using my new information on fuel flow, I am keeping a meticulous record of the fuel consumed by my own plane. It seems that our B-29 flies perhaps slightly "thirsty". I make the power settings, rpm and manifold pressure, while holding the throttles at mid-sector. That way Capt. Feil can speed-up or slow-down, as necessary to maintain our place in the formation, by advancing or retarding the throttle.

As best I can, I record the arc-size and elapsed time of each advance-and-retard event. I compute the average throttle lever displacement to be about three degrees of advance. Test reports give me no data as to how much this increases fuel consumption. I guess it to be about half of one percent.

Feil, Taylor and Malnove assess cloud-top altitude of a weather front ahead. Consensus is 7,000 feet. Flying at 5,000 feet, Capt. Curry leads the 9th Group planes into the clouds. The visual bond is broken. Airplane Commanders and Pilots maintain course, altitude, and air speed, via reliance on instruments. They maintain position in the linear formation by occasional brief sightings of lights ahead, but mostly by trust in flux-gate compass and directional gyroscope.

Thinking back to Boeing's B-29 factory school, I contemplate these two marvelous instruments. I thank the Air Corps and American technology for giving us the world's most technically advanced devices to guide Capt.

Feil and Lt. Taylor, as they fly steadily onward through the darkness and the storms of night.

Connor sits on the deck, beside me. We continue our flight-engineer training sessions.

Cotner. Connor, turn around and ask Caldwell to show you his compass instruments.

Connor. (*Complies, then turns back*). He's got three. He calls one the "flux-gate", another the "gyro" and the third the "radio" compass.

Cotner. Let's take them one at a time. The flux-gate compass is electronic. Its sensor is mounted horizontally in the left wing near the tip. A delta coil, five inches on each leg, is spun by a small synchronous electric motor. Each leg continuously cuts the earth's lines of magnetic flux. An electric current of successively varying strength is thus generated in each leg, and transmitted to the three delta terminal-connections.

Connor. Slow down.

Cotner. I'll draw a diagram.

On paper, I mark the three corner terminals of an equilateral triangle (a Greek letter delta) with a strong round dot. I connect each pair of dots with lines, each just sufficiently squiggly to indicate a coil of wire. I draw a magnetic north arrow. I draw straight lines through the triangle, each parallel to the north arrow.

Connor. Oh...yeah. I see it.

Cotner. Good. Each of the three sensor terminals is connected, via brush and shielded wire, and shielded through the wing, to a receiver delta coil behind Caldwell's compass-instrument dial. Currents, generated by the sensor, pass through the receiver coils. This generates a resultant magnetic field within the area of the receiver delta. This field is aligned with the earth's magnetic field. A free-to-rotate magnetized iron bar within the delta, thus points to magnetic north. The needle on the dial surface is attached to the bar's axle.

Connor. Tell me what flux is, and I think I've got it.

Cotner. Flux is flow. It comes from Latin. It is the jargon physicists use to explain that the power of a magnet to attract or to repel extends into the space around the magnet. I don't know how this is caused. The field of a magnet's attraction exists even in a vacuum.

Connor. Obviously it exists, whatever we call it.

Cotner. Let's finish the diagram.

At the other end of the paper, I draw a replica of the delta-coil. I label the second one the "instrument". I connect each terminal of the sensor to a respective terminal of the instrument. I draw a small bar magnet with an arrowhead on it, within the "delta" of the instrument.

Connor. (*Appreciative of the application of that which he remembers from his high school physics class*). Damn...Damn...It's so clever, and so damn simple. But why is it better than a simple magnetic compass?

Cotner. Masses of iron in the steel parts of engines, engine mounts and landing gears cause anomalies in the earth's magnetic field. Simple compasses are thus not accurate. Putting the sensor in the wing, far outboard of any iron, eliminates this problem.

Connor. Who invented the flux-gate compass?

Cotner. Well, in 1820 Oerstad, a Dane, sent a current through a coil of wire. "Voila", or whatever a Dane would say, a magnetic field surrounded

the coil. In 1831 Faraday, an Englishman, moved a coil in a magnetic field. "Behold", an electric current flowed in the coil.
I've never learned who the genius is who put these two phenomena together into the flux-gate compass. I hope he is soon properly celebrated. Minneapolis - Honeywell builds our compass. The B-29 is the only plane that has it.

Connor. So why do we need the second compass?

Cotner. Look at Caldwell's two compasses again.

Connor. (*After looking.*) The needle on the flux-gate bounces and flutters around a bit every time the plane bounces. The gyro is steady.

Cotner. Right. During every mission we spend at least two hours in rough weather. It's hard to track a course when the needle is fluctuating. It's always easy to follow the gyro.

Connor. Why not use just the gyro?

Cotner. We sometimes call it a gyrocompass but it cannot seek north. It really is a small gyroscopically stabilized platform that maintains a fixed position in space no matter what position the plane acquires around it. As you saw, compass numbers, zero to 360°, are marked on a cylindrical drum with a half inch high face. These numbers appear in the instrument's window. There is a "caging knob" below the window. With this knob the drum can be uncaged from the fixed platform and then the drum can be rotated until the number showing in the window is the same as the one to which the flux-gate needle is pointing. Due to friction in the gyroscope's bearing, the needle precesses with time. A reset is required about once every hour.

Connor. Wow.

Cotner. There is more.

Connor. I'm impressed. I'm glad to learn all this.

Cotner. I don't want this to get too complicated for one lesson; but, as you said, the B-29 has another compass, the radio compass.

Connor. I've heard of that. Its needle locates the station of a radio broadcast.

Cotner. Right. The radio compass has two antennas. One is a "loop" housed in an aluminum teardrop mounted on top of the fuselage. The other is a "whip." Schultz deploys it from the bottom of the fuselage, just aft of the forward gun-turret. Each antenna is aimed via an electrically driven gear system. Schultz monitors for broadcast strength at a sought for frequency. At max-response, the compass reads the heading from the airplane to the station.
Schultz has tables that match frequencies to Japanese cities. It's a great aid to Caldwell…I predict someday they'll make it even more useful. It'll tell us the heading <u>and the distances</u> to the source.

Connor. Three compasses and a really good Navigator and Radio Operator.

Cotner. Don't forget new and improved weather forecasts. We're lucky.

Connor. We guys in the back worry about gettin' lost somewhere over this huge, wet ocean. I feel better now. I'll tell them all about it when we get back to the tent tonight.

Cotner. Yeah, they need to know...Now for the Flight Engineer's responsibilities toward these compasses. The sensor delta-coil of the flux gate is rotated by an electric motor. The gyroscope of the "gyro-compass", and each of the other "flight-attitude" instruments is driven by a vacuum motor. The vacuum-system pump is driven by an electric motor. The radio compass antennas are each dependent on an electric motor.

Connor. Will I have to learn how to repair or replace these motors and directional systems in flight?

Cotner. We can't; they are not accessible. But if the flux-gate compass malfunctions, replace its motor fuse. Here's my screwdriver. Take the cover off that eight by twenty inch panel at the right of my instrument panel.

Connor. O.K....Wow, lots of fuses.

Cotner. Each one is named. Can you find "flux-gate"?

Connor. Yeah, but what if the fuse looks O.K.?

Cotner. We need these compasses! If Caldwell says one is not workin', put a new fuse in anyway. Spare fuses are on the inside face of the panel.

Connor. Yeah, I see them.

Cotner. If the gyrocompass malfunctions, put in a new fuse for the vacuum-pump motor-circuit. If that doesn't fix it, put a new filter in the vacuum supply-duct. I'll show you how to do that after we get home.

Connor. If you can't do it in flight, why not let the ground crew do it?

Cotner. We need those instruments in the air, and, we can change the filter in flight but the duct runs under Capt. Feil's feet and I can better show you how to make the change when the front of the plane is empty. The "change-fuse" procedure applies to malfunction of the radio compass antenna motor too.

Connor. That sure is one hell of a school at Boeing.

Cotner. The Air Corps wants these planes to do their damn job.

• • •

We drone our way through the night.

Warn. (*Breaking intercom silence.*) Hey, nobody's done no dang abortion.

Calhoun. (*Kidding Warn.*) I take that to be a dang-good omen.

Smith. I'm dang happy about our prospects on this dang mission.

Connor. (*Now in my seat, wearing my headphones and mike.*) Wait'll I tell you dang guys about the modern navigation instruments this dang plane's got.

Capt. Feil. We deserve a good run. I feel optimistic too.

I'm sittin' on the deck beside Connor. The engine instruments are showing perfect operation. I don't have a mike or earphones. My mood is good... *Does mood spread extra-sensorially*?
Caldwell hands me two cups. I read his lips, "tomato juice, for Schultz and me". I hand the cups to Taylor. He pours. He hands them back. I give them to Caldwell. We repeat the process for Connor and me, then again for refills all around.

Capt. Curry reaches the turning point. His navigator, Lt. Paul Gudgel, gives him a heading of 315°. Capt. Curry takes the controls from his pilot, Lt. Pattison. Curry gently turns the big plane around the gyro indicator until the number 315 is centered in the instrument's window. The line of 9th Group B-29s follows.

I send Connor back to his Right Gunner station. I climb down into my seat.

At Capt. Feil's command, Schultz employs the radio compass antennas. He tunes to Radio Osaka's frequency. Jap music comes on the intercom. Schultz mutes the music. Each of the plane's four radio compass dials reads

315°. Caldwell is happy to see that this checks the six degree magnetic-variation correction he used to verify Gudgel's 315° heading.

We are flying below cloud cover. Visibility of the ground is clear. At 220 mph ground speed we hasten through the sky. Our course carries us comfortably past the 6,300-foot peak of Bunkyo-Dake upon which the Japs are, obligingly, brightly flashing the lights of the mountain-peak warning-signal system.

Feil, Taylor and Malnove see the lights of Osaka ahead, and of Kobe twenty-five miles to its east north- east. We will soon be approaching Osaka's outskirts. Each of the five Airplane Commanders sees the city's nighttime glow in the sky. The Captain orders Schultz to cease operation on the radio compass, and to "stow" all parts of the system.

Just beyond Bunkyo-Dake, Smith comes on the intercom.

Smith. Lt. Caldwell, I've got a great picture of Osaka on radar.

Caldwell. It's beautiful Smitty. Osaka Bay and Osaka Harbor are really clear. Congratulations. (*To Feil*). Capt. I can take you to Osaka by flux gate compass, gyro, radio compass, or by radar. Do you have a preference?

Feil. I hate to disappoint you, Claude, but we've got Osaka in sight. I am in awe though of this plane's navigation systems. Don't feel bad. We'll be happy to let you take us back to Tinian.

Capt. Curry leads the 9th over Osaka's eastern edge. No citizen, or soldier, seems aware of peril. No city light blinks out. No searchlight flashes on. No anti-aircraft gun fires flak. Municipal illumination allows Airplane Commanders to read the smoke from factory chimneys. A strong street-level wind blows northwest. Curry guides us toward the southeast sector. Near the far end of that sector's edge, at precisely 0200, he orders Steinberg to drop the bombs.

Shenefiel, number two, sees bombs fall from Curry's plane. He yells "bombs away" to Maurice Bettinger, his Bombardier. Reaction down the chain of planes ensues.

Capt. Leon Smith, a lead crew commander, flies last in line. He is Col. Huglin's "last-chance" assurer, that at least one 9th Group plane will ignite the target. Smith sees a line of fire blowing toward the city's core. He marvels at the accurate work accomplished by the crews ahead. His bombs fall upon the end of the fire.

In Osaka, lights go out. Searchlights come on. Anti-aircraft barrages begin. Following Capt. Curry, the 9th Group planes make a climbing turn away from the danger. I give Capt. Feil climb-power. Our retreat passes over Osaka's neighbor city. It shines bright and clear. Will the little town of Wakayama be safe tonight? Maybe...But it is an enticing target of opportunity for any crew which may somehow miss its chance to bomb Osaka. At 7,000 feet we fly into the bottom of the cloud cover.

While we rise through the fog, I update my log. I muse, in mist induced mood. "Bombs away" ended our outbound flight, and began our homeward cruise. From our "start-engines" gross weight of 137,000 lbs., I subtract 20,330 lbs. of fuel consumed, 16,000 lbs. of bombs dropped, and zero rounds of ammunition fired. Gross weight is now less than 100,670 lbs.

At "start", each of the four engine-feed-tanks was full, and so was our wing center-section reserve-tank. Total fuel volume was 6,732 gallons. By "bombs away", 3,677 gallons had become smoke. We now have a little less than 3,055 gallons to get home on.
I feel good. We're only a little heavier than the 95,000 lb. gross weight-limit at which Boeing designed the B-29 to fly.. We have almost as much fuel as it took us to get here. We have a thirty-mile per hour tail wind.

Only the Air Corps can stretch the load-carrying capacity and extend the cruising-range of that frailest class of any industrially manufactured transport-machine, the aeroplane, and make it perform successfully as a weapon of power. I luxuriate in the bliss of esprit de corps...Oops! Sanity strikes. American Airlines cannot take such chances; United Air Lines can't. The cost of our cargos of bombs and bullets is borne by additions to the national debt. Our crews, and our passengers if any, are expendable. Commercial airlines are regulated by the Civil Aeronautics Administration. Airlines dread judgments of the courts and damages assessed by jurors. Intimidated civilians don't buy air-travel tickets. Prudent merchants minimize the risks of air-freight shipments. This is only the 9th Group's fourth mission, and some of our beautiful B-29s and some of our beautiful buddies' lives have already been spent.

Capt. Curry levels out at 10,000 feet. He leads us due south toward the safety of the Pacific Coast.

0212: Mission planners grant us a 225 mph indicated-air-speed getaway. With 300 plus airplanes trailing us, they want no traffic jams piling up behind. I make a new power setting of 2100 rpm and thirty-one point five inches-of-mercury manifold-pressure. We are burning 420 gallons of fuel per hour. Our true air speed, corrected for altitude, is 234 mph. With our thirty mph tailwind, per the weather officer, our ground speed is 264 mph. The fraction 264/420 yields miles per gallon. As a decimal it is .628 mpg. I talk to Capt Feil.

Cotner. Captain, we're burning too much fuel. With that tailwind we're supposed to slow down and let the wind give us ground speed.

Feil. There's nothing we can do about it until Capt. Curry dismisses the formation. He won't do that until we are over the ocean.

Cotner. I know. Everyone has to follow the flimsies until we are on our own. I just wanted you to be aware. (*Muses*). *Curry can't dismiss us till we get into clear air. A collision with a friend would be worse than gettin' hit with flack or a zero's bullets...We don't know where cloud top is. I feel lucky* *that Feil and Caldwell are skilled at piloting and navigating in instrument flight conditions.*

Caldwell. Capt. Feil, it's about a half-hour to the coast. It's time for you, Taylor and me to reset our gyros.

Taylor. Roger.

Feil. Let's do it.

They perform the procedure. Caldwell allows the six degree magnetic variation charted for this part of Japan. Having no way yet to check wind speed and direction, he makes no allowance for lateral wind drift. He arrives at a heading of 186°. He reads his gyro:186°.

Caldwell. Capt., I checked our heading. Are we still in line?

Feil. We are. We get a brief glimpse of McClintock's turbo-wheels now and then.

Caldwell. Good, I guess my buddy, Gudgel, is usin' the same wind I am.

Feil. Roger, thanks.

Caldwell. (*Planning ahead*). Malnove will you be ready to take a drift reading through the bombsight in case you see a hole in the clouds, and can find a strong light on the ground?

Malnove. Roger, I'm ready. I hope we do find a hole. Maybe we will at the coast.

Caldwell. Smith, try to find a distinct point on the coast, or on an offshore island, or even a large sea-going vessel that we can get a radar drift reading on.

Smith. Roger, Lieutenant.

Caldwell. My E.T.A. for the coastline is ten minutes. It will lie at an acute angle to our heading. Do the best you can with it, guys.

0258:

Warn. Hey, we're crossin' the coast.

Cotner. (*Looks at watch, 0258*). *Are we a little late?...Oh well, Caldwell's "half-hour" was just conversation, not a calculated ETA.*

Malnove. I saw a light for one or two seconds. If I can get one for thirty seconds, I might give you a guess on the drift. I'll keep looking.

Caldwell. Roger, Malnove. (*To Smith*). Your picture was good, Smitty. I saw the shore clearly but it was too damn smooth and straight, and too near parallel to our line of flight. I couldn't pin point any feature I could read drift on. Keep the radar going. Let me know if you get a big blip, bright enough to be a ship or an island.

Smith. O.K., Lieutenant, but a ship would probably be moving. Don't you need a stationary object?

Caldwell. Stationary is preferable but a ship's velocity is so small compared to ours, that I can get a workable approximation off of it.

Smith. O.K., I'll keep alert.

Caldwell. Gunners, watch the skies above us. Let me know if a hole opens up that I can shoot a star through.

A chorus of Gunners. Roger...Roger...Roger.

Calhoun. Lieutenant, the sky's opening up ahead right now.

Caldwell. Good. Thanks, Calhoun.

Caldwell gets a quick "time-tick" via radio. He takes off his parachute. He anchors the aluminum access ladder in place. With sextant in hand, he leans back against the ladder. He climbs three backward steps up. He sticks his head and shoulders into the three-foot diameter tunnel that serves as passageway to the rear compartment. He sits up. His feet and lower legs dangle out the mouth of the tunnel. His head is in the two-foot diameter Plexiglas dome on the roof.
He finds a star. It's so bright, he thinks it must be *Deneb*. He focuses the telescope. He begins to adjust the vertical-tube bubble...carefully,... carefully,...WHAM! Turbulence knocks him loose from *Deneb*.
He leans back on his elbows to ride out the rough air. Finally the turbulence calms. He sits up, head in the dome. He looks up. ..he sees clouds.

Caldwell. (*Back at his table*). Keep looking for holes in the clouds.

Gunners chorus. Roger, Roger, Roger.

• • •

0318: Capt. Curry flies into cloud-free air. He radios Airplane Commanders that each crew will be on its own, as soon as it enters the clear air space. Caldwell hustles to give Feil the heading to Tinian. To make room on his table to spread his map, he gently lays his sextant on the deck near his feet. Capt. Feil relays Curry's message to the crew.

Crewmembers shed flak suits. One by one we proceed to the relief tube. To gain a little space near the tube, we stow the ladder. On the way back to our station, each of us chats a word or two with Caldwell. Parade over, we settle down to work.

Caldwell. Capt. Feil, the heading to Tinian is 175° on the gyro.

Feil. Roger.

Cotner. What's the wind doing, Claude?

Caldwell. I haven't gotten a drift reading yet. I'll get a star shot soon to check our position. Then I'll compute what the wind has been since we leveled out at 10,000 feet. Right now I'm using a thirty-mile per hour tailwind, straight on.

Cotner. Same as briefing?

Caldwell. Roger.

Cotner. Roger.

Cotner. Let me know what's blowing.

Caldwell. Roger.

Cotner. Captain, I'm gonna cut the power all the way to 1900 rpm and thirty point three inches manifold pressure, that should give us about 200 miles per hour indicated air speed. I may adjust that, when Claude gives me the wind.

Feil. Roger.

Calhoun. Lt. Caldwell, there are a billion stars out now. There's no moon though.

Caldwell. Roger. Moonset was forty-five minutes ago. That'll make star-shots easier.

Malnove. Claude, there's a solid layer of clouds below us. I can't see the ocean.

Caldwell. Roger, keep scanning. Maybe we can get a drift reading on a U.S. Navy ship or perhaps you can find a whitecap if we leave these under-clouds behind.

Malnove. Roger.

Caldwell. Sergeant Schultz.

Schultz. Roger, Lieutenant.

Caldwell. Can you give me another "time-tick"? I want to make double sure my time is accurate.

Schultz. Roger, "time-tick" coming up.

Schultz tunes to the "U.S. Armed Services Greenwich-Time Short-Wave Network", which continuously broadcasts to any spot on earth where U.S. military personnel will need to know international time to the nearest tenth of a second.

Signal sounding in his headset, Caldwell precisely matches his special-issue navigator's wristwatch with Greenwich time. Caldwell consults his copy of the "Air Almanac of Star Positions", published by the U.S. Naval Observatory. He selects *Kolchab*, a bright star in the constellation *Ursa Minor*, popularly named "Little Dipper." We're lucky; Caldwell learned ready identification of the constellations as a Cub Scout and was a member of the Astronomy Club at the University of California. I watch Caldwell bend forward to retrieve his sextant from the deck. I see him rise, then disappear behind the forward turret. Up the ladder. In the tunnel. Head in the dome. *Kochab* in the telescope. He fine-tunes the screw-knob till the bubble is centered in the sextant's vertical tube. He records the angle of celestial declination and Greenwich time, 1001.3. At 1003.5, he records his fifth shot.

Back at his station, Caldwell averages times and angles. He enters the results in his log. He consults the "Air Almanac". He reads the "Sidereal Hour Angle and Angle of Declination", precalculated for *Kochab* at the averaged time of his shots. With the data from sextant observation, and that taken from the Almanac, he uses "Sight Reduction Tables for Air Navigation", a supplement to the Almanac, to determine latitude and longitude of our position at the time of the shot. The Sight Reduction Table yields the most rapid solution. The method is accurate only to one-half of a degree. In the air, speed of result is more important than slowly derived rigorous precision.

Before he plots them on his map, Caldwell knows his coordinates are "queer": 143°, longitude...impossibly eastward. Twenty-seven degrees latitude...too north to be true. He has been continuously monitoring his compasses. Feil and Taylor have steadfastly held the course. As a first check, using the same data, Caldwell computes the position using the perfection of spherical trigonometry, a branch of mathematics which he mastered at Berkeley: 139° 59' Lat, 26° 01' Long.

He observes an oddity. He sets his compass point on Osaka, its pencil on his plotted dead reckoned course on the point, at which he shot *Kochab*. He swings an arc counterclockwise. It passes through the "queer" location. He ponders...Is this coincidence?...yes...It can't be verification of distance flown, and thus of a thirty mph tailwind?

Caldwell. Capt. Feil, I took a star shot, and it shows an incorrect position, too far east and not far enough south. I'm gonna shoot another one.

Feil. Roger.

Caldwell elects to shoot *Polaris*. With Schultz' help he checks his watch. In the dome, he notes that, to his bare eye, *Polaris* seems high in the sky, to the rear of our line of flight. That's about the way it looks sighted through his telescope.

He returns to his table. He computes, by dead reckoning, and plots the position at the time of his Polaris shot. He computes, by spherical trig, the coordinates per *Polaris*. The latter reads two degrees east and three degrees south of the dead reckoned position. Caldwell ponders again...*On the map this almost looks like verification of dead reckoning, except that one degree of longitude, or latitude in this location is each more than 100 miles in length...If we are on a course that has already brought us 200 miles east of the true course, we'll fly too far east of Tinian to see it as we go by .and if we are 300 miles too far south, it means our tailwind must be 100 miles per hour...The only consolation I can get from these two star shots is that we probably have a tailwind. I'm gonna have to continue to call it a thirty mile per hour wind until I get a drift reading.*

Caldwell. Capt. Feil, I took a shot on *Polaris*. It was better than my earlier shot on *Kochab*, but neither result is believable. Hold the present course.

Capt. Feil. Roger.

Cotner. (*Also on line*). What shall I use for wind?

Caldwell. I'm trusting Captain Brown. I'm gonna use his thirty mile per hour tailwind.

Cotner. Roger.

I convert our 200 mph indicated, to 209 mph true air speed and with tailwind, to 239 mph sea-level speed. I read fuel consumption on my new charts to be 346 gallons per hour. Dividing 239 by 346 I get .691 miles per gallon.

Cotner. Capt. Feil, we're gettin' a little better gas mileage than we were before I slowed us down.

Feil. Good work, Don.

A half hour later I compute miles per gallon at 195 mph indicated. It's 336 gph and 234 mph (sea level), which yields .696 mpg.

Cotner. Capt., I computed a 195 mph cruise. It'll save only .005 mpg but I want to get the longest ride we can on this thirty mph tailwind. I'm gonna cut rpm to 1800 and keep the manifold pressure at twenty-eight. I'll keep checking it every half hour.

Feil. Roger. Good idea.

Our engines, and all other systems, perform perfectly as we steadily progress toward Tinian.

Malnove. Hey, Claude, I can see ocean below us. I'm searchin' through my bombsight telescope for whitecaps. As Calhoun says, the sky is bright with stars but below the horizon, that is one black sea surface down there.

Caldwell. Roger, Paul, but keep tryin'.

Malnove. Roger, willco.

0353: We don't stop, and neither does time. Between my half-hour checks on fuel consumption, and maintenance of my log, I have delightful moments when I think about my pregnant Jeanie and our babe in her belly.

...

0513:

Caldwell. Capt. Feil, Iwo is due east now. (*To Smith.*) It's about 100 miles out, Smitty. Can you verify it on radar?

Smith. I'll switch to maximum range. Give me a minute.

Caldwell. Roger

Cotner. (*Listening.) This may be good data for me.*

Smith. There is snow from electrical static at that location. Iwo may be experiencing one of its frequent storms but I find no island blip under the snow.

Caldwell. Thanks, Smitty. (*To himself.) I can't assume that is Iwo...storms happen on "open" sea.*

0543:

Malnove. Is it getting lighter?...Or am I getting lightheaded?

Calhoun. Dawn is breaking.

Warn. By golly-dang, you're right.

Connor. Concur.

Caldwell. Sunrise is due at 0602. Dawn is usually fifteen minutes sooner. At 10,000 feet, dawn and sunrise are each about four minutes earlier than at sea level. We should see the sun come up at 0558.

Caldwell. Schultz, give me a quick time-tic. I want to shoot the sun the instant it cracks the horizon.

Schultz. Roger (*within seconds*). Here it comes, Lieutenant...

Caldwell is in the dome, watch on wrist, sextant in hand. A sliver of Sol's rim appears. "Shaded" lenses protect Caldwell's retinas. He centers the bubble. He reads the vertical and horizontal angles of the bright bit of our nearest star. This instantaneous vision of the brilliant blip is the most useful sighting of the solar day.

Back at his station, he solves the mysteries encrypted within his spheric-trigonometrical equations. *Shit!...Wrong answer!...Again!...Someone must have stepped on my sextant .How come there's no room in the biggest bomber in the world for the Navigator to store his sextant. It's my fault though. Not Boeing's. not the Air Corps, not the guys...Well, I still think my dead-reckoned position is close to being right.*

We hold course, steadily cruising. Each half hour, if the charts lead me to a better mile per gallon figure, I reduce power to slow our speed.

Malnove searches for white caps. Over deep waters it takes "just-so" wind to whip up "just-right" waves. He finds <u>no</u> white caps. Caldwell and I continue to define the wind as "thirty miles per hour, following".

Sunrise progresses. Sky colors dazzle. Their glories energize our spirits... even Caldwell's.

Caldwell. Capt. Fiel, here's my E.T.A. for Tinian: 0907.

Warn. Hooray dang!...Oh...Excuse me, Captain.

Feil. Glad to hear it, Claude. (*To Warn).* You're excused, Warn, we're all glad to hear a good Tinian E.T.A. (*Back to Caldwell*). Claude, my watch reads 6:01. Is it right?

Caldwell. It's three seconds slow, Captain.

Feil. That's good enough.

Caldwell. Roger.

Feil. How's our fuel, Don?

Cotner. It's good. We have 1896 gallons. We'll only use half of that gettin' home from here. I suggest we begin a thirty-foot per minute let down, to about 3,000 feet.

Feil. I agree.

Feil starts the descent.

Cotner. Captain, I'd like to cut power a little, to save fuel, even though we have plenty. I'll maintain speed to meet Caldwell's E.T.A.

I reduce rpm to 1600 and manifold pressure to 27.5 in. Hg. I close cowl flap openings to a slit to maintain minimum engine temperature. Caldwell carefully plots our track. It shows that we are even with Faralon de Pajaras, the northern-most island of the Mariana chain.

Caldwell. Smitty, Pajaras is about 100 miles due east. Can you pick it up?

Smith. I'll try.

Smith tunes the radar to maximum range. He searches for Pajaras.

Smith. Lieutenant Caldwell, the electronics are clear, no "snow" from storms, no static, but there is no blip, no island, nor any ship. Do you see anything on your screen?

Caldwell. No. No blip. Nothin!...Pajaras is tiny. Keep lookin' for islands in the chain. Let me know when you find one.

Smith. Roger, willco.

0815:

Caldwell. We're fifteen minutes from Tinian...It's straight ahead.

Feil. Roger. That's good to hear. Keep your eyes open, crew.

0830:

Feil. Anybody see Tinian?

Malnove. Not yet.

Warn, Connor, Calhoun. No, Sir.

Feil. Caldwell, better check our position.

Caldwell. (*Already working.*) Roger.

With creased brow, clenched jaw, grim mouth, Caldwell furiously iterates his numerical data.

0836:

Caldwell. You'll see Tinian dead ahead in twenty minutes.

Feil. Roger. I'm gonna set up a watch: Malnove and Taylor, sweep a ninety degree sector straight ahead. Warn, watch near and far from 9:00 o'clock to 12:00. Connor, watch 3:00 to 12:00; Richardson, go back to the tail and take 9:00 to 3:00, rearward. Rich, if we fly by without seeing Tinian, we want you to turn us around damn soon.

Feil asks each man in turn for verification of his assignment. Each responds correctly.

Feil. Schultz, tune the radio compass to the Armed Services Radio tower on Saipan.

Schultz. Roger, Sir.

Schultz deploys the radio-compass antenna. He tunes the receiver.

Feil. Caldwell, does the radio compass check your heading to Tinian?

Schultz. Excuse me, Sir. I tried the local broadcast. I can't bring it in. We're too far away.

Feil. Not even enough to get a heading?

Schultz. No, Sir, but I probably can get Air-Sea-Rescue on Saipan.

Feil. That's good. Get it.

Schultz. Roger...I've got it.

Feil. Caldwell, does the radio compass check your heading to Tinian now?

Caldwell. Yes, Sir. The tower is on Saipan's highest point, about twenty miles west of Tinian. The radio compass needle is a hair west of the course we're flyin'...*Thank God...But if my course is so perfect,why is my position so putrid?*

Feil. Caldwell, can we get the distance to the Saipan tower?

Caldwell. No.

Feil. Schultz, I thought we can we get distance on the radio compass.

Schultz. Only on low frequency beams. Armed Services broadcasts on short waves of a very high frequency, so it can reach ships far out at sea. The Saipan station also beams its programs locally, in a 150 mile-or-so radius, at low frequency. I couldn't pick up the local broadcast. We must be out of local range. I switched to Air-Sea-Rescue, which broadcasts only on VHF short wave.

Feil. Why can't we read distance on short wave broadcasts?

Schultz. A short-wave broadcast sends off beams in all directions. There is a "ground-wave" which follows the earth's surface. Other fractions of wave energy are received after being refracted by, and reflected from, various layers of the ionosphere. We don't have a radio receiver that can translate these mixed signals into a sea-surface great-circle distance, source to receiver.

Feil. Thanks, Schultz, good explanation. (*To Caldwell.*) Claude, it seems we've got the course right, but we still don't know where we are on it...is that correct?

Caldwell. Yes, Sir...but I want to rework the E.T.A.

Feil. Go ahead...

Caldwell. Roger. *(To himself, he repeats what seems to have become his mantra.) If my course is so faultless, why is my position so poison?*

In his own mind, each crewman silently asks Caldwell's question, plus a few queries of his own invention... *Are we on course?...How do we know we're on course?...How come nobody has seen Tinian?...Are we east of Tinian, or west of Tinian?...Has Warn been asleep?...Has Connor been asleep?...Has Malnove been asleep?...Have we passed Tinian?...Should we turn around?...*

0934:

Feil. It's ninety seconds to your E.T.A., Claude. We should be able to see it. (*To crew.*) Has anyone seen Tinian?

Crew. No, Sir.

Caldwell. I know we're on course. I'll recompute the E.T.A.

Feil. I believe we <u>are</u> on course. Go ahead and recompute our position.

Cotner. ...*We can be on course and <u>still</u> run out of fuel...*

Caldwell. Our new ETA is 1047.

Silence...Silence...Silence...

The plane drones its own way onward, whichever way its way is.

• • •

1047:

Feil. Your third E.T.A. is here, Caldwell. That's an hour and forty minutes we've been lookin' for Tinian.

Caldwell. By all indications, including high frequency radio, we <u>are</u> on course.

Feil. Schultz, Try again to get Saipan's low frequency beam.

Schultz. Roger.

The whole crew waits...in silence...

Schultz. Can't get it, Sir.

Feil. Damn...I guess that means we're more than 150 miles out. (*To Cotner.*) We got enough gas?

Cotner. We can go 150 miles, but not much farther.

1119:

Smith. Lieutenant Caldwell, see those two blips eighty miles east on the scope?

Caldwell. Yes.

Smith. Aren't they Tinian and Saipan?

Warn. Hot-dangedy dang!!!

Caldwell. I see them...The tiny one is Pajaras and the relatively big one is Maug.

Cotner. How far is it to Tinian?

Caldwell. 372 miles.

Cotner. Are you sure we're that far from Tinian?

Caldwell. Yes.

Cotner. Well...we don't have enough gas to fly that far.

Caldwell. I thought you said we had plenty of gas to get to Tinian.

Cotner. I did,, but,that was when you were giving us E.T.A.s, that are no damn good now.

Feil. Hey throw no stones, guys.

Caldwell. Yes, Sir.

Cotner. You're right, Sir.

Feil. How many gallons of gas do you have?

Cotner. Well, my log says 504 gallons...That's barely enough to fly 372 miles, if we're lucky. But, at Boeing's B-29 school we learned that during descent, twenty-seven gallons are trapped in the lower corner of each tank, and are not available to the fuel pumps. 504 less 108 leaves 396 gallons. That's not enough. How far is it to Pagan?

Caldwell. (*Solves a simple right triangle.*) 183 miles.

Cotner. I suggest we fly to Pagan and ditch near the shore. It's the largest island in the northern chain. We should be able to paddle our rubber rafts to shore. It's uninhabited, but I think we can survive there till they rescue us.

Feil. I don't want to depart from a course that I believe is true. I'm headin' straight for Saipan and Tinian. I propose to ease down slowly to 500 feet, and cruise there. When we spot Tinian, I want to make an extended almost flat approach. I plan to come in at fifteen feet above the edge of the cliff.

Cotner. Well, you won't trap much fuel., Captain. But, what if we have less fuel than I think?. Wouldn't it be better to ditch under four-engine power, than to lose an engine during landing...whether on land, or on water?

Feil. Maybe...But, what if we have more gas than you think?

Cotner. I think we should prepare for ditching now. It takes a while to throw everything loose overboard.

Feil. I concur, but I want to talk to Air-Sea Rescue first. (*To Schultz.*) Schultz, get me Saipan Air Rescue, voice to voice.

Schultz. Roger. Go ahead, Captain. Major Lindsay* is on air.

Feil. Major Lindsay*, this is Captain Feil, B-29 Airplane Commander, Ninth Bomb Group.

Lindsay. Hi, Captain, Major Lindsay* here. We're damn glad to hear from you. Major Luschen has already reported you missing. Where are you?

Feil. Our heading is 186 degrees, on course to Saipan and Tinian. We're 365 miles from Tinian. We're low on fuel. I'm gonna land on Tinian if we make it that far. If not, I'll ditch on this course. Can you send an escort to mark us if we go down and a PBY to pick us up?

Lindsay. Roger, willco. I'm scrambling two escort planes and one PBY immediately. What is your altitude?

Feil. We're at 3,000 feet. We're descending fifteen feet per minute.

Lindsay. Keep flyin' in. We'll take care of you.

Feil. (*To crew.*) Prepare to ditch.

Ditching preparation is a procedure we have exhaustively rehearsed toward achieving inerrant performance.

Feil. Malnove, you're the front compartment collector. Calhoun, you're the rear collector. O.K., crew, we're gonna throw everything loose overboard. Hand all gear that's not "crash-landing" anchored to your collector.

Feil polls the crew. He gets mostly "willcos".

Warn. Captain, I got my dang forty-five in my pocket. I don't think it will come flyin' loose in a crash.

Feil. Intelligence advised us to surrender unarmed to Jap authorities, if we get shot down. Remember?

Warn. Roger. I just want to take a few dang authorities with me.

Feil. Warn, this is an order. Give your forty-five to Calhoun. We'll throw it overboard. I'll try to see that you won't have to pay for it. I also order you to carry no weapon on any future mission. You are a brave young man but I can't let you endanger any of us, who might be captured with you, if we're ever afoot on Japan.

Warn. Yes, Sir. Roger, Sir.

Feil. Malnove, Calhoun, pile all collected gear on the deck, by the bomb bay porthole door. Let me know when you're ready to toss it out.

Malnove, Calhoun. Roger, Sir.

Cotner. I'll have to keep my papers, my clipboard and my slide-rule, Captain. I've got a lot of fuel-use calculating to do.

Feil. Roger, O.K.

Caldwell. Captain, may I save my sextant?

Feil. Why? We won't need it.

Caldwell. It's out of alignment. Someone stepped on it. I want it as proof to Captain Roth, 99th Squadron Navigator, that I am a competent Navigator.

Feil. Give it to Malnove. Tell him I asked to see it. That way, I can vouch that it's bent. Then Malnove can throw it overboard.

Caldwell. Thanks, Captain.

Calhoun. Captain, I've got everything loose back here piled up by the bomb bay door.

Feil. Good, stand by. I'll get Malnove to open the rear bomb bay doors.

Malnove. Here's the sextant, Captain. It does look bent to me.

Feil. Roger, I concur. Throw it out. While you're here, open the rear bomb bay. Show Taylor how to close it, and how to open and close the forward bomb bay door.

Malnove opens the rear door. He instructs Taylor. He returns to his "collector" task. Taylor returns to his pilot station.

Feil. Calhoun, get Warn and Connor to help. Get all that loose gear overboard as soon as you can. Let me know when we can close the door.

Flack suits, tomato juice cans, Warn's pistol and all other loose objects go into the sea.

Calhoun. All gear overboard, Captain. O.K. to close rear door.

Feil. Taylor, close the rear bomb bay door, and stand by to open the forward door.

Taylor. Roger, willco.

Caldwell. Malnove says he's ready to clear out the front compartment.

Feil. Open the forward door.

Taylor. Roger, willco.

Malnove, with Caldwell's help, soon gets all loose gear on its way to the sea. Taylor closes the door.

I estimate that eleven flack suits, plus miscellaneous other equipment makes us 1400 lbs. lighter. Malnove passes my station on his way back to his forward post.

Cotner. Our fuel situation is grim. I'm desperate to know what the wind is doing. Do all you can with the bombsight.

Malnove. O.K., Don.

Back at his station, Malnove finds a prominent whitecap. He follows it through his bombsight lens for sixty seconds. He recites a running account of numbers. Caldwell records drift figures and times. He computes wind velocity and direction.

Caldwell. Hey, Captain! Hey, Don! We've got an eleven-mile an hour tail wind. It's blowin' us right on course to Tinian.

Cotner. Roger.

Feil. The watch for Tinian is still on. I don't want to waste even two feet of distance, or of altitude, gettin' lined up with that runway.

Assigned watchers. (*In chorus.*) Roger, Roger, Roger.

Malnove. Two planes are flyin' directly toward us. They're so far away I can't identify them.

Calhoun. I see `em. They're P-47s.

Taylor. They're closin' damn fast.

Cotner. The P-47 has a 2,000 hp Pratt and Whitney eighteen cylinder radial engine. It's one of the world's fastest fighter planes.

Warn. They're flyin' faster than the dang Zeros.

The talk of speed alerts a caution in Capt. Feil's mind. He is reluctant to utter it, but is afraid to commit a silent default.

Feil. No gunner shall practice tracking fighters on those planes! Keep all guns stowed!

Warn. We wouldn't shoot at these guys, Captain.

Feil. Are you questioning the order, Warn?

Warn. No, Sir.

Feil. Good.

Taylor. They're slowin' down as they get closer. They are about fifteen miles out now. They're 500 feet higher than we are.

Voice (*in the headsets.*) Greetings, Capt. Feil. I'm Major Hill*! My wingman is Lieutenant Williams*! We're your Air-Sea-Rescue escort.

Feil. We're damn glad to see you guys.

Hill. Captain, we're gonna split and go past you. We'll turn around and come back beside you. I'll be on your left. Williams will be on your right.

Feil. Roger.

At half a mile out they accelerate into a shallow dive. I recognize full-throttle engine roar, as they zoom into a tight inside-loop behind us. At the top of the loop they do a 180° roll. They throttle back and settle slowly down to our altitude and speed.

Cotner. Did you see that? They did an Immelman! The historic aerobatic military maneuver evokes visions of dogfights among World War I biplanes. Visions stored in my subconscious brain since my pre-teen addiction to 1930's pulp fiction.

...It's 1918. I'm in my Spad. I'm on the German side of the lines, I have Ober Lieutenant Max Immelman in my sight. I pull the trigger. My gun jams. I grab my wooden mallet. I reach over my windscreen into the slipstream. I pound on my gun barrel. The gun backfires. The mallet sails toward my head. I duck...

I look up. Bullets are shredding my upper wing. I look back. A Fokker D-7 is on my tail. My God! It's Immelman. No wonder he has twenty-five kills.

I look out my window. It's First Lieutenant Williams. He's flyin' so slow, he opens his canopy. He salutes. I salute. I do an Immelman with my right hand. I give him a left thumb up. He wags his wings.

I sort things out...At last, I have an accurate reading on the wind. I have radio compass assurance that we're on course. The flight-plan flimsy has been invalid since we dropped our bombs. Nestel's charts alone won't get us to Tinian. I think of Jeannie and the babe. Some guys die in ditchings. I don't care whether John Nestel or Curtis Le May approve or not. I shall continue to use the laws of aerodynamics.

Applying these verities of nature, using Caldwell's eleven mph tail wind, I compute our maximum fuel-saving sea-level speed to be 149 mph.

Cotner. Captain Feil, I'm gonna slow us down to 149 mph indicated. That's just fifteen miles per hour above our stalling speed, at current gross weight. Is that O.K. with you?

Feil. It'll keep me awake but I can do it. I want to ask Major Hill if the P-47s can fly that slow. (*To Hill*) Major, my flight engineer wants to fly at 149 mph indicated. Can you guys fly that slow?

Hill. No, too close to stalling. If you need it, do it. We can fly slow circles out and around you.

Feil. Roger. We'll do it. (*To Cotner*.) Go ahead, Don. Slow us down.

Cotner. Roger.

I make the power settings. *I'm down to 1300 rpm. and twenty-six inches manifold pressure. The Engine Operation Limit Chart tells me not to fly at less than 1400 rpm and 33.5 inches m.p. The accompanying memo tells me that to fly at lower power will ruin the engines, by causing them to overheat. I've been flyin' for several hours at lower than recommended manifold pressure. Now, I'm also dropping below the rpm limit. I have faith that the engines will last till we get to Tinian. I don't care if they are ruined when I get there, even if some officer who outranks me puts a memo in my 201 file that says I'll have to pay the cost of four new engines.*

It looks to me like they are wrong about overheating anyway. I am having trouble keeping them warm enough.

The air is smooth. The engines are humming gently in perfect synchronization. I make the power settings. We slow... *Are we floating in the air? Are two P-47s drifting in orbit around us?...All is surreal...It's not such a bad dream...except that...will it never end?*

Every half hour I slow us one or two miles an hour. The eerie reverie endures. No one speaks. All four fuel gauges read zero, or so close to zero that it looks like zero.

Cotner. Captain Feil. Each of my fuel gauges is on zero. We've been instructed that they are not necessarily accurate. According to my log, we still have 434 gallons. I have no sure way to tell how it's distributed among the four engines.

Feil. Thanks, Don. I'm gonna keep on flyin'.

Cotner. Roger.

The drone of the orbiting "satellites" reassures us. *Why then does the smooth and synchronous sound of our own precious engines seem somehow alien? Or are our spirits intimidated by dread that their song may soon cease?...Starved in their throats....................*

Lt. Williams comes round my side of the plane, one more time.
No Three coughs...it hiccups...it coughs...it sputters....it coughs...it dies... its propeller windmills.

Cotner. Feather No Three!

Taylor. Roger!

He mashes the button. The prop slows. I shut off fuel. I turn off ignition. I close cowl flaps...The prop stops.

Instant thought! *Transfer fuel from other tanks*. Second thought, and immediate action prevails! *Set fuel-transfer valves. Energize pump. Transfer any fuel trapped in No. Three tank into No. Four.* Thought process: *I don't know how much fuel, if any, is in any tank. I do not want another engine to quit. I especially do not want No. Four to stop.*

Next I intuit new power settings for each remaining engine. I give 900 horsepower to No. Four, to stop our rapid descent. I give 500 h.p. to No. One and 600 to No. Two.

Cotner. Captain Feil, you may have to use a little trim for a while. I've guessed at the engine settings. I'll compute a trim-free balance of thrust as soon as I can.

Feil. Roger. It's not too bad now.

I get out of my seat. From across the deck, I retrieve Boeing's four-inch thick book, <u>B-29 Specifications and Technical Orders</u>. Back at my seat, I find the dimension, from the centerline of each engine to the longitudinal centerline of the fuselage. I want to maintain the total horsepower of the three engines at 2060, the same as it was before No. Three quit running. I want to set No. One at a minimum of 530 hp.

I have the information to set up the three equations relating to horizontal rotation of the airplane about the vertical axis of its center of gravity. I solve the equations for hp required for engines Two and Four.

Rationality grabs me. I'm taking the wrong approach...*I'll be getting too many horses out of number Four...It will run too high on the fuel consumption curve...number Four might soon run out of gas...leaving only two engines running...both on the same side...*

Cotner. Captain. I'm gonna set One, Two and Four at 690 horsepower each. You'll have to use a lot of rudder to maintain course. I don't have enough fuel to balance thrust via unequal horsepower settings.

Feil. Roger, Don. Will do.

Cotner. We'll see what air speed we get.

Feil. Sounds good.

...

I analyze fuel use. I check fuel remaining. I monitor gross weight. It is a continuous rigorous audit...yet...I have too much time...Too much damn time to think.

I am not a Pilot. My knowledge of what it takes to maneuver a plane is intellectual. There is no learned sense of touch, of movement or of reflex and equilibrium stored in my bones, muscles, nerves or brain.

Back at McCook, Captain Feil once asked me to take the wheel-yoke and rudder pedals for five minutes. I was anxious. The 9th Group's forty-five aircrews shared training time in only three B29s. Our mechanics were learning the B-29 too. The three planes seemed seldom ready for flight, so I wanted Feil and Taylor to have as much time at the controls as they could possibly acquire... Is this the source of my fear?.I know Captain Feil is an excellent pilot but can any pilot land a B29 if an engine quits at a critical instant before contact?

I visualize us miraculously making it to Tinian...*We are in line with the runway...We approach...Captain Feil holds his fifteen-foot altitude above the rim of the cliff...No. Four dies...the right wing dips...the plane drops...Captain Feil pulls the wheel firm left and hard back...the plane drops...it smashes into the cliff...we die...the crumpled mass of aluminum and gore falls to the coral below...*

Captain Feil should set us down on the water, while we have enough fuel to power the last-second surge of speed needed to raise a dragging tail, to lift a drooping nose, or to level a dipping wing.

I've got to survive this war. I have to go home. I want to love, honor and obey Jeanie. I want to get acquainted with our baby. I want to love, and to raise, the babe. I must support my little family.

I know PBY's are slow but I hope to hell ours arrives soon. Maybe then Captain Feil will decide to ditch.

. . .

Taylor is faithful on watch. A speck appears in the southern sky. It expands into a silhouette. He recognizes the distinct form of a twin-engine high-winged flying boat.

Taylor. PBY, 12 o'clock at 1500 feet!

We expend pent tension in cheers of elation.

After a long, long while, the PBY is near.

A new headphone voice. Captain Feil. This is Commander Easton*, U.S. Navy. What is your situation?

Feil. Hi, Commander. We're very low on fuel. I want to fly straight to North Field on Tinian, and land as soon as possible. If we can't fly that far, I want to ditch on course. I hope you will land on the water, and get us aboard your plane right away. Can you do that?

Easton. Aye. We will do it. We've saved three B-29 crews. Do you and your crew know your airplane escape procedure?

Feil. Roger, or shall I say, aye, aye.

Easton. No formal protocol. Whatever is easy. We've been watchin' the sea since takeoff. Near Tinian the sea is rough...fifteen foot swells. They're only about ten feet here. Ditching, and rescue, would be easier sooner than later.

Cotner. (*Silently.*) *Thank you, Commander Easton. I want to abandon this plane in the ocean, and fly to Tinian in yours. I guess you land in Saipan Bay, though...but...That's O.K.....Close enough.*

Feil. I think I can make it to Tinian. I'm gonna try. Thanks for standing ready to save us, if we need it.

Easton. It's your call.

Feil. Aye, aye. (*To himself.*) *That's what Col. Wright said yesterday when he was briefing us Airplane Commanders. He had statistics on the 21st Bomber Command, all Wings. So far, twenty-seven B-29s have ditched .Of all crew members and passengers, thirty-five have been seriously injured and nineteen have been killed. One B-29 sank before anyone aboard could get out .I haven't told the crew. I'm damn sure not gonna tell `em now.*

Our slow-flying four-plane "squadron" proceeds toward Tinian.

Cotner. Malnove, with ten-foot waves, you've got plenty of whitecaps to get drift readings on, haven't you?

Malnove. Roger, Don. I'll keep you posted.

Cotner. Thanks. I hope we never again have a head wind that we keep callin' a tail wind.

Malnove. Me too.

...

We're flying at Capt. Feil's chosen 500-foot altitude. The P-47s are with us. The PBY is at 1,000 feet. I check, check and recheck my calculations. I look hard at my fuel gauges.

Cotner. Captain Feil, we're out of gas. My log says zero. The gauges say zero. I don't know what the hell One, Two and Four are runnin' on.

Feil. Well, as long as we're gettin' some thrust, I'm gonna keep flyin'. (*To the crew.*) Everybody except Schultz get into ditching position.

Crew. (*A chorus*) Roger.

Feil. Schultz, check my contact with Commander Easton. Then get ready to ditch.

Malnove comes back to my station. I get up. He sits in my seat. He slides far left. I sit at his right. It's crowded but my right hand is free if I need it. Our backs are supported by the sheet of one-fourth inch-thick steel armor plate behind my seat.

Caldwell and Schultz sit on the deck with their backs against the gun turrets. In the rear compartment, Connor and Warn sit with their backs against the bomb bay bulkhead. Calhoun, Smith and Richardson have their backs to the upper turret. Those men who sit sans intercom connection are in voice contact with a neighbor who is "plugged-in." Feil and Taylor depend on"four-point" seat belts to halt their bodies' forward impetus, if the plane is halted by impact with the sea.

The cramped closeness of crewmates comforts, but it inspires little conversation. Like athletes preparing for a championship match, I mentally rehearse. *Unscrew the three- inch diameter knurled knob at each corner of the window. Open the window. Follow Malnove out the window. Inflate my life jacket. Swim to the wing. Climb onto the wing. Dive off the trailing edge. Swim to one of the two life rafts, which will be inflated in the water because Schultz in the front and Calhoun in the rear, will have pulled the "release-handles" before leaving station. Grab an oar. Row to the aid of non-simmers, Calhoun and Warn, and help anyone in need.*

Those of us on intercom report our readiness to Capt. Feil. He acknowledges. Feil contacts Easton*, Hill* and Williams*.

Feil. Gentlemen, we're in ditching position. The Egineer, the Pilot and I are the only men aboard who are at our stations. The Pilot and I are the only two who can see forward. We will depend on you to help us find Tinian. Give us all the warning you can, on all conditions: weather, heading, E.T.A., and sightings.

Easton. Roger, Captain. You look good from here. How's your fuel?

Feil. My Engineer tells me I don't have any but I'm gonna fly as long as enough propellers turn to keep me in the air.

Easton. Trust us to do what we can, Captain.

I run through the escape procedure again. I speak to Malnove.

Cotner. Paul, check those knobs at each corner of my window. Make sure they are not rusted shut.

Malnove. They each turn easily. Shouldn't we open the window now?

Cotner. No. It would cause drag and the closing mechanism is designed to add structural integrity, which might help prevent collapse of the fuselage from the stresses of the sea landing.

Malnove. O.K.

We resume our own thoughts. Mine are of Jeannie and the babe.

Easton. Captain Feil, my Navigator, Lieutenant Roberts*, has a good fix on Tinian. His E.T.A. is fifteen minutes. Keep on flyin'.

Feil. Thanks.

Cotner. *Fifteen minutes?...Oh God...I know there is fuel. The engines are running...but how much fuel? I guess each has ninety-five gallons..Why do I guess ninety-five? Is it because I hope they have that much?*

I calculate gallons-per-mile of fuel-use one more time. I decide to cut power again.

Cotner. Captain Feil, I'm gonna make new power settings on One, Two and Four. I want to make whatever fuel we have take us as far as it will.

Feil. What's our stalling speed? We don't get airborne on take-off till 144 miles per hour.

Cotner. We take off with a gross weight of nearly 140,000 lbs. Our weight now is only about 70,000 lbs. Even at this relatively low weight, the B-29 has a high wing loading compared to most airplanes. Boeing lists stalling at 129 mph.

Feil. O.K. Let's try it. Do you think I should use flaps on the landing?

Cotner. I don't have a feel for it. What do you think?

Feil. The pilots' manual says to use flaps but my intuition says no flaps.

Cotner. The manual probably doesn't consider a condition like ours. My intuition says no flaps too. Flaps cause a hell of a lot of drag.

Feil. O.K. I won't use flaps.

At the new power setting the indicated air speed decreases two miles per hour. The altimeter needle flickers.

Feil. Don, I don't think we can hold altitude at this speed.

Cotner. We'll be ready to land in about fourteen minutes. If this is too early to letdown, I can increase the power. If this letdown is flyable, it will conserve a little bit of fuel.

Feil. Don't change it. This may be just what I was looking for.

Cotner. Roger

There's nothing to do now but wait. We're coming down in thirteen minutes or less. Where will it be?...In the ocean?...Against the cliff?...On the runway? Our survival chances are fair, zero and good...Is my clock stuck...or is Einstein right about time?

Easton. Captain Feil. I've contacted North Field tower. Visibility is perfect. The wind is ten miles per hour from the east. I presume you want to land against the wind.

Feil. No. For once in my life I want to land with a tail wind.

Easton. O.K. Do you want me to guide you to the east side of the island?

Feil. Yes. I'll do my own runway line-up. (*To North Field tower.*) This is Captain Feil. I'll be there in twelve minutes. Which runway shall I use? I'm gonna land downwind

Colonel Wright. Captain Feil, thank God you're still in the air. Use any runway you choose. The whole field is yours. We've got fire trucks, rescue crews, and ambulances standing by.

Feil. Thanks, Colonel. I hope we make it. We're ready to ditch if we have to.

• • •

Malnove and I watch the clock. After a while he says...

Malnove. Don, in case we don't make it, I'm glad I got to fly with you.

Cotner. Me too, Paul. I've been hopin' Captain Feil will ditch. I think we'll make it now.

...

Easton. Captain Feil! Land ho! Seaman Wills* sees Tinian in his telescope.

Feil. Hey, crew. A PBY crewman has Tinian in sight. Taylor and I don't see it yet.

I watch my instruments. Cylinder head temperatures on One, Two and Four are too low. There's nothing I can do about it...*Engines are not supposed to be able to run if they are this cold...Will they keep going?...How many separate miracles will the fates allow us?...*

...

I look around to give Capt. Feil a thumb up...*He's too busy...*

...

We're on the approach. The landing gear is down. Capt. Feil is letting down a little faster. I turn and raise partly out of my seat. I look out the nose. I see Feil is centered on Runway A. I sit down. I nudge Malnove.

Cotner. It looks good, Paul.

...

I watch instruments...

Feil. POWER!

He shoves all throttles full forward. I do the same with turbo-boost levers. The plane leaps upward. No. One quits. The plane drops. It bounces hard. It drops again. It bounces. It drops. It bounces in an attenuating sequence of jounces. The tires and gear hold. We roll forward. I look out my window. We're on Runway A. The crew yells. *Jeannie, I made it.*

Feil taxis toward our parking stand. I expect Two and Four to quit. They don't. We park. We rush out of the plane. We kiss the good earth. Hill and Williams buzz us. Easton gives us a wing wag.
Szarko arrives in a jeep.

Szarko. I waited an hour and a half. I gave up and went back to my hut.

He hugs each of us. He pats his airplane. He sobs.

Szarko. How did you guys fly so long?

He climbs to the wing. He measures fuel with his dipstick. He stands. He yells down to us.
Szarko. There's no fuel in these tanks. I poked into every corner. I can't find a drop.
Colonel Huglin and Major Chappel arrive in Huglin's jeep. They shake hands all around.

Chappel. Lt. Cotner, you did a damn good job of engineering the fuel.

Cotner. Thank you, Major. Just lucky, I guess.

.What I don't tell the Major is that I made a great error by making corrections for tail-wind, when no one aboard knew we had head-wind instead. Nor do I tell him that in the end, flying by the laws of aerodynamics, instead of by flimsies and charts, got us to Tinian on fumes.

Blitz Four, Kobe

15 March 1945, 0900 hours:

Our crew is in a debriefing session. It's the one we missed yesterday because of our late arrival. Major Morris Riley, 9th Group Combat Intelligence Officer, heads the team.

We tell our story. The officers congratulate each of us for being alive. Claude answers seventy-seven questions. They don't know what to ask me. I appreciate the opportunity to keep my individualistic approach to cruise control off the record. I've heard and read a bit of the history of military flight. I know the experience of Billy Mitchell, and his ardent advocacy of air power. I know that a genuine genius-hero can be scorned, vilified and persecuted by men mighty of rank, but weak of vision.

I have not yet explained to Captain Feil that I used my own methods of cruise control to accomplish our miraculous return from Osaka. I resolve to confess my "sin", to explain my method, and to receive Feil's absolution in the form of permission to go and "sin", whenever I think it best.

One purpose of debriefing is to pass along information learned from successful crews.

Major Riley. Three other crews had trouble with the wind. Captain Archie Nash's crew is one. Lt. George Bennett is Navigator. Bennett was lucky. Major Nole, 9th Group Navigator, was aboard as a passenger.

Cotner. *Good passenger to have,*

Riley. Jack Nole has 700 hours in Pacific skies on `17s and `24s.

Caldwell. Wow!

Cotner. *Outstanding!*

Riley. Nole talked via radio to Lt. Ed Smith, Navigator on Captain Maurice Ashland's B-29 flyin' nearby. Ed Smith said he <u>had</u> taken a drift reading at the Japanese coast and found a thirty mile per hour head wind. He had to let down to find a more favorable wind.

I restrain my impulse to stub my palm against my skull. I look at Caldwell. Caldwell looks at me. *Is he a little shriveled?...I feel shriveled... Are we thinkin' the same thought?...Is self-reliance a good trait in an airman? Yes. Excellent...Can ego kill you? Yes, if you fail to rely on your comrades when you should.*

The debriefers dismiss us. We go to brunch. We learn there is no mission tonight. Capt. Feil grants my request for a post-brunch conference. I run to our tent. I run back with my aerodynamics text, my engine operation charts, my slide rule, pencil and paper.
Over after-brunch coffee, I explain my cruise control system.

As an Army Air Corps Cadet Flight-school graduate, Feil knows the rudiments of aerodynamics. He has 353 hours of four-engine pilot time in B-17s and `24s. On those craft he had to pilot the plane, plus operate the engines. He knows well that wind affects range.

Feil. Don, that's a beautiful system.

Cotner. Thank you, Sir.

Feil. You've got a reputation among the Airplane Commanders. They're all askin' me how you did it. Now I know enough to talk a little bit about it. You have my permission to fly your own way anytime you wish. I have confidence in you, Don.

Cotner. I can only do it on the homebound leg of our missions. We'll have to fly by the flimsies to coordinate our target arrival times with the other airplanes.

Feil. O.K.

We go to our tent. I write to Jean, and to my folks. It's my turn to read our circulating copy of Forever Amber. It's a novel set in historic England, i.e., plague, London fire, et al. We hear it's a best seller.

Amber, a poor orphaned peasant, is energetic, intelligent and beautiful. At age fifteen she learns the joys of sexual love. By applying her natural attributes and by spreading joy among men, she attains wealth and influence. Her story is in continuous demand among us maximally-ripe, sexually-dispossessed young airmen.

I read till lunchtime. After lunch I play cribbage with Ken Lobdell. I've never won. I lose now.

I go to supper with Caldwell and Malnove and from there to the movie. We see "A Song to Remember", about Frederick Chopin and his lover, George Sand, a famous French (female) novelist.

We are tired at bedtime. We hit the sack early. Themes of the "A-Flat Polonaise" flow from Tinian's distant open-air theaters. Their notes float upon tropical night breezes. Their melodies waft into our tents.*Is this paradisiacal?...Yes...Can I stay awake?......zzz...*

16 March 1945:

After brunch I read that we have an 1800 briefing. I see that gunners have a 1400 training session scheduled. I presume it is for aircraft recognition. *Have the Japs got a new fighter plane?*

I play catch with Bill Duft. He checks out a catcher's mitt. He wants to see my "stuff". My fastball isn't fast, but it does "slide" a bit. After I get warned up, one hits him on the wrist. He yells, "No more in-shoots". I start throwin' "out-drops". They break slower, but farther, than my "in-shoots". One hits Duft on the wrist. He quits.

1700: Briefing. The arrow on the map points to Kobe.

Colonel Huglin. Greetings gentlemen. General Le May congratulates you on your success at Osaka. He is pleased to report that reconnaissance photos show ten point two square miles of the city are burned to the ground.

Cotner. *Does this mean we will never have to go there again?*

Huglin. Your performance made me proud. Every 9th Group plane took off. Each completed the mission. No aborts.

Cotner. *Hey, I'm a little proud too.*

Huglin. Our leadership role was perfectly executed.

Cotner. *Captains Curry, Shenefiel, Chapman, McClintock and Feil were great. I'm proud to be on Feil's lead crew.*

Huglin. We got in easy, and out quickly. No 9th Group plane suffered flak or fighter damage.

Cotner. *I'm so proud I'm conceited.*

Huglin. General Le May is sending us to Kobe tonight. It will be another low-level fire blitz.

Cotner. *I wish General Le May could elevate* his *self-esteem by granting us more altitude to maneuver in. This will be our fourth ground-grazer in seven nights. That's every other night. Can we keep this up?*

Huglin. The Kobe operation will be similar to that of the previous blitz missions; however, we shall employ a new defensive procedure.

Cotner. *Night fighter escort?*

Huglin. Intelligence suspects that the Japs have radar. They may employ it to aim searchlights and anti-aircraft guns. The Germans do.

Cotner. *Somethin's workin' for them.*

Huglin. Captain Rogan. In your 8th Air Force tour, did your B-17 crew use chaff against the Germans?

Rogan. (*Airplane Commander, Dave Rogan*). We never flew at night. The Brits took the night runs. We tried chaff on daylight flak. I think chaff was British Intelligence fantasy.

Cotner. *Careful, old Dave. Don't be too much of a curmudgeon. You want to make Major.*

Huglin. Thanks, Dave. Here's Lieutenant Charles Carpenter, the 9th Group's new Radar Officer. He'll tell us about chaff.

Carpenter. (*Stands. He is replacement for Major Conley, who was killed 9 March when Captain Keene ditched*). Chaff is strips of aluminum foil an inch wide. We use varying lengths. We try to bracket the Jap's radar-broadcast wavelengths. The strips reflect the waves to the receiving unit. Receivers are fooled. They sense many airplanes. They cannot recognize a true image.

Cotner. *Okay...Okay...Hooray.*

Carpenter. Chaff works on radar guided searchlights and guns. The conflicting reports about effectiveness originate because some weapons are radar guided and some are not.

Cotner. *Let's throw it at the Japs.*

Carpenter. The gunners have been trained on how to put chaff overboard. It will go out through the reconnaissance camera-port in the deck of the aft unpressurized section.

Cotner. *I was wondering how we were supposed to throw foil out the bomb bay, into the slipstream.*

Huglin. Major Luschen, give us the procedure.

Luschen. Thank you Colonel Huglin. On each plane, the three-man chaff squad shall consist of the Left and Right Side Gunners, plus the Central Fire Control Gunner. The latter shall be Squad Leader. In action, the leader shall assess the situation and keep the side gunners on post, or ask permission of the Airplane Commander to send one Gunner back to stuff chaff out of the camera-port.

When a Gunner is stuffing chaff, the C.F.C. Gunner shall cover fighter attacks from above, plus attacks leading into the absent gunner's side. The Airplane Commander can, of course, initiate or veto the use of chaff. There will be a cardboard box full of chaff, near the camera-port in each plane. Good luck.

Cotner. *Hey, it might work.*

• • •

Ashland, Brown and Spaargaren fail to leave their parking stands for takeoff due to mechanical problems. Thirty-four 9th Group planes get into the air.

Captain Bertagnoli, 1st Squadron, leads this typical blitz mission in a single-file cruise toward Kobe. Captain Feil leads the 99th Squadron. Feil's "lead" is a paper title. Our portion of the "file" is sandwiched between the 1st and the 5th Squadrons.

Capt. Curry is the first Airplane Commander to abort. Captains Scheaffer, Collins and Bowers also turn back along the way.

• • •

We start over Kobe. The 9th Group's thirty-one planes are spliced into the middle of the 20th Air Force's long, long line. The central city is blazing brightly by the time Bertagnoli leads us over the untouched outskirts. Capt. Feil heads for a dark spot on the edge of the fire.

Feil. Open the bomb bay doors.

Malnove. Roger, Captain.

We hear and feel the shock as hydraulically actuated doors snap into the lock-open position. Brilliant, blinding instant glare flares into every interior space of our plane.

Cotner. (*Stricken brain yelling inside his skull*). *Oh God! They hit us in the bomb bay before we could get rid of our bombs!*

Malnove. Bombs away!

Silence among the crew.

Schultz. Front bomb bay clear. Doors shut.

Connor. Rear bomb bay clear. Doors shut.

Cotner. *See, Don. You weren't panicked. You only thought you were.*

The Jap searchlight crew holds us fast, or is it radar that's got us? Concussions from antiaircraft shell explosions bat us around. Spent flak shrapnel rains on the skin of our roof.

Calhoun. Capt., there are no night fighters out there. Can I send Connor out to stuff chaff?

Capt. Feil. Yes.

Calhoun. Connor, go get some damn chaff in the air quick.

Connor unplugs his intercom connection. He opens the spring-loaded snaps that fasten his parachute to his one-man life-raft seat cushion. He grabs his flashlight. He rushes out the rear door into the unpressurized compartment.

The box is open. Connor opens the camera-port. He stuffs chaff. Everything goes black. The searchlight beam releases us. The gunners watch a 40,000 candlepower concentration of blue-white lumens dance a weird searching course through the ash-soiled soot of a saturated sky.

Connor. Hey! The chaff worked. (*He then remembers to plug his mike and earphones into the intercom jack. He repeats*). Hey! The chaff worked.

Warn. Yeah. We dang well noticed.

Feil. Good job, Connor. Stay out there and be ready to throw out chaff again, if we need it.

Connor. Roger, Captain.

Feil. Caldwell, I'm going left to avoid the smoke cloud. Give me the escape route heading, when I ask for it.

Caldwell. Roger. Smitty's got me a great radar picture. Kobe Harbor and Osaka Bay are beautiful.

Cotner. Be sure to get a drift reading, Caldwell.

Malnove. Tracer's comin' at us from two o'clock high.

Connor. Tracer's crashing through the plane out here.

Feil. Get back to your gun Connor. Forget chaff.

Connor. Roger, I'm comin' in.

Calhoun. The fighter came under us. He's flyin' an arc. Can you see him goin' away, Rich?

Richardson. I saw his exhaust, when he came out from under us. I've lost him now.

Feil. Give me 230 miles per hour, Don.

Cotner. Roger, Captain.

Feil. Make it 240.

Cotner. Roger.

Caldwell. Captain Feil, we're out here over Kobe harbor. We'll have to go way around, behind the smoke, to get onto the briefed escape route. I can give you an over-water shortcut to the Pacific, if you want it.

Feil. Good, Claude, give me the heading.

Caldwell. Roger. 177°.

Feil. Roger.

Caldwell. We're cruisin' down the center of Osaka Bay. Bear left eleven degrees. We'll split the Kijan Strait.

Feil. Yeah. I see it. Why the hell don't the Japs use blackouts?

Caldwell. Maybe it's dangerous for ships.

Feil. You'd think the ships could damn well sit out the bomb raid.

We enter the narrow strait. Searchlights and flak-bursts come at us from each bank of the narrow strait.

Feil. Give me emergency power!

Cotner. Roger.

I shift fuel-mix from lean to rich. I advance throttle. I increase turbo boost and prop-pitch. I don't take time to synchronize the engines. With 2,000 throbbing horses beating a different pulse from each engine, we flee at 310 mph above Kijan Strait.

Richardson. The goddamn night-fighter is back. He's firin' tracers at us. I can't see him in the dark. Wish to hell we could turn those damn lights off.

The flak ceases. The night fighter flies into the searchlight beams.

Richardson. I see the son-of-a-bitch...I've got him in my sight.

He squeezes the trigger. His twin fifty caliber machine guns and his twenty-millimeter cannon crash in cacophony. Alien tracers smash into his bullet-proof slab of a rear window. The slab cracks and crazes. It does not yield. Twenty-millimeter shells from Richardson's canon collide with the fighter. The shells and the fighter explode. Fighter debris splatters our rudder, our elevators and Richardson's compartment. Through his veined and scarred rear window, Richardson watches the Jap plane's ruined engine fly toward him. He hears jagged iron rip the skin of the B-29's tapered tail, barely beneath his butt. He feels the chill of slipstream-induced draft in his loins. It trembles his thorax. It shakes his shoulders. It rattles his skull. It addles his thought waves in their crazed quest for rationality.

Richardson. *(Thinking) Did I get a fighter?...Am I dead?...Am I dreaming?... Am I alive?...Am I freezing? Am I freezing or am I scared, or both .Are my eardrums ruptured?...*

Calhoun. I saw it, Rich. I can swear it's yours!

Crew. Congratulations, Rich!

Richardson. What?

Crew. (*Shouting in unison*). CONGRATULATIONS!

Richardson. Ouch! Thanks. I don't know if I ever want to get another one. He damn near got me, after I killed him dead.

Feil. Hey Rich, you saved the whole damn crew. You're our hero.

Richardson. Thank you, Captain.

We escape Kijan. We've been at emergency power our allotted three minutes.

Cotner. I gotta reduce power.

Feil. Give us as much speed as you can.

Cotner. Roger.

I set up 1800 horses each engine, and at 295 mph we fly above Kii channel to the free Pacific air. Feil orders 220 mph. I reduce power. As we fly by the beacon on the spiked point of Cape Murota on Shikoku's east coast, Caldwell gets a reliable drift reading.

We set course for Tinian with a six mph tail wind. Using Caldwell's wind and the laws of aerodynamics, which saved us on our last mission, I compute a maximum range cruise. I set up the power. We've spent too much fuel on extra speed, but I am confident I can get us home.
Capt. Feil gets each crewman's report: Excitement?...Enough...Injuries?... None...The airplane?...Flak holes and bullet holes...Systems and equipment?... All apparently working well....Except...

Richardson. There's a hole in the plane under me, Captain. I can't see it but I don't think it's too bad. Can I come up to the rear pressurized compartment, sir?

Feil. Roger, Rich.

We feel relaxed and safe. We silently ponder the new question. *Is it better to have every gunner man his weapon, or to deploy one gunner to chaff duty*? I thank God Captain Feil will make the decisions.

We're the last plane on the ground again at Tinian, but we're not so late that we draw a worried welcome-crew greeting.

The debriefing team is still in session. They tell us most aircrews believe that chaff is effective. They say a few 9th Group B-29s were attacked by night fighters, but none seriously. Richardson does not laugh. He tells the debriefers he could not identify the plane he shot. They tell him he'll be sure to get credit, with Calhoun as witness.

The standing joke among gunners is that "credit for a fighter won't get you rank, money or a medal but it'll be a great thing to tell your grandchildren". The sequitur is: "By the time you're a grandfather you'll be claimin' you shot down twenty fighters, left-handed."
We go to the tent. We're soon in the sack.

Again I contemplate the one I left at home. *It was exciting, Jeannie. After the war, I'll share my adventures. I might even write a book, so our children and grandchildren will know what the old guy did in the great war. I love you...*

Blitz Five - Bomblets Away

18 March 1945, 1900 briefing:

The arrow on the map shows us it will be Nagoya redux tonight.

Col. Huglin. Greetings gentlemen. General Le May likes what you did at Kobe. I like what you did. I'm proud of the Ninth Bomb Group.

Cotner. *Nagoya...Nagoya...Is it seven days since our crew had to abort the first Nagoya blitz because of a fire in No. Three?I still don't want to burn the city of the song but I damn sure prefer to burn down Nagoya than to have another fire aboard the airplane.*

Huglin. Tokyo, Nagoya, Osaka.,Kobe: Japan's four largest cities. Each is a huge industrial center. Each is hurt bad but parts of each are still standing. Tonight we will burn down some more of Nagoya. We'll show the Japanese that we shall keep bombing and burning until they understand that surrender is the only thing that can save them.

Cotner. *I hope to hell they see it soon.*

Huglin. Col. Luschen, give us the particulars on tonight's mission.

Luschen. It's incendiaries again. Single file again. The 313th Wing will be about three quarters of the way back in the line. The 9th Group will be in the last third of the Wing. Our altitude will be 8,500 feet.

Cotner. *That high, huh? Does Le May know that?*

Luschen. Lieutenant Carpenter, Group Radar Officer has a report.

Carpenter. There will again be a box of foil strips aboard each plane. Whether you use foil or not will be up to each Aircraft Commander.

Cotner. *To stuff, or not to stuff?...*

Carpenter. Most crews report that they like the way it worked at Kobe. A few think it's better to keep all guns manned.

Cotner. *Whatever.*

Luschen. Capt. Moore, 9th Group Armament Officer, has a surprise for us.

Cotner. *Any surprise in the briefing room is not a surprise of joy.*

Luschen. When you see what's in the bomb bays, you'll think you're deliverin' toys but the Japs won't think it's funny.

Cotner. *No one will laugh...Remember?...Sherman?...*

Luschen. Capt. Moore.

Moore. In the past eight days, the 20th Air Force has dropped 21,639,001 pounds of incendiary bombs on Japan. That's 111 more pounds of IBs than all of the Army Air Corps Armament Officers of Guam, Saipan and Tinian reported on their total manifests before we bombed Tokyo.

Cotner. *Do Armament Officers get letters in their personnel files for faulty, or fraudulent, accounts?...No...I retract the question...That's damn good counting.*

Moore. Our friends of the U.S. Navy have saved the day.

Cotner. *Is he gettin' ready to say they made this mission possible?...Is that what Navy friends do for Air Corps flyers?*

Moore. They made this mission possible. A U.S.S. Armament carrier happens to be in port at Guam. It did not bring us 500 lb. incendiary bombs but guess what it did have in its hold?

Cotner. *I'm not gonna guess...I might be namin' my own poison.*

Moore. An M-13 is a small incendiary bomb. A single M-13 weighs seventeen lbs., is twenty-three inches long and is nine inches in diameter.

Cotner. *All that big, Huh?*

Moore. We don't know for whom these bombs were intended but General Le May persuaded the Navy to let the 20th Air Force have them.

Cotner. *What for?...Is Connor gonna stuff them out the camera port?*

Moore. The U.S. Cincinnati is moored in Saipan Harbor. It's fitted out as a floating machine shop.

Cotner. *Yeah. We know. They're the guys who rebuild our worn-out Dodge-built R-3350 engines. It's too bad Dodge doesn't have any machinists as good as these guys.*

Moore. The Navy machine shop worked thirty-six hours straight, manufacturing 5,600 cables so we could fasten these little bombs into B-29 bomb racks. They cut quarter-inch steel cable into seven-foot, three-inch lengths. They swaged a six-inch loop on each end.

Cotner. *Don't tell us Rube Goldberg is General Le May's Armament Officer.*

Moore. When you look in the bomb bay, you'll think "Major Rube Goldberg" is the 20th Air Force's Armament Officer.

Cotner. *I can hardly wait to get down to the flight line.*

Moore. At each bomb bay's four bomb-rack stanchions, a pair of cables is latched to bomb shackles at the bottom and at the top. Each draped arc of a cable-pair is stuffed taut by forty-four M-13s.

Cotner. *Sounds more like Col. Mickey Mouse's work than Major Goldberg's to me.*

Moore. The good news is that your total bomb load will be only 6,084 pounds.

Cotner. *He's right. In case of a mechanical malfunction during takeoff, we will be slightly less dead at 127,000 pounds gross weight, than we would be at 137,000, but I feel devalued to know that my life will be at risk for 6,084 pounds of jelly instead of the usual 16,000 pounds. What if we had no bombs left anywhere at all in the Mariana Islands, except three M-13s? Would General Le May assign a B-29 crew to drop them on Tokyo?...Two M-13s?... One?...*

Huglin. Thank you, Captain Moore. Captain Brown, what kind of weather will we have?

Brown. You'll have clear weather over the target tonight, men, and a tail wind on the way home at the 8,500 foot bombing altitude. There will be a weather front 100 miles south of Iwo, and another one 200 miles south of Japan.

Cotner. *Doesn't sound too bad...Shall I believe that he might know?*

The G.I. truck stops at the Hon. Spy's parking stand. We hop off. We sprint for a bomb bay view. We look. We laugh.

Malnove. Hey. Don't laugh at my bombs, guys.

Warn. I'm dang well sorry I laughed, Lieutenant, but your little bomblets are so dang cute.

Caldwell. Yeah, Malnove, they don't look too damn bright, but they sure are cute.

Smith. Did anybody test this rig? What if we take these goddamn ugly-little-duckling bastards all the way to Japan, and have to bring `em all the way back, because we couldn't make `em leave their mama?

Feil. O.K., men. It's twenty-one minutes to take-off. Get your pre-flights done and get aboard. We don't want to be late.

Cotner. *I'll be damned. Capt. Feil doesn't want a letter in his personnel file either.*

. . .

We've been in the air two hours and twenty minutes. Most of that time Malnove has been in the bomb bays unwinding a cute little propeller in the cute little nose of each of his cute little babies. Thus he has set each little bomblet to explode 500 feet above Nagoya. They may be small but to the Nagoyans they will be nasty little monsters.

On his way from the bomb bays to his station in the nose, he lurches into my lap as we hit the rough air of our first weather front. I save him from hurt, and save myself also, by catching him in my arms.

For fifty minutes the air is rough and the visibility is poor. Captain Feil is busy. Finally we reach calm air. He can see for sure that he is still in place in the 9th Group's line of B-29s.

. . .

We hit the second weather front. It's rougher than the first. Again, Captain Feil gets us through.

. . .

We approach from Nagoya Bay. The city lies ahead.

Malnove. My God, what a fire. The damn little bomblets are demons.

Taylor. They're better than real bombs.

...

Feil. Open bomb bay doors.

Malnove. Roger.

Feil. Drop `em when you think best, Malnove.

Malnove. Bombs away!

Connor. Rear bomb bay clear. Bomb bay doors closed.

Schultz. Front bomb bay clear except that the right rear bombs are still hangin' in the cables.

Feil. Try `em again, Paul.

Malnove. Roger. (*He hits number four switch. He hits the salvo switch).* Did they go, Schultz?

Schultz. No they're still hangin'.

Feil. Shut the doors, Paul. We've got to get outta here.

Malnove. Roger.

Schultz. Front bomb bay doors closed.

Feil. What's the heading?

Caldwell. 180° for ten minutes.

Feil. Roger. Take us east to fifty miles offshore before you give me the heading to Tinian. I want to get clear of Japan. We damn sure won't think those goddamn bomblets are cute or funny if we get hit while they're still in the plane. (*To Cotner*). Take us up to 9500 feet in our fastest climb.

Cotner. Roger.

I give him 1800 hp per engine. We climb at 750 feet per hour. That's fast for us. I watch cylinder head temperatures.

We reach 9500 feet. Feil levels off.

Feil. Caldwell, give me the shortest course to get offshore.

Caldwell. Roger. Ninety-six degrees.

Feil. Give me emergency power, Don.

Cotner. Roger.

With 8,000 horses pulling strong, we escape the evil island empire.

Cotner. It's three minutes, Captain. I've got to cut power.

Feil. Roger. 220 mph is good.

Cotner. Roger.

. . .

Caldwell. We're fifty miles out, Captain. The course to Tinian is 169°.

Feil. Roger. (*To Schultz*). Take a look at our bomblets. How are they ridin'? Leave the bomb bay lights on.

Schultz. Roger, Captain. (*He turns the lights on.*) Captain! One of the bombs has fallen out. It's lyin' on the bomb bay doors.

Feil. Malnove, I'd like to open the bomb bay doors, and get the hell rid of it. Any reason we shouldn't.?

Malnove. No.

Feil. Go ahead then. (*To Schultz*). Keep an eye on it.

Schultz. Roger. (*The doors start to open*). It's out, Captain.

Feil. Close the doors, Malnove.

Malnove. Roger.

Schultz. Front bomb bay doors closed.

Feil. Connor, check that rear bomb bay just to make sure there's nothin' "cute" lyin' around.

Connor. Roger, Captain. (*He turns the bomb bay lights on. He opens the door. He sticks his head into the bomb bay. He searches*). There are no bombs back here, Sir.

Feil. Roger. Thanks, Connor. (*To Schultz*). Check the front bomb bay again.

Schultz. Roger, Captain. (*He performs the search routine*). They're all still in the cables, Sir.

. . .

Feil. When will we hit that northern cold front, Caldwell?

Caldwell. I don't know which direction, or how fast, the front is movin'. I think we may be hittin' rough air in about half an hour.

Feil. Thanks. Comin' north, that was mean turbulence. We'll have bomblets yawing, pitching, rolling, careening, colliding all over that damn bomb bay. (*To Malnove*). Paul.

Malnove. Yes, Captain.

Feil. We need to get rid of those bombs.

Malnove. They won't go off, Sir, until they've fallen 8300 feet.

Feil. Can you guarantee that?

Malnove. No, Sir.

Feil. Do you know anything about M-13s?

Malnove. No, Sir, I never heard of them before this mission.

Feil. Neither did I. How do we know they're not left over from World War I?

Malnove. Well, they damned sure burned Nagoya.

Feil. Yeah, and they might burn us. They were loaded by hand, and they can be unloaded the same way.

Cotner. Let me check the fuses for those bomb release circuits, Captain. I can take a look at Paul's switches too. Maybe I can make the electrical system work.

Feil. O.K., but hurry it up. We're approaching' the front.

Cotner. Roger.

The fuses look good. I replace them with new ones anyway.

Malnove opens the bomb bay. He toggles each of his four switches.

Schultz. Nothin' happened.

Malnove pulls the "salvo" lever.

Schultz. Nothin'.

I crawl up to Malnove's station. I check the wiring and the switches. It's all working.

Cotner. Control circuit wiring and switches are O.K., Captain. The malfunction, if electrical, is in the power circuit.

Feil. Can you "jump" a solenoid?

Cotner. Well, Captain, I'd have to go out into the bomb bay. You saw the four cable loops holdin' the damn bombs. Two at the top and two at the bottom. Each loop is secured in a solenoid-actuated shackle. Paul's electric circuits can release the four shackles simultaneously. I can only actuate the solenoids one at a time if I "jump" them manually.

Feil. But you <u>can</u> do it, can't you?

Cotner. Yes. But the bombs wouldn't fall straight down. They might fall on me. I'd be lyin' on that nine inch wide catwalk. That runs behind the stanchions. They might knock me right out the bomb bay. If we hit any rough air, I might fall out before I can get any cables loose...*I damn sure do not want to go out there.*

Feil. Well, Malnove, Cotner didn't volunteer to jump any solenoids. I'm not gonna order him to. Will you go out there and throw those bombs out one by one?

Malnove. I don't think I can do it by myself.

Feil. Do you think it's your responsibility?

Malnove. Yes, Sir. I am the crew's Armament Officer.

Feil. O.K. This is an order. Get out there and throw those bombs overboard.

Malnove. I don't think I can do it by myself.

Feil. Why not?

Malnove. I will have to hold on to the stanchion with one hand. I don't think I can lift a seventeen-pound bomb, drag it free of the cables and throw it out of the bomb bay with my other hand.

Feil. Is seventeen pounds that heavy?

Malnove. Well, those bombs are streamlined. They don't have any handles on `em.

Feil. How many guys do you need?

Malnove. Two of us can do it, Sir.

Feil. O.K. Who do you want for a helper?

Malnove. Well, Cotner is the best man. He's a damn good engineer.

Cotner. *Goddamn!...What the hell does engineering have to do with it?*

Feil. O.K., Cotner, you and Malnove get out there and get those bombs overboard before we hit the weather front.

Cotner. *Goddamn!*...Yes, Sir.

Malnove, sans parachute comes by my station. I get up. I take off my parachute. We can't climb into the bomb bay or maneuver about in there with chutes on our backs. The groin straps and the shoulder harness straps are too tight. The mass of the pack overbalances us rearward. The volume of the pack over-crowds the minimal spaces allotted for humans to creep about in.

Beside, what good would it avail us to float safely down 9,500 feet, from the "security" of the bomb bay, through the cold black air, of a coal black night, to the cold black water of a black, black sea, with no flotation or survival gear?

I follow Malnove to the two and a half foot diameter door, in the center of the bulkhead, which separates our compartment from the forward bomb bay. He calls Schultz into the conversation. He shows and tells Schultz the hand signals we will use. There are no intercom jacks in the bomb bay.

Malnove. Keep this door open all the time we're out there.

Schultz. Roger.

Cotner. Don't leave this door. Keep your eye on us all the time.

Schultz. Roger.

Malnove swings the circular door 180 degrees into the cabin. He gets onto his hands and knees, ass up and doorward. He extends his right leg into the bomb bay space. By downward search and touch, he puts the toe of his right foot onto the five-inch wide ledge, which runs across the forward end of the bay. He shifts partial weight to the right foot. He reaches backward toward the door with his right arm. He finds a handhold on the bulkhead opening. He grabs a similar hold with his left hand. He supports his weight at three points. He finds the five-inch ledge with his left foot. He pulls his shoulders and head into the bomb bay.

Malnove leans his body against the bulkhead. He slowly slips, one foot at a time, toward the next weight- bearing point of pause, as he sidles toward the right side of the bomb bay.

He arrives at the ten-inch wide longitudinal ledge, which traverses the right side of the bomb bay, front to back. He steps up three inches. He grabs new handholds. He pulls himself into a stance on the ledge facing the concave curve of the fuselage skin. He bends his body to match this surface.

Using the side-ways sidle, he moves toward the rear of the plane. He passes behind the forward stanchion. He reaches the rear stanchion. He grabs the vertical rails of the rear stanchion. He shuffles his feet, in successive small arcs of rotation until he completes an about face.

On hands and knees, I "ape" my bombardier. I enter the bomb bay. My God, it's icy out here. The frigid handholds "ache" my gripping hands. The holds are slippery with dew. So is the foot ledge. They told us flight engineering students, at the Boeing B-29 school in Seattle, that the bomb bay doors will remain shut and will structurally support the weight of a man. I am afraid. What if I slip and fall onto them? What about the load of my impact? Did the structural engineers consider that in their calculations?

My progress toward Malnove is exceedingly slow.

Malnove. Hurry up, Don!

Cotner. I can't.

Malnove I don't want to be out here with the doors open, when the turbulence starts bouncin' us around.

Cotner. Neither do I.

Malnove. Then hurry up, damn it!

Cotner. I won't.

Malnove. Goddamn!

Cotner. Goddamn?...*What the Goddamn hell am I doing out here? I'm the only flight engineer on board. If I fall into the ocean, who the hell will run the engines? Who will manage the fuel? Throttles are the only engine controls Feil and Taylor have. They can't get to Tinian using nothing but the throttle levers. One of the gunners should be doing this.*

I'm married. Jean is carrying our baby. None of the gunners is married. Why in the goddamn hell didn't I tell Capt. Feil to send someone else out here? Why do I have to have so damn much false pride ego that I let them continue to believe that I know every god damn thing there is to know about the fucking B-29?

Malnove. God damn.

Piss on him....I try to move a little faster. I want to get this over with.

• • •

I reach the rear stanchion with its cabled nest of bomblets. I shuffle through a ninety-degree rotation. I grip the forward leg of the stanchion with my left hand. I hold the stanchion within the vise of my inner thighs, gripping all the way from my knees to my loins. My grasp of the stanchion is a reverse handed-and-footed copy of Malnove's.

His left hand is free to reach around the stanchion and grab the finned end of a bomb. My right hand is similarly free to reach and lift the front end.

Malnove. Give Schultz the signal.

Cotner. Roger.

I look back to the door. *God, this is one long bomb bay.* Schultz is looking at me. I extend my right hand, fingers horizontal, nail side up, thumb against forefinger. I lower my thumb. Schultz signals a thumbs-up O.K.

Schultz. (*On intercom*). Lt. Taylor, Lt. Cotner says to open the bomb bay doors.

Taylor. Roger. Doors comin' open.

Taylor flips the salvo switch. Hydraulic pressure slams the doors open. The bomb release mechanism again fails to function.

Schultz. Bomb bay doors open.

Cyclonic cold-cold slipstream air blasts the bomb bay. Eddies and vortices swirl about us. Undercurrents suck us toward bottomless space.

I stare downward. I strain to focus. Beneath the feeble rays of our limited lighting system, I see blackness. My left leg trembles. *When did that start? Stop...stop...*but my will has no power.

Malnove. Let's get started.

Cotner. I can't.

Malnove. I want to get outta here. Quit it! You're shaking the whole damn stanchion.

Cotner. I can't. I have acrophobia.

Malnove. How'd you get in the Air Corps?...Why?

Cotner. *Yeah...Why?*...I thought I'd outgrown it.

Memory kicks in. I'm in grade three, Benjamin Franklin Elementary School, Tulsa, Oklahoma. Raymond Strickland and I are running free. We're on the flattop of the modified gambrel, which roofs the classroom wing. The bell rings. Recess ends. Kids in the schoolyard run inside. Mrs. Kingsbury wants to know where Raymond and Donald are. Our footprints race overhead, across room three. She knows.

She sends Jean Vinall to tell the Principal. Jean doesn't want to go. She likes me. I like Jean. She is the prettiest little girl I know. Jean doesn't know how to disobey Mrs. Kingsbury. Besides, Mr. Denney probably already knows.

Mr. Denney does know. Robert Ireland is telling and pointing now.

Raymond and I decide to come down. On our butts, we ease down the forty-five-degree slope of the gambrel. Raymond, on his belly, legs dangling, hangs over the gutter which projects from the eighteen-inch eave overhang. He braces his feet against the brick wall, one foot on either side of the downspout. He reaches, right hand first, under the gutter. He grabs the sloping arm of the downspout. He follows with his left hand. Foot by hand, by hand by foot, he rappels to the wall, then down the vertical pipe.

Belly on the gutter, feet against the wall, hands on the sloping gutter-arm, I emulate Raymond.

Mr. Denney. (*Profundo fortissimo*). Raymond Wade Strickland, Donald Lee Cotner, get down from there!

I turn my head. I look. Twelve feet down, Mr. Denney stands on the gravel yard. He holds his heavy wooden paddle at "right shoulder arms". My left leg shakes violently. I try to stop. The harder I try, the more it shakes and the more it shakes, the more scared I get…

With a start, I return to the present. I grip the cold, slippery stanchion with both hands. Reminiscence now races into August, 1936. I am fourteen years old. Mother, Dad and I search for roots in Wilmar, Arkansas, a town near the Mississippi River just north of Louisiana. Dad and I were each born here. Mother and Dad were wed here.

The morning is hot, humid and heavy with the essence of magnolia. My second cousin, Mary Lynn White, thirteen years old, rides Robbie, a big gelded fellow. They put me, the city boy, on Ginnie, a young filly. Born blind, Ginnie always follows Robbie with exquisite caution.

Mary Lynn leads us the length of second cousin (once removed) Walter Anderson's 14,000-acre cotton plantation. She leads us deep into cousin Walter's virgin growth southern pine timberland. We stop at the base of the 110-foot tall wood-framed fire-watch tower. We dismount. We tie the reins. We climb the tower. The topside view is magnificent.

Mary Lynn crosses the platform to the guardrail edge. I sense wind-forced sway. I cling to the rustic newel post. Mary Lynn turns back from the view. She beckons me to come. The breeze blows her blond tresses. She is the prettiest girl I've ever seen. I think she wants me to kiss her. I walk to her. The tower shivers in the wind. I grab the guardrail. I look down...far down. My left leg shakes. I can't stop. I don't try to kiss her. A coward wins nothing.

Malnove. God damn it, Don. Are you some sort of a coward or something?

Cotner. Sort of.

Malnove. Shall I signal Schultz to close the bomb bay doors?

Cotner. No.

My fear of being "coward" outweighs my acrophobia. I control my leg.

Cotner. I'll be O.K. Let's start throwin' the bombs.

With his left hand, Malnove lifts the butt of the top bomb. With my right hand under the nose, we move the bomb rearward till it clears the cabled stack.

Malnove. Drop it on three. I'll count: one...two...three.

We let go. The bomb falls. We work steadily. Employment conquers phobia. We rest thirty seconds or so between each bomb. We throw out fourteen bombs.

Malnove. I've got to rest a while.

Cotner. O.K., me too.

We rest three minutes.

Malnove. (*Checks his watch*). We threw out fourteen bombs in nineteen minutes. Why can't we work any faster?

Cotner. We're at 9,500 feet. Air Corps Regulations tell us to go on oxygen above 8,000 feet. We're gettin' rid of a bomb every one point four minutes.

If we can keep this up, we'll finish in forty-two minutes. I'm ready to go again, whenever you're ready.

Malnove. Roger. Let's try to do sixteen before we rest.

Cotner. O.K.

We throw out twelve.

Cotner. Let's rest.

Malnove. O.K., but what's wrong with us? We're only liftin' eight and a half pounds apiece.

Cotner. We're squeezin' these damn stanchions with all our force. It cuts off the circulation and tires the hell out of me. We're lifting that weight with our arms extended. That puts huge stress on our arm and shoulder muscles.

Malnove. That's enough. Don't make me more depressed.

Cotner. We're burnin' a lot of nervous energy fightin' our fear.

Malnove. Shut-up! How many more we got?

Cotner. We've thrown out twenty-six. There are eighteen to go.

Malnove. Let's do `em all this time.

Cotner. I'll try, but I'll stop if I have to.

We drop number twenty-seven. Actually, it's in Malnove's hand when the plane lurches in rough air. We grab the stanchion. It takes a while for us to be able to talk.

Cotner. You O.K., Paul?

Malnove. Yeah.

Cotner. Didn't sprain your wrist?

Malnove. No, thank God. Let's get busy. I hope this is not the weather front.

Cotner. OK. Let's go.

We drop eleven. By silent consent we rest four minutes.

Malnove. I'm ready.

Cotner. OK.

Malnove drops the last bomblet. I fling a kiss. *I hope the bomb strikes no sea creature.* Malnove's left hand and my right, grip in soldierly bond. I look toward the window. Schultz's thumb is up. I signal, thumb to forefinger. He tells Taylor. The bomb bay doors close...*Relief.*

I do a slow catwalk exit-shuffle. At the pressure bulkhead, I repeat the handhold foot-ledge creep. Schultz has the door open. I climb into the cabin...*Thank God.*

I move out of the way. Malnove enters. With orthodox grip, we repeat our "soldiers" handshake. I shake with Schultz. I shake with Caldwell, as I pass his station. I shake with Captain Feil, with Taylor.

I climb down into my seat.

I read each instrument. I check the position of each control lever, each electric switch. I look out Caldwell's window at engine numbers One and Two. I look out my window at Three and Four. I listen.

I bring my fuel-use log up to date.

Cotner. Captain Feil, by instrument, by sight and by sound, the engines are operating perfectly. We have plenty of fuel to take us to Tinian.

Feil. Thanks, Don. My compliments to you and Malnove. That was a brave job you guys did in the bomb bay.

Cotner. Thanks, Captain.

I relax...I really relax...I'm sleepy...I can't stay awake. *Amphetamine!*

I hand my mug to Taylor.

Cotner. Hey, Chuck. Tomato juice.

Taylor. Roger.

He fills my mug. He hands it back. The plane instantly falls out from under me. My left leg trembles. I spill a little tomato juice.

WHAM! The plane whumps me hard with a big bump in my butt. I dump tomato juice on my lap. I hang on to my pill.

Feil. We've hit the weather front. Be prepared for bad turbulence.

I relax again. I know this B-29. I trust it will withstand turbulence-induced stresses and strains. I am inside a cabin; I have no fear.

Cotner. Chuck, fill it half way.

Taylor. Roger, Don.

I wash my amphetamine pill down.

It's wham!...wham!...wham!...and...wham!...whump!...whump! for an hour and a half but I'm happy. I made it back inside before we hit the weather front. I'm warm and I will make it to Tinian alive.

I'm almost one mission nearer the time I can go home to dear, dear Jeannie and our sweet, sweet baby.

Blockade 101

27 March 1945. 1700 Briefing:

Col. Huglin. Men, you did an excellent job with the little M-13 bombs. Nagoya burned well this time. You earned General Le May's congratulations again.

Cotner. *Does he congratulate Malnove and me? We bombed Nagoyans by hand, just like the pictures we see of Lafayette Escadrille flyers bombin' Germans in W.W.I...Well, we bombed some fish anyway.*

Huglin. We have no 500-pound fire bombs in the Marianas, nor any seventeen-pounders now.

Cotner. *Praise the Lord. The Navy can't pass us that ammunition again.*

Huglin. We still have our friends, the U.S. Navy.

Cotner. *Yea Navy!*

Huglin. General Le May has promised the Naval Command the use of the 313th Wing's B-29 crews and planes, as deployers of anti-ship mines. The 9th Bomb Group is assigned the special target of the Shimonoseki Strait.

Cotner. *Special target smells like special danger.*

Huglin. Japan's fleets, both naval and merchant marine, now use their Inland Sea as a safe haven. (*Using his pointer on the map*). Kii Strait and Bungo Strait connect the Inland Sea to the Pacific Ocean. Our Navy has a task force near the Pacific Ocean mouth of each of these straits. The Japs do not elect to challenge either task force.

Cotner. *They were brave enough sneaks to attack Pearl Harbor.*

Huglin. Shimonoseki Strait gives access from the Inland Sea to the Sea of Japan, and thus to Chinese and Korean ports.

Cotner. *Does our Navy feel that Shimonoseki Strait is "special"?*

Huglin. Our Navy feels that Shimonoseki Strait is especially vulnerable to a mining blockade, because it is so narrow.

Cotner. *Hi ho! Hi ho! It's off to work we go...but...isn't it "specially well defended", because it is so narrow?*

Huglin. Shimonoseki Strait is the second most heavily defended area of Japan. Our assignment is hazardous.

Cotner. *Hi! Ho!*

Huglin. This will be our first time to the Shimonoseki area. Intelligence tells us there will be night fighters and anti-aircraft batteries.

Cotner. *High Li! Hi Low! We know! We know!*

Huglin. We will dedicate the months of April and May to this endeavor. We will saturate the entire fifty-seven-mile length of Shimonoseki, and all its harbors, with mines. Japan shall have no access to outside sources of supply.

Cotner. *If we work well and hard, and if we are lucky, can we maybe do it in two weeks?*

Huglin. Our navigators, bombardiers, and radar operators have had intensive training the last two days from naval counterparts, who are expert in deploying mines by parachute. Timing and wind drift are special problems in achieving accuracy.

Cotner. *I'm convinced. It's a "special" mission...But, hey, I am proud to do it. If we don't let the Japs outta the Inland Sea, the war won't last long.*

Huglin. To minimize wind drift induced errors, we will drop our mines from 5,500 feet.

Cotner. *I thought five low-level blitz missions in eight days was an eon...Now we graduate to two months of low-level mining...B-29s should be crewed by seven small men carrying picks, hi-ho!...*

...

1900:

With briefing, takeoff, and a 1400 mile single-file flight to the mouth of Bungo Strait behind us, the 9th Group's linear phalange follows Capt. Ben Nicks' B-29 on a course over Bungo. We maintain equal distance from Kyushu on the south, and Shikoku on the north. We thank God, one more time, for our wondrous radar equipment. It gives our navigators a precise picture of the waterways and land-lays below. We keep as far as possible from shoreline anti-aircraft gun emplacements.

Nicks flies a large left quarter-circle around Kunisaki Peninsula. He heads south down the center of Sua Bay, the southern arm of the Inland Sea. At Sua's end, he flies over the mouth of Shimonoseki Strait. He follows the Strait's curving course toward its Japan Sea outlet. Shore guns shoot at us. Apparently not expecting low-level attack, Japs set their shells to explode 15,000 feet above us. Concussion from the explosive blast is less severe than usual but shrapnel beats in furious anger upon our topside.

WHUMP! An immense mass of moving matter smites our fuselage. Every crewman hears the shock and senses the plane's shudder.

Feil. What the hell was that? Anybody know what happened?

Calhoun. (*From his topside Plexiglas dome*). A huge piece of something' hard and heavy hit the roof of the rear bomb bay, right in front of me.

Feil. Did it go through into the bomb bay?

Calhoun. I don't know. It was right in front of me. It bounced right by my bubble. I didn't have time to be scared but I'm scared damned silly now. What if something' falls on my head? This Plexiglas ain't gonna stop it.

Feil. Connor, turn the light on in the bomb bay. Check it out through the window in the door.

Connor. Roger. (*He checks*). There's a dent in the roof. I can't see much. Those four 2,000 pound mines, and their parachutes, are in the way.

Feil. Calhoun, do you see the dent? Is any light shinin' through?

Calhoun. I see light shinin' through six holes and I can see the dent, but no light is shinin' through there.

Feil. Whatta you think, Don? It doesn't sound to me like we need to salvo the mines and abort the mission.

Cotner. I concur, Captain. The B-29 is a strong airplane. Plus, I doubt if any more big chunks of flak are gonna fall outta the sky.

I damn sure do not want to fly this far and get no credit for a mission. I want to go home to Jeannie and the babe.

Oh God...I hope the release mechanisms work for those 2,000-pound mines. Malnove and I can't throw them out by hand. I'll make him help me though, if I have to jump solenoids.

Searchlights grab us. The Japs lower the range. Concussions jolt us. Shrapnel tattoos us. We fly out of the light. The Japs shoot at Captain Emmons, who follows us. He survives. Captain White makes it through. They shoot at Lt. Lewis.

Taylor. There are searchlights and heavy flak ahead.

Cotner. Where the hell is our target?

Caldwell. It's ten minutes ahead.

Richardson. (*On the gunner's intercom circuit*). Night fighters are after Capt. White!

Calhoun. They're after Emmons too!

Richardson. White got a Jap! He's on fire! He's gonna crash.

Calhoun. I'm takin' the upper-forward and the upper-rear turrets.

Richardson. Fighter comin' in, at five o'clock high.

Calhoun and Richardson track the Jap in their gun sights. Richardson fires his two fifty-caliber machine guns, and his twenty-millimeter cannon. Calhoun fires the four fifties in each upper turret. The Jap pilot fires his six thirty-caliber machine guns and his twenty-millimeter cannon. Opposing streaks of tracers blaze across the sky.

Calhoun. I got him!...I think I got him!

Smith, Warn, and Connor hear Jap bullets crunch through our plane's aluminum skin. The bullets scream through rear compartment space. They punch exit holes in the plane's skin.

The Jap pilot knows he is outgunned. He feels the momentum of our head-on bullets slow his plane's speed. He zooms up and away from the line of B-29s.

Calhoun. Looks like he got away. I know I got him. He'll crash before he makes it back to his base.

Connor. I saw it, Walt. He ain't goin' far.

The battle is a standoff. A standoff we win. We maintain place in our inexorably advancing line of aggression.

A moon, five days away from full, brightens the night.

Malnove. I can see both banks of the Strait through the bombsight, but there are clouds ahead. We may have to drop our mines by radar.

Caldwell. In case we do, give me a drift reading now.

Malnove. (*Sighting on a left shore sea wall*). Drift is sixty-seven degrees at eleven miles per hour.

Caldwell. Roger. Smitty's showin' a good radar picture. We're two minutes from mine drop.

Malnove. We're in the clouds. I can't see the ground or the Strait.

Caldwell. I've still got a picture. I'll use your drift, and tell you when to drop it. It's thirty seconds away.

Malnove. Intervalometer is set for fifteen seconds. Bomb bay doors comin' open.

Schultz. Front doors open.

Connor. Rear doors open.

Caldwell. Drop `em, Malnove.

Malnove. Roger. Mines away.

The first 2,000 pounder drops. The plane whumps us in the ass. We get seven repeats at fifteen second intervals, as each of our remaining mines is sent to do its dire duty to Jap ships and Jap sailors.

Schultz. Front bomb bay clear.

Connor. Rear bomb bay clear.

Connor. Rear doors closed.

Cotner. *Thank God.*

The mines will fall freely for 4,500 feet. Parachutes will open and set them gently into the water.

Smith records the time and place each mine was dropped. When the war is over, and the U.S. occupies Japan, the Navy will need this information in its work of sweeping Shimonoseki Strait clear of mines.

Richardson. I saw eight chutes open. I believe they were ours. They were all headed for the water.

Feil. Congratulations, men.

Nicks leads the line of planes in a climbing right turn. At 11,000 feet, he turns onto the exit course, Sua Bay, Inland Sea, around Kunasaki.

A Jap cruiser fires at us, as we streak across Bungo. We lose no planes. We fly into free Pacific Air.

Nicks dismisses the formation. Caldwell gives Capt Feil the heading for Tinian. I set up the engine power. We're on our way home.

Connor. Which do you guys prefer, blitzing or mining?

Smith. What the hell kind of a question is that?

Warn. It looks like I'll get more dang chances to shoot me a ding dang Jap fighter on a mining mission but the dang Jap will probably get better chances at me, so I'm dang well gonna leave it to General Le May. That's what he gets paid for.

Smith. If we have to come down on a blitz, we'll land in a firestorm. If it's a mining mission, we'll land on the water or crash into the side of a mountain.

Cotner. *It's probably better to die, than to become a prisoner. I think I'd rather die instantly in a mountainside crash...I'll think about surviving in the air instead.*

Our flight to Tinian is good. Even the turbulence in the usual two weather fronts is less severe than it ordinarily is.

...

28 March, 1100:

We land on Tinian. We taxi. We park. We disembark. We kiss the earth in our favorite religious ritual.

We ride to our encampment. We talk to the debriefing officers. They tell Calhoun that they can't give him credit for shooting down the Jap until they can find a 9th Group flyer who saw the Jap's plane go down. White, Loy, Thimlar, Dolan, Wienert and Hutchison haven't reported for debriefing yet. Perhaps one or more crewmen saw the Jap plane explode or crash.

They tell us that occasionally Japanese anti-aircraft shells are defective and instead of shrapnel, we get hit with huge chunks of iron. I say nothing but my thoughts are dour. *Damn, that could ruin a propeller, and its engine too. I believe an iron chunk will never come through the aluminum skin but Calhoun, and the other guys who sit under Plexiglas, ride in hazardous locations. The crew might survive the demise of Malnove and the gunners but if Feil and Taylor get conked, no one could fly the airplane.*

I shower. I lie on my bunk. I can't sleep. *Two months of Shimonoseki will give the Japs enough time to think of some way to knock us out of the air. We don't have any fighter escort. I'll be lucky if the amphetamine wears off by midnight.*

I think of Jeannie and the babe. I obtain repose.

Ken

30 March 1945, 1655 hours:

It is the 9th Group's second mining mission. Tonight our mines will blockade the Inland Sea approaches of Hiroshima. Twenty-four 9th Group B-29s taxi from their parking stands. Twenty-seven were scheduled, but the planes of Lts. Klemme, Barneback and Carver have mechanical problems.

The "Hon. Spy Report" is not scheduled for this mission. Colonel Huglin holds one or two of each squadron's lead crews out of certain missions, when doing so does not compromise success. He does not want to be sans a lead crew when he needs one. So far, he has not designated a replacement for either of the two we have lost.

As Capt Feil's lead crew airmen, we accept the resultant longer time our overseas tour of duty will last. There are benefits. We may live longer. The war might even end before we have to fly all of our missions.

Malnove. Let's go up to the flagpole and watch takeoff.

Caldwell. Yeah, and stay for the sunset. It's at 1847 tonight.

Cotner. It's gonna be another good one. Look at the way Pacific winds aloft are sculpting those clouds.

"Flag Pole Park" is about a quarter of a mile from our tent. "Ground" elevation is fifty feet higher there than the ground at the tent. It is ninety feet higher than that of North Field. We will have a good view of takeoff, and of sunset. Three days ago the Seabees bulldozed the eighteen-foot tall sugar cane crop that blocked our northward vista. Too many Japanese soldiers were hiding in there. The brass was afraid some Japs might creep out at night and slay a sleeping airman or two.

When the dozer started on the last clump of cane stalks, seven dirty, skinny little Japs ran out. They quavered in submission before our big grim Marines. They were thinking...*torture...or worse.* Instead, they got plenty of good food and humane treatment.

Caldwell, Malnove and I watch Lieutenant Raymond Tutton lead twenty-four B-29s westward along the southern edge of the field. At the taxi-strip's end, he turns ninety degrees right, onto the transverse strip that approximately follows the rim of the precipice that defines the western limit of North Field. The eighty-five-foot vertical face of this cliff backstops narrow White Beach 2 below.

Tutton proceeds past the western end of Runways D and C. He rolls toward B. Runway A is never used for takeoff. It is held in reserve for any B-29 in trouble, which may need to come around for an emergency landing.

Captain Bill Wienert, second in line, turns and taxis toward Runway C 1st Lieutenant Alvin Bowers turns and heads for D. The three Airplane Commanders, with simultaneous precision, turn right, into an eastward alignment with the unmarked longitudinal centerlines of the three runways. Each Commander instantly halts his huge airplane.

Each Commander, and each Pilot, pulls back hard on his long-leveraged brake handle. Each man is on zealous guard against forward creep. Each is in jealous lust of every possible millimeter of takeoff space.

Each of these three B-29s is scheduled to simultaneously begin takeoff runs at 1820.

Tutton. (*To M. Sgt. John Chambers, Flight Engineer*). Chambers, check engines for takeoff. (*To Lt. Richard Gerdau, Pilot*). Proceed with takeoff checklist.

Chambers and Gerdau. Roger.

Chambers reads all engine operation gauges. He makes a visual and audio check of each engine.

Chambers. All four engines O.K.

Tutton. Roger.

During this interval, Tutton and Gerdau test the flight controls, and check flight instruments. All are O.K.

Tutton. Give me half-flaps.

Gerdau. Roger. Flaps comin' down.

Dick Mitchell. (*Right Gunner*). Right flap half down.

Nick Valeno. (*Left Gunner*). Left flap half down.

Tutton. Roger.

Tutton checks the time with Gerdau. From the briefing room "time hack", their watches differ by only one second.

1658:30

Tutton. Chambers, you've got thirty seconds to give me takeoff power.

Chambers. Takeoff power comin' on.

Chambers sets cowl flaps full open. He sets mixture control on auto-rich. In small, alternating increments, he adjusts throttle levers, turbo boost levers, and propeller-pitch switches. Each engine soon runs at full throttle, at forty-eight inches of manifold pressure, and at 2,800 rpm. Each engine is producing its maximum rated 2,200 h.p.

Chambers. All four engines at takeoff power.

Tutton. Roger. (*To Gerdau*) It's 1819:00, give me a 1820:00 time tick.

Gerdau. Roger.

Gerdau latches vision onto the sweep second hand of his aviator's watch.

Tutton and Gerdau maintain maximum brake pressure. The plane shakes in fury to be free. Engine/propeller roar deafens.

1819:50:

Gerdau. (*Yelling his count*). 10...9...8...7...6...5...4...3...2...1...hack!

Tutton and Gerdau instantly release the brakes. Despite takeoff experience, the crewmen, in their hope to become safely airborne, always expect the plane to leap forward.

It leaps...about four millimeters. The sixty-second run-up is to warm moving parts to full-power temperature and to test each engine's ability to perform at full power. The only potential energy accumulated is stored in the brake linings.

The mass of the 137,500 pound gross overload exerts an initial inertial precedence over the strength of the engines. Yet, the 8,800 horses inexorably screw the four bladed propellers into the damp, dense sea level air, and motion begins. Acceleration is slow, but inevitable. Gerdau calls out the indicated air speed at five mph increments.

Tutton grips the throttle knobs in his left hand. At slow speeds, steering down the runway is accomplished by retarding engine power on one side or the other or by braking the wheels, left side, or right. The best Pilots use a little of each technique, both of which reduces the rate of acceleration.

At twenty-two miles per hour, the B-29's giant rudder begins to be a partially effective steering device. At intermediately increasing accelerative velocities, balancing the effect of throttles, brakes, and rudder requires a rigorously monitored sensitivity of steering touch.

A few 313th Wing Airplane Commanders have accidentally aborted their B-29, and its load of bombs and gasoline, and immolated its crew of brave airmen in a runway-side crash and explosion. Ninth Group flyers have lost but one plane and crew, Lt. Sullivan's, to this hazard.

Tonight Tutton and each of his winged comrades, Wienert and Klemme, rolls down the center of his assigned runway. Each reaches the 145 mph takeoff airspeed in time to be airborne as he flies over the rim of the eighty-five-foot cliff, which forms the eastern border of North Field. Seventy-five seconds later, Hobaugh St. Dennis and Malo, start. So it goes until twenty-five B-29s are airborne and on a single-file course toward Hiroshima.

At takeoff, the cylinder head gauge of each engine of each B-29 registers a temperature that frightens Flight Engineers. As he clears the precipice, each Airplane Commander dives for acceleration. Each flies at fifty feet or so above the water, until the engineer tells him the engines are cool enough to begin the climb to the mission's cruising altitude.

This evening the perfection of this dynamic panorama performed by our comrades-in-arms, maneuvering the world's most aerodynamically exquisite military airplane, stirs our deep sense of esprit de corps.

Caldwell. God! Those guys are good.

Cotner. Hey, those guys are <u>us</u>!

Malnove. It's beautiful. I love it.

Herb Hobler, Navigator on Capt. Flemming's crew is among the twenty-three people gathered at Flag Pole Park.

Hobler. Hi, Claude.

Caldwell. Hi Herb, you guys aren't flyin' tonight?

Hobler. Obviously.

Caldwell. I thought maybe it was just you.

Hobler. Our plane wasn't flyable. Oh, look. Ooh, damn. The sun's startin' below the horizon.

We turn toward the west.

Malnove. Those planes were out of sight and out of sound but I was still seein' and hearin' them. I guess it was all imagination.

Cotner. What is this we're seein' now? It must be imagination. Can anything real be this beautiful?

Malnove. I think not.

Over the western sea, earlier this day, multitudes of towering alto cumulus thunderheads formed. Fresh winds from the north blow forth at altitude. Wind forces strew acres and acres and acres of sky with north-south parallel rows of vaporous assemblages. Cores of the rows retain the solidly overclouded mass of their origins. The edges trail off through dense wintry brume into nebulae of fairy spume. The spume is torn and tattered by intermittent holes, where the purple deeps of the darkening sky show through. Misty foams of varying densities refract the rays of the sinking sun into pastel pink and lavender hues. The heavily hydrated cores reflect the fiery reds and burning oranges, fiercely radiated by the vanishing orb.

Thirty-one men of the 9th now stand in Flag Pole Park. We watch the sky in silent awe. The Color Guard comes. Our emotions are torn. Do we worship nature, or do we participate in military ritual? Patriotism wins. We love our flag. Duty is duty. At attention, we salute as the guard lowers the flag, folds it precisely and carries it reverently toward shelter for the night.

We turn again toward the sea.

Caldwell. I don't think I've ever been so emotionally high.

Cotner. Not even on your wedding night?

Caldwell. (*Holding his right arm in horizontal alignment with compass azimuth seventy-seven degrees*). Well, I'll tell you. Looking out over this ocean I'm thinking of my faithful, beautiful, dearly beloved Coral, waiting for me in California.

Cotner. You've said it, Claude. My Jeannie, and our babe in her womb, are waiting across this ocean.

Malnove. You guys are making me wish I was married.

The last segment of the solar disk sinks below the horizon. We see the instantaneous green flash. Is this real? Or is it, too, imaginary illusion? Dusk lasts. We linger…Darkness…

Hobler. Is that an airplane out there on the water?

Caldwell. God, Herb. Your eyes are good. Where?

Hobler. (*Points*). Way-out, two o'clock, if due west is considered to be 12:00.

Malnove. I see lights. I can't tell if it's a boat or a plane. It looks like it's on the water.

Cotner. The two lights look like B-29 landing lights. If it's a plane in, or on, the water, we wouldn't be seein' lights.

Hobler. I think it's comin' this way.

Cotner. It is a B-29. It <u>is</u> comin' this way. I hear faint engine noises. It has engine problems. It doesn't have enough power to climb.

Caldwell. It must be one of ours. I wonder who it is.

Cotner. I didn't see any planes in trouble on the runway, or after takeoff. They all got airborne.

Malnove. I haven't seen or heard any explosion of mines or bomb bay gas tanks they might have dropped.

Cotner. I hope to hell they've dropped them.

Hobler. Everything looked perfect. Maybe it's not one of ours.

Caldwell. Maybe it's one of the Navy's B-24s, or whatever "PB" number they call it. It's headed toward West Field.

Cotner. No. It's a B-29. I don't think he can land on West Field.

Hobler. He better change course soon.

Malnove. He better get some altitude.

Caldwell. Who is it?

Cotner. He's swingin' left. He's gonna try for North Field. He must still be carryin' his mines and his gasoline.

Malnove. He's higher than I thought.

In the chatter of the small crowd we hear consensus that it must be one of our crews comin' in for a landing on Runway A.

Hobler. Someone must have alerted the fire suppression and ambulance crews.

Sirens keening and emergency lights flashing, they race to the western end of Runway A. They park facing each other. Headlight beams give the poor devil in the plane a target to aim at.

Caldwell. He's on course now. It looks like he'll make it.

The thirty-three men in Flag Pole Park are silent. Each in his own way prays. Each still wonders...*who is it?*

Malnove. Pull up! Pull up!

Hobler. Up! Up! Man!

Caldwell. My god! I think that's Frank Maxwell's plane. Get up Frank!

Rumor spreads.

Crowd. It's Captain Rogan's plane.

Maxwell is Navigator on Rogan's crew. Rogan is a survivor of an 8th Air Force B-17 tour over Europe and, a volunteer for this B-29 tour. The irony that "Old Dave" Rogan is the Airplane Commander in trouble "certifies" the truth of the rumor in our minds.

I have no close friend on Rogan's crew but through Caldwell I know and like Maxwell. I add my voice to the chorus yelling advice to Captain Rogan.

1943:

Wham! Violence of sound, violence of flame. Rogan does not make it. His plane flies into the precipice. 2,000-pound mines and 640 gallon gasoline tanks explode in successive blasts. What remains of the B-29 and of its cruelly fated crew falls to the sand and coral of White Beach Two at the base of the cliff.

A few metal pieces land on the taxi strip and the beginning of Runway A. The fire trucks quickly extinguish the fires scattered topside. The ambulance crews and medics search for humans or parts thereof.

The rescue vehicles soon proceed, with sirens sounding and lights alit. They head south on Riverside Drive. They turn right onto a narrow road cut into the cliff face. It yields a slow way down, seemingly as though in grudge of passage. Eventually, trucks and crews are on the beach. They proceed north toward the burning wreckage.

They spray all the water from fire truck tanks. There is no beach area source of pumpable water. They can't search the wreckage. It's too hot. They search the beach in hope of finding crewmen who, dead or alive, have been blasted free of the central holocaust.

They find a man. He breathes. His dog tags are legible. The medics radio the North Field control tower, via clear channel.
S/Sgt. Ralph Purvis receives the message. It's garbled with static. Purvis repeats it for the benefit of the two men with him in the tower.

Purvis. Colonel Perry, Captain Forburger, they've found Joseph C. Trullo, Jr. He's alive, but unconscious. He has third degree burns. He's in the ambulance. It's headed for the Tinian Joint Services Hospital.

Perry. Forburger, look him up in the crew rosters.

Forburger. Roger (*He searches lists*). He's tail gunner on Captain Marvin White's 99th Squadron crew.

Perry. Col. Huglin, Col. Perry here in the tower. We just got a message from the medics on White Beach Two. They found Joseph Trullo alive. He's on the way to the hospital. He's Tail Gunner on Captain White's crew.

Huglin. Is it White's plane?

Perry. We presume that it is but it's too early to be certain. We'll keep you posted.

Huglin. Yes, please do. I'm comin' down there. Call me in my jeep.

Perry. Roger.

Huglin instructs his driver to rush to the cliff-top at Runway A. The security guard tells him it's too dangerous to get near the edge.

Huglin. I have to see. Those are my men.

He walks to the rim. He peers downward. The scattered pieces of the ruined plane are still burning. He feels his eyebrows and the hairs in his nose beginning to singe. He returns to his jeep. He proceeds to the tower.

Medic Perce Peerson* hears a groan. He finds a man lying on some loose sand. He kneels. The man speaks.

Man. Where am I?

Peerson. You're on White Beach Two.

Man. How'd I get here?

Peerson. You were on the plane that crashed. Can I look at your dog tags?

Man. O.K. Whose plane crashed?

Peerson. We're not sure yet. Is your name James Landgraf?

Landgraf. Yes. But, we didn't crash.

Peerson. We're gonna get you to the hospital.

Landgraf. Did I fall off the cliff?

Peerson. No. You climbed out of the wreck.

He knows he got blown out in the explosion, but being a wise medic, he knows not to emphasize the crash. He sees Landgraf's burned face.

Peerson. Are you hurtin' anywhere?

Landgraf. No.

Peerson. Hi, Schuster. This man is James Landgraf. Call that in to the tower.

Schuster. Tower, this is Cpl. Sam Schuster, Medic. We've found another survivor of the crash. He is James Landgraf. We're gonna get him to the hospital

Landgraf. There wasn't any crash. We were just comin' in for a routine emergency landing. Captain White wouldn't crash.

Peerson. Let's give him morphine. He needs to relax and get some sleep. We don't want to hurt him when we move him.

Schuster. Look at the direction that left foot is pointin'. If that left knee is not hurtin' now, it will be later.

The medics administer the shot and get Landgraf onto the stretcher and into a second ambulance. The driver departs.
The search continues. No more survivors are found.

Colonel Huglin departs the tower. He tells his driver to head for the hospital. He wants to make sure his two men get the best possible care.

Caldwell, Malnove and I, along with Hobler and other officers return to our tented area. Enlisted men return to theirs. We guess from the sound of the sirens that some survivors are on their way to the hospital. We still think it is "Old Dave Rogan" who crashed.

Most 9th Group flyers are on the way toward Hiroshima Harbor. Those not in the air and not with us are gathered outside Captain Feil's tent. Feil is there.

Caldwell. What happened, Captain?

Feil. We don't know. Nobody here was watchin'. We all heard the explosion and saw the fire. Do you guys know what happened?

Caldwell. One plane had trouble. The airplane commander came around for an emergency landing. We think it was Dave Rogan. He didn't have enough altitude. He flew into the cliff.

Feil. Rogan...Damn...Should'a quit after his tour in Europe. Poor guy. I liked Dave...How'd you find out it was him?

Caldwell. I thought I saw his *Spearhead* nose art just before he crashed.

Lloyd Welken. *(Hobler's A.C.)* You're not sure?

Caldwell. I think I'm sure, but it was damn near dark.

Walken. How will we find out for sure who it was?

Caldwell. We'll probably have to wait. The people in the tower may know, or at the hospital. The lights in the tower are on.

Spaargaren. I don't think I want to know tonight. What if it's Beeman Emmons? He's my best buddy.

The wisdom spoken in Sparky's truth quiets us. We break up. Each of us has a best buddy or two. I go to my tent. I lie on my cot. I think about my three best buddies. We are four young men with a kinship of experience. Each of us was called from an engineering life, as a student or practitioner when the Air Corps Reserve summoned us to active duty as non-flying aviation cadets. Each took cadet basic training at Boca Raton, Florida. The four of us studied together, and graduated on 2 March 1944, from the Air Corp's Aircraft Maintenance Engineering School, at Yale University. Each of us was commissioned 2nd Lieutenant that same day. Each of us volunteered for flight duty on the B-29.

The four of us were together in attendance at, and graduated from, the Boeing B-29 Factory School in Seattle, and the Air Corps Flight Engineering School at Lowry Field, Colorado. Each of us was assigned for combat training with the 9th Bomb Group, at McCook, Nebraska. Each of us has a new young wife. Each of us is the father of a new young baby in his new young wife's womb.

Jack Jewett, one of our four, is now safe from danger. He survived the 9 March ditching crash of Captain Keene's plane near Pagan. John Conly, Bernard Ladd and Marshall Long were killed in that crash. The survivors damn near drowned. Jack and the crewmates who endured till the next day rescue, are now relieved from flying duty.

Eddie Delahanty and Ken Lobdell are each on tonight's mission...I pray that each of them will return safely to Tinian.

I try to think of Jeannie. I think of her all right, but I can't help thinking also of Polly Jewett, Jane Delahanty, and Lorna Lobdell. These four formed the Flight Engineer's Wive's Chapter of the Pregnant Wive's Club at McCook. Each is now enduring the separation from the father of her babe at the home of her parents: Jean in Tulsa, Oklahoma; Polly in New Haven, Connecticut, Jane in Bloomfield Hills, Michigan; and Lorna in Seattle, Washington.

They are lucky to have the support of their parents. Some pregnant wives of soldiers can't go home.

Feeling great sympathy for all pregnant wives, I fall asleep.

31 March 1945:

When I awake, last night's story pours into my ears through the disquiet conversations of men walking past my tent on their return from breakfast.

It was Captain White and crew who crashed. Trullo and Landgraf survived. Trullo has not yet regained consciousness.

My thought: *Ken Lobdell was Flight Engineer. Ken is dead.*

Second thought: *Maybe Ken wasn't on the plane. Maybe there was a last minute substitution for some reason. Maybe Ken had an emergency appendicitis attack.*

Third thought in the strange way the brain performs*: I'm glad they didn't come get me to fill in as Engineer.*

I go to brunch. I'm not hungry. I want coffee and I want company. Eddie Delahanty is there. I sit by him.

Delahanty. Ken Lobdell is dead.

Cotner. Are you sure?

Delahanty. He's listed on the memo.

Cotner. Where is the memo?

Delahanty. (*Points to the tent post.*) It's posted.

I go read it. It is brief. It lists the time and location of the crash. It lists the survivors, Joe Trullo and James Landgraf and it lists those killed:

Captain Marvin L. White	1st Lt. Frank K. Bachelder
2nd Lt. William J. Frank	2nd Lt. Edward J. Maycomber
2nd Lt. Kenneth C. Lodbell	2nd Lt. Howard E. Crawford
S. Sgt. Earl W. Garrison	Sgt. Forrest H. Wadsworth
S. Sgt. Howard P. Winters	Sgt. Victor Dreeb

I return to my seat.

Cotner. Your tears are showin', Eddie.

Delahanty. I know. Jane and I shared a house with Lorna and Ken in McCook.

Cotner. I remember those card parties at that house.

Jack Jewett enters the tent. He comes over. He sits across the table. We have a three-way greeting.

Delahanty.. Have you read the bulletin?

Jewett. Yes. I read it up at headquarters. You're cryin' Eddie.

Delahanty. I know. You guys gonna write your wives?

Cotner. I'm not. I don't tell Jean anything that will make her worry.

Jewett. I don't tell Polly anything either.

Delahanty. Doesn't she know you ditched?

Jewett. I told her but not until they grounded our crew. I tell her that we will never have to fly again but she worries that the Air Corps will get short of aircrews, and they'll put us back on flying status.

Delahanty. I don't want to tell Jane but what if Lorna writes her? She'll want to know why I didn't tell her.

Cotner. I didn't think about Lorna writing. Jean will want to do what she can to comfort Lorna. I'd better tell her so that she can write Lorna.

Jewett. At headquarters there's a sign-up list for pallbearers. They want a detail of four men for each coffin. It's gonna be at 1000 hours, on the 2nd of April. I signed up.

Delahanty. I'm gonna sign up.

Cotner. Me too. Let's do it now, Eddie.

Delahanty. O.K. Don. We'll be back, Jack.

We walk in silence. We sign. We return. We sit with Jewett.

Delahanty. Well, that's three.

Jewett. I wonder who'll be the fourth.

Cotner. Why did we volunteer to fly? We would'a had it made by now, if we'd'a been content to be maintenance engineering officers. It was really a stupid thing for a married man to do.

Jewett. Yeah, it wasn't fair to do that to our wives.

Delahanty. I didn't get married till after I graduated from Yale.

Cotner. Yeah, but you had the wedding planned for right after.

Delahanty. Yes, I did but you know, Ken didn't even meet Lorna till he got to Seattle.

Cotner. Yeah, he was already committed to flyin' then. He's the only one of the four of us who didn't betray his wife.

Delahanty. I wish I didn't have to fly anymore.

Cotner. Me too, but we're stuck now. I feel no commitment to General Le May but I am loyal to Capt. Feil and to my crewmates; to all the crews in the 9th Group, for that matter.

Jewett. I'm glad it's over for me but I would rather still be flyin' if that would make Conly, Ladd and Long be alive.

Cotner. Well, I'm gonna go try to write to Jean. I don't know what to say.

Delahanty. Neither do I.

We depart and go our separate ways.

1 April: We each wash a short sleeve khaki shirt, and a pair of long legged khaki trousers. I let Eddie and Jack use the wind powered washing machine that Caldwell and I built. We hang our clean clothes to dry in the sun and breeze.

2 April, 0830: Those participating in the funeral meet in the briefing room. Briefers tell us that Joe Trullo died at 0504 this morning. They say the doctors believe James Landgraf will live. This means we will bury ten men. Bill Chamberlain, Flight Engineer on Captain Shenefiel's crew is the fourth pallbearer on our detail. Eddie, Jack, and Bill elect me "detail leader". I am honored to do it for Ken. I try to listen to instructions.

My dad had fought in France in World War I. In high school I had played a bugle in the Tulsa, Oklahoma, Post of the Veterans of Foreign Wars "Sons of the V.F.W. Drum and Bugle Corps". In the late 1930's, Spanish American War Veterans were dying regularly. Wives or family sometimes asked the V.F.W. to give their hero a "military funeral." Seven times, I played taps on my bugle. Three times I was behind a distant shrub playing "echo". Four times I played "source" at graveside. The latter was more difficult but, my sensibility was protected by my teenage stoicism over the death of an "old man" not personally known to me.

I learn that the Air Corps funeral protocols are much the same as those of the V.F.W.

Captain Richard Chambers, 9th Bomb Group Chaplain, will conduct the religious rites. He asks for volunteers to give a personal eulogy for each man. I tell him I will do it for Ken. Chambers gets his quorum.

Chambers tells us volunteers that he is an ordained minister of the Presbyterian Church. As Chaplain, he wants to be accessible to any man in the 9th Group. He knows that there are men of many religious persuasions, and he does not wish sectarianism to discourage any man from seeking council on a personal problem. He tells us that he wants each of our friends to have as much individual consideration as possible. His own words will be brief and his invocations and supplications will be to the universal God. He will read a few words from the Book of Psalms for each man, and each of us may speak as long as we wish. Within our level of knowledge, and of comfort, we should invoke the personal beliefs of our friend. He will call on us by the alphabetical order of our friend's last name.

The funeral is set for 0900 tomorrow. It will be out of doors, near the flagpole, at Tinian's Armed Services Military Cemetery.

3 April, 0800:

Captain Feil asks Caldwell, Taylor, Malnove and me to ride with him. Early on he checks out a jeep. There aren't enough jeeps for everyone. Some men will have to ride in G.I. trucks. Feil departs camp north onto Riverside Drive. He turns left onto the cliff-face road. At bottom he drives north along White Beach Two at the widest and highest part of the shore. Prior to the invasion of Tinian, the U.S. Navy bombarded White Beaches One and Two with sixteen, eleven and five-inch shells. Air Corps P-47s strafed it, each firing eight fifty-caliber machine guns. Fifty yards inland from high tide, palm trees and lush jungle had previously thrived. Flora is not yet re-established.

We see the cemetery. It lies in lonesome silence on bleak earth. Its 867 plain white wooden crosses stand at perfect attention, row upon row, backstopped by the face of the cliff. An armed Marine Guardsman directs Feil to the parking area. We are the first to arrive. We park.

We walk past the cemetery. At ten new holes, ten mounds of sandy soil are slumped into static repose, except for the few grains of sand stirred into brief flight by breezes from the north. The breezes stir our olfactory senses with ugly odors of the cremated carcass of the crashed B-29, lying a quarter of a mile north of us.

The names on the crosses are fading but we can read them. Six hundred and twenty eight crosses mark graves of our country's men who were killed in the Battle of Tinian. Flyers, crashing on takeoffs and landings, account for most of the rest. Japanese dead lie buried unmarked, elsewhere on the island. The name on the cross, at the head of each new rectangular hole, is freshly stenciled in capital letters. I spot Ken's: LOBDELL, K.C., 2ND. LT. 0-869146.

I note, his serial number is smaller than mine by a count of 202.

We pass ten wooden caskets. Each is covered by an American flag. The field of stars is at the head. Each casket rests on a low bier. On an engraved brass plate, I find Ken's casket. I take up my vigil. I stand at parade rest at Ken's head, on his right side.

A Marine guard armed with a rifle stands security watch. He sends Captain Feil and his other officers to the assembly area. They take the center spots right behind a line in the sand. Chaplain Chambers arrives. He stands between the flagpole and a bare bier. He holds his Bible in his right hand. Flagpole, Chambers, bier, and Feil are aligned on the centerline of the cemetery.

Col. Huglin and staff arrive. Captain Feil and entourage yield their front row center spot.

Men arrive. I signal those of my detail. They take their place by Ken. I watch men gather. I estimate that 250 men are here to pay their respects. Most are flight crew people. The ground crewmen are not here. We take that to signify that we will fly a mission tonight. I do see Master Sergeant Frank Naquin, Crew Chief of Captain White's plane, arrive with his mechanics. They bear a double bereavement, loss of their beloved flight crew and regret that White's plane had not been made ready.

Snare drums beat a cadence. A Staff Sergeant, leader of the Honor Guard, marches a double-line of Honor Detail Sergeants into the assembly area.

Three men lead the right line, each one carrying a rifle at right shoulder arms. Next a bugler carries his horn in his right hand, elbow bent. Three drummers complete the line.

The left line is lead by a bugler carrying his horn. Six Color Guardsmen follow.

The Honor Guard leader separates his lines. He halts each line ten feet from, and parallel to, the empty bier. He faces each line toward the bier.

Honor Guard Leader. Color Guard, raise the flag.

The Color Guard marches to the flag, in cadence with the drummers.

Honor Guard Leader. Sound "To the Colors".

The buglers sound it clearly, in perfect unison. The drummers play a lively roll. Echoes from the cliff meld and magnify the music. The flag is hauled spiritedly to the top.

Col. Huglin steps forward three paces.

Huglin. Salute the flag!...Pledge your allegiance!

He leads the throng in his "West Point" voice.

"I pledge allegiance to the flag of the United States of America, and to the Republic for which it stands, one nation, indivisible, with liberty and justice for all."

Color Guard Leader. Lower the flag to half-mast.

The flag is lowered slowly, while the drummers play a soft, slow tattoo. Colonel Huglin steps back into line.

Chaplain Chambers.[5] Comrades of, and friends of, the 9th Bomb Group. We meet on this battle-scarred beach, before God, to remember those who gave their lives in the cause that motivates us. Their names will always be on our honor roll.

We remember our comrades because they shared with us our faith...our faith that in our commitment to arms and military action, terrible and destructive as its consequences are proving to be, we are protecting our beloved country, the United States of America, and all that she stands for in terms of freedom, democracy, and the recognition of the rights and dignity of man. We believe that we are fighting for the whole human race, that men shall not be overwhelmed by the diabolical domination of Nazi Germany under Hitler, or the repressive conquests of Imperialist Japan.

We remember our comrades because of the deep personal friendships we developed as we shared in risk and danger, in homesickness, in commitment to patriotism, and in hope of a better world of peace and opportunity for all.

Abraham Lincoln at Gettysburg eloquently gives a model for our remembrance of our comrades:

> "It is for us, the living, rather, to be dedicated here, to be dedicated to the unfinished work which they who fought here have thus far so nobly advanced; that we here highly resolve that these dead shall not have died in vain; that this nation under God, shall have a new birth of freedom, and that government of the people, by the people, and for the people shall not perish from the earth."

> May we sum up our mood on this memorial occasion with the words of the third and fourth verses of, Katherine Lee Bate's "America the Beautiful".

5 I used (with some minor modifications) Chaplain Chambers' words and procedures from an address, entitled "Creative Memories", delivered to 9th Bomb Group Veterans at the 1987 Reunion, Tucson. D.C.

In perfect pitch, in the baritone range, Chambers leads. The male chorus of tenors, baritones, and basses joins. There is no instrumental accompaniment. Men with choir or glee club experience sing in three-part harmony. Men sans musical sophistication, sing the melody, sometimes on Chamber's note, sometimes an octave higher or lower.

"O beautiful for heroes proved in liberating strife,"

I try to follow. I'm too choked. I listen to the blended voices, and the reverberations. It's like an organ being sounded in chords of low register.

"Who more than self their country loved and mercy more than life.
America! America! May God thy gold refine
Till all success be nobleness, and every gain divine.

Oh beautiful for patriot's dream that sees beyond the years.
Thine alabaster cities gleam, undimmed by human tears.
America! America! God shed his grace on thee,
And crown thy good with brotherhood, from sea to shining sea."

Silence................

Chaplin Chambers. (*Loudly*). Frank K. Bachelder, 99th Squadron Navigator.

Bachelder's bearers lift his casket. They march to drummed cadence. They place his casket on the bier of honor. The Chaplin begins to read from Psalm 100.

I intend to listen to the words of the psalm. My mind instead tries to organize the irony in the many tales Caldwell told us when he returned from a wake held by some of the Navigators.

6 March 1945:

Lt. Frank Bachelder, Navigator on Lt. Christie's crew, is knocked to the ground in a game of Tinian touch football. He gashes his left knee on an outcrop of coral. Capt. Eppes removes him from flying status.

7, 13, & 16 March:

Capt. Roth, 99th Squadron Navigator flies as Christie's navigator. On the 16th, Christi, crew and Roth fail to return to Tinian.

17 March:

Bachelder, still grounded, is appointed 99th Squadron Navigator. He tries to refuse the promotion. He does not want to possess the position vacated by death of the man who substituted for him…but…this is war! Someone has to do the squadron navigational paperwork…Doesn't someone?…

In my mind I review the story told by Ed Maycumber, Captain White's Navigator. *White lands safely on 11 March from the 9th Group's mining mission to the Shimonoseki Strait. He taxies to his parking stand.*

White. *Lobdell, cut engines. Crawford, open bomb bay doors.*

Lobdell/Crawford. *Roger. (They comply).*

Maycumber. *(To Sgt. Earl Garrison, Radio Operator, whose station, like his own, is near the bomb bay bulkhead). I'm in a hurry. I'm goin' out the bomb bay.*

Garrison. *Be careful, Sir.*

Maycumber crawls through the circular door, into the bomb bay. He stands on the ledge below the door. He steadies his balance with his left hand on the bulkhead. He leaps through the open bomb bay doors.

His shriek resonates in the bomb bay before his feet hit the ground. He looks at his left hand. It has a thumb and three fingers. He grabs his wrist with his right hand. He looks up at the bulkhead. His finger still wears his wedding ring. The ring is somehow caught on the door latch.

Garrison sticks his head through the bomb bay door.

Maycumber. *Get my finger, Earl. Bring it to me. Keep it clean. Call the medics.*

Garrison. *Roger. Meet you at the front wheel.*

The flight line ambulance arrives. On the way to the hospital, the medics give Maycumber a shot of morphine. They sterilize his knuckle joint and his separated finger.

Emergency Room Doctor. *(After a quick examination). Lt. Maycumber, I apologize for my science's inadequacy. The separation is within the knuckle joint. We don't know how to reattach your finger.*

Maycumber. *(Groggy with pain, morphine and shock, mumbles). Notify the 9th Bomb Group.*

E.R. Doctor. *They know. Captain Eppes, your 99th Squadron Flight Surgeon, has already taken you off of flying status for three weeks.*

Maycumber. *(Moans).*

16 March:

Capt. White bombs Kobe with T.N.T. Capt. Milne Schmid, 9th Group Headquarters, navigates for him.

18 March:

White drops T.N.T. on Nagoya. Capt. Jack Nole, 9th Group Navigator substitutes for Maycumber.

24 March:

Nagoya again. Lt. M.V. Arnold[6]*, of Capt. McNeils crew, navigates.*

27 March:

Mining. Lt. Robert Wilson of Capt. Jacobsen's crew, navigates.

Maycumber chafes. He wants to finish his tour of duty. He wants to go home to his beloved wife.

30 March:

Maycumber learns the 9th Group will mine Shionoseki Strait again tonight. He tells Captain Eppes that his left hand is strong and free of pain. Eppes immediately returns him to flying status.

Bachelder and Maycumber are close friends. Bachelder knows the hand is weak. He wonders if Maycumber can hold the sextant steady enough to shoot a star.

Bachelder tells Captain Eppes his knee is strong. Eppes puts him on flying status. He volunteers to fly as passenger with Capt. White. He wants to be able to navigate in case Maycumber needs help.

My mind runs Claude Caldwell's tale back to its beginning.

---

6 M.V. Arnold is later lost at sea. See Chapter 6.

9 January 1945:

The 9th Group having completed its "staging" for overseas duty, deploys westward, in formation, from Herrington, Kansas. Capt. White flies with a brand new crewmember, Sgt. Howard Winters, Central Fire Control Gunner. Sol Sher, the crew's regular C.F. C. Gunner suffers a persistent pneumatic affliction. Captain Eppes keeps Sher grounded. Winters is a recent graduate from gunnery school.

14 January:

Capt White and crew are two hours out of John Rodger's Field, Honolulu on their way to Kwajalein. Number Three engine fails. John Rodger's tower directs White to Johnson Island. He lands there. A C-47 brings a new engine. Ken Lobdell directs local mechanics in its installation. The White crew proceeds to Kwajalein and Tinian.

The enlisted men of White's crew build a wind-powered washing machine.

The tub is a steel drum, sans lid. It brought fifty gallons of 100-octane aviation gasoline to Tinian.

29 May:

The breeze blows. The men orient their machine. They gather firewood from the forest. They build a fire. They fill their helmets with water from the lavatory. They heat the water. At boiling, they empty their helmets into the tub. Sgt. Albert Sklenka, Right Gunner, burns both hands. He scalds his bare belly. Captain Eppes grounds him. Sgt. Victor Deeb is assigned to substitute for Sklenka.

29 March:

Capt. Howard McNeil who flies B-29, "The Big Wheel", goes diving in deep ocean waters. He ruptures his left eardrum. Capt. Eppes grounds him.

30 March:

Capt. White and crew are assigned to drop mines again on Shimonoseki Strait. No. Four engine on his unarmed B-29 performs poorly. Master Sergeant and Crew Chief Walter Naquin, works on it all day. He has to report that the plane is not flyable.

Capt. White and crew are ordered to fly the mission aboard Captain McNiels' "Big Wheel". Most airmen are superstitious…I personally do not believe there exists an omniscient all-powerful entity, who preordains life…and death… or even injury to soldiers…to sailors…to airmen…but to young men who desperately want to survive this war, this final flight of the "Big Wheel" will to some appear to have been predestined to a dreadful doom, by a long accumulation of maleficent portending events.

I return to the present with the first volley of three, fired by the riflemen. "Taps" follows the rifle salute. I concentrate with appreciation. Reverberations from the cliff sound an echo of the source, and an echo of the "echo"...moving...beautiful...

Captain Chambers. 2nd Lt. Howard E. Crawford, Jr., Bombardier.

Crawford's bearers lift his casket. They march to the drumbeat...In alphabetical order, each crewman will receive his individual rite: personal eulogy, rifle salute, multi-echoed, four-toned, bugle blown requiem and rhythmically cadenced march to graveside.

After Crawford comes Sgt. Victor Dreeb, Right Gunner. Then it will be 2nd Lt. William J. Frank, Pilot. Next will be Sgt. Earl W. Garrison, Radio Operator.

I have trouble understanding the words of the eulogies. Some are spoken too softly, some too swiftly...

Mostly, the problem is that I am continually recomposing the words I'll use in Ken's eulogy. I know by experience and training, that to be heard outdoors, I must speak loudly and clearly. I thank my parents for seven years of "expression" lessons. Ardent Christians, they dream that I will be a preacher. Delivering Ken's funeral oration will be the nearest I'll ever come to fulfilling their hope.

. . .

Taps sound for Garrison.

Chaplin Chambers. 2nd Lt. Kenneth C. Lobdell, Flight Engineer.

Cotner. (*To bearers*). Lift... *Why is this casket so light?*

We march. We reach the bier of honor.

Cotner. Rest casket.

We ease the casket onto the bier.

Cotner. Ten hut.

We stand at attention. I take two paces to the rear.

Chambers. The Lord is my shepherd. Though I walk through the valley of the shadow of death, I will fear no evil.

Cotner. (*I salute.*) Kenneth Cameron Lobdell...Ken...(*I return to attention. I face left. I look at the listening throng*). Ken was my buddy. He was my buddy in the sense of that word that we all know from the World War I song, "My Buddy". The song that we hear sung on the radio many times every Memorial Day. It's chorus says, "My Buddy...My Buddy...Your Buddy misses you."

Some things I know about Ken from our many talks together. Ken was born on 24 March 1919, in Vermont. He was an only child. He grew up in Lebanon, New Hampshire. He went to public schools there. He graduated from the University of New Hampshire in June, 1941, with a Bachelor of Science degree in Mechanical Engineering. His major option was Aeronautical Engineering. He spoke well of the fine teachers he had learned from. He attended Sunday School and church with his parents at the Lebanon Congregational Church.

He remembered what his parents, his schools and his church taught him. He was a New England gentlemen. He did not curse, smoke, drink or gamble. Most of us soldier/air-men learned in our youth to abstain from these evils. Most of us here today are now addicted to all four.

Ken was brave. From college he took a job with a defense manufacturer in Maryland. His firm's President found Ken's energy and creativity to be so valuable to the production of military arms that he prevailed upon the officers of the Selective Service System to exempt Ken from the draft. Ken did not have to serve in the Armed Services for the duration of this war. He chose to enlist in the Army Air Corps.

Some things I know about Ken from our association as Aviation Cadets, and as 2nd Lieutenants, learning our trade as B-29 Flight Engineers.

Ken and I met during Aviation Cadet Basic Training in Boca Raton, Florida. We both enjoyed the rugged physical training, and the close order drills. We especially liked the latter when the band marched with us. Sans the band, we sang as we marched. Each of us had an aversion to being as underclassmen the recipients of, or as upperclassmen the perpetrators of, the silly, sadistic hazing the Air Corps forced us to participate in.

Ken and I survived our torrid summer in Southern Florida, and the stupidities of hazing. We were sent to the Army Air Corps Technical School at Yale University. We studied the theory and practice of maintaining the operational integrity of military aircraft. The aim of the program was the production of Maintenance Engineering Officers. Intellectual discipline was severe but fortunately there was no time to waste on hazing.

Ken told me how much fun it was to have these knowledgeable civilian instructors, and these richly endowed laboratories. He realized that only "Uncle Sam" could afford to supply such a meritorious staff, and such an exhaustive variety of military aircraft, and their component systems, to work on. As an aeronautical engineering graduate, he was in paradise.
It was the school's policy to have a test every Friday. Ken always made the highest grade in our class.

On Saturday the instructors reviewed the tests. They frequently asked Ken to explain something the rest of us needed help on.

Going from class to lab, and from lab to class, we marched the campus streets. We sang with energetic volume. Vehicles yielded to our formations.
The Army Air Corps Band was stationed at Yale. Colonel Glen Miller, <u>the</u> Glen Miller, was the Director of the Band. Several times a week, we cadets marched "Retreat Parades" on the historic New Haven Village Green, adjacent to the Yale Campus. Col. Glen Miller strutted out front with the baton. We marched to the "St. Louis Blues, Alexander's Ragtime Band, the Jersey Bounce, and Buckle Down Windsocky". We were, of course, honoring the flag. We marched in respectful earnestness but each cadet's face was grinning in joy.

Physical training was rigorous. Yale, in peacetime, ranked low in intercollegiate athletic competition but its facilities for the development and practice of individual fitness rated with the best in the world.
In body build, Ken was a perfect ectomorph. Light, lean, agile, quick and wiry. He loved Yale's famed "obstacle course". He would dash between hazards. Climb ropes. Swing like Tarzan. Leap low fences. Scale high ones. Vault chasms. Sprint to the finish line. He always finished first. I'll bet his record elapsed time still stands.

Two weeks before our class graduated at Yale, the brass called us into a room. They swore us to secrecy. They told us, "Boeing is building a new bomber. It will be the biggest, and the fastest, bomber in the world. It will have remote-control gun turrets. It will have pressurized cabins. Like a Navy ship, it will have an Engineering Officer. The Engineer will be a very important member of the crew. It is the wave of the future. After the war, airlines will vie for trained Flight Engineers to fly their new post-war airplanes."

Ken volunteered. I volunteered. Eddie Delahanty and Jack Jewett volunteered. Thirteen others signed up. Ken was thus doubly courageous. He had already forsworn protective asylum from military service. Now he had given up the relatively safe haven of service "back at the base" for the dangerous business of seeking violent action in unknown aerial fronts.

On 2 March 1944 our class graduated. We were sworn in as Commissioned Officers, of 2nd Lieutenant rank. We were ordered to attend the Boeing B-29 Factory School. We were issued rail passes for the five-day train ride to Seattle.

Jack had married Polly, and I had married Jean, as cadets, in New Haven. Eddie and Jane were married between train stops. In Seattle we married couples found dwellings in town. The Air Corps assigned Ken to the Bachelor Officer's Quarters. At a bachelor's party at the Officer's Club, Ken danced with beautiful "townie" Lorna Doll. Magic was instantaneous. On 14 April 1944, Lorna and Ken were married.

At Boeing we studied the maintenance and operation of the B-29. We met the airplane. Its beauty awed us...*I hesitate...this is not the place to praise the airplane that these air crewman lost their lives in.*

As at Yale, Ken made the top grade on every test.

From Seattle, the Air Corps sent us on to Flight Engineers School at Lowry Field, Denver, Colorado.

We worked six days a week at Seattle and at Denver but these halcyon days were like honeymoons to us young married couples. In Denver, Lorna, Jane, Polly and Jean each became pregnant.

We husbands, flying in the rear of B-24s, seated at mocked-up B-29 Flight Engineer Consoles, learned fuel management, and engine operation. Ken, of course, was the best student.

At graduation we were awarded Flight Engineer Wings, and were assigned to Groups for combat training. Our foursome went to the 9th Bomb Group at McCook Air Force Base, Nebraska.

Ken, Jack and I were assigned to the 99th Squadron, and to the crews of Captains White, Keene, and Feil. Crew training was a series of missions in a B-29, each with a specific learning objective. The most significant mission was to fly a non-stop 3,000-mile circuit. All crews tried it at least twice. Captain White's crew, with Ken as Flight Engineer, was one of only two crews to accomplish this important achievement.

As most of you know, there were many days and hours at McCook, while we waited on base for our turn to fly one of the three available B-29s. Ken and I spent a lot of time in earnest conversation. Our most discussed subject was our love for our wives.

On Tinian we dwelt first in neighboring tents and then in adjacent huts. Ken taught me to play cribbage. We did not gamble, but we kept a record of points. (*I turn my head toward the casket*). Ken, unless I make it to heaven, I'll owe you 13,333 points throughout eternity.

The subjects of our conversational sessions were seemingly unlimited: wives, fatherhood, religion, politics, science, engineering, art, music, literature but mostly we talked of our dear wives and the anticipated joys of fatherhood.

I told Ken how much I enjoyed our social get-togethers as couples, how sweet it was to observe his and Lorna's mutual adoration. I remind him of how Jean and I were always amused, but always touched, by Lorna's demonstrations of admiration of his "beautiful, long, dark eyelashes", and how he blushed.

(*I pause*). This next subject...fatherhood...drew Ken and I close. So close that I will be brief. Ken knew that "Joy Mary" or "Kenneth Cameron Lobdell, Jr." woul be born in the middle of May, about six weeks from today. My "Donna Marie" or "Donald Karl Cotner" is due in two weeks. Ken and I agreed that our wives had earned the right to name our first-born child.

Each of us present has lost a true and faithful comrade-in-arms. Eddie Delahanty, Jack Jewett, Bill Chamberlain and I have each lost a best friend. The Air Corps has lost its Top-Ace Flight Engineer. Our country has lost a man of our generation who will be missed throughout post-war years. A man whose courage, wisdom and strength will not be replaced...

Lorna Lobdell will be deprived forever of her dear, dear love...her husband Ken.

Joy Mary or Kenneth Cameron Lobdell, Jr. will never know the man whose precious genes have given her or him life.
(*I face right.*)

Detail, salute. . .Ken...Goodbye...End salute.

I step forward. I face left. Three rifle shots ensue. Taps resonates.

Chaplain Chambers. Sgt. Joseph C. Trullo, Jr., Tail Gunner.

Cotner. Detail...Lift...Forward march.

We march to the grave.

Cotner. Detail...lower.

We place the casket on the graveside bier.

Cotner. Remove and fold the flag.

We fold it into a military triangle. I tuck it under my left arm. I will give it to Col. Huglin. He will send it to Lorna along with his personal condolences.

The casket is light. Lest it become contaminated by salt-water infusion, the grave is only three feet deep. We four lower the casket by hand. Eddie places a photo he had taken in Denver of Ken and Lorna as newlyweds on the top. Jack Jewett tosses a Tinian wild flower blossom. I place a handful of polished “cat eyes”, the beautiful shells of Tinian sea-creatures. Chamberlain has torn “The Unknown Citizen” from a book of poetry. He weights it with a few of my cat eyes.

Delahanty. Let’s each say a silent prayer.

We comply. After the prayer, soldiers with shovels approach.

Jewett. Let’s each throw a handful of dirt.

Each man does.

Chamberlain. Ashes to ashes.

The soldiers arrive. They cover the grave with earth.

Cotner. Let's maintain a silent vigil till the ceremony is finished.

We stand, at ease, until Sgt. Forest H. Wadsworth, Left Gunner, Capt. Marvin L. White, Airplane Commander, and Sgt. Howard R. Winters receive due honors, and are interred.

Chamberlain has no return ride. We wait with him for a G.I. truck. We catch the last one. I sit just inside the tailgate. I watch the cemetery recede. The scene is bleak.

Why are we abandoning the best of America's young men, to the silence of this lonesome desolate nether world, on the barest site on this island, in the remotest spot of this earth's surface...

My muse returns me to 1938. Miss Esther Larson, Tulsa Central High School's marvelous teacher of 12th grade History, "knows" her students will fight soon the world's most destructive war. She assigns us to read St. Augustine's twelve "justification points". Augustine's purpose was to justify the wars of fouth Century Roman Emperors, with Christian philosophy. The Bishops did not want fear of the Church's "fires of hell" to cause the newly Christianized Emperors to backslide into Paganism.

Miss Larson. (*Next day*). Mr. Cotner, can a war be just?

Cotner. (*I think of my Dad, who fought in France in World War I. I want him justified*). Yes, Ma'am. I am impressed with St. Augustine. I didn't know he was so smart.

Larson. Those who rule countries seem always to make aggressive demands on other nations. In time, confrontations develop into wars, "justified" or not. What if we had leaders who could avoid demands?...Miss Collins?

I was glad she asked Dorothy Collins instead of me but I wonder now... *If in 1852, President Millard Fillmore had <u>not</u> ordered Commodore Perry* *to use big black warship intimidation to secure a trade treaty with Japan's reigning Shogun, would the Japanese have learned to build a huge Navy, and have decided to attack Pearl Harbor, so that they too could become a great world power?*

The truck levels out at the top of the cliff. I see the B-29s on North Field. My thoughts speak to Miss Larson. *Thank you for the inspired lessons. I hope post-war salvation for our world can be accomplished through some sort of unity...maybe a more effective successor to the League of Nations.*

Reality is here. The only way we can end this war is to defeat Japan. Will there be a mission tonight? Will I be on it? Will I survive it? Will I ever see Jeannie again?

Ken's Funeral Service
Chaplain Richard Chambers with Bible. Don delivers a eulogy for his buddy.
Courtesy of Joy Lobdell Wallace

Tinian's Military Cemetery
Air Corps Photograph

Air Corps Photograph

Joy

Made a part of this book by permission of Joy Lobdell-Wallace

Talk at the 9th Bomb Group Reunion
Tucson, AZ · October 7, 2000

Joy Lobdell-Wallace, Daughter of 2nd Lt. Kenneth C. Lobdell, killed 3/30/45

My Father is 2nd Lt. Kenneth Lobdell. We never got to meet. He died in a crash on Tinian, March 1945. I was born in June 1945. My being here today is part of a wonderful journey I started in January 1999. That's when I read an article in the *Oregonian*, my local paper, about an organization - the American WWII Orphans Network (AWON). The article told the story of Ann Mix, then of Bellingham, WA, who created AWON to support orphans in their search for information about their fathers.

Fathers who died during WWII left children who grew up surrounded by silence and secrecy. We orphans knew not to ask questions because talking about our Dads was painful for our Mothers and for our new Daddies. Furthermore, we grew up in a time when personal issues like this were not discussed. Our Moms were told to "get on with your life" because people did not want to dwell on the war.

I was lucky. I always knew I had a Father who died before I was born. Mother called him "Daddy Ken", and I knew from her voice that she loved him very much. I also knew my grandparents and cousins in VT and NH. But, I never knew much about my Dad...and I never realized that this void profoundly affected my life in many ways.

In January 1999, I sat at my computer and went to the AWON Website (www.awon.org) and looked at a section called "Our Fathers"...tributes written by adult orphans about their Fathers. It took me two seconds, and I was a heap of tears. Reading what orphans had to say about their dead Fathers opened up a floodgate of tears, grief and pain that had been locked in me for over fifty years. I had found a group of people like me, all trying to reconstruct their own heritage; trying to learn as much as possible about their Fathers. These other orphans inspired me! I quickly joined AWON and received forms that helped me organize the information I did have about my Dad, and helped me know what to search for. In June 1999, I submitted the tribute to my Father to the AWON Website.

Because I have a photo of my Dad's plane with signatures of all the crew, I knew that James Landgraf was the only survivor of the crash that killed my Father. I decided to search for him on the Internet, since his name is unique. I came up with a list of ten James Landgrafs around the country. Rather than calling all of them, I decided to try something else. Next, I went to a Website called Heavy Bombers (www.heavybombers.com) where one can search WWII Bomb Groups. I was so excited, because here I found the 9th Bomb Group and the name of Herb Hobler, president, and Larry Smith, historian, with a link to send Larry an e-mail message.

In June 1999, I sent Larry an e-mail message. I told him who I was and asked if he knew how to contact James Landgraf. He immediately wrote back saying he would contact James and tell him that I wished to talk to him about my Dad. Larry also told me about the book, *History of the 9th Bomb Group*, and asked if I would like to order a copy. I said yes, and almost before I could mail a check, the book was on my porch.

In a day or so, Jim called me and we visited. He explained that enlisted men and officers did not mix much during the War, but he told me about the crash and about living conditions on Tinian. At the same time, Bonnie sent me an e-mail message from Herb that described the crash and my Dad's funeral on Tinian. I had never heard an eyewitness account of the crash or anything about the funeral.

I asked Jim if he would be willing to take a photo of my Mother and Dad with their wedding party to your reunion last year. I have never known who the men are in the photo, and hoped one of them might be at the reunion. Jim didn't find those men, but he connected with the Cotners and Delahantys. As soon as the Cotners got home, they telephoned me. The conversation was overwhelming to me...I had never discussed my Mom and Dad with people who had known them both. They told me stories about traveling across the country with them; what living conditions were like at the Air Bases; what they all did in their spare time. Don, especially, has given me some insight into the kind of man that my Father was; a special gift from Don. In the past year, I have spoken with the Cotners, the Delahantys, and with Jim. They have all told me stories over the phone, and sent me information in the mail.

Last Veteran's Day, I contacted the *Oregonian* and suggested that they do a story about WWII orphans. I ended up being interviewed by Marge Boule, my favorite columnist, about being a war orphan and AWON. Two days later, I traveled to Seattle to visit family, and went to see a B-29 that is being restored at the Museum of Flight. One of the restoration volunteers took me on-board and let me sit where the flight engineer sat on the B-29. I think he was embarrassed that I could not contain my tears.

Last May, I traveled to Vermont to my Father's grave for a mini-memorial service to honor him. I had been there before, but never so keenly felt his absence in my life. Some cousins joined me, as well as the minister of my Grandma's church, Rubin, a man who enlisted with my Dad, and two other war orphans who came to share this experience with me. This service for me was a public way to claim my Father. Being here is another public declaration of being his daughter.

Months ago, when I told Don that I was considering coming to the reunion, he suggested that he would like to make arrangements to present me with my Dad's medals. Now, here I am. After eighteen months of searching for my Dad, you, his special friends surround me. I will leave here feeling closer to him than ever before.

Addendum:

Joy's story is unabridged and unedited.

Our President, Herb Hobler, suggested that we 9th Bomb Group regulars bring as many as possible of our family members with us to the Tucson Reunion. Jean and I brought our three daughters, Donna Marie, Laura Jean and Frances Irene. Jane and Eddie Delahanty won the prize. They brought sixteen people, counting children and grandchildren. For the Reunion's featured breakfast assembly, the audience exceeded 450 people.

On the dais, Jane Delahanty, James Landgraf, and I each spoke our remembrances of Ken. Joy then delivered her story. When she finished, every person in the room was crying.

The disorientations of battle cause discontinuities in the perfection of records. Many brave soldiers go unrecognized as heroes. So it was with Ken. Lorna, Ken's widow, received none of his decorations. James Landgraf did receive all of his medals except one. I acquired all of the missing medals. General Henry Huglin, who as Colonel Huglin, was the 9th Group's W.W. II Commanding Officer, presented the medals to James and to Joy.

James was awarded the Presidential Unit Citation Badge with one Bronze Oak Leaf Cluster.

As Ken's survivor, Joy was awarded Marksmanship Medals for skill and accuracy with Thompson Sub-Machine Gun, Carbine and Pistol, and Medals for valor: Purple Heart, Air Medal, Presidential Unit Citation Badge with Bronze Oak Leaf Cluster, Asiatic Pacific Theater Medal with four Battle Stars, American Campaign Medal, World War II Victory Medal.

Thank you, Joy, for permitting me to use your story in my book.

Donald Cotner

A Memorial Tribute to Ken Lobdell, 9th Group's Tucson Reunion, Aug. 2000

Standing (L. to R.):
Jim Landgraff, Sole Survivor of the crash
Joy Lobdell Wallace
Jane Delehanty
Don Cotner
Seated:
Herb Holder

Credit: Jean Cotner

Joy Lobdell Wallace, Gen. Henry Huglin, and Don Cotner at the Tucson Reunion
Joy wears the medals earned by her father, Ken Lobdell
Ken's Medals:
Purple Heart; Air Medal; Presidential Unit Citation with Oak Leaf Cluster; Asiatic Pacific theater Medal with 4 Battle Stars; American Campaign Medal; and World War II Victory Medal.

Credit: Jean Cotner

MORE BOMBINGS, BURNINGS & BLOCKADINGS

1 April 1945: Fools Day is not a fun day. We, the crew, and Captain Fiel, have completed thirteen missions. *Is thirteen a lucky number? It is a big enough number to have brought us to a constant state of weariness and apprehension? Will we survive our tour of duty?*

As we continue to fly, each mission has its distinctive terrors; yet they run together in a continuum of maleficent memories:

3 April 1945: We fly to Ota. We drop 2,000 lb. T.N.T. bombs on the Nakijima Aircraft Factory. We encounter much flak and many Zeros. It is our first mission with Lt. Karl Pattison as Airplane Commander. Captain Feil rides as "Check-Pilot".

4 April 1945: Once again we fly a Lead-crew practice mission. We bomb by-passed Rota. We feel that we deserve a day off. Except...Pattison is happy. He loves to fly. He will have no Check Pilot today. He gives me permission to bring my Seabee friend Pete Ayers aboard as a passenger.

Pete sits on the deck by my station. He has no intercom headset. He watches Pattison, Caldwell and me get the plane into the air and on course to Rota. With engines synchronized at a relatively slow cruising speed, I beckon Pete to near. I speak into his ear.

Cotner: Jean writes that she and her doctor believe our baby is due soon. I want to pass out cigars but I cannot find one damn cigar for sale on Tinian. I believe General Le May has commandeered the entire Mariana Island's stogie supply.

Ayers: (*In my ear*) There's a surplus of cigarettes but cigars are damn scarce. Seabees have sources that generals and admirals don't know about.

7 April 1945: We fly to Nagoya again. We put T.N.T. on the Mitsubishi Aircraft Engine Factory. Flak and Zeros seek us. Connor sees two B-29s from the 73rd Wing rammed by Zeros. All four planes burn. They fall.

Will this be a Jap tactic? Will we be able to dodge Zeros? Will we be able to shoot them down before we collide? Well, we won't see many more Nakijima planes with Mitsubishi engines in them.

Pattison is O.K.

8 April 1945: Pete Ayers stops by my hut. He gives me a sealed box of Corona Coronas.

Cotner: Gee thanks Pete. Where in the Pacific Ocean did you get this?

Ayers: There is a British Merchant vessel in Tinian harbor. I walked aboard and found the supply officer. I traded him a "blood stained rising-sun flag, taken from a dying Jap soldier, at the battle of Tarowa." He was glad to get it, I shoulda asked for two boxes.

Cotner: Damn Pete, how many Jap corpses have you stolen a flag from?

Ayers: None. Sometimes we had to bury Japs. But all the souvenirs were gone by then. Hell Don! I can make a Jap flag in thirty minutes. I can put that gobbledy-gook Jap writing on these flags faster than any Jap ever could. I can't read any of it butI don't believe they can read it either.

12 April 1945: Shimonoseki Strait. Our crew parachutes six 2,000 lb. T.N.T. anti-ship mines into the water. Caldwell is accurate.

15 April 1945: Nagoya, once more, Kawasaki Engine Factory. Our gunners see B-29s shot down all around us, four of them are 9th Group crews: Malo, Carver, Jones, Sullivan.

Debriefing officers confirm the lost crew identities.

The officers hand me a special confirmation: a cablegram from O.K. Riesinger:

I opened envelope quietly. I read in silence.

> 14 APRIL 1945:
>
> CONGRATULATIONS DON
> LITTLE DONNA MARIE BORN TO JEAN APRIL 13TH 9:35 AM
> 6 LBS. - ZERO OZ STOP JEAN AND BABY WELL.
> DAD RIESINGER

I lose command of the code of military conduct. I sing too loudly, "Off I go into the wild blue yonder." Instantly I apologize. Quietly but with intense zeal I meditate...I praise God...I praise Dad Riesinger...I praise Jean...I praise little Donna Marie.

After the session ends I invite everyone to my hut. I gather a small entourage along the way. I give everyone a cigar. We smoke a little while. I show pictures of Jean. The soirée ends.

I take my cigar to the washbasin. I carefully extinguish the fire with slow drips. I want to smoke as much as I can tomorrow, but I don't want it to be soggy.

I hit the sack. I talk to Jean. *You did great honey. I'm proud of you. I love you...*I talk to Donna Marie. *Welcome to life sweet baby daughter. Daddy wishes he had been there to greet you. He'll come home to you as soon as he can.*

18 April 1945: Kokubu Air Field, Kyushu. B-29s from the Marianas fly in support of the Okinawa Campaign. Our assignment is to booby-trap

runways to keep Japanese home-island based planes on the ground. We drop 250 lb. T.N.T. bombs, with fuses set for randomly timed explosions. Hair triggers set them off at de-fusing attempts.

This is the first mission we fly with 1st Lt. Ted Littlewood as our Airplane Commander. *We liked Pattison. We wish we could have kept him. Littlewood doesn't like us...Will he warm up?...Thirteen-hour missions are long, even with congenial crewmen.*

22 April 1945: We are on our way to booby-trap/blockade the runways of Hishira Airfield, Kyushu. Number Four engine swallows a valve. We abort. We return to Tinian.

29 April 1945: A new Fighter Group joins the Seventh Fighter Command on Iwo Jima. The Command is now 240 P-51s strong, with Pilots.

Fitted with a 256-gallon disposable gasoline tank under each wing, the P-51 has a 2000-mile range. A P-51 can fly to any part of Japan, drop the wing tanks, shoot up everything on the ground and return to Iwo, with fuel in reserve.

Occasionally, P-51s fly as B-29 defenders. Our crew will be beneficiary of P-51 protection on six of our thirty-three missions. More often, P-51 Groups are assigned targets of their own. With three fifty-caliber machine guns mounted in each wing, and sans wing tanks, the P-51 is superior in aerial combat to any Japanese airplane.

P-51 strafing-sweeps devastate trains on the rails, demolish trucks on the roads and decimate airplanes in the air, or on the tarmacs. Sweeps are coordinated with B-29 missions. B-29s lead the fighters to Japan, and back to Iwo.

Abort, Personnel

3 May 1945:

Caldwell and I swing by the bulletin board. We read that Littlewood and crew are scheduled for a 1900 briefing.

This will be our nineteenth mission. It will be our fifth mission with Lt. Littlewood as our Airplane Commander.

We flew ten missions with Captain Feil our original Commander. Feil liked me, and trusted me. I trusted and admired him. Feil was promoted to 99th Squadron Operations Officer when Major Chappel, flying as an observer on Lt. Carver's crew, failed to return from the third of April bombing of the Nakajima Aircraft Plant.

Young Karl Pattison, promoted from Pilot on Captain Curry's crew, replaced Feil for four missions. Pattison was bright and talented. He and I trusted and liked each other.

The brass then decided that Lt. Littlewood should be made a Lead Crew Airplane Commander. They switched Littlewood and Pattison. Our crew was assigned to Littlewood. Littlewood's crew was assigned to Pattison. Littlewood kept his airplane and his ground crew.

Littlewood is <u>not</u> pleased. He trained at McCook, and flew fourteen missions with his original crew. He thinks they are the best air crewmen in the 9th Group. He thinks that if the brass needs another lead crew, it should be "his" first crew with himself as its Airplane Commander.

A B-29 Airplane Commander and his Flight Engineer must work in close harmony. I receive no positive comment from Littlewood. He gives no instruction about how he wants me to perform. He seems to expect me to know what he is thinking.

I know he has over 300 hours as a B-17 Instructor Pilot. Don Connor, our Right Gunner, tells me his older brother is the "Flight Engineer" Gunner on a crew in the 8th Air Force. I know that the B-17 has no Flight Engineer's station. Connor can't tell me what his brother's duties are. *Does Littlewood have a condescending attitude toward B-29 Flight Engineers? Is he proud of his ability, to combine in his person, engine operation ability and aerodynamic control of a four-engine bomber? Does he feel that B-29 Flight Engineers are usurping power rightfully belonging to Airplane Commanders?*

Or, is it a personality problem between Littlewood and me? Is it my fault?

John Dreese is the new Crew Chief. It is imperative that he and I cooperate. I like John. I respect him. I believe he likes me and respects me.

One Flight Engineer duty is to write a report in the Airplane Operation Log at the end of each flight. The report is written just prior to disembarkation. I am required to delineate any mechanical malfunctions that occurred during the flight.

The Crew Chief is required to read each report, and to certify that all problems are corrected, before a succeeding flight can occur.

In my reports, I include brief discourses on diagnosis of causes of malfunctions. Maurice Szarko, Crew Chief of the "Honorable Spy Report", in which we flew fourteen missions, prior to being switched to Littlewood's B-29, always thanked me for my helpful reports.

At 1000 hours, Captain Art Smith, 99th Squadron Aircraft Maintenance Engineering Officer, sends word. He wants to see me at his flight line office. I check out a jeep. I drive to his office tent. 1st Lieutenant Howard Fiedelman, Smith's assistant, is there.

Fiedelman. Hi Don, come in. Art will be right back. I know you went to Yale. What class were you in?

Cotner. (*Salutes*). Hi Howard, I graduated 2 March '44. Did you go there?

Fiedelman. Yeah, I graduated 3 November '43. They weren't lookin' for Flight Engineers then.

Cotner. You wanta trade jobs?

Fiedelman. No, thanks.

Smith walks in.

Smith. Hi, Cotner. Fiedelman is gonna join us.

Cotner. (*Salutes*). What did you want to see me about?

Smith. John Dreese tells us he doesn't like for you to make diagnoses in his log.

Cotner. He has never said a word to me about it. I thought it was our log.

Smith. Since the log stays with the airplane, all Crew Chiefs feel proprietary about it. Master Sergeant Dreese is a good soldier. He probably feels his immediate supervisory officer, that's Fiedelman, is the proper channel for expressing his feelings. We had a three-way conversation about it.

Cotner. I thought Dreese and I were gettin' along fine.

Smith. He says he likes you. He says no other Flight Engineer reports diagnoses. I can verify that, for the 9th Bomb Group Flight Engineers. He says no B-17 Pilot ever did a diagnosis. You know that before there were Flight Engineers, the Pilot always wrote the log report. None of them ever attempted a diagnosis.

Cotner. I'll admit that the regulations don't say anything about diagnoses. Maybe I am being too "creative". I'll quit. It will shorten my work.

Smith. Thanks. John Dreese is a good Crew Chief.

Fiedelman. He'll make sure your plane is safe to take off in.

Smith. You always have the last say. If it doesn't pass your pre-flight inspections you don't have to fly it.

Cotner. O.K., Captain...Lieutenant. Thanks for sharing this information. Our flight crews' lives are in Dreese's hands. I damn sure want him to be happy.

I drive back. The Seabees have built good roads for us on Tinian. Like our runways, they are built of gravel-sized chunks of live coral. They are saturated with ocean water and the coral is compressed with rollers. The coral chunks grow together. They make a smooth, strong, hard surface.

I'm somewhat let down. *I thought I was being a damn good Engineer. I don't seem to be pleasing anyone.* I punch the gas pedal. The jeep jumps ahead. It's fun. I drive fast. Unexpectedly, before I realize where I am, I whiz past the motor pool, my little engine whining, my little wheels spitting crumbled coral. I slam on the brakes. The wheels skid. I make a U-turn. I go back to the entrance and drive into the motor pool "yard".

A Sergeant comes out of the tent.

Cotner. I'm turnin' this jeep in.

Sergeant. Sign the log. Write the date and time.

Cotner. Roger. (*I write*).

Sergeant. No comments?

Cotner. (*I thought these "Crew Chiefs" didn't want me messin' up their logbooks.*) O.K. Sergeant. (*I write, "performance perfect"*).

Sergeant. Lieutenant, there are speed limits on Tinian roads.

Cotner. Thanks, Sergeant. I didn't see any posted.

Sergeant. The military police won't accept ignorance as an excuse.

Cotner. Thanks. (*I ride a lot in the back of trucks. Are they allowed to go faster? Or, does it just seem faster, because we get bounced around so much?)* I seldom have a reason to be a driver. I'll go slower next time.

I go toward the brunch tent. I muse, as I walk. *It's true, 2nd Lieutenant is the lowest rank in the Army. I used to think Aviation Cadet was.* Inside the tent a few small conversational claques are going. I see none of my close friends. I see only 1st Lieutenants and Captains. I sit in the corner. I get a cup of coffee. It's cold. A Captain speaks.

Captain. Electricity is out for this part of the camp.

Cotner. Thanks, Captain. (*Oh well, at least he didn't blame it on me*).

I go by the mailroom. I have a letter from Jeannie. Her letters always cheer me. I take the letter to our tent. Jean's sweet words of affection always bring an instant observable arousal. My tent mates always laugh and comment. Most men are crude, and some are rude, but I think it's funny too. *I am proud to be married, and I am proud of Jean's beauty.*

Today I'm not in the mood to be kidded, so I sit down to read the letter. The first sentence slays the erection. It subsides faster than it arose.

"Oh, Don, why don't you write more often. Nadine across the street gets a letter every day from her boyfriend, Jack. He's stationed in Hawaii."

I've thought about mailing Jean at least a note every day.. But, what if I skip one day?...Two days? Maybe it won't even be my slip-up. But...will Jean think I got shot down? I resolve to write more often.

I nap. I oversleep. I run to the Officer's mess hall. I'm five minutes late for supper. Captain Smith gives us a seventy-five-minute window of time to find a seat and be served. There is no evening chow line. The waiters are enlisted men on Captain Smith's staff. I sit at the end of the nearest table. One of his men promptly brings me a plate.

Smith is quickly beside me.

Smith . You're seven minutes late, Lieutenant.

Cotner. Yes, Sir. (*I was only five minutes late when I came in*).

Smith. I shouldn't let you have anything to eat.

Cotner. Yes, Sir.

Smith. Are you flyin' on tonight's mission?

Cotner. I believe I will be. I haven't been to briefing yet. I don't know if there is a mission.

Smith. There is a mission. Col. Huglin told me to be sure to serve something that would go down quickly and be easy to digest.

Cotner. Yes, Sir.

Smith. Since you're flying, and since I presume you'll be on a long mission, go ahead and eat. Be through in half an hour.

Cotner. Yes, Sir.

Smith. My men get up early every morning. They work hard every day. They deserve to get off duty on time.

Cotner. Yes, Sir.

Smith. When you were in Officer Candidate School didn't they emphasize the importance of promptness in any military situation?

Cotner. I was never in the O.C.S. program, Sir. I was an Aviation Cadet.

Smith. Didn't they stress punctuality?

Cotner. Yes, Sir. (*Why doesn't he let me eat?*)

Smith. Try to be on time from now on.

Cotner. Yes, Sir.

Smith departs. *I would leave but I don't want to be hungry in mid-Pacific air.* I eat. I know everyone in the mess hall is watchin' me. I know I was wrong to be late. I know that battles can be lost by failures of timing. *Was Capt. Smith right to humiliate me so publicly? Maybe he was using me to demonstrate a point. Well, I'll be able to ingest enough calories to feel comfortable and to perform well.*

2100 hours:

We report for a relatively late briefing. I am in my seat early.

It's a mining mission, Shimonoseki Strait again. The only thing different from the others we've flown is the late takeoff time. I worry about flyin' that same course again but the only way we could vary the course would be to fly over mountains, and altitude would mean more gasoline,,fewer mines and less accuracy.

Throughout the briefing I half expect to be berated by a briefing officer, or to be asked a question I can't answer, but I escape any kind of castigation. *Has my luck changed*?

It's dark of night as we ride in trucks to the flight line. *Is this the reason our usual high-spirited repartee, with its humor based on spoofs of personal traits of character, is muted? I am not scolded even in jest. Is this a good omen?*

I resolve to try especially hard to communicate well with Littlewood. I look forward toward completing one more mission.

At the plane, I give Dreese a cordial greeting. He responds. We air crewmen complete our exterior pre-flight inspections. Littlewood orders us to board.

2130 hours:

Littlewood. Start engines.

Cotner. Roger.

I open all cowl flaps. I set all mixture control levers on Auto-Rich. I set all throttles at mid point. I set all propellers at minimum angle of thrust. I turn on the No. One engine magnetos. I turn No. One starter switch to "energize". With a moan, the starter motor begins to spin its heavy flywheel. I hold the switch in this position. The moan grows louder and increases in pitch to a whine.

After ninety seconds, I flip No. One starter switch in the opposite direction to "engage". The motor continues to run. Through a clutch, the momentum of the flywheel and the continuing electrical power of the motor are transmitted to the shaft of the eighteen-cylinder engine. No. One propeller begins to rotate. It speeds. The spark plugs fire. It runs.

I flip the starter switch to off. I adjust throttle and propeller pitch. I obtain an 800-rpm idle speed. No. One sounds good.

I repeat the starting procedure for engines Two, Three and Four. Each is soon idling at 800 rpm. It's beautiful music. In about three minutes the temperature of each engine sits on normal.

Cotner. Captain, the engines look good. I'm gonna make the magneto checks.

Littlewood. Roger.

Henry Ford had a good knowledge of electricity. He used a magneto to generate, and to time, the spark that fired in the cylinders of his Model T automobile engines. It is one reason the Model T was a dependable automobile. Reliability is the reason magnetos are in the ignition systems of airplane engines.

To increase the probability that an engine will not cease to produce power during flight or takeoff, designers provide each engine with two magnetos. It is the flight engineer's responsibility to test the magnetos prior to departure from the parking stand.

Via throttle lever, I advance the rpm on engine No. One to 2000. I let it run for ten seconds. It's smooth. I turn the left magneto off. The rpm quickly drops to 1700. It runs steadily. I turn the left magneto on; rpm rapidly returns to 2000. I let it run ten seconds. I turn the right magneto off. No. Two drops again to 1700 rpm. It runs steadily. I turn the right magneto on. Rpm rapidly resumes a steady 2000. With the throttle I set it again at its 800 rpm idle speed. I listen three seconds to the song.

Cotner. No. One is perfect.

Littlewood. Roger.

I repeat the magneto test procedure, and set idle speed on engine No. Two. I listen again.

Cotner. No. Two is perfect.

Littlewood. Roger.

I repeat on engine No. Three. *Have I found the lost chord...again?*

Cotner. No. Three is perfect.

Littlewood. Roger.

I run No. Four up to 2000 rpm. The left magneto operation test is perfect. I turn the right magneto off. Rpm's drop to 1300 slightly uneven revolutions per minute. I increase rpm to 2400. I turn the right magneto on. I run the engine for fifteen seconds. It smoothes out.

This is standard procedure to clear a "fouled" spark plug. A plug becomes fouled when foreign matter (usually motor oil) shorts-out the gap between electrodes.

I reduce rpm to 2000. I turn the right magneto off again. It's suddenly 1300 rough rpm's. I "clear the plugs" again.

I start the right magneto test one more time. Crew Chief Dreese's head pops up, from the front wheel well beside me. He watches the test. It is again a failure.

Dreese. Let me try it, Lieutenant.

Cotner. Roger.

I get out of my seat. Dreese and I trade places.

Dreese. The left mag was O.K., wasn't it?

Cotner. It was perfect.

Dreese tries the test. His result is the same as mine. He wears a scowl. *Is he mad at me? Does he think I screwed it up?* He tries a second time. No success. He begins a third try.

Someone grabs my foot on the ladder. I look down. It's Howard Fiedelman, my friend from the morning conference. He wants up. I climb down. He climbs up. I find Captain Smith standing there.

Cotner. Hi, Captain

Smith. Hi, Cotner.

Smith moves into the wheel well. Dreese comes out. Smith waits his turn on the ladder. Fiedelman gives up. He trades places with Smith. Smith tests the magneto. He tries to clear the plug.

A jeep drives up. Major Weinberg, 9th Group Aircraft Maintenance Engineering Officer steps out. I salute. He returns.

Weinberg. Fouled plug?

Cotner. I think it's more serious than that, Major.

Weinberg. Naw. That's all it is.

Cotner. Well, neither Sergeant Dreese nor I can clear it. Lt. Fiedelman tried. Capt. Smith is tryin' now.

Weinberg goes to the wheel well. He grabs Fiedelman's foot. Fiedelman climbs down. Weinberg climbs up. Tests continue. I've counted eighteen failures. Col. Luschen, 9th Group Operations Officer arrives in his jeep. Smith and Weinberg climb down from the plane. I'm to the right of No. Four. I'm looking up toward it. A circle assembles around me. All faces glower. *Why is my flight crew mad at me?*

Luschen. What's the problem?

Weinberg. The flight engineer abandoned his post.

Cotner. No, Sir. I yielded to the command of Lt. Fiedelman. He outranks me.

Smith. That's right.

Luschen. Is the plane O.K.?

Cotner. No, Sir. No. Four won't run on right magneto.

Weinberg. It's just a fouled plug. It'll clear up when you put takeoff power on it.

Cotner. It might, but it could be something else that is malfunctioning.

Weinberg. It was O.K. this afternoon, wasn't it?

Fiedelman. I didn't check it. Dreese reported it ready to fly tonight. I trust him.

Weinberg. Did it run right this afternoon?

Dreese. It was perfect, Sir.

Weinberg. Well, you guys better get back in. You're runnin' late now.

Cotner. I'm not gonna try to make this plane fly.

Weinberg. Not even if Colonel Luschen orders you to?

Cotner. No. Not even if Colonel Huglin, General Davies and General Le May order me to. *Not even if F.D.R. orders me to.*

I get glares from some, and inscrutable stares from others. I endure them silently. The worst they can do is court marshal me and kill me. I'll be just as dead if I start down the runway in this B-29.

I must have spoken blasphemy. I don't care. I know I am right. Why is it so important to gamble the cost of a million and a half dollar airplane, plus the cost to train an aircrew against the chance that we'll have thirty-two B-29s in the air instead of thirty-one?

The silence has no end...Finally, Caldwell speaks.

Caldwell. If Don's not going, neither am I.

Luschen. Well, that settles it. All the rest of the planes are gone. We've got enough jeeps here. We'll take you men back to camp. Cotner, you ride by me.

Weinberg. Sgt. Dreese, get this plane buttoned up for the night. Lieutenant Fiedelman will come back and give you a ride.

Dreese. Roger, Sir.

Our small parade of jeeps departs.

Luschen. You know, Cotner, I've flown 17's and 24's. I've taken off a time or two when the mag check on one engine wasn't perfect.

Cotner. No, Sir. I didn't know.

Luschen. I got away with it, obviously.

Cotner. Were the planes overloaded, Sir?

Luschen. No. In fact, they were only lightly loaded.

Cotner. Well, many four-engine planes can take off on three engines, if the load is light.

Luschen. Weren't you afraid not to fly?

Cotner. I was afraid to fly. My wife delivered little Donna Marie, our first child, on 13 April. I want to be husband and father to my family.

Luschen. But you volunteered to fly, didn't you?

Cotner. Yes, Sir. I know now that I made a mistake.

Luschen. You're not saying you're gonna quit flyin' are you?

Cotner. No, Sir. But, I was obeying orders tonight. The Flight Engineer's B-29 Operation Manual says, "Do not attempt takeoff in a B-29 unless all four engines pass the magneto test".

Luschen. I know that. I've been wondering when you would say it. I was beginning to think you didn't know your manual.

Cotner. I was wondering if Captain Weinberg knows it.

Luschen. I'll make sure that he reads it. I complement you, Cotner, for knowing what was right, and for standing up against pressure. I'll see that you're not in any trouble. There is pressure on the mechanics to get as many B-29s in the air as possible. You remember Crew Chief Roger Tricot, don't you?

Cotner. Yes, Sir. Back when Karl Pattison was our Airplane Commander, we flew one mission in his plane. He was a hell of a nice guy. His plane flew perfectly for us.

I visualize the night of 3 April.

Thank God we flew to the Nakajima Aircraft Factory in our own plane, on that night. We hear the story from our Crew Chief, Maurice Szarko, as soon as we disembark on our return to Tinian.

In Tricot's B-29, the aircrew is ready to taxi, from the parking stand toward takeoff. Tricot holds his good-bye salute. He stands in "Crew Chief position", aligned laterally with the Airplane Commander's window, outboard of No.One engine. Captain Scheaffer, the Airplane Commander, does not increase power... Does not increase power...Does not increase power .He opens his window. He beckons to Tricot. Tricot comes near. Scheaffer yells, "The bomb bay doors won't close!"

Tricot frowns. He runs toward the bomb bay, to see why his doors have failed him. One of No. Two engine's 17' 9" propeller blades slices downward through the top of his head.

Capt. Scheaffer orders Lt. Bob Bates, Flight Engineer, "Stop all engines." Bates complies. Scheaffer calls the tower. The ambulance arrives. The medics gently load poor mangled Roger Tricot into the ambulance. Sirens screaming, they race to the hospital. They race back to the field. They may be needed.

Col Huglin arrives. He asks Scheaffer. "Can you fly the mission, if the plane can be made ready?" Scheaffer says, "Yes, Sir."

Capt. Smith arrives. He sets men to work on cleanup. A mechanic tells him, "The bomb bay door safety switch had been left on." Smith says, "Turn it off."

Smith tells Capt. Scheaffer, "Start engines, the plane is O.K." The engines are soon idling.

Scheaffer asks Smith, "Is No. Two O.K.?" Smith says, "Run it up to 2,000 rpm." Sheaffer relays to Bates. Smith watches the engine closely. He signals for idle speed. Scheaffer opens his window. Smith yells, "It's O.K. No vibration."

Schaeffer commands Lt. Varg Frick, Bombardier, "Close the bomb bay doors." They shut perfectly. Scheaffer taxis. He catches the end of the line. He completes the mission.

Luschen lets Caldwell, Malnove and I out near our hut. We thank him for the ride. We salute. We walk to the tent. Taylor is already there. He gripes because we didn't fly.

Cotner. Are you mad at me?

Taylor. No, no. I'm mad the plane wasn't ready.

Malnove. Look at it this way, Chuck. Any mission we don't fly now might be one we will never have to fly.

Caldwell. I'm proud of you for standing up to the pressure, Don.

Cotner. Thanks for your support.

• • •

October 1991: Jean and I are at the 9th Bomb Group Reunion in St. Louis, Missouri. Ralph Pattison is attending the reunion with his father, Karl Pattison. Ralph and I peruse 1945 military documents that Larry Smith, 9th Group Historian, has set on display in our "mementos and relics" room.

We go through a summary of 9th Group missions flown. Ralph says his dad never talks about the war. I comment to Ralph and answer his questions. We find the four missions that our crew flew with Karl as our Airplane Commander. We continue through the pages. Every time we see his dad's name, I tell Ralph what I remember about that particular mission. I've never seen this document before. It's a great reminiscence generator. I look for the names of Feil and Littlewood. The other two of the three Airplane Commanders my own crew flew with. I tell Ralph some of our experiences.

We come to page nineteen. In the column headed "Mining, 3-4 May" (Shimonoseki Strait), I see, "Littlewood Abort - Personnel".

Ironic memory floods my brain...*Abort - Personnel! I am the person! Damn! Damn! I did get a letter of condemnation in my file. No wonder I didn't get promoted to 1st Lieutenant till 25 June 1945, two months after every other 2nd Lieutenant, including Chuck Taylor who was still a Flight Officer when we arrived on Tinian. I'll never know who wrote it...Weinberger? No! .Littlewood?...??*

I had finally asked Littlewood why I hadn't gotten promoted when all the other Flight Engineers had. I remember his response, "You don't ask your immediate superior why you don't get promoted." My silent response: *Who the hell do you ask? How else do you correct your "malfeasance and malperformance?*

In college, R.E. Means had been the brightest, and most influential, of my architectural professors. Raymond Means was a liberal, and a skeptic. When he spoke of the evils inherent in all organized religions, I could not refute him with experience or with logic. In those days I had agnostic,, and sometimes atheistic thoughts.

I wonder now, are injustices upon my innocent psyche, and insults to my intelligent performances, partial causes of the growing ascendancy of agnostic personal philosophy over my war-generated religiosity?

Irony. Irony. I never knew what I had done to be denied the timely promotion I deserved. I guess I am lucky I got my silver bar in time to wear it home. Wearing my gold bar solo had seemed at first like wearing a sign, "I am a fuck-up". But soon I wear it with defiance. I polish it daily.

...

2005:

"The Army will make a man of you", is an American adage. The Romans spoke a Latin equivalent. Warring cave clans sounded it in primitive grunts. I am convinced of its truth, so long as one is not killed, demoralized by debilitating injuries, emotional disturbances, or mental derangements.

...

Subsequent to 17 October 1945, the bureaucracies in which I have served have been peopled by civilians. Most of these, who have been in positions "superior" to mine, have fairly and generously assessed my performance. A few have not.

...

Now, in old age, the gold of my self esteem glows; and the silver of my self-reliance shines.

Thanks for the memories, Army Air Corps...

But, while playing "old soldier" and "war hero", let me never forget that the true heroes are the host of men like Master Sergeant Roger Tricot and Lieutenant Ken Lobdell who gave all: life, youth, love, and fatherhood...in tribute to the God of War.

The Three Big Bad B's Rebid and Redoubled

We seek capitulation. We burn down cities of less than 100,000 people.

We drop leaflets: 10,000 plus in May; 20,000 plus in June; 30,000 plus in July. "EVACUATE YOUR LITTLE TOWN! WE ARE COMING IN OUR B-29s TO GET YOU!"

But...Where can they go?...How can they get there?

Their planes and their ack-ack shoot some of us down. Their Zeros ram a few of us. Our strength grows. Their resistance, though briefly fierce at times, fades.

16 May 1945: The 315th Wing of B-29s arrives on Guam from its training base in Kansas. The 315th will share Guam's northwest field with the 314th Wing.

17 May 1945: Our crew is well on the way to Maizuru. The 9th Bomb Group will booby-trap Maizuru's Bay and harbor, by parachuting it full of 2,000 lb. T.N.T. naval mines.

Our No. One engine swallows a valve. We have to abort,again.

I wish we were still flying with Captain Feil in our "good-ole Honorable Spy". This never-named airplane of Littlewood's has aborted with us three times already...Is it some sort of illegitimate offspring of the Boeing Company, or whichever company built it?

18 May 1945: We fly to far Northern Honshu. We mine the harbor of Tsuruga Bay. Caldwell tells us we are only 400 miles from Russia.

We fly into searchlights and flack. Connor is busy stuffing chaff out the camera port, while Caldwell and Malnove are busy parachuting mines.

20 May 1945: We fly to far Western Kyushu. We parachute mines into Miyazia Bay and Maizuru Bay. Yawata's Harbors will have no access to open seas. Fighter sweeps will close rail and road traffic in and out of Japan's steel producing area. This siege will soon halt the manufacture of war's indispensable material. Our blockade tightens. Caldwell says we are only sixty-three miles from Korea. *Are we telling the Japanese there is no place they can hide from the B-29? Is there any Jap who is listening?*

22 May 1945: We fly our "Superdumbo" mission. (A tale told previously). We guide Joe Lewis and crew to the submarine, *U.S.S. Toro.* Caldwell cues the men in their stricken B-29 when to make their desperate leaps into the darkness of the night and their dire parachute descents into the blackness of the sea. When dawn arrives we search for hours at 500 feet altitude. We finally find three men: Canova, Smith and Stein. We guide Toro to these three. the submarine crew takes them aboard. Eight airmen - Fiedler, Victery, Row, Arnold, Dixon, Yarewick, Dutrow and Lewis - are never seen again.

23 May 1945: Our crew leads a three-plane flight of B-29s. We circle Ha Ha Jima, a small island seventy miles north of Iwo Jima. Our assignment is to furnish navigational escort to Japan, for P-51s. We will wait offshore till they complete their strafing sweeps. We will then lead them back to Iwo, and, we will return to Tinian.

We circle "Ha Ha" for hours. We never see a P-51. We fly back to Tinian. We learn that headquarter people on one or both sides failed to "understand." We get no credit for a mission.

26 May 1945: The 58th Wing of B-29s is deployed to Tinian from India. The 58th's planes will use West Field, newly enlarged by the Seabees. The Mariana Islands' B-29 strength is increased again. The 58th was not effective flying from India. It will be now.

1 June 1945: We attack Osaka, at 20,000 feet altitude, in a daylight formation fire blitz. The 20th Air Force puts 458 B-29s over the city. Our gunners fire

at Tojo fighters. We shoot no Tojos down. The Tojos shoot no B-29s down. An outdated design, the Tojo is slower and less maneuverable than the Zero. *The Tojo pilots seem reluctant to fight. Are the Japs out of Zeros?*

5 June 1945: The 20th Air Force hits Kobe in a daylight formation incendiary blitz of 473 B-29s. It is the biggest strike in the history of aerial bombardment in terms of tons of bombs dropped. We fly at 13,500 feet. It is the lowest altitude we have had yet to bomb from, in the daylight.

A Zero puts a twenty-millimeter cannon shell through the No. Four fuel tank in our right wing. We are lucky. The shell does not explode; but, the self-sealing gas tank cannot "heal" a cannon-size hole. For lack of fuel, we lose No. Three and No. Four engines. We fly to Iwo Jima on engines One and Two. We make an emergency landing at Iwo on the P-51 field.

8 June 1945: The 509th B-29 Group arrives at North Field. It is made a part of our 313th Wing. Our Wing now has five Groups. All other Wings have only Four The 509th Group has fifteen B-29s. All other Groups have forty-five to forty-eight. The 509th planes are "funny". They have no gun turrets. Their propeller blades can be reversed after landing. It slows them down on the runway, a great safety feature. We have lost two B-29s and their crews on landings, when the brakes failed and they rolled over the cliffs at the end of the runway.

Marines, armed with rifles, guard their parking area and their living area. We can't enter their space. We cannot converse with them...*Who are these guys?*

9 June 1945: The 9th Bomb Group bombs the Aichi Aircraft Factory, Nagoya...*Is Nagoya Gen. Le May's favorite target?*...We fly at 16,000 feet, in daylight formation. We drop 4,000 lb. T.N.T. blockbusters. Zeros put bullets through our fuselage. They injure no crewman. They cause no serious damage to our plane. Reconnaissance photos show big holes in the earth, but the factory facilities appear to have survived.

10 June 1945: Rumor spreads. "Captain McClintock's crew is going to be transferred to Tinker Field, Oklahoma City, for special training"...*Why them?... What training?*...I find my friend, Russell McFee, McClintock's Flight Engineer.

Cotner: Hey Russ, is the rumor true?

McFee: Yeah, Don. My name is on the order.

Cotner: Any other crews goin'?

McFee: I think we're the only one.

Cotner: Man. I'd sure love that assignment. I could visit my wife and baby in Tulsa every Sunday, or I could move them to Okie City with me. What are you guys gonna do there?

McFee: We don't know. McClintock isn't talking.

Cotner: Will you send a dozen roses to my wife in Tulsa? It's only 100 miles north northeast.

I give him the address of Riesinger's Jewelry Shop and I give him a twenty-dollar bill. I write a note: "I love you, Jean, Don."

11 June 1945: McClintock and crew depart.

12 June 1945: A memo is posted.

> "12 June '45. To 9th Group personnel:
>
> The tour of duty of air crewmen flying missions to Japan, from Tinian, Saipan and Guam is increased from twenty-five to thirty-five missions, effective 12 June 1945, by order Hdqtrs. 20th Air Force.
>
> Col. Henry H. Huglin, C.O. 9th Bomb Group"

Can they do this?...Yes... "This is the Army, Mr. Jones." We think we feel low; then an information leak spreads: "20th Air Force statisticians have computed that air crewmen losses are so small that more than fifty percent of crewmen will survive twenty-five missions. They estimate that by flying ten more missions, we can reach the desired fifty-fifty death rate"...Now we "know" we are "low". *Are these statisticians aware that we have lost more planes and crews from mechanical malfunctions and operational mishaps than we have from enemy action?...or...do these kinds of losses count against us, because they might be our fault?...Oh....God...Why wasn't I sent to Tinker Field?...Oh well...Jean will have a dozen roses to remember me by.*

15 June 1945: Littlewood and crew are scheduled to fly another daylight formation incendiary raid over Osaka. We are supposed to burn down the Amagasi area of the city...*Is this an area we have failed, so far, to incinerate?...*

We taxi toward our takeoff runway. Littlewood senses a soft left-brake pedal. He manages a right-hand turn, out of the taxi line, at the first cross-strip. He is able to maneuver a sloppy, but safe stop. I shut down the engines. We disembark. They will tow the plane to its parking stand. It is another mechanical abortion for us.

Well...at least we won't get killed on this mission. Thanks, Littlewood, for your caution. We would not have appreciated being the third Ninth Group B-29 to go over the cliff for lack of brakes on a landing roll.

I'd better tell Jean about the roses. She may want to press the dried petals in her Bible like W.W.I widows did.

19 June 1945: The 313th Wing incinerates Fukuoka this night. The new 509th Group participates. The searchlights capture our plane. Connor stuffs chaff. It works. As far as we can tell, the 509th drops the same bombs we do...*Why then are these guys so special?*

20 June 1945: The 316th Wing flies into Guam from its training base in Kansas. It will use Guam's North Field. The number of B-29s in the Marianas is now 1101. *How soon will we announce this, via leaflets, to all of Japan?*

26 June 1945: Col. Huglin assigns our crew to lead the 9th Group on another attack on the Aichi Aircraft Works, Nagoya. He instructs us to obliterate it this time. To make sure we will, he flies as our passenger.

At our assigned altitude of 16,000 feet, Nagoya is covered with clouds. Malnove cannot find the target. Ice forms on the gunners' Plexiglas blisters. Huglin orders Littlewood to find clear air. We descend. The formation follows. We find cloud bottom at 12,000 feet. Malnove sees the Aichi factory. He sets his bombsight cross hairs on it. Zeros attack. No plane in the formation can fly an evasive maneuver during the bomb run. Ice from the storm at our former altitude remains on our Gunners' Plexiglas blisters. It spoils their aim. The Gunners conserve ammunition, but they fire a few rounds in hopes of intimidating the Zero Pilots.

Malnove holds a steadfast course..."Bombs away"...Seven 2,000 pounders fall from each B-29. Littlewood asks for power. I give it. At 239 miles per hour we escape to nearby Pacific air space.

Next day's photo reconnaissance shows ninety-four percent damage. Our crew will be awarded the Distinguished Flying Cross. Col. Huglin will have won his second DFC.

3 July 1945: We burn down Himeji. The cities get smaller. There are no fighters. Flack is meager.

7 July 1945: Shimizu is the target city. We abort. No mission credit but we live to fly again.

8 July 1945: We fly solo. It is our turn to do a Radar Surface Mapping mission. Caldwell and Smith cooperate on obtaining a number of radar view photos of the area surrounding Mount Fuji.

It is eerie to fly slow circles around the most sacred of Japan's mountains. Fuji stands alone. Its perfect cone rises 15,000 feet above the valley floor. The highest point in Japan lies on the mount's nearly perfect rim. In July, the snowcap extends downward 500 feet. We fly all alone. We are fearful at first. People on the ground must know we are here.But no searchlight seeks us. No fighter plane challenges our presence. No anti-aircraft gun fires. We drone our repetitive aeronautical meanderings. Caldwell, Smith and Malnove find, identify and photograph our targets below.

We never learn to what purpose intelligence will use our pictures, but it is almost fun and it will be a credited mission.

12 July 1945: We incinerate the City of Tsuruga. We survive a long mission through bad weather. Despite rain, the winds of storm seem to make the fires burn better. It is our twenty-seventh mission. *Will we ever reach thirty-five? Since Jean hasn't mentioned anything about the roses in her letters, perhaps I should write again.*

19 July 1945: Target: Chosi. Objective: incineration. Performance: mechanical-failure abortion.

20 July 1945: Fifty fighter pilots fly into Iwo Jima from their training base in Iowa. They fly P-47 N Thunderbolts. The 7th Fighter Command is now 340 planes and pilots strong.

With disposable wing tanks, the P-47 has a range equal to that of the P-51. The P-51 is a few miles per hour faster than the P-47 and it is slightly more maneuverable. The P-51 has a liquid cooled V-12 Merlin engine, an engine that is more vulnerable to enemy fire than the air-cooled radial engine of the P-47. One bullet through the radiator will down a P-51. Like the P-51, the P-47, in aerial combat, is superior to any Japanese plane. The P-47 has four fifty-caliber machine guns in each wing. It is a more deadly strafing airplane than the P-51.

24 July 1945: Col. Huglin tells us in briefing that the 313th Wing will send 206 B-29s over Isu. *We hope the people of that little town will have heeded our warning leaflets. We hope they will be gone by the time we incinerate the place...but, where can they go?...How will they get there?...*

Thirteen of the 206 planes will be from the 509th Group. We are glad to have these new flyers join us, even though their numbers are small.

It turns out to be a great day for the U.S.A. At least 400 other B-29s hit other Japanese towns. It is our first 600-plus B-29 day. More than 200 P-51s fly strafing sweeps on targets of opportunity.

Just as Col. Huglin told us,Admiral Halsey supports our attacks with a 1,000 planes from the 3rd Fleet aircraft carriers. Everywhere we look we see B-29s, P-51s, P-47s, naval dive bombers, torpedo bombers, Corsair gull wing fighters, and Gruman Hellcats. We don't count airplanes but we are impressed and proud. We see no Japanese plane in the air.

Damn it, Japs, surrender. I've got six more missions to fly. I might get killed even though you are defenseless. American planes may start having air-to-air collisions.

1 August 1945: Today is "Army Air Forces Day". It is not a national holiday. The Air Corps' observance of the day does not include granting time off from duty to air crews, nor to ground crews.

We of the 20th Air Force celebrate "our day" by attacking Japan with a maximum effort number of war planes: 235 P-51s, forty-one P-47s, and 826 B-29s. The fighters, from Iwo Jima, fly devastating daylight sweeps. The P-47s, each armed with eight fifty-caliber machine guns, explode the boilers of five steam locomotives. A few Zero pilots attempt to challenge. No Zero escapes aerial destruction. P-51 pilots claim nineteen kills. P-47 pilots claim seven. One P-47 is shot down. Many planes, trains and trucks are destroyed on the ground.

Each of the six B-29 Wings is assigned a different city to burn in nighttime raids. Two B-29s fail to return to the Marianas. In debriefing, no airman reports seeing any B-29 fall from the sky. We think that they were not shot down, nor rammed by the Japanese.

The 313th Wing incinerates Nagaoka. The 9th Bomb Group puts forty-seven B-29s over the target.

Japan!,...Japan!..., We tell you we are coming...surrender before we annihilate you.

2 August 1945: Many 9th Group airmen sleep late. The brunch tent is crowded. Excited conversations flow. We know that General Le May is an advocate of the thesis that air power can alone conquer a nation.

Le May, of course, has credited all of the men, of all the U.S. Armed Forces, who won the many victories that have given us the Mariana Island B-29 bases and the Iwo Jima P-51 and P-47 bases.

Le May has acknowledged that the now total blockade of Japan is a joint effort of the U.S. Navy's third and fourth fleets and of the 20th Air Force. Any Jap vessel that attempts to sail from an eastern coast port, or out of either the Kii or Bungo Straits will be sunk by submarines, by carrier-based airplanes, or by surface vessels. No vessel can depart westward. The western harbors, bays, rivers and straits are full of mines, deposited by B-29s.

Brunch-tent air-crewmen comments support our concurrence with General Le May that Japan is defeated now. We wonder. *Are the Japanese too stupid to surrender? Do they fear mistreatment from American conquerors?*

Is their government hijacked by bushido-code Samurai idiots who envision a glorious death for every Japanese soldier and citizen in defense of Emperor and country?

Perhaps prompted by my desire not to die, I ask my comrades:

Cotner. Why don't we cease attacking the Japs? Let's just hold the siege. The Japanese economy will not provide subsistence income to the people. Japanese agriculture will not feed the people. Infrastructure and housing will not be rebuilt. Japan's wet and cold winter will soon be here. People will die of famine, exposure and disease. Even the Samurais can't make such death glorious. Japs who don't die will unite in a surrender plea.

My Comrades. (*Speaking almost as one*). I want to take my chances with flying my thirty-five missions and going home soon.

Caldwell. This is pointless. Our vote doesn't count. Gen. Le May will send us out to burn towns and hamlets as long as there are any not yet burned.

6 August 1945: A B-29 called "Enola Gay", from Tinian's 509th Bomb Group drops "Little Boy" on Hiroshima. The 509th's secret is out; except... *Who the hell knows...What is an atomic bomb?...*

Photos of Hiroshima are quickly distributed. We ordinary airmen admit that with our ordinary ordinance it would have required 100 B-29s to do to Hiroshima what the Enola Gay did with one bomb. *The Japanese will surrender now...won't they?...*

8 August 1945: The Japanese do not respond to U.S. demands for immediate unconditional surrender. *Can't they imagine what will happen when every one of our 1101 B-29s simultaneously drops an atomic bomb on their country?*

The 313th and the 58th Wings from Tinian send 517 B-29s to Yawata. Our crew is among them. The 517 planes incinerate the Japanese steel producing "capital city". Homelessness of the surviving population is additional certainty, that goes with flattened mills and mined ports, that Japan will manufacture no more steel. A few Zeros come up...*Are the Japs still trying to fight?* We have a P-47 Thunderbolt fighter escort. The P-47s shoot down twelve Zeros.

In the afternoon, the 314th Wing bombs the Tokyo arsenal again.

During the night, the 58th Wing incinerates Fukayama. Recon photos will show that not one structure in the little town survives.

9 August 1945: "Bock's Car" of the 509th Group drops "Fat Man" on Nagasaki. The U.S. again demands unconditional surrender.

10...11...12...13...14 August 1945: There is no Japanese response.

14 August 1945: Three 9th Group crews, Capt. Littlewood's. Capt. McClintock's and Capt. Nash's, (*Why three?.Why me?*) are sent to drop firebombs on Kumagaya, a small city. It is our crew's thirty-second mission. My worry is earnest...*Why doesn't Japan capitulate .Why does the U.S. risk the lives of thirty-three good air crewmen on a mission of such puny significance?I don't want to die so near the end of the war.*

1 & 2 September 1945: Our crew is one of twenty from the 9th Bomb Group assigned to carry food and supplies to American prisoners of war, at a camp north of Nagasaki. The drop is by parachute. It is successful. The drop precedes by sixteen minutes the signing of the Japan surrender treaty aboard the *U.S.S. Missouri.*

We are credited with mission number thirty-three. It is our last. The war is over. I survive. *How soon can I get to Tulsa to see Jeannie and Donna?*

Epiquotes

"I fear we have only awakened a sleeping giant, and his reaction will be terrible."

Admiral Isoroku Yamamoto, after his attack on Pearl Harbor

"Praise the Lord and pass the ammunition."

Navy Chaplain, Howell M. Forgy, during the attack on Pearl Harbor

"Anyone, even a coward, can commence a war, but it can be brought to an end only with the consent of the victors."

Gaius Sallustius Crispus, in his history of the Roman war with Numidia, Bellum Iguruthinum, written between 46 and 23 B.C.

"When there was peace, he was for peace; when there was war, he went."

In the poem, "The Unknown Citizen", Wystan Hugh Auden

PART III: PEACE

WING CHANGE

1000 Hours, 22 September 1945

The war is over. Japan surrendered twenty days ago. Caldwell, Taylor, Malnove and I sit on the "front porch" of our Quonset hut. We have cool shade, a sea view and a sea breeze. We have no military duties. Are we in paradise? Yes...But...No!...No!...We want to go home!!

Malnove is single. Caldwell, Taylor and I are married. I will have the double bonus of sweet, loving wife Jean, and beautiful, intelligent six-month-old daughter, Donna Marie, to welcome me.

To relieve the ennui of what seems like suspended animation, we try to play what has been our favorite game of cards, Hearts.
We wait for Taylor to accumulate sufficient gumption to gather, shuffle and deal the cards. I look around. I get lost in a daydream.

I admire the neat and comfortable improvements we have added to our Quonset hut dwelling. I am prejudiced. I was the architect and the landscape architect. I was the procurer of material, the foreman of construction, the inspirer of labor. My comrades did work hard, toward my support.

I had completed my fourth year of the five-year Bachelor of Architecture curriculum at Oklahoma State University before being called to active service by the Air Corps. This is the first of my designs to become a constructed reality.

I look up. I approve the canopy, with its wide overhangs east, south and west. Its canvas was provided by a Supply Sergeant who bent rules to "salvage" a tent (per his record). I created its ingenious lightweight framing system from "sticks" salvaged from the Harbor Master's lumber scrap heap. The "genuine battleship-grade teak" decking was purchased with a bottle of whiskey from an itinerant Seabee. I knew he exaggerated but it was flooring...tongue and groove flooring. Soon after we nailed the deck to the joists, a Seabee with two big buckets of "genuine Aircraft Carrier deck-finish" came by. He guaranteed a "100% waterproof" paint job, labor and materials, all for only one bottle of whiskey. We got a beautiful battleship-gray deck.

On the eastern edge of the deck, from a planter-box of my design, native vines bloom upon a latticework trellis. In the "yard", beyond the trellis, three transplanted guava trees thrive.

A coral pathway connects our front stoop to a "Japanese Garden" bridge, spanning in graceful arc, the drainage ditch between yard and coral-paved street.

Rumors, about our "place", attract visitors from other squadrons and groups. Most men are complimentary. A few laugh at my lightweight system of roof support. Some sneer and predict the wind will blow it away.

The critics do not bother me. I know them. I call them "passenger-type aviators". They think they are superior aeronauts to the Wright Brothers, because the B-29's wingspan of 141 feet is greater in length than was Orville's first flight.

Like the way the Brother's light and delicate aeroplane resisted aerodynamic forces of flight, my roof has survived strong winds from the sea.

...

Malnove. Hey Don, pick up your damn cards. You're holdin' up the game.

Taylor. Yeah. What the hell are you doin', thinking about your wife again?

I pick up my cards. I pass the Queen of Spades, the Jack and Ten of Hearts to Taylor on my right. I pick up two deuces and a four, all clubs, from Caldwell. *Uh oh, he's goin' to try to "shoot the moon."* I warn no one. I'm tired of this game anyhow.

Cotner. I want to thank you guys for helping me improve our real estate.

Caldwell. You can probably volunteer to stay on here awhile, if you love it so much.

Cotner. No. I'm looking forward to that ocean cruise excursion, even though it means I'll be on the same boat with you guys.

The armed services has devised a point system for determining priorities of homeward rotation, and of separation from the service. Our thirty-three combat missions and our assortment of decorations for valor give us enough points to be sent home immediately but we know well by now that with the Army, immediately sometimes takes a while.

Taylor chuckles as he drops the Queen of Spades on Caldwell's trick. He is not yet aware of Caldwell's maleficent intent.

A Sergeant walks across our bridge, and down our path. He steps onto our deck. He salutes. We return.

Sergeant. Lieutenants Caldwell, Malnove and Taylor?

Response. Roger/Roger/Roger.

Sergeant. Colonel Wright asked me to deliver these orders to you. (*He hands each man a copy*).

Caldwell. I hope this is not some Court Martial Warrant you're serving us.

Cotner. *Caldwell is gettin' back to thinkin' like a damn lawyer. He's gonna resume his studies toward a law degree at the University of California at Berkeley as soon as he can get there.*

Sergeant. It's not. It's good, but you'll have to act fast. That's why the Colonel sent me.

Cotner. How come I didn't...

Malnove. Wow! Oh! Wow! "At 1400 hours, 22 September 1945, the following men shall be transported by troop truck from 99th Squadron Headquarters to the west end of Runway D, North Field. Shall proceed via air aboard Tinian Taxi to Isley Field, Saipan. Shall ride Saipan Armed Forces shuttle truck to Coast Guard Headquarters. There to be enrolled, by the Harbor Master, as personnel eligible for U.S.A. transport via troop ship."

Malnove, Caldwell and Taylor dance. They shout. The cavort like demented apes!

Cotner. Why wasn't I on the list?

Sergeant. I don't know, Sir.

Cotner. I've got just as many points as these guys.

The Sergeant shrugs.

Cotner. Is Col. Wright at headquarters?

Sergeant. He was when I left, Sir.

I run to 99th Squadron Headquarters. I save no time. It takes too long to catch my breath. But, the exercise banks the fire of my rebellious anger.

I enter the tent. I address an orderly.

Cotner. Lt. Cotner requests permission to see Col Wright.

Wright hears me.

Wright. Yes, Lieutenant?

Cotner. Sir, I believe I was inadvertently left off the order of my crewmates to depart at 1400 for Saipan, and home to separation.

Wright. No, Lieutenant. Today we received 313th Wing Special Order 242, signed by Colonel Mundy, on 22 September 1945. It transfers you to the 58th Bomb Wing. (*To orderly*). Give Lt. Cotner a copy of the order.

Cotner. Thank you, Sir.

Salute/return.

I read the order. It is brief. It says I'm "relieved from assignment and duty here and am assigned to the 444th Bomb Group, 58th Bomb Wing, and will report to the C.O. 23 September 1945, no travel involved".

Cotner. Col. Wright, is there any appeal for relief from this assignment?

Wright. No, Lieutenant. Why would you want to?

Cotner. I've been lookin' forward to a nice ocean voyage home with my crewmates.

Wright. Haven't you heard? The 58th Wing is flyin' home. They're taking off the twenty-fourth. They were short a Flight Engineer and asked us for one. Major Feil says you are our best one. He says you have a wife and new baby waitin' for you. We're doin' you a favor.

Cotner. Well, I will like to get home sooner, but how do I know I'll get a fair shake on early separation?

Wright. I believe they'll let you go once they get all their B-29s parked at their stateside home field.

Cotner. Sir, I've got this feeling that I've used up all of my flyin' luck.

Wright. Major Feil was very high on your courage and your intelligence. I don't believe you'll get superstitious. Anyway, I'm not goin' to send a revision back to Colonel Mundy.

Cotner. Yes, Sir. Thank you, Sir...Oh. What about the enlisted men on my aircrew? Are they leaving today?

Wright. Yes, they are. Capt. Littlewood's staying though.

I salute. Wright salutes.

I walk to the enlisted crewmen's hut. I say goodbye to Sgt. Connor, Sgt. Warn, Sgt. Richardson, Staff Sgt. Schultz, Tech Sgt. Calhoun, and Tech Sgt. Smith. The scene is on the edge of being teary.

I walk back to my hut. My mates each have their handbag packed. They think I'm lucky. I agree that maybe I am. We eat lunch at the Officer's Mess Hall. There is "goodbye type" excitement. Several other crews are leaving.

At 1400 I shake hands, as my crewmates and friends board the truck. They depart. We wave.

It's back to my hut again. I'm lonely. I pack my handbag. I write to Jean. I don't tell her I'm flyin' home with the 58th Wing. I know she wants me to stay on the ground, or on the sea. If I do fly, my arrival may be delayed.

I do not want her to worry. I walk to the 9th Group mailroom. I drop the letter in the slot.

I check out a jeep. I drive to the flight line. I shake hands goodbye with Master Sgt. Dreese and Tech Sgt. McAffee. I thank them for taking care of me. I pat a goodbye on "Old 574's" side.

I drive to the "Hon. Spy Report". Master Sgt. Maurice Szarko and I trade hugs. I shake hands with Staff Sgt. Kyger. I climb up the nose wheel well ladder. I salute my old instrument panel. I climb down. Capt. Art Smith and Lt. Howard Fiedleman are there. I thank everyone for taking care of me. We shake all around. I drive to camp. I return the jeep.

I walk to the hut.

Lieutenants Ed Piatek, Wilbourne Gromatsky, Ed Swanson, and M.L. Godfrey are playing Hearts on my porch, or should I say their porch. Tomorrow I will be gone. They will have to stay awhile. These four are the Officer airmen on Air Plane Commander Lacy Bobo's crew. They were assigned to the 9th Group on 8 May 1945 as a replacement crew. They haven't had the opportunity to fly many missions, and thus accumulate "rotation-points".

Piatek is the best buddy I have left on Tinian.

Piatek. Join the game, Don.

Cotner. Thanks, but I'm not in the mood.

Godfrey. Neither are we. Whatcha say we quit guys?

Gromatsky and Swanson. Roger, let's quit.

Piatek. Sit down, Don. What the hell's goin' on.

Cotner. Well, Caldwell, Malnove, and Taylor, and all our enlisted crewmen are on Saipan, waitin' for a boat to the U.S.A.

Swanson. Yeah, we told them goodbye.

Godfrey. What about Littlewood?

Cotner. He didn't get on the truck. I think he wants to be a career Air Corps man.

Piatek. How come you're still here?

Cotner. This will be my last night. I'm assigned to the 58th Wing.

Gromatsky. How come?

Cotner. Col. Wright says they're gonna fly home. One crew was short a Flight Engineer. Col. Mundy signed my transfer order but Major Feil and Colonel Wright selected me.

Piatek. You'll get home in a hurry.

Cotner. I'll be in the U.S.A. soon but will the 58th Wing C.O. let me separate?

Swanson. Pharaoh, Pharaoh, let my people go.

The afternoon and evening are endless. Saipan Sam has gone home. Tokyo Rose is off the air. I saw the movie last night. I hit the sack. I talk to Jean. I fall asleep.

0700 23 September 1945

I rise early for once. Early enough that I can eat breakfast in the mess hall. I'm glad to find Major Feil there. I didn't find him anywhere yesterday.

We reminisce. I thank him for all his efforts in my behalf. We talk about our wives, Mary and Jean. He gives me Mary's phone number. He asks me to call her when I get to the U.S.A. He wants me to assure her he's O.K. I promise.

I return to the hut. I gather my gas mask, my bayonet knife, my canteen, my blanket and my pillow. I go to the supply hut. I rap on the window. A Sergeant comes. I show him my order. I turn in the mask, knife, blanket and pillow.

I pick up my parachute, my C-1 life vest and my Mae West life preserver. I carry them to the hut.

Back at the hut, I pick up my handbag. I say goodbye to Ed Piatek. I walk out to the street. I look back at my handsome front porch and yard. I walk down to Riverside Drive. I'll try to hitchhike the seven miles to the 58th Wing camp. *Damn, I'm carryin' a load. Couldn't they at least have spared a driver to take me over in a jeep?*

A Sergeant in a jeep stops.

Sergeant. Hop in, Lieutenant. Where you headed?

Cotner. 58th Wing Headquarters.

Sergeant. I'm goin' to West Field. It's not far to the 58th Wing camp. I'll take you to Headquarters.

He lets me out at Headquarters. I thank him. I walk into the tent.

Cotner. I'm Lt. Donald Cotner, Flight Engineer, from the 9th Bomb Group, 313th Wing. I'm ordered to report to the Commanding Officer, 58th Wing.

Sergeant. He's not here now, Lieutenant.

He hands me two copies of an order dated 23 September 1945. It starts out, "Having reported to this Headquarters in compliance with..."

Sergeant. One is your copy. Just sign above your name on my copy.

I note that they have assigned me to the 444th Bomb Group. No mention of Squadron or Airplane Commander. I sign and return the order.

Cotner. Are there any further orders? I don't know where to go.

Sergeant. I apologize, Lieutenant. We're flying home in a couple of days. I'm behind in my typing. You are assigned to the 677th Squadron, and to Captain James C. Gallagher's aircrew. I'll show you how to get there.

I follow him out of the tent. He points south.

Sergeant. Captain John Gallagher and his officers live in hut number nine. Second block down this street.

Cotner. Thank you, Sergeant.

He salutes. I return.

I walk down the street. I find number nine. *Where is their porch?* Nostalgia grabs me. I go in. A man about thirty years old sits reading a book. He wears double barred insignia.

I salute. He returns.

Cotner. I'm Lt. Cotner, Sir. Are you Captain Gallagher?

Gallagher. Yes. Are you my new Flight Engineer?

Cotner. That's what the Sergeant tells me. I have no written order.

Gallagher. We're behind with the formalities. You may be in the U.S.A. before the order sendin' you there reaches you.

Cotner. Shall I report to the 444th Group Commander?

Gallagher. He's gonna give us a briefing at 1900 tonight. I'll introduce you to him and to the C.O. of the 677th Squadron..

Cotner. Thank you, Sir.

Gallagher. (*Pointing*). The last cot on the right, there, is your sack. The blanket and pillowcase are clean.

Cotner. Thank you, Sir.

Gallagher. The latrine and the shower are out the back door. You won't have any trouble findin' them.

Cotner. Roger.

Gallagher asks the details of my training and experience. He tells me he's lucky to get such a qualified engineer. I learn that he's got 600 hours piloting multiple engine planes. He flew out of Houston for Humble Oil Co. Inc. before the war. He was with the 58th Wing in India. He bombed Japan seven times from China. The B-29s had to fly over the "hump" from Karachi, land in China to refuel, fly round trip to Japan, refuel again, and get over the "hump" again to Karachi. I tell him I'm lucky to fly with an Airplane Commander who can do that.

I'm tired. I lie on my sack. I had forgotten how uncomfortable an army cot is. I think of my Seabee built bunk bed. I wonder who has claimed it. I think of Jeannie. I fall asleep.

Captain Gallagher wakes me. He introduces me to his Pilot, 1st Lt. Bill McClendon, and to his Navigator, 1st Lt. Bob Leffert. Gallagher says we will fly without a Bombardier. I feel good about flying. These guys all seem well qualified. We won't need anyone to aim bombs at Dallas, or to shoot down any P-38's flying escort.

We all wash up and go to dinner in the Officer's Mess Hall. Their chef serves the same New Zealand lamb and Tinian vegetables that I got in the 9th Group. The crew makes me feel welcome.

We are fifteen minutes early at the briefing. So is everyone else. *Does this tell me something?*

At 1900 we stand and salute as the C.O. strides in. He is tall. His hair is blonde. His shirtsleeves are cut off at the shoulder seam. *Does he lift weights somewhere? He wears eagles on his epaulets. He wears his ribbons of valor on his chest. Is he younger than I am? Is this the guy Warn told us about?*

He leaps two steps to the dais deck. He smiles. He radiates energy.

Gallagher. (*In my ear*). This is Col. Wood, the 444th Group's C.O.

Wood. Good evening gentlemen. I am Del Wood, C.O. 444th. I especially welcome those of you who have recently joined our Group.

Cotner. *Does he mean I'm not the only new man?*

Wood. We asked for the best people the 313th Wing could send us. The 58th Wing is commanded to fly each of our B-29s to the U.S.A. Some of our crews had unfilled positions.

Cotner. *So far, so good.*

Wood. We depart Tinian 0900 24 September 1945. Our first stop will be Kwajalein.

Cotner. *That's the way the 9th Group got here.*

Wood. Here's the good news.

Cotner. *I wish he had said somethin' else.*

Wood. I received approvals this afternoon for the 444th's Special Mission.

Cotner. *I wish he had said somethin' else.*

Wood. This will be a surprise for you new people.

Cotner. *Hey, Col. Wood! Surprises sprung in briefing are never good.*

Wood. On all our 444th planes, insignia and lettering are freshly painted. You'll be proud to be in the 444th Group.

Cotner. *I'm here but my loyalty and my pride are still with the 99th Squadron and the 9th Bomb Group.*

Wood. Listen up, new people. You will have the honor of flying with us in our thirty-day aerial victory parade in the skies of the United States of America.

Cotner. *I can't believe a rational man would have said that.*

Wood. We'll fly in formation every time we're in the air.

Cotner. *Don't tell me anymore, Col. Wood.*

Wood. We'll fly over a different big city every day.

Cotner. *Big cities like New York? Chicago?*

Wood. We'll land at each city and have open house for the public.

Cotner. *Don't tell me we'll give free rides to civilians.*

Wood. A few lucky citizens will win rides in B-29s.

Cotner. *Won't somebody tell this madman this is illegal?*

My brain ceases to hear more. It's too busy visualizing.

We are flyin' from fields where there are too few mechanics; worse, there are no mechanics that know how to service the B-29. We are flyin' from fields where there is no stock at all of any B-29 spare parts.

Engines fail on takeoff; flight instruments fizzle in mid-air; control surfaces flap futilely in the wind during tight turns of flight. Propellers run loose in flailing fiascoes. On landing, brake systems go bankrupt.

Horny young airmen, some of them Airplane Commanders, some of them Pilots, search too many bars, buying too many drinks. matching too many women drink for drink or worse, matching women two drinks to one.

Some of them finally find a woman too drunk to say no. They flop around trying to gain sufficient arousal to consummate their lust despite the detumescent effect of alcohol saturation upon their central nervous systems. They lose too much sleep.

Hung-over airmen on the base try to entertain voyeuristic civilians.

Hung-over, dead-tired "performers" take off in freshly-painted B-29s. We try to assemble in glorious formation. I see two B-29s collide in the sky. I see a three-way collision. I see a B-29 fly into the Empire State Building.

I return to reality, as I hear Col. Wood say, "The Flight Engineers will meet with Capt. Wiley, Group Flight Engineer."

Briefing has broken-up into ad hoc assemblies of specialists. Captain Gallagher points out Capt. Wiley to me. I go to his corner. I salute and introduce myself. He gives me a Flight Engineer's flimsy for the flight to Kwajalein. I tell him it's the same form we used in the 9th Group.

I go back to Hut Nine. I wait for Captain Gallagher. He soon comes in carrying the Pilot's flimsy.

Cotner. Captain, I feel like I've been shanghaied. No one told me you were going to fly an Aerial Victory Parade.

Gallagher. I apologize, Lieutenant Cotner. Col. Wood ordered us to keep it quiet, until he got it approved. I guess he finally sold the idea to General Raimey, C.O. of the 58th Wing.

Cotner. I've got to talk to Col. Wood and tell him how I feel.

Gallagher. How do you feel?

I tell Gallagher of my visions.

Gallagher. You have a great imagination.

Cotner. It may be intuition.

Gallagher. What will you say to Col. Wood?

Cotner. I'll tell him that I think I've earned the right, by surviving combat, not to gamble with my life in peacetime. I'll tell him I've used up all of my flyin' luck. I'll tell him about my wife and daughter, and how I want to be husband and father.

Gallagher. I have a wife and children. I feel much the same as you.

Cotner. Let's both go talk to him.

Gallagher. I know him. I know what he'd do to someone who would say the things you've told me.

Cotner. What could he do? What would he do?

Gallagher. He'd say you're a coward. He'd say you were tryin' to ruin his parade. He'd say you're not a civilian yet. He'd say he is your Commanding Officer, and, that it is a soldier's duty to obey his C.O. He'd say that it is your duty to make him look good.

Cotner. He could put that in my Personnel File but I don't want a military career anyway.

Gallagher. I've seen him be hard on men he accused of being cowards.

Cotner. That's difficult to believe.

Gallagher. When he finds out you're anxious to get home to your wife and baby after the parade, he could figure out someplace to send you, where you'll be stuck for months before you can get home, or get to a separation center. He would think he's making a soldier out of you.

Cotner. I'm tempted to confront him as a challenge.

Gallagher. Don't. I'm trying to save your ass.

Cotner. I'll sleep on it.

Gallagher. Sleep easy, Lieutenant. The "parade" won't be as dangerous as you envision it. I know these guys. None of them will want to bring a dose of clap or syphilis home to their wife or sweetheart. They're good flyers. You didn't hear him, but Col. Wood ordered us to do at least eight hours of formation flying between here and the U.S.A.
We're the designated lead crew of the 677th Squadron and the 677th will be lead Squadron of the Group. Out front is the safest place to be in any aerial formation.

I look at the Flight Engineer's flimsy. *They're givin' us a full fuel supply for each of the four wing tanks. We'll carry twelve men as passengers, but no other load. It's only 972 miles to Kwajalein. We'll only weigh 119,100 lbs. at take-off. We'll have plenty of gas. They've given us fast cruising speeds. It should be an easy flight.*

I see takeoff is scheduled at 1100 hours tomorrow. I hit the sack. I decide to say nothing to Col. Wood. I'll take my chances. I think of Jeannie and Donna Marie. I go to sleep.

Kwajalein

24 September 1945, 58th Wing, Tinian.

Captain Gallagher wakes me. I get out of the sack. I'm stiff. I sure miss my bunk bed. I go to breakfast with Gallagher.

Cotner. I've decided to at least partially follow your advice. I'm not gonna say anything before we get to the U.S.A.

Gallagher. That's wise.

1000. We ride in trucks to the flight line. I meet Tech Sergeant Clayton Ziegler, the Crew Chief. He and eleven mechanics will be our twelve passengers. If that is true for each of the Group's forty-five planes, one of my envisioned problems will be solved.

I perform my pre-flight inspections. Everything is perfect. I compliment the Crew Chief.

Cotner. I see that your plane has the new Curtis electric propeller-pitch control system.

Ziegler. All the 58th Wing planes have it. We deployed to India in June 1944. The Air Corps has gradually replaced all those old original worn-out B-29s we had.

Cotner. That's encouraging news. We lost several planes and crews in the 9th due to brake failure. Now when we land, and the Airplane Commander gives the order, I can reverse the propellers and slow us down.

I solve the weights and balance equations. I put one passenger up front.

Cotner. Ziegler, you want to sit on the deck beside me?

Ziegler. Yes, Sir.

Cotner. (*To Captain Gallagher*). I'm puttin' one passenger up front. Is it O.K. if Ziegler rides there?

Gallagher. Roger. (*To the crew*). Let's board.

We climb in. We do our in-cabin pre-flight inspections. Everything is in order.

Gallagher. Start engines.

Cotner. Roger.

I warm up the engines. I check the mags.

Cotner. Engines O.K., Captain.

Gallagher. We taxi in two minutes. Nice timing, crew.

Gallagher taxies to "lead-off" takeoff position. He orders takeoff power. We start down the runway. We accelerate. Lift off is easy. Our heading for Kwajalein is ninety degrees, almost due east. I feel good.

Gallagher calls for a slow cruise. He orders each Squadron to close into separate formation behind its lead plane. We fly as squadrons for an hour.

Gallagher orders the leader of the 676th Squadron to close in, 500 feet high, on our Squadron's right. He orders the 678th leader to close in 500 feet low, on our left. We fly for an hour in group formation. Commanders and Pilots are good flyers. Everything that happens makes me feel better.

Ziegler shows great interest in what I do. I tutor him in flight engineering. He knows the B-29 and its engines well. I show him how to manage fuel consumption, and to maintain the log. I share time with him in my seat.

We cross no cold fronts, and except for a five mph headwind, the weather is perfect. Gallagher orders the formation to spread. On intercom, Lt. Leffert, Navigator, gives an E.T.A. of fifteen minutes.

Gallagher begins letdown. He sees the island. It's long enough for a runway, but it's only a few hundred feet wide. Its length is parallel to our course. Gallagher lands smoothly. A sergeant in a jeep guides him to a parking spot. There's going to be barely enough room for forty-five B-29s.

Where the hell has the time gone?

We climb down to the sandy coral surface. We watch the rest of the planes land and taxi. I notice that around the huts palm trees are growing. I hadn't seen a live plant on our stop here on the way to Tinian. The naval barrage had killed every living thing.

We find ping-pong tables, horseshoe pits and volleyball courts. We blow off a little energy. We go through a supper chow line. The mess hall is crowded. We stay for a debriefing/briefing meeting. Spirits are high, especially Col. Wood's spirits.

Kwajalein has showers with hot running water. I spend about an hour in my bath. I hit the sack in my assigned cot. *I'm getting closer, Jeannie.*

JOHN RODGERS FIELD

25 September 1945, 0700, Kwajalein.

An electronic bugle wakes us. We shave, dress, breakfast and walk to our re-fueled planes. At 0900 Gallagher leads the takeoffs. Every B-29 gets airborne. Our heading to John Rodgers Field, Honolulu, is sixty-three degrees, roughly east, northeast. Our distance will be 2,619 miles.

Gallagher gets us through the formation flying early. The rest is mostly boring "airplane driving". I'm happy to share time with Ziegler.

After we eat our sack lunches, we go through a weather front. Ziegler tosses his lunch.

Ziegler. I'm sorry. I couldn't help it.

Cotner. You didn't get any on me.

Ziegler. Well, so much for my budding career as a Flight Engineer.

I thank my parents for the genes that have given me a cast-iron stomach. I've never experienced motion sickness from any movement source, any auto, boat, airplane or other vehicle.

I remember Edwin Pomeroy, a fellow flight-engineering student at Lowrey Field, Denver. He flew in the same plane with me. There was always rough air over the Rockies. Edwin always vomited. He always had to clean it up, of course. Once he threw up in my lunch sack. To save himself a clean up, I suppose. Even seeing it happen didn't make me sick. I got really hungry that day though.

Just before dark we hit Oahu on the nose and on schedule. We land at John Rodgers Field.

We have the next day off. With my crewmates I ride the bus to Waikiki. I rent a surfboard. It's two and a half inches thick, ten inches wide, and twelve feet long. I stagger under its weight as I carry it to the water. The waves are apparently perfect. The brown beach boys are dazzling a bunch of haole girls, as they ride the surf from half of a mile out, blown by a strong onshore breeze.

I drop my board into the water. I lie down on it. I paddle seaward. It's hard going. I work to exhaustion. I stick my left arm down. I'm in about a foot and a half of water. I look back at the shore. I've hardly gone anywhere. My comrades and I return our boards. We shower and dress. We eat a fabulous lunch in the Halekalani Hotel. We return to John Rodgers.

At an evening briefing, we learn that takeoff tomorrow will be at 1000 hours, for Mather Field, California, U.S.A. The briefing officer finally silences our cheers.

I hit the sack. *I'm on Oahu, Jean. I'm on my way...*Fatigue won't let me finish.

MATHER FIELD

26 September 1945, 0700, John Rodgers Field.

A live bugle and a real bass drum, get us out of the sack. Col. Wood tells us at a post-breakfast briefing that there will be a slight delay in the scheduled 1000 takeoff for Mather Field. We are commanded to pre-flight our planes and stand by until ordered to take off. At 1000 hours we are standing by. We stand until 1100 hours. At 1200 hours they send us to lunch.

Rumors crisscross the mess hall. The rumor that becomes accepted as the truth, is that Col. Wood is seeking permission for a change of plans. We believe that the Colonel wants us to enter the U.S. in Group Formation over the Golden Gate Bridge. He wants us to fly south over the eastern shore cities of the Bay. He wants us to fly over San Jose and north over the Peninsula Cities. He wants us to circle San Francisco two or three times. He is seeking FAA approval and newsreel coverage.

We are excited. Even I want to do it. I am finally realizing that after a war, soldiers want to play conquering hero. Giuseppe Verdi even wrote an opera about it.

1330 hours.

The order comes that we can use the recreational facilities but we are still on standby. We are forbidden to leave John Rodgers Field. So it's table tennis, horseshoes and volleyball again. The Honolulu afternoon is hot and humid. We don't have the energy for games. We try to rest on our sacks in the hot tents. "Milliards" of flies attack us. They don't bite. They crawl...they crawl...

1600 hours.

The order is delivered by sweating runners. "Take off at 1700."

We jog to our planes. We re-do pre-flights. We board. At 1700 Captain Gallagher takes off. We have fuel in the center wing-tank now. We are a little heavier than on our two previous flights. We are still much lighter than we flew in combat.

Gallagher reports to Col. Wood that the Group has done beautiful formation flying. He asks Col. Wood for relief from formation practice on this flight. Wood grants relief.

Captain Gallagher takes up the Navigator's course of sixty-one degrees to the Golden Gate Bridge.

Gallagher. Lieutenant Cotner, give me little extra speed, if you have enough fuel.

Cotner. I'd better play it safe, Sir. We don't know what kind of winds we will have.

Gallagher. Roger.

We'll have to fly all night, but I've done that before. This time I've got Clayton Ziegler. I can take a nap or two. Golden Gate Bridge...It was a beautiful sight when we left the U.S.A. It will be even prettier when we return.

We cross no weather fronts. We hit no rough air. Headwinds are mild. The plane performs perfectly. *How lucky can I get?* I trade with Ziegler. I nap.

27 September, 0601.

Light enters the cockpit. It wakens me from my uncomfortable, cold, restless sleep on the deck. I see Ziegler in my seat. I yawn. I get up and stretch. I look out the nose of the plane. The sun is rising from the sea. I miss the Mariana Island's sunrise colors but I know we're near the U.S.A. I ask Nelson where we are. He says we're two hours out of San Francisco Bay.

I greet Ziegler. I thank him for the nap. I greet Captain Gallagher and the Pilot. I visit the relief tube. I say good morning to the Radio Operator, Staff Sgt. John Eareckson. I go to my station. I swap places with Ziegler. I check his fuel figures.

Cotner. We've got a little extra fuel, Captain; do you still want to fly faster?

Gallagher. No. It was a bad idea in the first place. I've just ordered each Airplane Commander to catch up with the Group and find his place in the formation. Slow us down about ten mph.

Cotner. Roger.

I eat the rest of my sack lunch for breakfast. I drink tomato juice and coffee.

The planes begin to catch us. By 0700 the Group is in formation. The C.F.C. gunner, S/Sgt. Keene, reports that it looks perfect to him.

0742.

Bill McClendon (*Yells on the intercom*). I SEE THE BRIDGE! I SEE THE GOLDEN GATE BRIDGE!

Bill, the Pilot, is a native Californian. He thinks the bridge is his. I turn and look out the nose. No wonder he's proud. Silhouetted in the morning sunlight, it is a moving, beautiful United States of America sight.

We are at 4900 feet.

Gallagher. (*To the Group Formation*). I'm speeding up to 230 mph. Follow me. Keep the formation clean and tight. (*To me*). Give me the speed, Lieutenant.

Cotner. Roger.

Gallagher goes into a shallow dive. *What the hell? Is he gonna take us under the Bridge? He levels off at 4,000 feet.*

0817.

We are beyond the bridge. We expect a right turn. Gallagher turns left. *What the hell is happening? Did Gallagher get an order while I was asleep?*

Gallagher. What's the course to Sacramento?

Nelson. Two degrees. Why?

Gallagher. We're going directly to Mather Field and land there. Give me an ETA.

Cotner. *Who the hell gave the order? General Raimey, General Le May, General Arnold?*

Nelson. Damn soon. Follow the Sacramento River and you'll soon see it.

Gallagher. Eareckson, notify all group radio operators that we're landing at Mather right away. Instruct each Radio Operator to advise his Airplane Commander. Report back to me when each Airplane Commander has acknowledged the order.

I look out the window. I've heard of the Sacramento River Delta, but we're already up-river from there by now. Some fields are green. I guess they are irrigated, because most of the country below is brown. When we left for Tinian in January, California was green. I turn back to the instruments.

We are soon on the landing approach at Mather Field. Again, I feel lucky to be on the lead plane. Captain Gallagher bounces the plane on the landing. Maybe he's excited too. He doesn't look excited though.

Gallagher. Reverse the propellers.

Cotner. Roger. *What an invention. I know he means, "reverse the pitch of the propellers".*

We slow.

Gallagher. Give me thrust for taxiing.

Cotner. Roger. (*I comply*).

Gallagher follows a jeep. He parks.

Gallagher. Cut engines.

Cotner. Roger. (*I comply*).

A Sergeant signals Gallagher to open his window. Gallagher slides it back. The Sergeant salutes. He hands Gallagher a paper.

Sergeant. Instructions from the Base Commandant, Carl Mather Field.

Gallagher. Roger. (*He scans the paper. He comes on intercom*). Hold up a minute, crew. We're instructed to disembark the plane with all our personal belongings, and with all Air Corps flight gear. With belongings and gear we shall board bus No. One. I see the bus. It is waiting for us.

Cotner. Ziegler, you want to fill out the Airplane Performance Report, for a change?

Ziegler. Yeah, thanks.

I'm surprised. Before he changes his mind, I let him into my seat. I open the hatch. Still wearing my flight gear and carrying my flight bag, I climb down to the USA!

With all my gear, I struggle aboard bus No. One. My crewmates follow. Airmen from other crews follow. Bus No. One fills. We depart.

We ride into the neat little city of Sacramento. We ride down tree shaded residential streets. We park with the other buses in a lot beside a huge grassy park. Sergeants count us as we alight from the buses. They form us into lines on the grass.

When we are all deployed, a Colonel appears.

Colonel. I am Colonel Graeber, Commanding Officer of Mather Field Air Base. Welcome to the U.S.A., to Mather Field, to the city of Sacramento, and to Forty Niner Park. Our facilities on the base are overcrowded with war returnees. The city has graciously permitted us to use this park.

If you wish to proceed as soon as possible to the Army's Center nearest your home, for discharge from, or for separation from, the service, place all of your army owned equipment on the ground in the space beside you. Have your "Separation Points Service Card" ready. The card must bear the signature of your Group's Commanding Officer.

Great cheers fill the park. I wonder where and how soon I can find a phone.

A phalanx of Supply Sergeants comes down the rows. They look at our gear on the ground. They find our records on their clipboards. They line through and initial each item we turn in.

I recognize the sheets that I signed for this stuff,when we left the staging base back in January. How did they meet me here today in Forty Niner Park? I'll never disabuse the Army about inefficiency again.

The Sergeant finishes my paperwork.

Sergeant. Are you leaving the service, sir?

Cotner. As soon as I can, Sarge.

Sergeant. May I see your "Points Card"?

I'm ready. I hand it to him.

Sergeant. 187 points, wow! It's signed by Col. Huglin. He's not on my list of Group Commanders.

Cotner. He was my Commanding Officer when I was in the 9th Group, 313th Wing.

I show him my transfer order.

Sergeant. O.K. Get back on bus No. One.

He salutes. I salute. He moves to the next man. Free of Army gear. Free in spirit. I run to the bus.

Camp Stoneman

A sergeant by the open door salutes me. I return. I board the bus. I find a front seat.

The bus soon fills. The Sergeant and the driver board. We depart. We ride through Sacramento. We take the highway south.

The somber, sere landscape makes me wonder who, or what, rained on Col. Wood's Aerial Victory Parade. He flew as "passenger" (more probably as "Acting Airplane Commander") in the lead plane of the 678th Squadron, the last in the 544th Group aerial formation. Was that so he could shoot down straggling defectors from the 677th and the 676th?

I have not seen Col. Wood since I boarded Captain Gallagher's plane at John Rogers Field in Honolulu. *Was he as surprised as I was by the events at Mather Field?*

I decide to forget him. Then I think, if I ever write a book about my wartime adventures, I will put him in it.

Song breaks out. We sing "Off We Go Into The Wild Blue Yonder","Wait Till The Sun Shines Nellie", "Roll Me Over In The Clover", "Oh Maresy Doats", "Don't Fence Me In". Someone starts "Paper Doll", but we shout that one down. We <u>want</u> real live girls.

We go south on a highway that follows the Sacramento River. I look at the river and the green trees and shrubs that line its banks. I look at the tall grasses in the fields. They shine golden in the sunlight. Someone else is impressed. He sings, "California, Here I Come". I am, of course, an Okie and I want to go home to "Okie Land" but I sing as loud as I can.

The highway veers inland. The land looks barren, somewhat like a desert.

We turn off the highway. A big sign reads "CAMP GEORGE STONEMAN". We park near the buildings. The Sergeant asks us to sit tight a minute. He goes inside a big building.

The Sergeant returns. He steps aboard.

Sergeant. The mess hall is still open. They'll serve you lunch. It's not segregated. Officers and men can eat together.

The Sergeant leads us to the mess hall. I'm soon carrying my tray, looking for a seat. I see a 1st Lieutenant wearing Flight Engineer's Wings. I sit by him. He is John Tiernan. He was transferred to the 677th Squadron from the 505th Bomb Group, 313th Wing. He too, of course, arrived from John Rodgers this morning.

We find much in common. He was a Non-Flying Aviation Cadet at Boca Raton. He graduated from, and was commissioned at, Yale. He went to the Boeing School and to Flight Engineering School at Lowry. He trained with the 505th Group at Liberal, Kansas.

After lunch, the Sergeant takes us to the line that leads us to the "check-in" counter. They put Tiernan and me in the same double occupancy Bachelor Officer's Room. They tell us it will be three days before we can get on a train headed east. We will be free to leave the camp if we choose but they warn us to be here when our train leaves.

John and I find our room. We pass a battery of pay phones on the way. In the room, I put down my bag. We both run back to the phones. We get in what appears to be the shortest line. I have my quarters ready, and Jean's folk's phone number in Tulsa, lest I forget it.

The line barely moves. We ask the Sergeant ahead of us, "Why is everyone talking for such a selfishly long time?" He says, "The phone company cuts us off at three minutes. The long distance telephone operators are on strike.

Ma Bell is trying to maintain service, using supervisors as operators. What we wait for is to get hold of a supervisor."

We thank him. We wait. *Why will a "God" permit phone operators to do this to returning War Heroes?*

Two and a half hours later, I'm talking to Jeannie.

Jean. Hello.

Don. Surprise, Honey! I'm in the U.S.A.

Jean. Is this you Don? Where are you?

Don. Camp Stoneman.

Jean. Where's that?

Don. Less than fifty miles north of San Francisco, I love you, Jeannie.

Jean. I love you, Don. Why didn't you write or phone that you were coming?

Don. I didn't have time. I'll explain when I see you.

Jean. Oh, Don. I'm so happy.

Don. I'm happy too, Honey. I want to make love with you.

Jean. Oh, yes, Don, yes, yes, yes, yes, yes.

Don. How's little Donna?

Jean. She's wonderful, Sweetheart.

Don. Can I talk to her?

Jean. She can't talk yet. She's only five months old.

Don. Is she awake?

Jean. No, she's already asleep.

Don. Can't you wake her up?

Jean. No, that wouldn't be good for her.

Don. I want to hear her coo, and to make whatever sounds she does.

Jean. I don't think I should, Don.

Don. Won't she be able to go back to sleep?

Jean. Yeah, she will.

Don. Does she sleep in a crib?

Jean. Yes.

Don. Please go get her. Are your Mother and Dad there?

Jean. Yes.

Don. Let me talk to one of them, while you go get her.

Jean. Well, I guess I'll get her. Here's Dad.

Dad. Hi, Don. I heard something about Camp Stoneman. Are you gonna be stationed there? Where's that?

Don. Hi, Dad. Are you feeling as good as you sound?

Dad. Yes, I'm good. I'm sure glad the war's over. Where are you?

Don. I'm in Camp Stoneman. It's in California.

Dad. Here's Jean. She's got little Donna. She sure is a beautiful little baby.

Jean. Hi, Honey. You're gonna love our baby.

Don. Let me talk to her. Put the phone up to her ear.

Jean. O.K., Honey. Here she is.

Don. Hello, Donna Marie. This is your Daddy. I love you. I'll be home soon.

Jean. She's smiling. I think she knows it's her Daddy.

Don. Yeah, Donna. I'm your Daddy, Don. Jean, can you get her to say something? Or laugh maybe?

Jean. I'll tickle her a little.

Donna. Hee, hee, hee, hee, hee.

Jean. Did you hear her?

Don. Yeah, she laughed. She's got a sweet little laugh.

Donna. Waah, waah, waaaah.

Jean. She's crying now.

Don. I hear her. Is she all right?

Jean. Yes, she's all right, but I'd better get her back to sleep before she gets too mad.

Don. Does she have a temper?

Jean. No. She's the best little, sweetest little girl in the world but she's never been awakened before.

Don. Well, I don't want her to get sick.

Jean. She won't. She's very healthy. Here, say hi to my Mom, while I put Donna back to sleep.

Mom. Hi, Don. How are you?

Don. I'm fine, Mom. How are you?

Mom. I'm pretty good. Are you going to be discharged soon?

Don. Very soon. Is Frank gettin' out soon?

Mom. He doesn't know. He's stationed at Scott Field now. Across the river from St. Louis. Here's Jean.

Jean. Hello, Honey. I love you.

Don. Hello, Jean. I love you, and I love our baby.

Bell Supervisor. You've talked two minutes and fifty seconds. We're cutting you off in ten seconds.

Don. Roger...Jean, I'll try to call you tomorrow. I love you.

Jean. I love you, Don. Kiss, kiss, kiss, kiss.

Telephone. Click. Bzz, bzz, bzz.

I hang up. John completes his call to his sweetheart in Pittsburgh. We eat supper in the mess hall. We go to the evening movie. It's Humphrey Bogart in a gangster movie. I can't stand that ugly over-emoter. I sleep. John wakes me when the movie ends. We go to our room. We shower. We sleep.

0600: 28 Sept.

A trumpet, tuba, trombone, snare drum, bass-drum combo wakes us. Stoneman is a big camp. Over breakfast in the mess hall, John and I decide to hitchhike to San Francisco. We have no clothes, just khakis. We find out they are the official uniform in September in California. We each pin on our ribbons. They represent the only medals we've actually received so far: the Distinguished Flying Cross and the Air Medal.

Before leaving, John calls his girlfriend again, and I call Jean. It's lunchtime when we finish waiting in line and talking our three minutes each.

After lunch we walk out to the highway. We wait in the Service Men's Pickup Shelter. We get a ride soon. An Air Corps Captain picks us up. He doesn't talk like a Captain.

Captain. Where are you guys going?

John & Don. San Francisco

Captain. I can take you as far as Sausalito.

John & Don. Where's that?

Captain. It's at this end of the Golden Gate Bridge.

John & Don. Good.

We see that the Captain wears pilot's wings.

John. What did you fly?

Captain. B-17s.

Don. Where?

Captain. I was in the 8th Air Force. I bombed Germany from England.

John & Don. How many missions did you fly?

Captain. Three.

Don. Did the war in Europe end on you?

Captain. It did for me.

John & Don. What do you mean?

Captain. I got shot down on my fouth mission.

Neither John nor I know what to say. The Captain volunteers nothing. There is thirty minutes of silence.

We reach Sausalito.

Captain. Let me take you guys to meet my Aunt and Uncle. They live here.

John & Don. O.K.

The Captain drives up a steep hill. He parks. We walk to the door. His Aunt seems overjoyed to see us. She invites us in. We talk. The Uncle comes home. He and the Aunt came here from Iowa to work in a shipyard. They insist we stay for supper. It's Iowa home cooking. We each get all the blackberry cobbler a la mode we can eat.

After supper they open a fifth of bourbon. They laugh and cry at our war stories. The Captain opens up. He spent a year and a half in a German Prison Camp. Says he would have starved except that his guards sneaked food to them for "Red Cross" cigarettes.

Aunt and Uncle open another bourbon. We talk and laugh till we're falling asleep with our heads on the table. Aunt and Uncle have an extra double bed and a sofa bed. The Captain gets the sofa bed. John and I share the double bed.

29 Sept.

The shipyard is still on a wartime production schedule. Aunt and Uncle get up early and go to work. John and I and the Captain get up late. The Captain makes coffee and toast. John and I have queasy stomachs. We eat little.

The Captain drives us to downtown San Francisco. John and I forgot our razors. We get our first ever shaves in a barbershop. *Damn! Those towels are hot.*

We ride the cable cars. We try a seafood lunch at Fisherman's Wharf. We are still too liquor-queasy to enjoy food. We take a taxi to the servicemen's hitchhiking shelter near the Golden Gate's south tollbooths. We catch a ride to Stoneman.

We go to the office. We find out we are each scheduled for departure next day on a 0900 train to St. Louis.

We each take a long nap. We feel hungry. We eat supper in the mess hall. We go to the theater. We watch "Meet Me In St. Louis". John and I had seen it on Tinian. We enjoy it again. It stirs our anticipated joy of joining our little families. We shower and go to bed.

Meditations on the movie mingle with wistful thoughts of Jeannie and Little Donna….The movie fades…I think of Jean and Donna…z…z…

UNION STATION

The band wakes us at 0700. We dress. We breakfast. We pack our bag. We board the train. It chuff, chuff, chuffs out of Camp Stoneman at 0900.

I find that I'm in the lower berth on the right front corner of the second Pullman car. By chance, I share the facing pair of seats with a short young Sergeant named Keith Golden. We recognize each other as being of the Class of '39 at Tulsa Central High School, a class numbering 1413 teenage souls. We had shared only one class, Francis McCullough's Sophomore Mechanical Drawing Class.

Our reunion is briefly fun but Keith turns out to be one of those enlisted men who adopts a fawning subservient relationship toward officers, even toward Lieutenants. Sophomore Mechanical Drawing is a subject for less than a half hour's worth of conversation. I finally have to ask Keith to be silent part of the time.

The desert is beautiful, but solar energy soon warms our rail car. Keith and I combine our efforts. We get the ancient window open. The train is speeding. A strong wind blows in. It's warm, but its velocity cools. It carries particles of coal, soot and ash.

To avoid these irritants, Keith permits me to ride backward, sitting next to him. He offers to hold his magazine so we can each appreciate the photos of mostly undressed women. I decline but I thank him. I ask him if I can sit by the window. He graciously trades with me.

The grit doesn't get in my eyes now. I admire the panoramas as they roll by. I daydream of Jeannie and little Donna. The seat is comfortable, and since my first train ride as a child, I have loved the rhythm steel wheels play upon jointed rails. I doze off now and then.
Keith sleeps too. He snores with loud snorts but they are not loud enough to wake him. I let him sleep.

They had told us at Stoneman that troops will be the only people aboard but a genuine civilian negro Pullman Porter comes down the aisle. He has a lot of energy and great loud humor. He takes our rail passes. He punches the tickets. He sticks them in the holder at our seat station.

Porter. You taking good care of our Lieutenant, Sarge?

Keith. Yes, sir.

Cotner. *Keith says "sir" to a Negro? Does he believe that the Porter's uniform and his Pullman badge bestow officer's rank? Well, Don, in actuality, don't they? Is Keith aware that Negroes can outrank white people; or is he habituated to "Sir-ing" an imposing uniform?*

I note that the Porter speaks with no trace of a southern "darkie" dialect. Punching tickets as he goes, he works his way to the rear. He looks ahead. He soon adopts a broad, "black" brogue. A Colonel sits in the last seat.

Porter. Lemmee see yoh ticket, Boss.

Slight pause.

Porter. Wheah yoh goin', Suh?

Colonel. Boston.

Porter. Oh my! Colonel, dincho read yoh ticket?

Colonel. The destination is not shown on the ticket.

Porter. Oh, yessuh! It say right here "Sheecago! Sheecago, Illyonoise!

Colonel. Show me where it says "Chicago".

The Porter shows him the ticket. He points.

Porter. Raht dere, Boss.

The Colonel is not catching on. I guess that no one has ever kidded him since he first wore Major's, or maybe Captain's, insignia.

Everyone watches, but keeps a straight face.

Colonel. It doesn't say "Chicago". It doesn't say "St. Louis". It says "Atcheson, Topeka and Santa Fe Railroad. United States of America, Armed Services Railroad Pass".

Porter. Din't dey show yoh how to read dem numbers? Dats de code. How yoh get dem eagles, out yoh larn yoh codes? All dem Cohpls and Sgnts, and sum dem lutenints, back dere knowed dere codes.

We look away. We try not to let the Colonel see us tremble all over...*I believe the Colonel has caught on.*

Colonel. My Sergeant opted for a military career. If he was still with me, he would have checked my ticket. He knows everything. I don't know how I'll get by as a civilian without him to tell me what to do.

We explode!

The Colonel salutes. The Porter returns. The Porter comes back down the aisle. He tells us that lunch will soon be served. Keith and I resume our seats.

A Negro, in white apron and chef's hat, enters the car's rear door. *Is there a dining car on this train?*

Chef. Line up according to your seat and follow me. Forget rank.

Is the Army trying to civilianize us?

We go through the next car; it's empty. *How many dining cars do they have on this train?* We enter the next car. It's a kitchen with a chow line down one side. Negro "chefs" are waiting to serve us. Our "chef" leads us through into the next car.

Surprise! This rail car has been stripped of seats, and of Pullman berths. I see four rows of narrow, three-tiered iron-framed bunk beds. Their vertical stanchions are anchored to floor and ceiling. The aisles are narrow. The center aisle is passable enough for us to walk through. In nearly every bunk, a Negro G.I. lies on his back. A few pairs of men sit playing cards. They hunch over for lack of headroom. Their legs dangle into the aisles. All men wear fatigues. Most sleeves sport P.F.C. stripes. Many sleeves are bare of insignia of rank. *Buck Privates?*

A few of us stare, some with ill will showing. Most of us look straight ahead. Some with compassion. Some with embarrassment. We can't shut off peripheral vision. We see.

The next car is the same. We don't go past it. The third "Negro car" now contains the line from our third "white car". Our "first car" troops do not enter the car we are in.

Chef. (*In attempted humor*). To the Rear, Harch!

We proceed, at less than march pace, toward the front of the train. In the mess car, the chefs serve us as much as we ask for, of mashed potatoes, roast beef, rolls and butter, a variety of vegetables and of puddings, pies and cakes. We can have coffee or milk or both. *Is the Army trying to influence our memories of service in case they want us to fight another war?*

We carry our trays to our seats. Our porter has unfolded and set up our table. He has closed our window. Keith and I sit down to a meal. It is as good as those I remember eating in a dining car on a civilian train.

While we eat, a parade of Negro G.I.'s comes through our car. Next, a line of Negroes forms in our aisle. Most of them stare at our tables, at our padded seats, at the old, but still elegant, stained and varnished finishes of the woodwork. They see no sleeping facilities. *Do they know about Pullman berths? Some do. The word will spread.*

As they wait, the line of fatigue clad Negroes reverses. I read the unit insignia sewn onto the left sleeve, at the shoulder, of a Negro beside me. He looks down. Our eyes meet. He smiles. I smile.

Cotner. You're in the 811th Engineers?

Negro. Yes, Sir. The 811th Engineer Aviation Battalion.

Cotner. Where did you guys serve?

Negro. Asiatic Pacific Theater, Sir.

Cotner. What island?

Negro. A number of them, Sir. We started out in Australia on 13 April '42. Iwo and Okinawa were our last two.

Cotner. What did you do on Iwo?

Negro. We helped the Seabees build the P-51 field. They did the smart work. We mostly did pick and shovel work but we did build the control tower by ourselves.

I stand. I salute. He returns.

Cotner. You guys saved my life. My crew had to land on that P-51 field once. The P-51 tower officer "talked us in by radar-observation. The B-29 field was closed during a Pacific storm. The man in the B-29 tower said, "Ceiling zero, visibility zero. Ditch or bail out."

Chef. Forward, Harch!

Will their meal be as good as ours? How will they balance their trays as they sit hunched in their crowded bunks?

I had not seen black troops during my entire service. I knew before the war that Negroes lived in poor neighborhoods. I knew they went to different schools, to different churches. I knew they had to ride in the back of the bus. I heard many whites say that niggers are dirty, dumb and dishonest. I knew there were lynchings in the south.

I feel a bond with these black skinned men. They are my comrades-in-arms. They built those airfields while the war on Iwo was still going on. Construction workers were killed and maimed, by enemy fire and by construction accidents. They, like me, are on their way to Thomas Jefferson Barracks, a camp named after Thomas Jefferson, a man, who in our Declaration of Independence said, "All men are created equal." Why, in Jefferson's America, am I treated to a luxurious ride, while they, who also served America, ride as third class passengers?

Why does our Porter poke fun at whites of rank? Is it because Pullman portering is one of the few professions available to Negroes, that permits a black man the opportunity to earn a steady, dependable living wage, and thus a strong position of economic independence to relate to whites from?

Or is our Porter merely wise and wily in the ways of human nature? Does he know that the higher the status of a white person, the smaller the tip will sometimes be? Does he know the man of rank needs no ego gratification from generous treatment of subservient men? Does he know that lower ranking white soldiers will reward him for debasing, even in humor, an officer of rank? An officer whom, like some they may have served under, abused his privileges, and their rights? I am sure our Porter knows the arithmetic. There are a lot more Corporals than there are Colonels.

We bus our own trays and garbage.

Keith and I raise the window. He wants to play gin rummy, now that we have a table. He wants to gamble, of course. I resolve to treat him more respectfully. I agree, but to small stakes. When he senses respect, he retreats a little from his self-deprecating attitude.

I still get time to dream of Jeannie, to nap, and to watch a lot of scenery. The Porter comes by.

Porter. What time do you boys want to go to bed?

Cotner. 9:30.

Keith. 10:30.

We compromise on 10:00.

Porter. Roger.

That word clenches it. It's pure Air Corps. He is wily.

We ride. We have an excellent supper. The Porter comes to make-up our berths. Keith and I stand aside and watch him perform his magic. We are soon in our pajamas lying in our comfortable bunks. *Jeannie, how well I remember our five nights on the train from D.C. To Seattle.*

I think of the Negroes on their mattresses, and their sagging, coil-less springs. I think of Jeannie and little Donna. "Clickety clack" sings me to sleep.

A damn bugle blows. I stick my head out between the curtains. The Porter is by my berth. He's not blowin' a bugle. It's a trumpet. He plays, "I Can't Get `Em Up". Next he plays "The Boogie Woogie Bugle Boy of Company `B'".

Porter. Union Station, Union Station, Central Rail Hub of the United States of America, St. Louis! St. Louis! St. Louis, Missouri! All men disembarking here get up and shave, shit and shine your shoes. Use one of your G.I. meal chits for breakfast at Harvey House in the station.
All men going to points east stay in your bunks, out of the way. I'll get you up later.

Keith and I put our shoes and trousers on. We go to the Pullman toilet room/bathroom. It has six lavatories. Our wait is not too long. *How are all those Negroes gonna have time to shave?*

The Porter holds my hand as I step off the rail car. I leave a two-dollar bill in his hand. A standard tip is twenty-five cents. A big tip is fifty cents. Am I trying to atone for white America's sins? The Porter thanks me.

JEFFERSON BARRACKS

Keith and I carry our bags into the Harvey House Restaurant. We each order bacon and eggs and hot cakes. I've lost track of time. The calendar reads October.

We find the Union Pacific train to Jefferson Barracks. The ride is short. The train follows a siding into camp. We disembark. We report.

We get in line. Medical doctors examine me.

Doctor. How did you get your flat feet?

Don. When I reported for duty at Boca Raton, Florida, supplies were short. They gave me size twelve shoes. I wear ten and a halfs.

Doctor. That shouldn't cause flat feet.

Cotner. I was assigned to Squadron C. It was Squadron C''s turn to take the twenty-five-mile hike. We Cadets each carried a fifty lb. pack. When I took off my size twelve shoes after the hike, my feet were flat.

Doctor. Do you want Army medical treatment?

Cotner. What treatment is there?

Doctor. None that cures flat feet, that I know of. Shall I write that Lt. Cotner refuses Army medical treatment for flat feet?

Cotner. Yes.

I proceed to each doctor in the line of stations.

Doctor. How did you get your hemorrhoids?

Cotner. Sittin' 932 hours on a damn life raft.

Doctor. That shouldn't cause hemorrhoids. I don't believe you could'a survived 932 hours in a life raft anyway.

Cotner. I wasn't lost at sea. The life raft wasn't inflated. It was buckled to my parachute. I flew thirty-three missions from Tinian to Japan. The folded life raft was my seat cushion. It was hard and lumpy.

Doctor. Do you request Army medical treatment?

Cotner. What is the treatment?

Doctor. Surgery.

Cotner. Does it work?

Doctor. Yes, but I don't recommend it.

Cotner. I don't want it then.

Doctor. Shall I write that?

Cotner. Yes.

The medics raise no more issues. They say I survived the war well. Next I go to the dentist.

Dentist. You have a cavity on the back side of your left upper incisor. I'll have to fill that. I can do it today, 2:00 p.m.

Cotner. (*I want to go home.*) Just write that I refuse treatment.

Dentist. My conscience won't let me do that. I'll see you at 2:00 p.m.

Cotner. All right, Sir. (*Why did I say, "Sir". He's wearing gold bars. He must have just graduated from Dental School. I'll bet he got a deferment, and the promise of a commission, while I was gettin' shot at. Now he thinks he outranks me.)*

Next I go to "Personnel". A Captain shows me my personnel file. He shows a form that lists my awards for valor. I read. "Distinguished Flying Cross, Air Medal with Six Oak Leaf Clusters, Asiatic Pacific Theater Medal with Four Battle Stars, Army Commendation Medal, American Campaign Medal, World War II Victory Medal, The Presidential Unit Citation with an Oak Leaf Cluster". I read the list of my marksmanship medals, "Rifle, Thompson Submachine Gun, Carbine, Pistol":

Captain. I salute you. You are a hero.

We exchange salutes.

Captain. You're a good shot too. Did you kill any Japs?

Cotner. I've never fired a gun in my life, except on Army Target Ranges.

Captain. What's your secret?

Cotner. I have steady nerves and excellent eyes and, being a novice, I listened to instructions.

Captain. I think the Army needs you.

Cotner. We were told that we would receive all our medals at the Separation Center.

Captain. Lieutenant, you were in service long enough to know that the Army does not always deliver on its promises. With this form, however, you can purchase any medals listed thereon at the Post Exchange.

Cotner. Thank you, Sir.

Captain. This is your 201 file. When the dentist signs your medical release, I will give it to you. I will also give you a chit to take to the Payroll officer.

Cotner. Do I have back pay coming?

Captain. You may. Don't fail to see the Payroll officer.

I lunch in the mess hall. I find the telephones. I get in line. The long distance operators are still on strike.

At 1:40 p.m. *I'm getting used to civilian time*, I drop out of line. I report to the dentist. He's examining teeth. The line is long. I read his sign, "Dr. Young, D.D.S.".

Cotner. Will you be able to take me at 2 o'clock, Dr. Young?

Young. Yeah. Find a seat. My examination reliever will be here at 2:00 p.m.

I wait. *Where the hell is that damn relief man?*

2:45 p.m. I make a proposition.

Cotner. Dr. Young, how about me signing this statement, "I appreciate Dr. Young's examination of my teeth. I promise to get his recommended dental procedure promptly accomplished, at my expense, within one week after I arrive in my home town of Tulsa, Oklahoma."

Young. I can't do that.

Cotner. Doc! That tooth has never bothered me. I didn't even know I had a cavity.

Young. No!

Cotner. But, I've got a wife, and a baby who was born while I was on Tinian. They are waitin' to see me. I want to see them.

Young. You're still in the Army. You know regulations are regulations.

I am angry.

Cotner. I know that an officer who is not a coward can bend regulations. *Why is this guy so desperate for a patient to practice on?*

Young. I guess my relief man, who is a civilian dentist, had an emergency in his office. Just wait. I'll work on you as soon as I finish these exams.

Young has the power. How come every officer and non-com in the Army has some sort of situational authority over me, even those few whom I outrank? But, I'm too close to being outta here, to gamble on a protest now.

4:21 p.m.

Young. O.K., Lieutenant. Get in the chair.

I get in. He goes rapidly to work. He has no dental assistant.

Young shoots my upper inside gum with Novocain. He shoots my gum outside, above my tooth. He is not gentle. Too soon he drills. I make him wait till I'm numb. He drills again, again, and again. I jerk in reflex to sudden pain.

Cotner. Go-od! Da-amn!

Young. What's the matter?

Cotner. That hurt! I've never been hurt by a dentist before.

Young. You never had a filling in a front tooth before. I'm gonna give you more Novocain.

He gives me fore and aft shots again. He keeps testing until a total feeling of numb paralysis possesses my entire upper jaw.

Young. I may have hit a nerve. Nerves are not very deep in front teeth. It's quit hurting now, hasn't it?

Cotner. Oomhoo.

Young fills the tooth. He lets me out of the chair. Payroll has closed. I don't feel good. I go to my room. I lie in the sack. I go to sleep.

1:30 a.m.

I wake up moaning. The Novocain has let go. I've heard of toothaches but I have never had pain like this. My tooth throbs. My gum burns, it stings, it smarts. My forehead is split vertically between the eyes. The axe head is still buried.

I gradually get up. *I'm thirsty. Do I have a fever?* I struggle to the lavatory. I get water into my glass. I intend to open my mouth.

God! God! Damn! Why does it ache so violently to try to move the hinges of my jawbones. Is this lock-jaw? Does Tom Jefferson have a dentist on emergency call? Can I get there, if he does?

I crawl back into my sack. I moan and suffer. I moan and hurt. I moan in agony. I endure an eon of excruciation. It's unbearable. I ignore reveille. I scorn the thought of breakfast.

8:00 a.m.

I get out of the sack. I go to the Dentist's Station. No one is there. I wait. At 9:00 a.m. an officer arrives. He wears Captain's bars.

Cotner. Are you a dentist?

Captain. Yes, I'm Dr. Newman.

I open my mouth. I moan, I point inside.

Newman. Get in the chair, Lieutenant.

I obey.

Newman. Open your mouth. My God. what the hell happened to you?

Cotner. Doctor Young filled my tooth.

Newman. Here, swallow this pill.

He gives me a horse-sized pill, and a paper cup of water.

Newman. You've got two pustules on your upper gum where you were shot. I'm gonna lance them.

He picks up a small scalpel. He lances. The axe comes part way out of my skull. He squeezes all my pus out.

Newman. I'm gonna take this filling out. I'm not gonna shoot you. You're gums are too inflamed.
He drills a little. I feel the filling fall out.

Newman. I'm gonna put sulfa ointment on the lance wounds and in your cavity. Then I'm gonna put a sulpha-saturated desensitizing fluid in your cavity and fill it. These new sulfa drugs are medical miracles.

He completes the work.

Newman. You're ready to go, Lieutenant. You on your way home?

I feel almost good, physically and psychologically I am elated.

Cotner. Yes, Sir, as soon as you can sign my dental release.

Newman. Hand it here. I'll sign it.

Cotner. Lt. Young has it.

Newman shuffles papers. He finds mine. He signs it. He hands it to me. I thank him. I salute. He returns.

I go to Personnel. I pick up my 201 file and my Separation Certificate. I go to Payroll. They pay me $75.00 in greenbacks for September Flight Pay.

The Payroll officer gives me a copy of an order. It shows that my unused leave, plus my terminal leave will run until 19 November, 1945.

Officer. Technically, you're in the Army until then. Don't stupidly break any military rules of conduct. If you get caught, you can still be court-martialed.

Cotner. I'll be good.

The officer gives me a copy of a Payroll Voucher. It states that the War Department will mail me a check on 19 November, 1945 in the amount of $542.01. He claims that is the total due to me on 19 November for base pay, allowances, allotment to Jean, plus $300 mustering out pay.

It should be a lot more. Is he cheating me? I try to follow his arithmetic explanatory babble. The axe blade begins to press into my skull again. Oh, well. The war is over. I am alive. I'm out of the Army. I'm on the way home. What the hell?

The payroll officer tells me that if I show my Separation Certificate on any St. Louis train, the conductor will let me ride free.

Having missed a supper and subsequent breakfast, I am hungry but I forego the mess hall. I'm not ready to chew anything. I catch the first train for St. Louis.

ST. LOUIE, LOUIE

The train chuffs backward onto an auxiliary siding. Brakes clang. The train chuff, chuff, chuffs forward. It switches back onto the Jefferson Barracks track. We head north, northeast across some of the Barrack's many acres.

These rail cars are not Pullmans. All seats face forward. I choose one on the right side. I watched rolling hills and meadowlands on my ride down from St. Louis. I want a river view going back.

The track switches onto the Union Pacific main line. We roll along the edge of a bluff. Four hundred feet below us, the Mississippi River runs wide and swift toward New Orleans. Current velocity reveals itself as roils around snags, and as rapids over barely submerged sandbars.
The bank on the opposite side slopes upward from water's edge to the limitless spread of Illinois prairie.

I am awed but I try to imagine how beautiful it must have been in 1832, when Lewis and Clarke and their brave men began their western expedition.
Now, ugly barge trains loaded with ugly industrial products are pushed swiftly south by ugly motorized scows, while ugly loads of industrial raw materials pass slowly north in ugly barge trains pushed upstream by struggling, straining, ugly smoking scows.

The train speeds for four miles. The bluff dwindles down to water's edge.
We enter the city. We creep along.
In forty-five minutes our Negro conductor comes in.

Conductor. (*Singing*). St. Louie, St. Louie, St. Louie, Louie.

At Union Station, all men aboard hit the concourse running. *To the telephones?* I go out onto the sidewalk. I walk a block and a half. I spot a phone booth. It is vacant. I dial Braniff Airways, a local call. I've missed the morning flight to Tulsa. The best I can do is an 8:36 p.m. departure from Lambert Field with a 10:56 arrival at the Tulsa Municipal Airport. I make a reservation.

I phone Jean. The long distance operators are still on strike. It takes me fifteen minutes to get one but then I soon hear Jeannie's sweet voice.

Jean. Hello.

Don. Hello, Honey, it's me.

Jean. Oh, Don, I love you. Where are you now?

Don. St. Louie, Louie.

Jean. St. Louis, Missouri?

Don. Yes. I have a reservation on Braniff. My ETA for Tulsa Municipal Airport is 10:56 p.m. I love you.

Jean. I love you, Don. Are you out of the Army?

Don. Yes, Sweetheart.

Jean. Is that the soonest you can get here?

Don. Yes, isn't it terrible? I love you.

Jean. You want me to meet you at the airport?

Don. No. You stay there with the baby. I'll take a taxi.

Jean. Taxis are so expensive.

Don. We'll save money later. I love you.

Jean. I love you, Don: I can hardly wait.

Don. I love you, Jeannie.

Operator. Your time is over. Please hang up.

Don. Bye, bye, Sweetheart.

Jean. Bye, Don.

I go back to Union Station. I find the service men's hitchhiking shelter. I get a ride to Scott Field. My driver crosses the U.S. highway system's Mississippi River bridge. He follows U.S. 64. In thirty-seven miles he lets me out at the Scott Field Guard Shelter. The guard pages "Frank Riesinger" for me. Frank comes to the shelter. He salutes me. I salute him. We shake hands.

Frank. Hi, Don.

Don. Hi, Frank. You look good in uniform. I wish I had my wools. I'm not used to this icy weather.

Frank. You didn't take a winter uniform?

Don. They didn't tell us our destination till we were in the air headed west, over the Pacific but they did say, "You won't need anything but khakis where you're goin'."

Frank. How much time do you have?

Don. I'm catching Braniff at 8:36 p.m. to Tulsa.

Frank. You on leave?

Don. Yeah. Terminal leave. Can you go into St. Louis?

Frank. If my 1st Lieutenant brother-in-law will sign for me, I can.

Don. You wanta go?

Frank. After Hiroshima, they canceled the Cadet Pilot Training Program. They've been keeping "idle hands" busy with "make-work" projects. I'm sick and tired of scrubbing the barracks building every day whether it needs it or not.

I sign Frank up for an off-base pass. We walk to the ride-share shelter. We hitch a ride into St. Louis.

Don. I'm hungry, but my mouth is tender from that second class, Second Louie dentist who jerked me around at Jefferson Barracks. Can I treat you to a malt or something?

Frank. Yeah.

Driver. I'll drop you guys off at Dutch's Palace. It's a German bakery and ice cream shop. It's St. Louis' best.

Don. Roger.

Frank. I hear the guys at Scott Field talk about it.

Our driver stops at the curb. We get out. *Damn, that wind chills. I don't even have an undershirt on. Do I really want ice cream?*

I run inside. Frank follows. We sit in a booth. I look at the menu. Frank orders a banana split. I see "Hot Fudge Sundae". I order a jumbo.

Frank and I swap stories. He turned nineteen in August. He wanted to be a fighter pilot. He thinks he'll be out of the Air Corps soon, now that pilots, or any other class of personnel are no longer needed. He was disappointed not to become a flyer but he's glad the war is over.

I tell Frank this is only the second time I've had ice cream since I left the U.S. in January. I tell him the other time was on Tinian, when I traded a fifth of bourbon to an itinerant Seabee peddler for a quart of melting "home-made" ice cream. He wouldn't say how he "home-made" it. I shared it with Caldwell. Neither of us got sick, even though we wondered what those black globules were that looked like chilled axle grease. At least we didn't think they tasted like it.

There is no doubt that the dark stuff in and on Dutch's sundae is genuine fudge, mmm... mmm.

We leave Dutch's. *Is the wind colder? Or, am I colder on the inside now?* I tell Frank I haven't had a beefsteak since I left the U.S.

Frank. We're only a few blocks from a good steak house.

Don. I'm not sure my mouth can take it.

Frank. They serve a filet mignon that is so tender it will melt in your spit.

Don. Let's go. I've heard of filet mignon. Never eaten one.

By the time we get to the steak house, my teeth are chattering; but, it's warm inside. We're cozy in a booth. We talk as we eat. I have no trouble with my tender mouth. My hunger for beefsteak is satisfied.
Frank says he has to return to Scott Field. I walk with him to Union Station. The sun is low in the sky. The temperature is dropping. Frank hitches a ride at the service men's pavilion. We salute goodbye.

Lambert Field

I go inside Union Station to get out of the wind. I ask where the taxi line is. I go out the door nearest the front of the line. I get in the first taxi. I tell the driver, "Lambert Field".

It's a forty-five minute ride. The sun sets. It's 6:30 p.m. when I arrive at the airport. Braniff's schedule-board lists my flight as on time. I have hours to kill.

The walls of Lambert's terminal concourse are an aviation history museum. Photographic and written vignettes of places, of planes and of men significant in aviation history are posted. I learn that in my homeward bound odyssey from Tinian, I have encountered names and places that give me, a latter day aeronaut, connection with heroes of the past.

In January 1911, Naval Lieutenant John Rodgers "flew" upon a kite, towed by the U.S.S. Pennsylvania, as a gunnery observer for that battleship. Later in 1911, he trained in airplanes with Orville Wright in Dayton, Ohio. He was the second man to qualify as a Naval Aviator. On 31 August 1925, he lead a two-seaplane squadron from San Francisco west. The goal was to make the first flight from the mainland to the Hawaiian Islands. One plane had to "land" on the ocean just 300 miles out from San Francisco. Rodgers' plane ran out of fuel 400 miles short of Oahu. He and his crew made sails from the wing fabric. They "sailed" the plane to Kauai.

Carl Mather was an early day test pilot, during a time when the Army Aviation Service was under the aegis of the Army Signal Corps. On January 25, 1918, Mather was the first military test pilot killed in the crash of an experimental model he was testing for airworthiness.

Thomas Jefferson, during his term as Ambassador to Paris, witnessed significant early non-tethered hot-air balloon flights of Joseph and Jacques Montgolphier. On September 19, 1783, at Versailles, he watched a sheep, a rooster and a duck make a free rise and descent, with no ill effects to any passenger. On November 21, 1783, at Paris, he witnessed the first free flight and descent of human passengers in a hot-air balloon. The four men seemed to enjoy flying nearly as much as the animals. Jefferson studied the physical principles of balloon buoyancy and the related mathematical equations.

The first American military flying academy, through an association with Kinloch Field eighteen miles away, was established at Jefferson Barracks. Student pilots would take off at Kinloch and land on a grassy meadow at "J.B.". After lunch they would reverse the flight. The first parachute jump from an airplane was made over Jefferson Barracks.

Scott Field is named for Frank S. Scott. In 1917, Corporal Scott was the first enlisted man to be killed in the crash of a plane he was piloting.

John Lambert was St. Louis' first licensed civilian pilot. His instructor was Orville Wright. Lambert, with the help of St. Louis investors, bought Kinloch Field from the Army. He renamed it Lambert. "Lambert" has been St. Louis' commercial airport since that date.

There is no record of who Kinloch was. *Was he a famous early year aviator? Was he a farmer? A land speculator?*

A change of mood changes my muse. I consider my professional future. *I love architecture. I love aviation. I want to return to college. In one year, I can obtain a Bachelor of Architecture Degree. It will take me three years to get a Bachelor of Science in Aeronautical Engineering.*

I can complete a commercial course in pilot training in a few months but my 932 hours in the world's best airplane has taught me that the glamour of being a flyer ends after a few accumulated hours. Flying is really "glorified" chauffeuring, like driving a taxi, or a bus. The exceptions, I suppose, are stunt flying, test flying, or air racing but, why survive aerial combat only to get killed doing aerial stunts? I'll be just as dead as I would have been if a Jap Zero had gotten me.

My true longing is to be a husband to Jeannie, and a father to little Donna.

So, it comes down to architecture or aeronautical engineering? I don't have to decide immediately.

I sit some more. I think forward to Tulsa. I return to the historical mood. I recall the history of Tulsa Municipal Airport, where I will soon make the most important landing of my flying career. The Tulsa Airport is not included among the Lambert Aviation history exhibits but from boyhood, I have witnessed significant historical events there and I have read of its founding.

In 1918, Duncan McIntyre became a biplane fighter-pilot ace in a Spad over France and Germany. On 22 May 1919, barnstorming in his used W.W. I Jenny, he landed on a vacant plot of weeds near Sheridan Road and Apache Avenue. Impressed by Tulsa's status as leader of the Oklahoma oil boom economy, and by Tulsa's claim to be "Oil Capitol of the World", he bought the weed field and named it "McIntyre Airport".

In 1927, at the age of five, I went with my Dad to see Charles Lindbergh land at Tulsa's commercial airport, "McIntyre Field".
McIntyre Airport became Tulsa Municipal Airport on 3 July, 1928. Dad and I watched the twenty-five-plane squadron of Henry Ford's "Reliability Tour" land on 5 July. We returned on the sixth to see the takeoff. The next time I will see that many airplanes land and take off, I will be departing McCook, Nebraska Air Base, December 1944 as the 9th Bomb Group deploys for war.

Will Rogers, the humorist, social commentator and famous celebrity of the 1920's and 1930's, was born about eight air miles from the spot that became McIntyre Airport. Though never a pilot, Rogers was a champion enthusiast of aviation. Rogers and Wiley Post, the renowned pilot and native Oklahoman, were flying comrades. Between 1931 and 1934, Post flew several flights at record altitudes and twice circumnavigated the earth in record time. In the 1930's, Post, with Rogers as passenger, frequently landed his Lockheed Vega at Tulsa Municipal.

A husband returning home from the war cannot dwell long on aviation history. My mind leads me across McIntyre/Tulsa Municipal's northern boundary, into the almost limitless acres of Tulsa's marvelous nature preserve, Mohawk Park, a small portion of which includes picnic facilities.

On the 31st of July, 1941, Jean and I had our first date. My best friend, Truman Franklin, his girlfriend, Leah Plumly, Harold Franklin, Truman's younger brother, and Harold's girlfriend, Mildred Kelley, joined us in Mohawk Park for what we called a watermelon feast.

Thinking on and on, upon the story of our romance, I get relaxed, and finally thawed, I doze.

TULSA! TULSA! TULSA!

At 8:15 p.m., they call us Tulsa passengers. We are soon aboard. The airplane is a Douglas C-47, in Air Corps jargon. Douglas calls this civilian cousin the DC3. The plane is a twin engine, low wing monoplane. Except for the insignia and the paint job, it looks just like the Air Corps airplane.

I walk up the steps. I enter the plane. If this is a cousin to the C-47, it is a far, far distant relation.

The C-47 has unpadded, low-backed, wooden benches. The floor is plywood. The fuselage wall and ceiling construction is bare, in full organic glory, ribs, skin and all.

This city cousin has comfortably upholstered seats, with reclining backs and with adjustable head rests. The floor is carpeted. The walls and ceiling are upholstered and padded, undoubtedly with thermal and sound insulation blankets. There is an adjustable reading light for each passenger. Each passenger can summon a stewardess. Each stewardess is a Registered Nurse. *Can a plane this luxurious actually be tough enough to get off the ground, to fly through thunderstorms, hail and lightning strikes? To withstand the stress of landing, in the event it reaches its intended destination?*

The flight is less than half full. I find an aisle seat near the front. I'll be able to look over my left shoulder to see engine No. One. Over my right shoulder I'll be able to see engine No. Two. I'll be able to hear both engines. Technically, I'm still in the Air Corps through 19 November. *That must mean that I'm still a Flight Engineer. If there was a Flight Engineer station on this crate, maybe I could run the engines, and manage the fuel to make sure we had enough to take us to Tulsa.*

I believe the Pilot and Co-pilot must have completed their pre-flight checks by now. I hope civilians are civil enough to do these things.

The Pilot gets each of his puny little engines started well enough. He warms them up. He makes mag checks. Sound tells me each engine passes. We taxi. There is no other traffic.

The Pilot turns onto the end of the runway. Power increases. The plane rolls. Even though engine roar is rather soft, the plane eases into the air and into a climbing turn. We come out at what feels like 8,000 feet. *I hope we fly no higher because this plane is not pressurized.* On intercom, the Pilot welcomes us aboard. He says we are on course to Tulsa. My instincts tell me we are.

Thrum, thrum, thrum, thrum. *We've had that damn beat ever since we took off. I forgave the Pilot while we were climbing. After all, the poor guy has no Engineer. But, there is no excuse now. Doesn't the Pilot hear it? Hasn't Braniff instructed him to make the flight comfortable for the paying customers?*

Thrum, thrum, thrum, thrum. *Damn, this is uncomfortable and annoying. I summon the stewardess.*

Stewardess. Yes, sir, what can I do for you?

Cotner. Can you talk to the Pilot?

Stewardess. Only in an emergency.

Cotner. If I write a message, can you deliver it to him?

Stewardess. No, sir. What's your problem, sir?

Cotner. Someone should let him know he's annoying the hell out of all of us in the fuselage.

Stewardess. He is not annoying anyone, sir. He's just flying the plane.

Cotner. Don't you hear that terrible beat?

Stewardess. No, sir.

Cotner. Be still and listen to the engines.

She listens for a time.

Stewardess. The engines sound just like they always do, sir.

Cotner. You mean the Pilot, or the Co-pilot, never synchronize the engines on Braniff flights?

Stewardess. I don't know what you're talking about.

I see that she's looking at my marksmanship medals.

Stewardess. Are you armed, sir?

Cotner. No. I turned my pistol in to the Supply Sergeant at Mather Field. I'm separated from the service. I'm on my way to Tulsa to see my wife and my baby daughter.

Stewardess. Stand up and show me that you are not armed.

Cotner. I will, if you will tell that pilot to synchronize his damn engines.

Stewardess. If I go in there with some crazy story, he'll make an unscheduled landing at the nearest field.

Cotner. *Damn. I should have known she would outrank me. Doesn't everybody in uniform? (To the stewardess).* I'll be quiet. *I damn sure won't do or say anything that will slow me down from an on- time arrival at Tulsa.*

Why is this stewardess suspicious of me? Am I not a returning hero, home from the great war? Don't I wear the wings of a U.S. Army Airman? Don't I wear the Silver Bar of a U.S. Army 1st Lieutenant upon each shoulder, and on the side of my cap? Don't I wear marksmanship medals for each of four firearms, and ribbons representing medals of valor, on my left breast? Don't I wear the blue badge of courage with a bronze oak leaf cluster, signifying twice being awarded the Presidential Unit Citation on my right breast?

I notice the military aura of her presence. I see her beautifully styled uniform, its royal blue color, its red and white piping, its severe tailoring to match her slim, erect figure. there is not one run in her silken hose. Her seams are in perfect vertical alignment. Her medium-heeled navy-blue pumps are as clean, and as polished, as my brown dress shoes ever were, even when I was a Cadet. Her saucy little hat is a complement to her medium-length wavy-blonde tresses. During our conversation, I had noticed that her facial makeup and her manicured nails flatter the natural color of her skin.

I contemplate my persona. *I am in smudged, soot-soiled and wrinkled khaki shirt and trousers. Here in Midwest USA, wools have been the official uniform of each of the U.S. services, since the first of September. My cap has lost its official crease from too many train seat naps. My shoes are scuffed and dull. My tie bears the indelible stain of spilt coffee. The skin on my hands and face has faded, and peeled in irregular splotches, from the evenly tanned epidermal sheathing I so gloriously sported during those days on my Pacific Island paradise. I know, from the mirror in the Lambert Field washroom, that my eyes are still bloodshot from cinder particles that pollute the air in all environs in which coal burning steam engines operate.* Mirror memory prompts me to run a hand across each cheek, across my chin, across my upper lip. I feel stubble. I feel the scabs of partially healed shaving wounds. *Damn! Why didn't I take time to buy some new razor blades?*

No wonder this beautiful young woman thinks I might be an impostor. No wonder she doubts my motives. When Jean answers the knock on her father's front door, who, and/or what, will she see standing there?

Thinking of that moment soothes all my apprehensions. Will she know me? I think of Jeannie and Donna for the remainder of the flight. These thoughts remove all worries. These thoughts of declarations of love, and of kisses and of caresses, raise pleasurable, anticipatory tensions.

We land on time and taxi to the Tulsa Municipal Airport terminal building. The ground crew wheels the portable flight-of-stairs to the door. The impeccably uniformed Stewardess opens the door.

Bag in hand, I salute her, and rush down the steps. I run into the terminal and into the washroom. I remove my tie and shirt. Via paper towels and lavatory, I bathe. I have saved my second shirt. It is clean, but rumpled. I put on the shirt. I put the dirty shirt and tie in my bag.

I run to the curb. I catch the last cab. I get in. I don't wait to be invited.

Cotner. Thirty-three eighteen East Sixth Street.

Cabbie. Yes, sir.

Cotner. I'm in a hurry. You know the way?

Cabbie. Yes, sir.

Cotner. How will you go?

Cabbie. South on Memorial. West on Admiral. South on Harvard. East on Sixth Street.

Cotner. Wouldn't west on Apache or Pine to Harvard be quicker?

Cabbie. There probably would be less traffic and fewer traffic lights. Is Pine O.K.?

Cotner. Yes.

Leaving the airport on Memorial Avenue, we pass the mile long, 1,000,000 square foot building erected by the Douglas Aircraft Corporation in 1942. Douglas built Consolidated's B-24s, and their own A-20s there. Jean was one of the first employees. She scored high on the mathematics aptitude test. Douglas hired her as a timekeeper. She rode a bicycle all over the plant floor to pick up the time cards she tabulated hours from.

Next, we pass the Spartan Aircraft Company building. In 1942, I worked there during my summer vacation from college. I was the engineering aide of Robert Ernest, Industrial Engineer. The two of us were the Industrial Engineering Department. Spartan, a small factory, had created a small open-cockpit biplane design. The Navy had ordered 200 planes to use as primary trainers. Spartan was having trouble delivering. Spartan imported Robert Ernest from Consolidated Vultee. He replanned, then rearranged, the production line. Spartan rolled out three planes a day. The Navy was happy.

Mr. Ernest graciously credited my help. It was a great experience for me, a college sophomore.

The cab turns west onto Pine. I know this underdeveloped area of the city well. The airport had been the northern extent of the Tom Sawyer-like rural adventures my boyhood friends and I had ranged through on our bicycles, and afoot with our homemade trek cart.

I count the miles by the Section Line County Roads: Sheridan Road, Yale, Harvard.

Going south on Harvard we cross Apache, then Admiral. Now I count the blocks: First Street, First Place, Second Street, Third Street and Place, Fourth Street. I'm so excited, I count no more.

We turn left. It's Sixth Street. A half a block down the street, I point.

Cotner. That's it. Just stop at the curb.

He stops. I read the meter. I hop out. I hand him two one-dollar bills.

Cotner. Keep the change.

I run up the sidewalk. I leap up the steps. I ring the doorbell. I pound on the door. It opens.

Jeannie. Sssh. Everybody's asleep. Oh, Don.

We embrace. We kiss. Time passes.

Jeannie. I'm gettin' cold. Come inside.

I comply. She closes the door. We embrace. We kiss. We had always been able to hold kisses endlessly. We break all our old records.

Jeannie., Oh, Don. You're home.

Don. Yes, Jeannie.

Jeannie. Are you O.K.? You didn't get hurt?

Don. No injuries. At the Separation Center they told me I had flat feet and hemorrhoids; but, outside of that, I'm in good shape. I was lucky.

Jeannie. Oh, Don. I'm so glad. I was so worried.

She cries. I hold her, I kiss her tears.

Don. I wanta see the baby.

Jeannie. O.K.

She takes my hand. She leads me into the bedroom, to the crib. She turns on a night-light.

Don. Oh, she is beautiful. Can I hold her?

Jeannie. Yes. She might wake up and fuss. Do you know how to hold a baby?

Don. I've held several of my Aunt Ruby's babies.

Jean. Get ready and I'll put her in your arms.

Don. O.K.

I hold little Donna. Jean holds me. I know what love is.

Part IV Epilogue

By Way of Pre-War/Post-War Bio-Sketch

Epilogue

17 July 1922: Horse and Buggy Era: Vera Irene Cotner (Clark), wife of George Bird Cotner, gives me birth, in the vine trellised Cotner Cottage on Bird Avenue,[1] in the magnolia blossomed village of Wilmar, Arkansas.

We Cotners live the primitive existential joys of rural Southern Arkansas, sans benefit of plumbing and wiring. My tender bliss is from ignorance of the possible…I try to learn.

17 July 1923: I watch my mother light the first oil lamp of the summer evening. I speak my first sentence…"Dark outside."

17 Dec 1923: I sit in my highchair…I meditate…I astonish my parents with an impromptu recital of a poem oft read to me.

"Twas the night before Christmas; and, all through the house, not a creature was stirring, not even a mouse"…(I omit no word)…"and to all a good night."

17 July 1924: In the hen house, I fashion a nest of straw. I collect a clutch of eggs. I sit in "broody-hen" emulation…I sit…I sit…I sit…Mother finds me…*Why is she so frantic?*…She carries me away. I protest, "Mother the chicks haven't hatched."

17 August 1924: Gertrude Heflin, Dad's thirteen-year-old half-sister, recently orphaned, now lives with us. Aunt Gertrude rushes home one

day from town, "There's a monkey in front of Cousin Walter Anderson's Cash Store!"[2]

Dad scoops me into his arms. We three run to the store. A hurdy-gurdy is playing. Dad sets my feet upon a vacant arc of the circle. A monkey dances to the music. His master ceases to "grind" the gurdy. In silence, the monkey and I stand eye to eye…Our admiration is mutual…Our brain waves meld in the sacred bond of one small ape with another…My cup of happiness runneth over…I look up…"Daddy, that monkey knows me."

Do I remember?…I think I remember…Or, do I recall often heard parental tales?

June 1924: George and Vera buy our family's first automobile, a Model-T Ford Touring Car. Dad stows the surrey and pastures Barney.

July 1924: The Gates Brothers, wealthy by now, close their timber/lumber business. Each brother retires to Pasadena, California.

Wilmar residents flee in panic at the sudden loss of collective economic viability.

August 1924: Forsaking most possessions, but cramming sentimental necessities into the little Ford, we Cotners migrate to Oklahoma.

I am raised and publicly schooled in Tulsa. Ethical training by my parents is supplemented by the ministers and teachers of Boston Avenue Methodist Church. My intellectual interests are reading, mathematics, science and the arts.

Edgar Rice Burroughs is my favorite writer. My buddies and I improvise parodies on his work of genius. Being best at swinging through trees, I play Tarzan. My friends accept the roles of apes, lions, elephants and monkeys.

My quiet hobby is the building of model airplanes. My physical hobbies are: 1. Excavation and construction, with my buddies, of underground caves on neighboring properties, kept bare of "development" in the fiscal depression's miserly grip; and, 2. "sand-lot" and other amateur sports participation, my favorite being tennis. I am proud of my modest collection of baubles awarded for competitive success.

September 1939: I enroll in the School of Architecture at Oklahoma State University. To meet expenses, I wash dishes. I sweep classroom floors. I grade papers. I vend Coca Colas in school sports arenas and at campus dances.

July 1941: Jean Riesinger serves me homemade peach cobbler, and "hand-cranked" vanilla ice cream at an Ice Cream "Social" on a church lawn. We date. Summer ends. I return to school. Jean has to work.

7 December 1941: Infamy.

March 1942: I enlist in the Army Air Corps Reserve. I will continue in school until called to active duty.

25 December 1942: Jean Riesinger and I become engaged. Jean's Dad, a jewelry designer and craftsman, makes the ring. I stay in school. Jean's employer is now Douglas Aircraft Company, Tulsa.

23 May 1943: I am called to active duty. I am a non-flying Aviation Cadet. I am sent to the Air Corps' Technical School at Yale University, New Haven.

4 December 1943: Jean Riesinger and I marry in Yale's Dwight Memorial Chapel. Air Corps Chaplain William Green performs the ceremony. Jean's Dad makes our rings from a single meld of gold.

2 March 1944: I graduate from the Yale Technical School. I am Commissioned 2nd Lt. I volunteer for flying duty. I am sent to study the

B-29 at the Boeing Company's Factory School, Seattle. I graduate. I am sent to the Air Corps' B-29 Flight Engineering School, Lowrey Field, Denver. I graduate. I win my wings. I am assigned to the Air Base at McCook, Nebraska, for combat training with the 9th Bomb Group. Captain Harold Feil selects me as Flight Engineer on his lead crew. The 9th "stages" for overseas duty at Herrington Air Base, Kansas. Jean accompanies me to Seattle, Denver, McCook and Herrington.

9 January 1945: The 9th deploys to Tinian Island. Jean, who is pregnant, "deploys" to her mother and dad's house, Tulsa.

25 February 1945: We bomb a naval base in Tokyo Bay. It is our first mission.

13 April 1945: Jean delivers Donna Marie, our first child, while I am bombing Tokyo City.

2 September 1945: I fly my thirty-third, and last, mission.

15 September 1945: The Peace Treaty is signed. I am a survivor. I am awarded a number of decorations for valor. I am most proud of The Distinguished Flying Cross.

October 1945: I return to the U.S.A. I separate from the service. I come home to Jean and Donna. I separate myself for life from the service-connected habits of smoking and drinking. I cleanse my speech. I limit profane expressions to occasional phrases necessary to the resolution of an undeserved state of intolerable frustration.

January 1946: Under the G.I. Bill, I resume my studies at Oklahoma State. Jean, Donna and I dwell in a plywood hut in "Veteran's Village" on the edge of the campus.

June 1947: I graduate. My degree is Bachelor of Architecture. First in my class, I am awarded the American Institute of Architecture's "School Medal". I work in architectural offices in Tulsa.

13 April 1948: Daughter Laura is born.

September 1951: We return to Vet Village. I again enroll in O.S.U.

June 1952: I am awarded the degree, Master of Science in Structural Engineering. My profession becomes the architectural and structural design of buildings.

September 1960: We move to California. I teach in the Architectural Engineering Department of California State Polytechnic College, San Luis Obispo.

21 June 1961: Our bonus baby, Frances, is born. Jean delivers her "naturally", sans drugs.

June 1964: I resign at Cal Poly in order to practice architecture and engineering.

September 1965: San Luis Obispo does not support the practice. Jean, Frances and I move to Buena Park, California. Donna and Laura remain, as students, in San Luis Obispo. Frances begins kindergarten. I practice my professions. Jean becomes a yogini. Her profession as Yoga Instructor begins.

Our daughters grow up. Each graduates from college. Donna's degrees are Bachelor of Science in Biology and Doctor of Dental Surgery. She practices Dentistry. Laura's and Frances' degrees are Bachelor of Education. Laura teaches in public schools. Frances teaches in public schools. She resigns in favor of occupations that yield her more time for her sons. Pregnant couples seek Frances, and find her, to enroll in her home taught classes on "Natural Childbirth".

Our daughters marry. Our direct progeny are seven grandchildren and five great-grandchildren.

October 1987: I retire. Jean and I train for and compete in track and field meets. My events are the 1500-meter run, and the 5000-meter race walk. Jean race-walks. Competition is within five-year age groups. We amass a bushel of medals. In the 5000-meter walk, Jean is the U.S.A. Champion, Indoors and Outdoors in 1989 and in 1990. She is champion of the U.S.S.R. in 1991 and of China in 1993. I win the silver medal in the 1500-meter run, in the 1987 U.S.A. Championship Meet. I walk to gold in the 1992 U.S.A. Indoor meet. I win race walking silver in Japan and gold in China in 1993.

In the course of competition, and in the indulgence of our love for travel, we visit forty-seven of the fifty states, a few U.S. territories and fifty-one foreign countries.

As of this writing, Jean still teaches five yoga classes per week and I am trying to put my manuscript for this book into the hands of a publisher. Beyond that, our competitive zeal is consumed in maintaining our independent lifestyle to the end.

• • •

A Postscript to Jean...and to Our Progeny.[1]

Jean maintains her faith in Jesus, God and the Holy Spirit. She <u>will</u> be with you in paradise.

My faith is in the natural universe...If, however, I shall, upon some future time, awaken within the space of some supernatural Elysium...and...if the surprise thereof has scattered not the particles of my new ectoplasmic

1 A final word, unless perhaps I write another book.
Don

self…I shall immediately enlist in the collegium of saved souls who dwell therein…and…if Jean, or if any of you…have preceded me to that place, I shall search you out…and then…I shall stand by the gate to welcome the arrival of each one of the rest of you.

Don's Girls at the Tucson Reunion

Jean Marie Cotner with daughters:
Donna Marie Cotner
Laura Jean Spiers
Frances Irene Hill
in front bombay of restored B-29, Sentimental Journey, Pima AFB Museum, Sept, 2000, Tucson, AZ.

Credit: Don Cotner

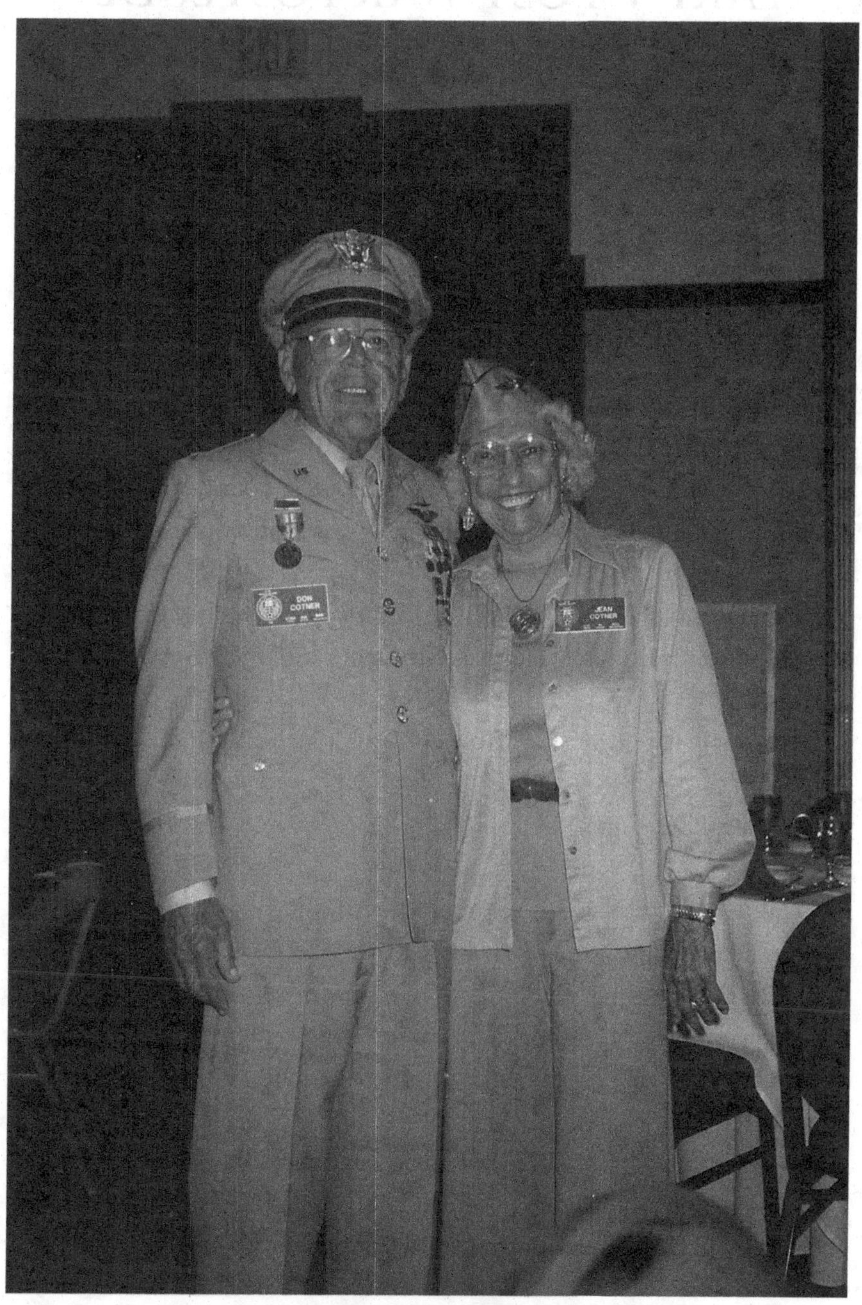

Jean and Don in "Uniform" at the Tucson Reunion
Credit: Jane Delahanty

Part V Post War Postlude

An American/Japanese Afterglow

9/7/45: America and Japan sign a treaty to end the war. Many American soldiers, sailors, and marines had been killed or injured. Japanese military personnel had experienced like casualties in greater numbers.

Other than in the Pearl Harbor surprise attack there had been very few American civilian deaths or injuries. American B-29s had poured thousands of tons of explosives, incendiaries, and radioactive poisons upon Japanese cities. Each of Japan's major cities, and most of its minor ones, were razed.

Rail facilities and other elements of infrastructure had been destroyed. Starvation was imminent. Douglas McArthur became governor.

Do the people hate America? Most do!

Do the people give up? No!

General McArthur, though at times in his military career has exhibited a proud and haughty mien, now shepherds the people with firm , fair, honest compassion. He guides them in the establishment of a democratic government. He helps the leaders write a new constitution. It limits militarism. It bans aggression against other nations.

America provides some financial assistance. For three years, American provides complete military protection. Then in a negotiated agreement, protection becomes somewhat mutual. America maintains military bases on Japanese soil.

The Japanese people respond with will. They work with zeal toward restoration. Their rail system becomes the best in the world. Their fifteen-car Shin-Kan-Sen trains (bullet trains in English) travel at 230 kilometers per hour. Their cities gleam with modern earthquake and fire resistant buildings. Their factories are new and efficient. Their electronic products are the world's best. Their automobiles compete with American, British, German and French cars. America had purposely spared ancient shrines and gardens, particularly those in Nara and Kyoto.

Loss of face was replaced with new pride. Tokyo won its bid to host the 1964 Olympic Games. The Tokyo Games were the best-organized and presented to date and so was the movie of the Tokyo Olympics, which was distributed to an appreciative world audience, which included this writer and his family.

All this while, old soldier, Don Cotner continued to tell stories of his W.W.II experiences. The audience often times included Don's daughters. Daughter Frances (affectionately Fran), younger by seventeen and fourteen years than sisters Donna and Laura heard the stories over a long period of her young life.

Among Fran's playmates and schoolmates were some of Japanese descent. She loved them and in some cases she knew and loved their Japanese mothers.

In her eighth school year, Fran's history class undertook a comprehensive six-week study of Japan. It included history, geography, economics, agriculture, architecture, the arts, governmental, and intellectual trends, from feudal to modern times. It included international relations form Shogun Isolationism to Commodore Perry's coerced opening of Japan to cultural and economic exchanges with the west, and on to Japan's military aggression in Asia and on through Pearl Harbor and W.W. II. The main focus was on Japan "now."

Fran fell in love with the beauty of the country, and of the people. She received an A-plus for her beautiful final report.

She wondered why her father, whom she loved, so often took delight in repeating the stories of his participation in the war. Fran held these "wonderings" within, until as a senior in high school she brought them to the school psychologist. He told her she was bearing her father's "guilt." He told her, she had no personal guilt, and to cease dwelling on the matter. Fran told me of this only when I started writing this chapter of my book.

Jean and I entered Fran in dancing school when she was five years old. She studied tap, ballet, and acrobatic dancing in a private studio, and in public school dances classes in high school and college. She loved to perform in recitals and school programs. She also loved drama, and to perform in plays.

At age seven Fran joined the "La Mirada Meteors" track team. She trained and competed in track and cross-country meets sponsored by the Amateur Athletic Union. A distance runner, she won, or placed highly in local, state and national "age group" championship meets.

On her twelfth birthday Fran asked to own a horse. Jean (and I with reluctance) complied. "Buddy," a big strong, gelded pony became Fran's best friend.

Fran was in her first semester of college when her dance instructor told her that Ringling Brothers, Barnum and Bailey Circus was holding tryouts for dance performers in Los Angeles. Fran tried out. She was selected. She brought home a contract, which I read. I would have preferred that she stay in school but she was eighteen, so Jean and I let her sign up with our blessing. She reported in early January to Ringling Brother's in St. Petersburg, Florida. She learned the tap dancing routines and an "aerial ballet," in which she climbed a ninety-foot rope to perform the complicated and beautiful poses and movements of the art-form, while a strong, young acrobat on the floor held the rope taut. She also learned to ride Rani, a large, young Indian elephant.

On the first day of February, Ringling Brothers, Barnum and Bailey loaded people, animals, costumes, props and everything onto a 107-car train; and started an eleven-month tour that included all major and many minor U.S.A. cities. Fran retired at tour's end.

She returned home and resumed college. Soon though, she joined six of her ex-circus girlfriends to serve a six-month engagement as the "American Show" at the resort hotel "Kanasaki," on the outskirts of Atami, upon the shore of the Sagami Sea. Atami is an hour's ride on the Shin-Kan-Sen, south from Tokyo.

Jean and Don traveled to the hotel to spend the last week of her "gig" with Fran. Fran and the "American Show Troupe" took us to a small restaurant in downtown Atami to meet the owner, a Japanese woman who had been their friend, protector, and advisor.

When we left Atami the three of us rode the Shin-Kan-Sen to Tokyo station where Fran's Japanese boyfriend met us and took us to his friend's travel agency. Two agents prepared for us a thirty-six-day tour of Japan. They made the reservations for all of our overnight accommodations. They prepared a travel guide. It was written English and Japanese and was illustrated by a line drawn pictograph showing our various modes of travel: bus, train, and boat. With this guide, and with Fran's rudimentary ability to speak Japanese we successfully completed all elements of the plan. We ranged as far north as Niko, as far east as Yokohama, west as far as Nagasaki, and south as far as Otoshima, a small island in the Yokishura Sea. At times we thought we were lost, but with Fran's pidgin Japanese, and help from the occasionally encountered Japanese person with pidgin English ability, we make each of our connections. Locally, we depended on taxis and their white-gloved drivers. Every driver is obsessed with the cleanliness of his cab, inside and out.

Every Japanese person we encountered was friendly, polite, courteous, and helpful, except that one lady we met in blind corner "surprise" in Osaka Castle could not contain her laughter at the length of our western noses. We looked at each other and laughed with her.

Japanese mountains are green. Timber is harvested in patterns that preserve forest beauty. All level earth and some terraced slopes are diked and flooded for the raising of rice. All cities are neat and clean. Autos, buses, streetcars, and trucks mingle on city streets and interconnecting roads. All drivers are courteous and patient and they never honk their horns, as they cautiously unravel the snarls and hang-ups induced by narrow roadways and square corners. On the outskirts of towns we sometimes pass a junkyard. Japanese junk is always precisely sorted, neatly stacked and partially shielded form view with plantings.

The Japanese code of individual honesty is publicly displayed. In their daily travels (to and from work, etc.) many people ride their bicycles for intra-city commutes. Cycles are parked at outside "public rack" areas. We never saw a bike with a security lock on it.

In Osaka we have a three-hour layover between boat and train. Having recently read *Shogun* by James Clavell, Osaka Castle was a "must-see" priority. Carrying our luggage, we taxied to the castle. We found no lockers in which to store the luggage. The clerk at the entranceway to an open-air souvenir shop told us (in English) we could leave our bags on her floor. We protested that we couldn't ask her to guard it. She answered, "I won't. No one will take it." "She's right," Fran said. So we left them unguarded for two hours. Each bag was there when we returned.

Jean, Fran, and I returned home to California full of warm regard for the people of Japan as individuals and, as a nation.

Fran returned to school and stuck to it. She graduated form California State University, Long Beach in 1986 with a Bachelor of Arts Degree, with a major in English, and a minor in Japanese.

Recruiters from Sony Corporation of Tokyo interviewed applicants on the Cal State campus for a position in Tokyo as an English instructor for Sony employees. Whom did they select? Frances Cotner. She signed a two-year contract and was soon established in Tokyo. Jean and I visited her on two occasions. Jean later made a third visit alone.

We accepted invitations to meals and to overnight stays in the homes of people who befriended us. I do not name them nor do I use photographs. They have had no opportunity to read the book or to even know I have written it. It would be impolite to identify them herein without asking their permission to do so.

Some of these people have accepted the hospitality of our California home and beaches. One was a young "Samurai" man from Yokohama, whom we met at the shrine of the Great Wooden Buddha at Nara.

One was the young priest of a Tokyo Shinto Shrine. Jean, Fran and I, attracted by the beauty of its garden, stopped for a rest during a Tokyo stroll. The priest came out to welcome us. In excellent English he explained the symbols of the garden elements and of the shrine building. His dwelling was on site, and he asked us to lunch with him. After lunch, he changed into priestly vestments, shed his slippers and "married" Jean and me in the shrine. He lit candles, he chanted, he danced, he fanned colored smoke upon us, and read scripture from scrolls, in a ceremony he said was so ancient that he didn't know the exact meaning of the words. He said the scrolls were seven hundred year-old copies of truly ancient scrolls and that he stored them in a fireproof vault. I supposed, but did not ask if they survived the Tokyo fires. The gardens, the shrine, and the home all looked old. Maybe the Japanese had given special protections to holy places.

Two years later, the priest wrote that he and his bride were coming to America on a honeymoon visit. Jean and I sent him an invitation to bring his bride and stay with us. They came, and we of course treated them to swimming sessions on the beaches.

In 1997 the City of Nagasaki hosted the Biannual World Championship Track and Field Meet of the World Federation of Veteran Athletes. Jean and I competed in the Race Walk events. It is our fourth and last visit to Japan. This was the fifth World Meet we have participated in. Which County proved to be the best host?...Japan!

The stadium was freshly painted. The track was resurfaced. The events were well organized. The schedules were well published, and all events were promptly started. Starters, timers, judges, etc., were efficient and effective. It was fun for the competitors. The medals were beautifully designed and crafted. Every competitor from last to first place finishers was awarded a gold medal commemorating their participation. No other country, including the U.S.A. had ever done this.

I want to close this chapter and end this book with a brief paean to the people, and the country of Japan. Jean and I have visited fifty-one of the world's countries (some visits have been extremely brief). We are as gregarious as is possible with limited abilities in foreign tongues. Foreigners who know some English are usually glad to talk to us. Jean and I are amateur readers of world history. Within these limits of expertise we speak.

We believe that no other people have ever forgiven an enemy who so nearly destroyed them to extinction as America did in W.W.II.

We also believe that Japan is one of the best friends that America has in this world.

ACKNOWLEDGEMENTS

I. HELPFUL CONSULTATIONS, FACTUAL VERIFICATIONS AND SCRIPTED DOCUMENTATIONS

I have a good memory, especially of the War Years...But..."Nobody's perfect"[1]...I have therefore relied upon the recall abilities of people of my generation, and of persons of a lesser age, who have acquired knowledge of those years.

Communication to me has been through conversations, letter exchanges, and by my perusal of written works.

The following listings are my endeavor to credit each person who has helped me get my stories onto these pages:

A. Consultants, Army Air Corps Veterans (9th Bomb Group, unless noted otherwise).

George Albritton
Maurice I. Ashland
Robert C. Bearden
George G. Bertagnoli
Winton C. Brown
Robert R. Canova
Leonard W. Carpi
Donald R. Connor
Edward M. Delahanty
James F. Drake
John H. Dreese
Russell J. Fee
Paul W. Gudgel
Henry C. Huglin
Wendell W. Hutchison
Howard Jarvis
Arthur P. Landry
Theodore P. Littlewood
Frank L. Luschen
Paul Malnove
Lorenzo S. Mancuso
John I. Nestel
Jack D. Nole
Karl M. Pattison
Richard J. Richardson
Dave L. Rogan
Arthur C. Smith
Charles W. Smith
George F. Smith
John P. Snyder
Edgar G. Specter
Howard E. Stein
Maurice Szarko

1 Joe E. Brown, Closing line of the movie, Some Like it Hot.

Richard Tolly
Joy C. Wallace
Coral Caldwell
Widow of Claude
Margaret (Chambers) Collins
Daughter of Richard
Ralph Pattison
Son of Carl
Margaret Campbell Boyes
American Red Cross Hdqtrs., Tinian, 1945

Philip True
Hal G. Worley
Joseph Cohen
313 Wing Headquarters
Mary Feil
Widow of Harold
Lawrence S. Smith
Historian, 9th Bomb Grp.
James Patillo
58th Wing

Don Van Inwegen
Lynn (Dreese) Breslin
Daughter of John
Margaret Chambers
Widow of Richard
Harry H. George
Historian, 6th Bomb Grp.
Sherman Wilkens
58th Wing

B. Consultants, Crew Members of the Submarine *USS Toro*, and Related Persons.

Roy Anderberg, Quartermaster 1st Cl
William Bruckel, Lt. Jg, Communications Officer
DeWitt Freeman, Radio Man 1st Cl
Allen Gresham, Chief of Boat
Edward Hary, Torpedo Man 1st Cl
Donald Kleinman, Electrician's Mate 1st Cl
Donald Koll, Gunner's Mate 1st Cl
Edward Logsdon
Burton McNamar, Fireman 1st Cl
William Ruspino, Lt. Jg Engineering Officer
Donald Shreve, Gunner's Mate 1st Cl
Hugh Simcoe, Lt. Jg, Electrical Officer
David Snyder, Chief Radio Man
Mark Van Auken, Son of Charles Van Auken, Electrician 1st Cl, Deceased

II. MILITARY MUSEUMS AND CURATORS[2]

A. AVIATION MUSEUMS

Wilbur and Orville Wright Museum, Wright Brothers National Monument, Kitty Hawk, NC.
Fly-in Exhibits of W.W.II Aircraft, presented by the Confederate Air Force, TX, CAF "Fly-ins" includes "Fifi", the only flyable B-29 remaining.
Air Museum, Davis-Monthan AFB, AZ.
Air Museum, Wright-Patterson AFB, OH., David N. Menard, Research Librarian.
National Air and Space Museum, Washington D.C.
Historical Museum, Travis AFB, CA, M. Sgt. Karl M. Schneider.
Strategic Air & Space Museum, Ashland, NE.
Air Museum, Hill AFB, UT, M. Sgt. Jack Dotson, Ret.
Air Museum, Langley AFB, VA

B. NAVAL MUSEUMS

National Maritime Museum, Pier 45, Fisherman's Wharf, San Francisco.
USS *Pampanito* S383, W.W.II Fleet Submarine. (Same class as USS *Toro*).

III. MILITARY ORDERS, LOGS AND REPORTS [3]

A. AIR CORPS ORDERS

My personal (201) file was bestowed upon me at separation from the Service.[4] This file includes all the special, operational and general orders issued by the respective Air Corps Authorities, who were required to control all aspects of my military service in W.W.II. The time frame is from my enlistment in the

2 I regret that I do not have the names of all persons who helped me on my visits to these museums.

3 Long since declassified

4 To my amazement, the file contained <u>no</u> "Letters of Condemnation."

Army Enlisted Reserve Corps, my appointment to active duty as an Aviation Cadet, my promotion to Second Lieutenant and later to First Lieutenant, my training along the way, my assignment to (and my travel to) the various training and performance units in which I served.[5]

Compiled, these orders state all details of my experience. I cite one example: My Flight Log accounts for every minute I was aloft, in training or in combat. This Log shows when, where, how long, and what kind of airplane I flew in.

I attempted to organize this total record of orders for listing in this space. It overwhelmed me. I write the following words instead. I believe most readers will find them preferable to a list. In the unlikely event that some rigorously oriented historian wants a copy of a specific order related to an event in one of the stories, I might send him a copy, if I am not too old or too deceased to accomplish it.

Despite the preceding paragraphs of protest, I list several orders as a sample.

15 Dec '44, Restricted, Roster of Officers, Statistical Control Officer, 9th Bomb Grp., McCook Neb. (A good source of officers' names, ranks, and duty assignments.)

27 Dec '44 Confidential, Deployment of 9th Bomb Grp. Air Crews, Colonel Castor, Hdqtr's. AAF, McCook. Neb. (A good source of crew rosters).

5 Jun '45, Secret, Pilots "Flimsy"/Air Squadron Assignments, Lt. Col. Henry Huglin, C.O. 9th Bomb Grp., Tinian. (Due to late acquisition

5 I think of the billions of printed pages, mostly inerrant, through which the Army Air Corps planned and directed the activities of each of its warriors. I am in awe of the perfection of organization. No wonder the Air Corps was so successful a fighting force.

of this resource, the story "From Dawn Into Darkness" sets the mission approximately seven hours later than shown in the "Flimsy". I have chosen not to do a rewrite).

31 Jul '45, Restricted, Roster of Officers, Hdqtr's. 9th Bomb Grp., APO 336, San Francisco, Calif.

6 Oct '45, Unclassified, Gen. Orders No. 85, Hdqtr's 20th Air Force, San Francisco.

B. AIR CORPS LOGS

1945 War Journal of the 9th Bomb Group, Colonel Henry C. Huglin.

1945 Mission Record, 9th Group Archives, compiled by Brig. General Henry Huglin, U.S.A.F., Ret.

C. AIR CORPS REPORTS

Air Sea Rescue Report No. 13, 313th's Wing Headquarters.
9th Bomb Group Mining Mission, 23 May 1945, General Davies, C.O.

D. U.S. NAVY ORDERS

? Dec. 1944[6] U.S.S. *Toro* (SS422) _Fleet Post Officer, San Francisco, Calif. From Commander J.D. Grant, the C.O. The below listed officers and men were aboard on this date of sailing. (A total of eighty-six people).

E. U.S. NAVY LOGS

The Commander's Log Book, U.S.S. Toro (SS422), J.D. Grant, Commander, commencing 1 May 1945, at sea, and ending 31 May 1945, at sea, pp. 276,

6 The date in December is unreadable in my copy.

277 and 278. *Entries cover the search for and the rescue of Canova, Smith and Stein.*

War Patrol Log, U.S.S. Toro (SS422), pp. 8, 9, and 10. *Entries cover the search for and rescue of members of 1st Lt. Joe Lewis' B-29 crew.*

IV. PERSONAL MEMOIRS, CORRESPONDENCE AND ASSOCIATION ROSTERS

A. MEMOIRS OF AIRMEN
(9th Bomb Group, Except as Noted)

Donald R. Connor, "Memories of My Combat Missions in 1945", an on the spot diary, unpublished.

Horatio W. Turner, 502nd Bomb Group, "Last Mission - Air Offensive Japan", unpublished.
Reminiscences About Missions, Arthur P. Landry, includes an account of being flipped upside down in the smoke column over Tokyo, on the 13 Mar 1945 raid, unpublished.

B. CORRESPONDENCE (A sampling).

14 Dec 1944, Christmas letter from: Crew Chiefs & Aircraft Mechanics (fifty-nine in all) to: "Lt. Smith" (Arthur C. Smith, Maintenance Engineering Officer, 99th Squadron). This letter was sent to me by my first Crew Chief, Maurice Szarko. It is my best "roster" of crew chiefs.

19 Jun 1995, Childhood memories of Margaret (Chambers) Collins of B-29s at air bases where her father was Chaplain and stories of his Tinian experiences as 9th Bomb Group Chaplain.

8 April 2000, Edward Logsdon, of the *Toro* crew, sent a beautiful drawing (by his own hand) of a longitudinal section of the *Toro*.

19 May 2005, Arthur Smith, 99th Squadron Maintenance Engineering Officer, reminiscences of Tinian experiences from the point of view of one responsible for keeping B-29s operable.

Undated, Donald Shreve, Gunner's Mate 1st Cl, sent names and duty stations of submariners on deck during the sea search for our downed airmen.

C. ROSTERS

9th Bomb Group Association Collected Rosters, Herbert Hobler, Assoc. President.
58th Bomb Wing Association Roster, Issue XXIII, John Misterly, Assoc. President

V. BOOKS

9th Bombardment Group History, 1995, Smith, Lawrence S., Compiler, 9th Bomb Group Association Historian, Writer, and Editor.

B-29 Superfortress, in Detail and Scale, ©1983, Lloyd, Alwyn T. Tab Books, Blue Ridge Summit, PA.

The Superfortress is Born, The Story of the Boeing B-29, Collins, Thomas, ©1945, Duell, Sloane, and Pearce, New York.

Saga of the Superfortress, ©1980, Birdsall, Steve, Doubleday & Company, Inc.

Bombers Over Japan, ©1982, Wheeler, Keith, World War II Time-Life Books, Alexandria, VA.

At The Controls, ©2001. Photography by Eric F. Long and Mark A. Aviro, edited by Tom Alison and Dana Bell, Smithsonian National Air and Space

Museum, the Boston Mills Press, an affiliate of Stoddart Publishing Co. Ltd., PMB 128, 4500 Witmer Estates, Niagara Falls, NY 14305-1386.

B-29 Superfortress, Pimlott, John, ©1980, Bison Books, Troy MI.And Now the News 1945, ©1994, Hobler, Herbert.

Dutton's Navigation and Piloting, 14th Edition, Maloney, Elbert S., Naval Institute Press, Annapolis, © 1985.

The Night Tokyo Burned, Hoito, Edoin, St. Martins Press, N.Y., N.Y. (Hoito, at seventeen years of age, experienced this holocaust).

United States Submarine Operations in World War II, Roscoe, Theodore, United States Naval Institute Press, Annapolis.

Tinian, © 1989, Farrell, Don E., Micronesian Productions, CNMI, Saipan. Note: In 1993, Jean and I visited Tinian on our way to L.A. from Hong Kong. Fred Castro, a resident of San Jose (formerly Tinian Town) gave a half-day of his time to be our guide. He refused our offer to pay. He gave us this book and would not let us pay its cost. Thanks, Fred.

The Bluejackets Manual, 1944. United States Naval Institute Press, Annapolis.

War in the Pacific, © 2000, Scuts, Jerry, Thunder Bay Press, San Diego

VI. INTERNET SEARCHES

Hans Haug, husband of our daughter Donna. Information subject: St. Elmo's Fire. Sites contacted: http://www.sciam.com/asktheexperts/physics35.html.

Darrell Hill, husband of our daughter Frances. Information subjects: Histories of the B-29 and of WWII. www.heavybombers.com; www.web-birds.com; www.b-29.org; www.warbirds resourcesgroup.org.

John Hicks, friend. Information subject: The patriotic song America The Beautiful. http:/bensguide.gpo.gov/3-5symbols/americathebeautiful.html; http://www.scoutsongs.com /lyrics/americathebeautiful.html.

Reference librarians of the public library, City of San Juan Capistrano, CA: Mercedes McCarthy, Chief, Laura Blasingham, Lori Lawson, Melisa Dolby, Nicole Orth, Laurie McIntyre, Dee Ann Hui, Nelda Stone Information subjects (and website addresses where available):

1. Sun and Moon data, U.S. Naval Observatory, 23 May 1945, at longitude E 32.5, longitude N 13.5, in universal times. Data includes: "begin twilight; sunrise; sun transit; sunset; end civil twilight; and moonrise, transit moonset, and following day moonrise/moonset; and, phase of moon/full moon data": http://www.usno.navy.mil/cgi-bin/as_pap. This precise data was used in the story "Shimonoseki, Superdumbo and the Submarine."

2. "Universal Sun Chart", ©1951, Halasz, Andre. A.I.A., is a graphic means of determining the time of sunrise or sunset upon any date at any point on the earth's surface. It is not intended for use by Navigators. It was excellent to my purposes.

3. Japanese Current: Data includes temperatures, velocities, and coursing. Data sent by the Metropolitan Cooperative Library System. MCLS credits Fact on File publications, Dictionary of Marine Science, Barbara Charton; and, 1968, Elsevier Publishing Co., New York, Ocean Currents.

4. Air Fields on Iwo Jima, The Corps of Engineers: The War Against Japan, Karl C. Dodd, Office of The Chief of Military History.

5. Port of Tinian, 1945, U.S. Coast Guard.

6. Early air heroes, John Lambert, Carl Mather, John Rodgers, Frank Scott, and air fields named for them. http://www.sacairports.org/mather/about/history.html.

7. United States Army in World War II, Special Studies, "The Employment of Negro Troops," Ulysses Lee, for sale by the Superintendent of Documents, U.S. Government Printing Office, Washington, D.C. http://www.army.mil/cmh-pgl/books/wwwii/11-4/index.html.

VII. PERIODICALS

Wings, Oct. 1973, "Super Bomber", Sentry Magazines, New York, N.Y. (A gift from Maurice Szarko, Crew Chief of the "Hon. Spy Reports").

Journal, American Aviation Historical Society, Fall 2000, printout, "The Beast, Living with the 3350", E.M. Gillium, M.D., publisher unknown to me. (Loan from Larry Smith, 9th Bomb Group Historian).

AAAS Journal American Aviation Historical Society, Fall 1988, printout, "Why the Boeing B-29 Bomber and Why the Wright R-3350 Engine?" Robert E. Johnson. Publisher unknown to me. (Loan from Larry Smith).

Air Power History, Spring 1994, "Will We Make Iwo", Phillip True, a story of the 7 June 1945 mission to Kobe told from a different point of view.

VIII. CRITIQUES

Orange County Writers Club, Martha Anderson, President and Hostess. I salute Martha, and the following members of the club, for giving me perceptive criticisms and encouraging suggestions toward success on a number of my stories.

Martha Anderson
Tom Anderson
"Mike" Christiansen
Julie Christiansen-Dull
Roger Coleman
Catherine Gardner
Rebecca Geneck-DeLo
Steve Harvey
Craig Innis
Tom Mason
Len Rugh
Luann Rugh
Christie Shary
Tom Skellett
Margie Taylor
Lois Tiller

I send Martha an especial second salute for her wartime service as a welder of stainless steel parts for B-29s in a Detroit defense factory.

IX. VIDEOS

B29s Against Japan 1999 Ashland Video, 9th B.G., Tinian WWII 1945, Maurice Ashland.

Thunder From Tinian 1995, Prof. Anderson Giles, University of Maine

Certain TV Airings (I made no notes and am unable to make specific citings) of the "Wings" and "History" Channels.

X. PHOTO PROCESSING

Cheryl Wayland and Harvey Tarango cleaned up a number of my tattered and torn snapshots from 1945.

Cheryl's father, Edward J. Pooler served as a B-29 Airplane Armorer in the Army air Corps in 1944 and 1945, in Harachi, India and on Tinian. Cheryl has served eight years of active duty, in the U.S. Navy. Harvey, fought in the U.S. Army's front line battles in Vietnam.

Marlene Voight, Specialist, Staples Copy Center, San Juan Capistrano created the final images of each photo in the book. Marlene's father, Walter Voight, and her Uncle Fritz Voight enlisted in the U.S. Army and Navy respectively (Fritz at seventeen had his father's consent). Each served until the war was over.

XI. TYPIST APPRECIATION

Bonnie Chiravalle, Secretary, 9th Bomb Group Association, who typed an error free, first-publication, version of my story "From Dawn Into Darkness" to prepare it for inclusion by, Larry Smith, Editor, in his 9th Bombardment Group History.

Gloria Lapwood, Owner, Wright Secretarial, San Juan Capistrano, California, who has faithfully typed all of my hand scribbled writings, and re-writings.

Granddaughter Jamila Ghoul typed a few pages.

Darrell R Hill, Son-in law, who has transcribed the entire finally corrected manuscript into beautifully arranged pages and who has created a final disc with all elements and files in suitable order for the publication of this book.

XII. BOOSTERS

Ten people have read my completed manuscript. Each has given positive support. Each has urged me to publish.

1. Jean Cotner, wife and comrade, may never be able to read the book. The years have taken her vision. I have read each chapter to her, as I finished writing it. I have read the completed book to her. Toward my endeavors of the last sixty-five years she has been a booster. She still is.

2. Larry Smith, Comrade, and 9th Group Historian, accumulated, organized and filed a treasure of authentic documents. He generously used a great amount of his time to respond to my request for prints. He has not had the opportunity to read my completed book; but, I name him a booster, because of his help.

3. Bill Fickling and Nonie his wife and comrade, are our dear friends from a younger generation. Bill and Nonie are semi-retired from the sport and business of auto-racing. She managed the finances. He was successful as a racecar driver, a racetrack engineer and a racing team owner. He now participates in events of selected interest. He is still a winner. Bill and Nonie support me with praise for the writing. He understands and appreciates its terse technical authenticity.

4. Paul Y. Burns, PhD. is "Forestry Professor Emeritus," Louisiana State University. After the year 1940, Paul and I did not communicate for 66 years. In 2006 we had phone conversations and traded W.W.II memoirs. Paul served the Army Air Corps as a Meteorologist for Fighter Plane Units in England, and later in France and Germany. Paul's three-page critique of my manuscript was supportive in detail.

5. Donna Cotner, my baby daughter in the book, is now a practicing Dentist. Donna's comments give a special boost, because I know from reading prose and poetry from her pen, that she recognizes good writing when she sees it. She also edited the book, line by line, and produced the artwork on the title page.

6. Laura (Cotner) Spiers, daughter, graduated from San Francisco State University. She teaches second grade in the public schools. Laura has read my book. She thinks it should be published. She is inspired to finish her own project, the writing and illustrating of a group of stories for children...on peaceful themes of course.

7. Frances (Cotner) Hill, daughter, graduated from Long Beach State University with a major in English, and with minors in Japanese and Dancing. She has helped me with publication issues. As a child she heard my war stories. Her reaction was to study Japanese culture, art, and language in school and on her own.

8. In 1981, Frances and four other girls danced a six-month "gig," as "the American Show," at a resort hotel in Atomi, Japan. In 1985 and 1986 she taught English in the Sony Corporation's English School in Tokyo.

9. Darrell Hill, son-in-law, has typed the final and the final-final, editions. He is close to the work. He has found errors and suggested helpful clarifications.

10. Rollin Maycumber, volunteer leader of the newly re-instituted 9th Bomb Group Association, composed of a few Old Soldiers and a growing number of younger generation patriots. Rollin is a first cousin of Edward Maycumber, Navigator on Captain White's crew, Edward was killed in the 30 March 1945 crash of Captain White and his Crewmen (Chapter 16). Rollin has been a good proofreader. He found a number of errors and helped toward correction. He gave me some individual ironic facts, which melded into the twisted fate of larger tragedies.

11. John Trice is my beloved first cousin. John flew F-80s and F-86s in Korean-War aerial combat for three and a half years. Surviving the war, he flew four-engine airliners thirty-four years with TWA, as Co-pilot ten years, and as Captain twenty-four years. For ten of the twenty-four years he captained overseas flights between the U.S.A., North Africa, Asia and Europe.

    Having read some of my early written chapters, John urged me to finish the book. Upon reading the final manuscript he told me it was an authentic story of overwater flying in the big, less technically advanced airplanes of former years.

ESPECIAL GRATITUDE

I am in earnest debt to the men and women of the Boeing Airplane Company, and to those workers of contributing subsidiary companies, for designing, building and delivering the B-29. I volunteered to fly and fight in it. Every time I took off in it, its power, strength, durability and flyability brought me safely back to earth.

Titles of Rear Cover Photos:

(See print of rear cover design, which is a collage of photos)

Top-Right & Center: "Don delivers a eulogy for his buddy, Ken Lobdell."

Top-Right: "Tinian's Joint Services Cemetery."

Left-1st Down From Top: "Ken Lobdell's grave."

Right-1st Down From Top: "Donna Marie Cotner, Donald Cotner, and Jean Marie Cotner in front of Jean & Don's home in San Juan Capistrano, California."

Left-2nd Down From Top: "Lt. Nick Bonack with Beeman, on Nick's quanset-hut porch, Tinian, 1945."

Right-2nd Down From Top: "Jean Marie Cotner holding Donna Marie Cotner, on the front lawn of Jean's parents home in Tulsa, Oklahoma."

Left-Bottom Corner: "Don Cotner and Jean Cotner, in 'uniform' at the Boston Reunion, 1999."

Right-Bottom Corner: "Jean Cotner with daughters Donna Cotner, Laura Spiers, and Frances Hill at the Tucson Reunion, 2000."

About the Author

Donald L. Cotner received bachelor of architecture and master of science degrees in structural engineering from Oklahoma State University. He is active in VFW and the 9th Bomb Group annual reunion. He lives with his wife of sixty-seven years, Jean Cotner, in San Juan Capistrano, California.